Houghton Mifflin · Reading

D1478100

Teacher's Edition
Grade 3

Horizons

Back to School

Theme 1 **Off to Adventure!**
Focus on **Poetry**

Theme 2 **Celebrating Traditions**
Focus on **Trickster Tales**

Theme 3 **Incredible Stories**

Theme 4 **Animal Habitats**
Focus on **Biography**

Theme 5 **Voyagers**
Focus on **Fairy Tales**

▶ **Theme 6** **Smart Solutions**

Senior Authors J. David Cooper, John J. Pikulski

Authors Kathryn H. Au, David J. Chard, Gilbert G. Garcia,
Claude N. Goldenberg, Phyllis C. Hunter, Marjorie Y. Lipson,
Shane Templeton, Sheila W. Valencia, MaryEllen Vogt

Consultants Linda H. Butler, Linnea C. Ehri, Carla B. Ford

HOUGHTON MIFFLIN   BOSTON

LITERATURE REVIEWERS

Consultants: **Dr. Adela Artola Allen,** Associate Dean, Graduate College, Associate Vice President for Inter-American Relations, University of Arizona, Tucson, AZ; **Dr. Manley Begay,** Co-director of the Harvard Project on American Indian Economic Development, Director of the National Executive Education Program for Native Americans, Harvard University, John F. Kennedy School of Government, Cambridge, MA; **Dr. Nicholas Kannellos,** Director, Arte Publico Press, Director, Recovering the U.S. Hispanic Literacy Heritage Project, University of Houston, TX; **Mildred Lee,** author and former head of Library Services for Sonoma County, Santa Rosa, CA; **Dr. Barbara Moy,** Director of the Office of Communication Arts, Detroit Public Schools, MI; **Norma Naranjo,** Clark County School District, Las Vegas, NV; **Dr. Arlette Ingram Willis,** Associate Professor, Department of Curriculum and Instruction, Division of Language and Literacy, University of Illinois at Urbana-Champaign, IL

Teachers: **Suzanne Clark,** Burlington, VT; **Leola J. Burton,** Vallejo, CA; **Kathleen Gousha,** Camden, NJ; **Angie Pink,** Independence, IA; **Anita Pohlman,** Memphis, TN

PROGRAM REVIEWERS

Linda Bayer, Jonesboro, GA; **Sheri Blair,** Warner Robins, GA; **Faye Blake,** Jacksonville, FL; **Suzi Boyett,** Sarasota, FL; **Carol Brockhouse,** Madison Schools, Wayne Westland Schools, MI; **Patti Brustad,** Sarasota, FL; **Jan Buckelew,** Venice, FL; **Maureen Carlton,** Barstow, CA; **Karen Cedar,** Gold River, CA; **Karen Ciraulo,** Folsom, CA; **Marcia M. Clark,** Griffin, GA; **Kim S. Coady,** Covington, GA; **Eva Jean Conway,** Valley View School District, IL; **Marilyn Crownover,** Tustin, CA; **Carol Daley,** Sioux Falls, SD; **Jennifer Davison,** West Palm Beach, FL; **Lynne M. DiNardo,** Covington, GA; **Kathy Dover,** Lake City, GA; **Cheryl Dultz,** Citrus Heights, CA; **Debbie Friedman,** Fort Lauderdale, FL; **Anne Gaitor,** Lakeland, GA; **Rebecca S. Gillette,** Saint Marys, GA; **Buffy C. Gray,** Peachtree City, GA; **Merry Guest,** Homestead, FL; **Jo Nan Holbrook,** Lakeland, GA; **Beth Holguin,** San Jose, CA; **Coleen Howard-Whals,** St. Petersburg, FL; **Beverly Hurst,** Jacksonville, FL; **Debra Jackson,** St. Petersburg, FL; **Vickie Jordan,** Centerville, GA; **Cheryl Kellogg,** Panama City, FL; **Karen Landers,** Talladega County, AL; **Barb LeFerrier,** Port Orchard, WA; **Sandi Maness,** Modesto, CA; **Ileana Masud,** Miami, FL; **David Miller,** Cooper City, FL; **Muriel Miller,** Simi Valley, CA; **Walsetta W. Miller,** Macon, GA; **Jean Nielson,** Simi Valley, CA; **Sue Patton,** Brea, CA; **Debbie Peale,** Miami, FL; **Loretta Piggee,** Gary, IN; **Jennifer Rader,** Huntington, CA; **April Raiford,** Columbus, GA; **Cheryl Remash,** Manchester, NH; **Francis Rivera,** Orlando, FL; **Marina Rodriguez,** Hialeah, FL; **Marilynn Rose,** MI; **Kathy Scholtz,** Amesbury, MA; **Kimberly Moulton Schorr,** Columbus, GA; **Linda Schrum,** Orlando, FL; **Sharon Searcy,** Mandarin, FL; **Melba Sims,** Orlando, FL; **Judy Smith,** Titusville, FL; **Bea Tamo,** Huntington, CA; **Dottie Thompson,** Jefferson County, AL; **Dana Vassar,** Winston-Salem, NC; **Beverly Wakefield,** Tarpon Springs, FL; **Joy Walls,** Winston-Salem, NC; **Elaine Warwick,** Williamson County, TN; **Audrey N. Watkins,** Atlanta, GA; **Marti Watson,** Sarasota, FL

Supervisors: **Judy Artz,** Butler County, OH; **James Bennett,** Elkhart, IN; **Kay Buckner-Seal,** Wayne County, MI; **Charlotte Carr,** Seattle, WA; **Sister Marion Christi,** Archdiocese of Philadelphia, PA; **Alvina Crouse,** Denver, CO; **Peggy DeLapp,** Minneapolis, MN; **Carol Erlandson,** Wayne Township Schools, IN; **Brenda Feeney,** North Kansas City School District, MO; **Winnie Huebsch,** Sheboygan, WI; **Brenda Mickey,** Winston-Salem, NC; **Audrey Miller,** Camden, NJ; **JoAnne Piccolo,** Westminster, CO; **Sarah Rentz,** Baton Rouge, LA; **Kathy Sullivan,** Omaha, NE; **Rosie Washington,** Gary, IN; **Theresa Wishart,** Knox County Public Schools, TN

English Language Learners Reviewers: **Maria Arevalos,** Pomona, CA; **Lucy Blood,** NV; **Manuel Brenes,** Kalamazoo, MI; **Delight Diehn,** AZ; **Susan Dunlap,** Richmond, CA; **Tim Fornier,** Grand Rapids, MI; **Connie Jimenez,** Los Angeles, CA; **Diane Bonilla Lether,** Pasadena, CA; **Anna Lugo,** Chicago, IL; **Marcos Martel,** Hayward, CA; **Carolyn Mason,** Yakima, WA; **Jackie Pinson,** Moorpark, CA; **Jenaro Rivas,** NJ; **Jerilyn Smith,** Salinas, CA; **Noemi Velazquez,** Jersey City, NJ; **JoAnna Veloz,** NJ; **Dr. Santiago Veve,** Las Vegas, NV

CREDITS

Cover
Cover photography © Eric Meola/The Image Bank/Getty Images.

Title page photography © Chase Swift/CORBIS.

Photography
Theme Opener © Zigy Kaluzny/Stone/Getty Images

Illustration
All kid art by Morgan-Cain & Associates.

ACKNOWLEDGMENTS

Grateful acknowledgment is made for permission to reprint copyrighted material as follows:

Theme 6
"Fastest Cat on Earth," from *Stories to Tell a Cat,* by Alvin Schwartz, published by HarperCollins Publishers. Copyright © 1992 by Alvin Schwartz. Reprinted by permission of Curtis Brown, Ltd.

"Run to the River," by Pamela Kuck from *Highlights for Children* Magazine, October 1998 issue, Vol. 53, No. 10. Copyright © 1998 by Highlights for Children, Inc., Columbus, Ohio. Reprinted by permission.

"Seven Foolish Fishermen: A Story from France," from *Noodlehead Stories: World Tales Kids Can Read & Tell,* retold by Martha Hamilton and Mitch Weiss. Copyright © 2000 by Martha Hamilton and Mitch Weiss. Reprinted by permission of Marian Reiner Literary Agency.

STUDENT WRITING MODEL FEATURE

Special thanks to the following teachers whose students' compositions appear as Student Writing Models: **Cindy Cheatwood,** FL; **Diana Davis,** NC; **Kathy Driscoll,** MA; **Linda Evers,** FL; **Heidi Harrison,** MI; **Eileen Hoffman,** MA; **Julia Kraftsow,** FL; **Bonnie Lewison,** FL; **Kanetha McCord,** MI

Smart Solutions

Theme **6**

OBJECTIVES

Reading Strategies evaluate; predict/infer; summarize; phonics/ decoding

Comprehension problem solving; drawing conclusions; making generalizations

Decoding Longer Words VCCCV pattern; VCV pattern; contractions; word endings -er and -le; words beginning with a- and be-; soft c and g

Vocabulary synonyms; antonyms; dictionary: spelling table

Spelling words that end with -er or -le; words that begin with a- or be-; contractions

Grammar adjectives; expanding sentences with adjectives; comparing with adjectives; using *good* and *well;* adverbs; expanding sentences with adverbs

Writing an announcement; ordering important information; a summary; paraphrasing; an essay; telling more with adverbs; process writing: persuasive essay

Listening/Speaking/Viewing resolve a conflict; give a persuasive speech; dramatize a story

Information and Study Skills bilingual dictionary; following directions; real-life reading (menus, signs, etc.)

Smart Solutions

CONTENTS

Pepita Talks Twice

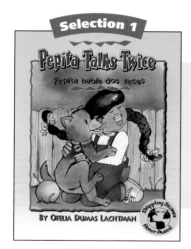

Realistic Fiction

Below Level   *On Level*   *Above Level*   *Language Support*

Theme 6

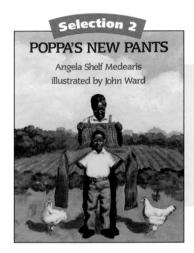

Selection 2
POPPA'S NEW PANTS
Angela Shelf Medearis
illustrated by John Ward

Realistic Fiction

Below Level

On Level

Above Level

Language Support

Selection 3
BEVERLY CLEARY
Ramona Quimby, Age 8
ILLUSTRATED BY ALAN TIEGREEN

Realistic Fiction

Below Level

On Level

Above Level

Language Support

Theme Wrap-Up
Monitoring Student Progress

Theme 6

Leveled Bibliography

BOOKS FOR INDEPENDENT READING AND FLUENCY BUILDING

To build vocabulary and fluency, choose books from this list for students to read outside class. Suggest that students read for at least thirty minutes a day, either independently or with an adult who provides modeling and guidance.

Key

 Science

 Social Studies

 Multicultural

 Music

 Math

 Classic

 Art

 Career

Classroom Bookshelf

WELL BELOW LEVEL

Barn Savers
by Linda Oatman High
Boyds Mills 1999 (32p)
A boy and his father take apart a barn, board by board, for recycling.

Inspector Hopper's Mystery Year
By Doug Cushman
Harper 2003 (64p)
A grasshopper private eye and his sidekick McBugg solve mysteries in every season of the year.

Stone Soup
by Marcia Brown
Aladdin 1987 (48p)
In a town where all the food is hidden, three soldiers begin to make soup from a stone and water.

Harley
by Molly Bang
SeaStar 2001 (48p)
A woman buys a cantankerous llama named Harley to keep her sheep safe from coyotes.

BELOW LEVEL

*Flatfoot Fox and the Case of the Missing Schoolhouse
by Eth Clifford
Houghton 1997 (32p)
When Principal Fox can't find his schoolhouse, he turns to Flatfoot Fox for help.

Pepita Thinks Pink/ Pepita y el color rosado
by Ofelia Dumas Lachtman
Arte Publico 1993 (32p)
Pepita, who does not like the color pink, eventually changes her mind when a new girl moves next door.

The Mud Flat Mystery
by James Stevenson
Greenwillow 1997 (56p)
Duncan's neighbors pry and poke at his special delivery box until they find out what's in it.

What About Me?
by Ed Young
Philomel 2002 (32p)
A boy follows the instructions of a Grand Master in the hopes of obtaining knowledge.

The Bow Wow Bake Sale
by Judith B. Stamper
Grosset 2002 (48p)
Four friends raise fifty dollars to adopt a dog who needs a home.

Mr. Tanen's Tie Trouble
by Maryann Cocca-Leffler
Whitman 2003 (32p)
When his school runs out of funds for the new playground, the principal knows just what to do.

Too Many Tamales
by Gary Soto
Penguin 1993 (32p) also paper
Maria fears she has lost her mother's wedding ring while making tamales. **Available in Spanish as** *Qué montón de tamales.*

ON LEVEL

Doctor De Soto
by William Steig
Farrar 1982 (32p) also paper
Mouse-dentist Doctor De Soto and his wife must find a way to keep from being eaten by one of their large and hungry patients. **Available in Spanish.**

The Gardener
by Sarah Stewart
Farrar 1997 (32p)
Through her love of gardening, Lydia Grace hopes to cheer up her unsmiling Uncle Jim.

Sparrow Jack
by Mordicai Gerstein
Farrar 2003 (32p)
John Bardsley brings one thousand sparrows from England to Philadelphia to save the trees from the inchworms destroying them.

Miami Makes the Play
by Patricia McKissack
Golden 2001 (96p)
Miami goes to baseball camp, where a bully strains his friendship with another friend.

Jake Drake: Teacher's Pet
by Andrew Clements
Simon 2001 (80p)
A third-grader is considered a "teacher's pet," until his school principal comes up with a solution.

---

* Included in Classroom Bookshelf, Level 3

Not My Dog
by Colby Rodowsky
Farrar 1999 (69p)
Ellie has always wanted a puppy, but instead she gets Preston, her great-aunt's fully grown mutt.

 Spaghetti Park
By DyAnne DiSalvo-Ryan
Holiday 2002 (32p)
Angelo and his grandfather help clean up a local park and create a bocce ball court for the neighborhood.

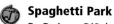 **The Upside Down Boy**
by Juan Felipe Herrera
Children's Book Press 2000 (32p)
An understanding teacher and a supportive family help Juan discover his talents. **Text in English and Spanish.**

Herbie Jones Moves On
By Suzy Kline
Putnam 2003 (80p)
Herbie comes up with a plan to stop his best friend Ray from moving to Texas.

 Nobody Particular
by Molly Bang
Holt 2001 (32p)
Diane Wilson takes on a polluting corporation in a quest to save the local bays and their ecology.

 Ramona and Her Mother
by Beverly Cleary
Avon 1999 (160p)
Ramona finds that she doesn't always like being the youngest.

 The Man Who Made Time Travel
by Kathryn Lasky
Farrar 2002 (32p)
John Harrison made history by inventing a seafaring clock, called a chronometer, to measure a ship's longitude.

BOOKS FOR TEACHER READ ALOUD

So You Want to Be an Inventor?
by Judith St. George
Philomel 2002 (32p)
A witty look at history introduces readers to inventors and their inventions, both successful and not.

A Far-Fetched Story
by Karin Cates
Greenwillow 2001 (32p)
A grandmother ingeniously uses her family's collection of stories to keep them warm during a cold winter.

Here's What You Do When You Can't Find Your Shoe
by Andrea Perry
Atheneum 2003 (32p)
These humorous poems describe uninvented inventions like spider spotters and foot floss.

 Freddy the Pilot
by Walter R. Brooks
Overlook 2000 (288p)
Freddy the pig and his friends look for a way to protect Mr. Boomschmidt's Stupendous and Unexcelled Circus.

Technology

Computer Software Resources

- **Get Set for Reading CD-ROM**
  Smart Solutions
  Provides background building, vocabulary support, and selection summaries in English and Spanish.
- **CD-ROM for Smart Solutions.** *Houghton Mifflin Company*

Video Cassettes

- **Beverly Cleary on Video.** *Media Basics*
- **Tops and Bottoms** *by Jan Stevens. Media Basics*
- **Doctor De Soto** *by William Steig. Media Basics*
- **Stone Soup** *by Marcia Brown. Media Basics*

Audio

- **Ramona's World** *by Beverly Cleary. Listening Library*
- **Ramona and Her Mother** *by Beverly Cleary. Listening Library*
- **Boys at Work** *by Gary Soto. Recorded Books*
- **Stone Soup** *by Marcia Brown. Weston Woods*
- **Zero's Slider** *by Matt Christopher. Recorded Books*
- **Ramona Quimby, Age 8** *by Beverly Cleary. Listening Library*
- **Mr. Pin: The Chocolate Files** *by Mary Elise Monsell. Recorded Books*
- **Freddy the Detective** *by Walter Brooks. Recorded Books*

Technology Resources addresses are on page R29.

Technology Resources addresses are on page R29.

Education Place®

www.eduplace.com *Log on to Education Place for more activities relating to* Smart Solutions.
- e • **Glossary**
- e • **WordGame**

Book Adventure®

www.bookadventure.org *This Internet reading incentive program provides thousands of titles for students to read.*

Accelerated Reader® Universal CD-ROM

This popular CD-ROM provides practice quizzes for Anthology selections and for many popular children's books.

Theme Skills Overview

	Selection 1	Selection 2
Pacing Approximately 4–6 weeks	**Pepita Talks Twice** Realistic Fiction pp. 297A–337R	**Poppa's New Pants** Realistic Fiction pp. 339I–367R
Reading **Comprehension** **Information and Study Skills** **Leveled Readers** • Fluency Practice • Independent Reading	**Guiding Comprehension** 🔄 **Problem Solving** T 🔄 **Evaluate** **Poetry Link** How to Read a Poem Bilingual Dictionary **Leveled Readers** *Tall Tony* *Talented Alex* *Paul the Artist* *The Tallest Boy in the Class* Lessons and Leveled Practice	**Guiding Comprehension** 🔄 **Drawing Conclusions** T 🔄 **Predict/Infer** **Media Link** How to Read a Diagram Following Directions T **Leveled Readers** *A Little Bit Hotter Can't Hurt* *The Mural* *Gampy's Lamps* *Chili for Lindy* Lessons and Leveled Practice
Word Work **Decoding** **Phonics Review** **Vocabulary** **Spelling**	🔄 **VCCCV Pattern** T **Word Endings -*er* and -*le*** 🔄 **Synonyms** T Words Ending with *er* and *le* T	🔄 **VCV Pattern** T **Words Beginning with *a-* and *be-*** 🔄 **Antonyms** T Words Beginning with *a* and *be* T
Writing and Oral Language **Writing** **Grammar** **Listening/Speaking/ Viewing**	✏ **Writing an Announcement** Ordering Information Adjectives T Resolve a Conflict	✏ **Writing a Summary** Paraphrasing Comparing with Adjectives T Give a Persuasive Speech
Cross-Curricular Activities	Responding: Listening and Speaking, Vocabulary, Internet Classroom Management Activities	Responding: Math, Social Studies, Internet Classroom Management Activities

T Skill tested on Theme Skills Test and/or Integrated Theme Test

Target Skills

Comprehension
Vocabulary
Phonics/Decoding
Fluency

Selection 3	Monitoring Student Progress

Ramona Quimby, Age 8
Realistic Fiction
pp. 367S–399R

Check Your Progress
Helen Keller
Nonfiction

Prairie School
Realistic Fiction

pp. 399S–413R

Guiding Comprehension

🎯 **Making Generalizations** T

🎯 **Summarize** T

Drama Link
How to Read a Play

Real-Life Reading (menus, signs, etc.)

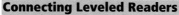

Guiding Comprehension

Theme Connections

🎯 **Comprehension Skills Review** T

🎯 **Summarize** T

Taking Tests: Writing a Story

Leveled Readers

The Dive
First Day for Carlos
Real Team Soccer
Christy's First Dive

Lessons and Leveled Practice

Connecting Leveled Readers

🎯 **Contractions** T

Soft *c* and Soft *g*

🎯 **The Spelling Table in a Dictionary** T

Contractions T

🎯 **Structural Analysis Skills Review** T

🎯 **Vocabulary Skills Review** T

Spelling Skills Review T

✏️ **Writing an Essay**
Using Exact Adverbs T

Adverbs T

Dramatize a Story

✏️ **Writing Skills Review** T

Grammar Skills Review T

Responding: Math, Listening and Speaking, Internet

Classroom Management Activities

Cross-Curricular Activities

Classroom Management Activities

Combination Classrooms

See the **Combination Classroom Planning Guide** for lesson planning and management support.

Writing Process

Reading-Writing Workshop: Persuasive Essay
- Student Writing Model
- Writing Process Instruction
- Writing Traits Focus

Additional Theme Resources

- Leveled Theme Paperbacks Lessons
- Reteaching Lessons
- Challenge/Extension Activities

Technology

Education Place
www.eduplace.com

Log on to Education Place® for more activities relating to *Smart Solutions*.

Lesson Planner CD-ROM
Customize your planning for *Smart Solutions* with the Lesson Planner CD-ROM.

Cross-Curricular Activities

Independent Activities

Assign these activities at any time during the theme while you work with small groups.

Additional Independent Activities

- Challenge/Extension Activities, Theme Resources, pp. R9, R11, R13, R15, R17, R19

- Theme 6 Assignment Cards 1–9, Teacher's Resource Blackline Masters, pp. 85–90

- Classroom Management Activities, pp. 300A–300B, 339Q–339R, 367AA–367BB, 399Y–399Z

- Language Center, pp. 337M–337N, 367M–367N, 399M–399N

- **Classroom Management Handbook,** Activity Masters CM6-1–CM6-12

- **Challenge Handbook,** Challenge Masters CH6-1–CH6-6

Look for more activities in the Classroom Management Kit.

Art

Make a Teamwork Collage

👤 Singles	🕐 30 minutes
Objective	Make a collage about teamwork.
Materials	Old magazines or newspapers, scissors, glue, large drawing paper

Think about ways in which people work together to solve problems. Then make a teamwork collage.

- Look through magazines or newspapers for pictures of people working together.

- Also look for words that tell about working together as partners or as a team.

- Cut out your pictures and words and arrange them on your paper to make a teamwork collage.

- Then write a caption that sums up the spirit of your collage.

Math

Race to 100

👥 Groups	🕐 15 minutes
Objective	Add numbers to 100.
Materials	2 hundred charts or grid paper, number cube, 2 game markers

Divide the group into two teams. Give each team a hundred chart or make your own. To make one, mark a 10-square wide by 10-square long square on grid paper and draw a box around it. Number the squares from 1 to 100. This is the game board.

To play the game:

- Teams take turns tossing the number cube and moving along the game board.

- On its first toss, a team adds the number on the cube to 0 and moves its marker to that spot on the board. One member of the team should show the addition on paper while another moves the marker.

- In its next turn, a team tosses the cube again. The team adds this number to the number of the space it is currently on and moves its marker to the new sum. Play continues until one team reaches 100 exactly.

Consider copying and laminating these activities for use in centers.

Science

Research Space Missions

Singles	30 minutes
Objective	Research past space missions.
Materials	Research sources

ny flight into space requires a crew f astronauts, with specialized roles, ho work together as a team to ake the mission successful.

Use reference sources or the Internet to find out about past space missions. Clicking the "Missions" button on the following NASA site might help in your research: http://www.nasa.gov.

Note each crew member's job title and special skills.

Then write a paragraph about the skills a team of astronauts needs to work together effectively.

Apollo 11
Neil Armstrong:
Mission Commander

Health

Make a Sports Poster

Pairs	30 minutes
Objective	Make a poster about a team sport.
Materials	Reference sources, drawing materials

Choose a team sport, such as soccer, basketball, baseball, volleyball, field hockey, or football. Research and make a list of the names of the team positions. Describe each position. Make a poster for your sport. Don't forget to include

- the name of the sport
- the name of each position
- the responsibilities of each player to the team

Soccer
5
Position: Goalie
Role: Stand by the goal and keep the ball from going into the net.

Language Arts

Agree on a List

Groups	30 minutes
Objective	Brainstorm items to take on a camping trip in the desert.

Your group is going on an overnight camping trip. The group is only allowed to take 20 items. Work as a group to decide what 20 items to take. Read these trip guidelines:

- The campsite is a desert area. Temperatures are in the 100s during the day and in the 30s at night.
- No services are available at the site. That means there is no water, no food, no medical supplies, and no shelter.
- Each person should wear a shirt, slacks, socks, shoes, and a light jacket. Any other clothes will have to be included in the list of 20 items.

Once your group has agreed on and listed the 20 things it needs to survive, each member of the group should write a paragraph about how your group process worked. Tell how any disagreements were resolved and what, if anything, you learned from the process.

Planning for Assessment

During instruction in Theme 6 . . .

1 SCREENING AND DIAGNOSIS

Screening
- Baseline Group Test

Diagnosis
- Leveled Reading Passages Assessment Kit
- Phonics/Decoding Screening Test
- Lexia Quick Phonics Assessment CD-ROM

2 MONITORING PROGRESS

ONGOING INFORMAL ASSESSMENT
- Guiding Comprehension questions
- Literature Discussion groups
- Comprehension Checks
- Fluency Practice
- Monitoring Student Progress boxes
- Writing Samples
- Observation Checklists
- Skill lesson applications

END-OF-THEME REVIEW AND TEST PREPARATION
- Monitoring Student Progress
- Assessing Student Progress

FORMAL ASSESSMENT
- Selection Tests
- Integrated Theme Tests
- Theme Skills Tests
- Fluency Assessment
- Reading-Writing Workshop

3 END-OF-YEAR ASSESSMENT

Additional opportunities for monitoring students' yearly progress at the end of the school year:

- Administer the **Benchmark Progress Tests,** a measure of students' reading and narrative and expository writing levels compared to a national sample.
- Review student performance in the **Integrated Theme Tests,** Themes 1–6, using the Integrated Theme Test Class Record form in the *Teacher's Assessment Handbook*.
- Compare the performance of students reading below level, on passages in the **Leveled Reading Passages Assessment Kit** and/or the **Oral Reading Record** for **Below-Level Leveled Readers** since the beginning of the school year. You may want to use the variety of oral reading checklist forms in the *Teacher's Assessment Handbook*.

4 MANAGING AND REPORTING

Technology Record each student's performance on the **Learner Profile® CD-ROM.**

National Test Correlation
Documenting Adequate Yearly Progress

SKILLS for *Smart Solutions*	ITBS	Terra Nova (CTBS)	CAT	SAT	MAT
Comprehension Strategies and Skills					
• Strategies: Summarize, Predict/Infer*, Evaluate*	O	O	O	O	O
• Skills: Problem Solving, Drawing Conclusions, Making Generalizations, Author's Viewpoint*, Cause and Effect*, Making Inferences*, Compare and Contrast*, Making Judgments*	O	O	O	O	O
Structural Analysis					
• VCCV Pattern	O	O	O	O	
• VCV Pattern	O	O	O	O	
• Contractions *n't, 'm, 're, 's 'll, 'd*	O	O	O	O	
Vocabulary/Dictionary					
• Synonyms	O	O	O	O	O
• Antonyms	O	O	O		O
• Spelling Table					
Information and Study Skills					
• Following Directions	O	O	O	O	O
• Real-Life Reading*					O
Spelling					
• Word Endings *-er* or *-le*	O	O			O
• Word Beginnings *a* or *be*	O	O			O
• Contractions *n't, 'm, 're, 's, 'll, 'd*	O				
Grammar					
• Adjectives (including *a, an, the*)	O		O		
• Comparing with Adjectives	O				
• Adverbs	O		O		
Writing					
• Formats: Writing an Announcement, Summary, Essay	O	O			O
• Reading-Writing Workshop: Persuasive Essay	O	O			O

*These skills are taught, but not tested, in this theme.

KEY

ITBS Iowa Tests of Basic Skills

Terra Nova (CTBS) Comprehensive Tests of Basic Skills

CAT California Achievement Tests

SAT Stanford Achievement Tests

MAT Metropolitan Achievement Tests

Launching the Theme

THEME **6**

Smart Solutions

If you run into a wall, don't turn around and give up. Figure out how to climb it, go through it, or work around it.

Michael Jordan

297

Introducing the Theme: Discussion Options

Combination Classroom

See the **Combination Classroom Planning Guide** for lesson planning and management support.

Read aloud the theme title and quotation on Anthology page 297. Ask:

1 What is a *smart solution*?
(Sample answer: an idea that solves a problem in a new or interesting way)

2 What does the quotation from Michael Jordan make you think about?
(Sample answer: Difficult situations can be overcome with hard work and creativity.)

3 Based on the quote and the title of the theme, what do you think the selections will be about?
(Sample answer: different people overcoming difficulties in interesting ways)

Smart Solutions

with Ofelia Dumas Lachtman

People solve problems in different ways. Here is how Ofelia Dumas Lachtman solves a problem that you might have.

Dear Third-Graders,

What do you do when you're already on the school bus, and you find that you're wearing one bright blue sock and a striped, white one? What do you do when you're served a giant helping of green peas again, and you can't stand to eat even one?

Maybe the first thing you do is to wish that you were somewhere else. Or maybe your wish is for an instruction manual that tells you how to solve problems step-by-step.

Let's say that you have the "Oh, no, not green peas again!" problem. Wouldn't it be great to have a guide like the one on the next page?

298

299

Building Theme Connections

Read aloud Anthology page 298. Tell students that Ofelia Dumas Lachtman wrote *Pepita Talks Twice,* a selection they will read in this theme. (See Teacher's Edition page 304 for more information on Ofelia Dumas Lachtman.)

Ask volunteers to read aloud the author's letter on Anthology pages 299 and 300. Use the following questions to prompt discussion.

1 Tell of a problem you had and what your smart solution was.
(Sample answer: My dog ran away from home, so I made flyers and left a bowl of food by the door, and before I knew it, my dog was home safe.)

2 What is your least favorite food? How do you avoid eating it?
(Sample answer: applesauce; I eat a whole apple instead.)

3 Have you ever made a deal to solve a problem? Tell about it.
(Sample answer: My friend and I wanted to play outside, so I asked her for help with my chores so we could go out sooner.)

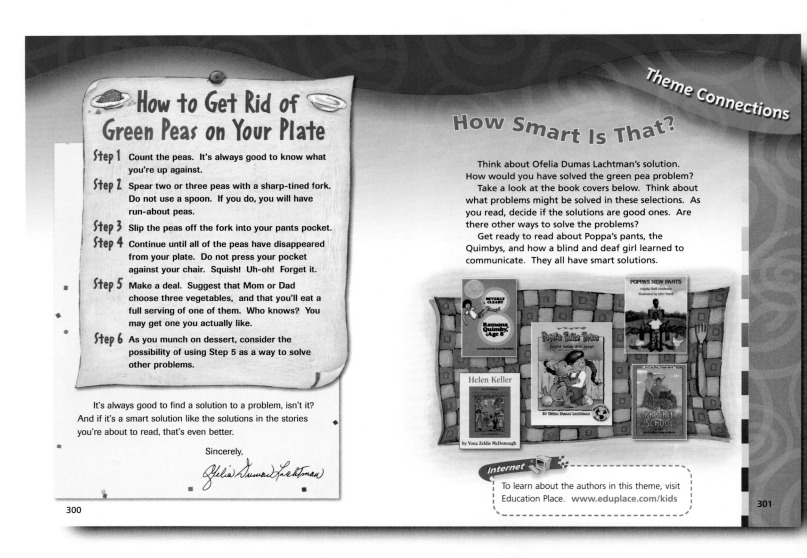

How to Get Rid of Green Peas on Your Plate

Step 1 Count the peas. It's always good to know what you're up against.

Step 2 Spear two or three peas with a sharp-tined fork. Do not use a spoon. If you do, you will have run-about peas.

Step 3 Slip the peas off the fork into your pants pocket.

Step 4 Continue until all of the peas have disappeared from your plate. Do not press your pocket against your chair. Squish! Uh-oh! Forget it.

Step 5 Make a deal. Suggest that Mom or Dad choose three vegetables, and that you'll eat a full serving of one of them. Who knows? You may get one you actually like.

Step 6 As you munch on dessert, consider the possibility of using Step 5 as a way to solve other problems.

It's always good to find a solution to a problem, isn't it? And if it's a smart solution like the solutions in the stories you're about to read, that's even better.

Sincerely,

Ofelia Dumas Lachtman

300

How Smart Is That?

Think about Ofelia Dumas Lachtman's solution. How would you have solved the green pea problem?

Take a look at the book covers below. Think about what problems might be solved in these selections. As you read, decide if the solutions are good ones. Are there other ways to solve the problems?

Get ready to read about Poppa's pants, the Quimbys, and how a blind and deaf girl learned to communicate. They all have smart solutions.

Internet To learn about the authors in this theme, visit Education Place. **www.eduplace.com/kids**

301

Building Theme Connections, *continued*

Home Connection

Send home the theme letter for *Smart Solutions* to introduce the theme and suggest home activities. (See the **Teacher's Resource Blackline Masters**.)

For other suggestions relating to *Smart Solutions*, see **Home/ Community Connections**.

Read aloud the first paragraph on Anthology page 301.

- Have students brainstorm ideas, images, and words they associate with a smart solution. Record their thoughts.
- Discuss how students' ideas compare with Ofelia Dumas Lachtman's.

Have students finish reading Anthology page 301.

- Explain that the books pictured on the page are the selections students will read in the theme *Smart Solutions*.
- Ask students to predict what kind of smart solutions might be discovered in each selection. (Answers will vary.)
- Allow students time to look ahead at the selections and illustrations. Have them revise their original predictions as necessary.

Making Selection Connections

Introduce Selection Connections in the Practice Book.

- Have students complete **Practice Book** page 165.

- Preview the **Graphic Organizer** on page 166. Read aloud the directions, selection titles, and boldface questions. Explain that when they finish reading each selection, students will add to the chart to deepen their understanding of the theme *Smart Solutions*.

Classroom Management

At any time during the theme, you can assign the independent cross-curricular activities on Teacher's Edition pages 296I–296J while you give differentiated instruction to small groups. For additional independent activities related to specific selections, see the Teacher's Edition pages listed below.

- Week 1: pages 300A–300B, 337M–337N

- Week 2: pages 339Q–339R, 367M–367N

- Week 3: pages 367AA–367BB, 399M–399N

- Week 4: pages 399Y–399Z, 411A–411B, 411C–411D, 413N–413O

Monitoring Student Progress

Monitoring Progress

Throughout the theme, monitor your students' progress by using the following program features in the Teacher's Edition:

- Guiding Comprehension questions
- Literature discussion groups
- Skill lesson applications
- Monitoring Student Progress boxes

Wrapping Up and Reviewing the Theme

Use the two selections and support material in **Monitoring Student Progress** on pages 399S–413R to review theme skills, connect and compare theme literature, and prepare students for the Integrated Theme Test and the Theme Skills Test as well as for standardized tests measuring adequate yearly progress.

Practice Book page 165

Launching the Theme
Selection Connections

Name _____

Smart Solutions

Describe a problem that you would like to solve. Tell why you think it is important to solve it.

(5 points) _____

What could you do to help solve this problem?
(5)

Practice Book page 166

Launching the Theme
Selection Connections

Name _____

Smart Solutions

Fill in the chart as you read the stories.
Sample answers shown.

	Pepita Talks Twice	Poppa's New Pants	Ramona Quimby, Age 8
What is the problem?	Pepita doesn't want to speak twice all the time. She wants more time to play with her dog, Lobo. (2 points)	Poppa needs his new pants to be hemmed. (2)	The Quimbys are crabby because they are stuck inside the house on a rainy Sunday. (2)
How is the problem solved?	Not speaking Spanish creates more problems, so Pepita decides it is good to speak two languages. (3 points)	Poppa's family makes his pants too short, so they give them to George. (3)	The Quimbys go out for dinner, have a nice meal, and learn to enjoy being together again. (3)

Lesson Overview

Literature

Pepita Talks Twice
Pepita habla dos veces

BY OFELIA DUMAS LACHTMAN

Skipping Stones Honor Award

Selection Summary

Pepita, who speaks both English and Spanish, decides that she doesn't want to "speak twice" anymore. Her decision creates problems she hadn't anticipated. A close call makes Pepita realize that it's great to speak two languages.

1 Background and Vocabulary

2 Main Selection

Pepita Talks Twice
Genre: Realistic Fiction

3 Poetry Link

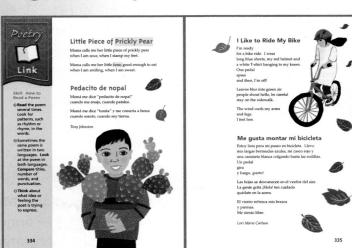

Instructional Support

Planning and Practice

- Planning and classroom management
- Reading instruction
- Skill lessons
- Materials for reaching all learners

- Independent practice for skills, Level 3.6

- Newsletters
- Selection Summaries
- Assignment Cards
- Observation Checklists
- Selection Tests

- Transparencies
- Strategy Posters
- Blackline Masters

Reaching All Learners

Coordinated lessons, activities, and projects for additional reading instruction

For
- Classroom teacher
- Extended day
- Pull out
- Resource teacher
- Reading specialist

Pepita Talks Twice

Technology

Audio Selection

Pepita Talks Twice

Get Set for Reading CD-ROM
- Background building
- Vocabulary support
- Selection Summary in English and Spanish

Accelerated Reader®
- Practice quizzes for the selection

www.eduplace.com

Log on to Education Place for more activities related to the selection, including vocabulary support—
- e• Glossary
- e• WordGame

Leveled Books for Reaching All Learners

Leveled Readers and Leveled Practice

- Independent reading for building fluency

- Topic, comprehension strategy, and vocabulary linked to main selection

- Lessons in Teacher's Edition, pages 337O–337R

- Leveled practice for every book

Technology

Leveled Readers
Audio available

Book Adventure®

- Practice quizzes for the Leveled Theme Paperbacks
  www.bookadventure.org

● BELOW LEVEL

Tall Tony
by Lucy Floyd
illustrated by Diane Hearn

▲ ON LEVEL

Talented Alex
by Lee S. Justice
illustrated by David Austin Clar

● Below Level Practice

Name _____

Tall Tony
Key Vocabulary

Vocabulary

Find and circle four words from the box. Write the words on the lines below.

Vocabulary
mural
coach
captain
super

```
T  S  G  C  O  A  C  H
M  U  R  A  L  Q  U  Q
X  P  P  P  O  U  E  W
B  R  E  F  T  P  V  J
R  C  F  C  A  D  C  H  F
H  I  S  I  E  J  K  V
M  H  D  N  O  B  M  B
O  G  X  Y  C  G  O  J
```

Order may vary.
1. ____mural____   3. ____captain____
2. ____coach____   4. ____super____

Write three sentences about a school activity. Use at least three of the words from the box.

▲ On Level Practice

Name _____

Talented Alex
Key Vocabulary

Vocabulary

Use the words from the box to complete the sentences. Write the answers in the puzzle.

Vocabulary
talented
program
salsa
fashion
Spanish

1. The ____program____ shows that there are three dances in the recital.
2. My ____salsa____ recipe calls for 2 cups of chopped tomatoes.
3. My sister is a ____talented____ soccer player.
4. I learned to speak ____Spanish____ before my trip to Mexico.
5. I wonder what the next ____fashion____ in clothing will be.

Write the letters from the circles to complete this sentence:
Once you solve a problem, the answer seems as clear as ____glass____.

● Below Level Practice

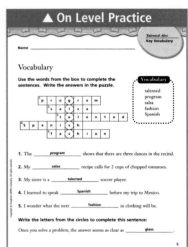

Name _____

Tall Tony
Comprehension Skill
Problem Solving

Comprehension

Read about a problem that Tony has with a player on the basketball team. Write pros and cons for each solution shown. Then write your idea for a solution and write its pros and cons. Responses will vary.

The rule on Tony's basketball team is that if you don't come to practice, you can't play in the game on Saturday. Frank misses basketball practice all the time. Then he gets mad at all the other players when he doesn't play in the game.

Possible Solutions	Pros (+) and Cons (−)
Tony could go over the team rules with Frank.	(+) Tony could be sure that Frank knows about the rule.
	(−) Frank probably already knows the rules, but doesn't follow them.
Tony could ask the coach to talk to Frank.	(+) Frank might listen to a grownup.
	(−) Frank might be angry that Tony got him in trouble with the coach.
My solution: Responses will vary.	(+) Responses will vary.
	(−) Responses will vary.

▲ On Level Practice

Name _____

Talented Alex
Comprehension Skill
Problem Solving

Comprehension

Read about Alex's problem. Write pros and cons for each solution. Then write your solution and write its pros and cons. Responses will vary. Possible responses are shown.

It is Saturday morning and Alex realizes he has a problem! His parent's dance recital is at 3 o'clock. He promised his dad that he would be there to hand out programs. But he forgot about that promise when he told his friend he could go to the movies at the very same time.

Possible Solutions	Pros (+) and Cons (−)
Alex could ask his friend to go to a later showing of the movie.	(+) Alex would be able to keep his promise to his father.
	(−) Alex's friend may not be able to go to a later showing of the movie.
Alex could ask his father to have someone else give out the programs.	(+) Alex would be able to join his friend at the movie.
	(−) Alex's father may get angry that Alex is breaking a promise.
My solution: Responses will vary.	(+) Responses will vary.
	(−) Responses will vary.

Leveled Theme Paperbacks

- Extended independent reading in Theme-related trade books
- Lessons in Teacher's Edition, pages R2–R7

Below Level

On Level

Challenge

■ ABOVE LEVEL

Paul the Artist
by Floyd Messmer
illustrated by Liz Callen

◆ LANGUAGE SUPPORT

The Tallest Boy in the Class
by Lucy Floyd
illustrated by Diane Hearn

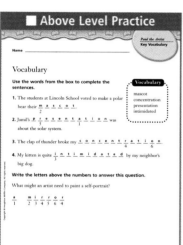

■ Above Level Practice

Paul the Artist
Key Vocabulary

Name _____

Vocabulary

Use the words from the box to complete the sentences.

Vocabulary
mascot
concentration
presentation
intimidated

1. The students at Lincoln School voted to make a polar bear their m a s c o t
2. Jamil's P r e s e n t a t i o n was about the solar system.
3. The clap of thunder broke my c o n c e n t r a t i o n
4. My kitten is quite i n t i m i d a t e d by my neighbor's big dog.

Write the letters above the numbers to answer this question.

What might an artist need to paint a self-portrait?

a   m i r r o r

◆ Language Support Practice

The Tallest Boy in the Class
Build Background

Name _____

Build Background

Use the picture to answer the questions.

1. To play this game, does it help to be tall? Why or why not?
yes; because you can reach the basket and hold the ball over other people's heads
2. What other things might help in this game?
running, jumping
3. Think of some other times it helps to be tall.
Answers will vary.
4. When might it help to be short?
Answers will vary.

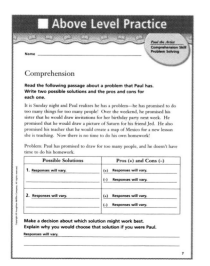

■ Above Level Practice

Paul the Artist
Comprehension Skill
Problem Solving

Name _____

Comprehension

Read the following passage about a problem that Paul has. Write two possible solutions and the pros and cons for each one.

It is Sunday night and Paul realizes he has a problem—he has promised to do too many things for too many people! Over the weekend, he promised his sister that he would draw invitations for her birthday party next week. He promised that he would draw a picture of Saturn for his friend Jed. He also promised his teacher that he would create a map of Mexico for a new lesson she is teaching. Now there is no time to do his own homework!

Problem: Paul has promised to draw for too many people, and he doesn't have time to do his homework.

Possible Solutions	Pros (+) and Cons (−)
1. Responses will vary.	(+) Responses will vary.
	(−) Responses will vary.
2. Responses will vary.	(+) Responses will vary.
	(−) Responses will vary.

Make a decision about which solution might work best. Explain why you would choose that solution if you were Paul.
Responses will vary.

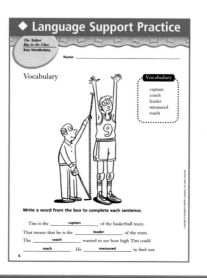

◆ Language Support Practice

The Tallest Boy in the Class
Key Vocabulary

Name _____

Vocabulary

Vocabulary
captain
coach
leader
measured
reach

Write a word from the box to complete each sentence.

Tim is the ___captain___ of the basketball team.
That means that he is the ___leader___ of the team.
The ___coach___ wanted to see how high Tim could
___reach___. He ___measured___ to find out.

Daily Lesson Plans

Technology

Lesson Planner CD-ROM allows you to customize the chart below to develop your own lesson plans.

T Skill tested on Theme Skills Test and/or Integrated Theme Test

	DAY 1	**DAY 2**
50–60 minutes ## Reading **Comprehension**  **Leveled Readers** • Fluency Practice • Independent Reading	**Teacher Read Aloud,** 301A–301B *Run to the River* **Building Background,** 302 **Key Vocabulary,** 303 language　　salsa　　　tamales Spanish　　tortilla　　tacos enchiladas **Reading the Selection,** 304–331 🔵 **Comprehension Skill,** 304 Problem Solving **T** 🔵 **Comprehension Strategy,** 304 Evaluate .... **Leveled Readers** *Tall Tony* *Talented Alex* *Paul the Artist* *The Tallest Boy in the Class* Lessons and Leveled Practice, 337O–337R	**Reading the Selection,** 304–331 **Comprehension Check,** 331 **Responding,** 332 Think About the Selection 🔵 **Comprehension Skill Preview,** 319 Problem Solving **T** **Leveled Readers** *Tall Tony* *Talented Alex* *Paul the Artist* *The Tallest Boy in the Class* Lessons and Leveled Practice, 337O–337R
20–30 minutes ## Word Work **Phonics/Decoding** **Vocabulary** **Spelling**	**Phonics/Decoding,** 305 Phonics/Decoding Strategy **Vocabulary,** 304–331 Selection Vocabulary **Spelling,** 337E Words Ending with *er/le* **T**	🔵 **Structural Analysis,** 337C VCCCV Pattern **T** **Vocabulary,** 304–331 Selection Vocabulary **Spelling,** 337E Words Ending with *er/le* Review and Practice **T**
20–30 minutes ## Writing and Oral Language **Writing** **Grammar** **Listening/Speaking/Viewing**	✏️ **Writing,** 337K Introducing an Announcement **Grammar,** 337I Adjectives **T** **Daily Language Practice** 1. pepita is abel to speak too languages. (Pepita; able; two) 2. We found out latter that she knows an word for almost anything. (later; a) **Listening/Speaking/Viewing,** 301A–301B, 315 Teacher Read Aloud, Stop and Think	✏️ **Writing,** 337K Writing an Announcement **Grammar,** 337I Adjectives Practice **T** **Daily Language Practice** 3. Even in Winnter, Pepita's mother made an enchiladas. (winter; the; enchiladas) 4. Tomatoes, with their red cullar, are a important part of salsa. (color; an) **Listening/Speaking/Viewing,** 331, 332 Wrapping Up, Responding

Target Skills of the Week

Comprehension	Evaluate; Problem Solving
Vocabulary	Synonyms
Phonics/Decoding	VCCCV Pattern
Fluency	Leveled Readers

Pepita Talks Twice

DAY 3

Rereading the Selection

Rereading for Writer's Craft, 315
Mood

Rereading for Genre, 329
Realistic Fiction

Comprehension Skill, 337A–337B
Problem Solving **T**

Leveled Readers

Tall Tony
Talented Alex
Paul the Artist
The Tallest Boy in the Class

Lessons and Leveled Practice, 337O–337R

Phonics Review, 337D
Word Endings -er and -le

Vocabulary, 337G
Synonyms **T**

Spelling, 337F
Vocabulary: Making Inferences; Words Ending with er/le Practice **T**

Writing, 337L
Ordering Information

Grammar, 337J
Adjective Game **T**

Daily Language Practice
5. She takes a litel more than a hour to prepare the tamales. (little; an)
6. She also likes to use a aple in her cooking (an; apple; cooking.)

DAY 4

Reading the Poetry Link, 334–337
Poems in English and Spanish

Skill: How to Read a Poem

Rereading for Genre, 336
Poetry

Comprehension Skill Review, 309
Author's Viewpoint

Leveled Readers

Tall Tony
Talented Alex
Paul the Artist
The Tallest Boy in the Class

Lessons and Leveled Practice, 337O–337R

Phonics/Decoding, 334–337
Apply Phonics/Decoding Strategy to Link

Vocabulary, 337M
Language Center: Building Vocabulary

Spelling, 337F
Spelling Game, Proofreading **T**

Writing, 337L
Writing Game

Grammar, 337J
Adjectives Practice **T**

Daily Language Practice
7. Last sumer, Pepita helps to prepare an spanish feast. (summer,; helped; a; Spanish)
8. In novemmber, she made up a new recipe for Tortillas. (November; tortillas)

Listening/Speaking/Viewing, 337
Discuss the Link

DAY 5

Rereading for Fluency, 327

Responding Activities, 332–333
Write an Opinion
Cross-Curricular Activities

Information and Study Skills, 337H
Bilingual Dictionary

Comprehension Skill Review, 311
Making Inferences

Leveled Readers

Tall Tony
Talented Alex
Paul the Artist
The Tallest Boy in the Class

Lessons and Leveled Practice, 337O–337R

Phonics, 337N
Language Center: Scrambled -er and -le Words

Vocabulary, 337M
Language Center: Vocabulary Game

Spelling, 337F
Test: Words Ending with er/le **T**

Writing, 337L
Sharing Writing

Grammar, 337J, 337M
Expanding Sentences
Language Center: Use Adjectives to Describe

Daily Language Practice
9. Have you evver seen Lobo runs after an bouncing ball. (ever; run; a; ball?)
10. Pepita learns an useful lesson when she travvells to school. (a; travels)

Listening/Speaking/Viewing, 337N
Language Center: Resolve a Conflict

Managing Flexible Groups

Leveled Instruction and Leveled Practice

	DAY 1	**DAY 2**
WHOLE CLASS	• Teacher Read Aloud (TE pp. 301A–301B) • Building Background, Introducing Vocabulary (TE pp. 302–303) • Comprehension Strategy: Introduce (TE p. 304) • Comprehension Skill: Introduce (TE p. 304) • Purpose Setting (TE p. 305) **After reading first half of *Pepita Talks Twice*** • Stop and Think (TE p. 315)	**After reading *Pepita Talks Twice*** • Wrapping Up (TE p. 331) • Comprehension Check (Practice Book p. 169) • Responding: Think About the Selection (TE p. 332) • Comprehension Skill: Preview (TE p. 319)

SMALL GROUPS

	DAY 1	**DAY 2**
Extra Support	**TEACHER-LED** • Preview *Pepita Talks Twice* to Stop and Think (TE pp. 304–315). • Support reading with Extra Support/ Intervention notes (TE pp. 305, 307, 314, 320, 330).	**Partner or Individual Work** • Reread first half of *Pepita Talks Twice* (TE pp. 304–315). • Preview, read second half (TE pp. 316–331). • Comprehension Check (Practice Book p. 169)
Challenge	**Individual Work** • Begin "Smart Comic Book Solutions" (Challenge Handbook p. 46). • Extend reading with Challenge notes (TE pp. 313, 330).	**Individual Work** • Continue work on activity (Challenge Handbook p. 330).
English Language Learners	**TEACHER-LED** • Preview vocabulary and *Pepita Talks Twice* to Stop and Think (TE pp. 303–315). • Support reading with English Language Learners notes (TE pp. 302, 306, 309, 314, 317, 318, 323, 324).	**TEACHER-LED** • Review first half of *Pepita Talks Twice* (TE pp. 304–315). ✔ • Preview, read second half (TE pp. 316–331). • Begin Comprehension Check together (Practice Book p. 169).

Independent Activities

- Get Set for Reading CD-ROM
- Journals: selection notes, questions
- Complete, review Practice Book (pp. 167–171) and Leveled Readers Practice Blackline Masters (TE pp. 337O–337R).
- Assignment Cards (Teacher's Resource Blackline Masters pp. 85–86)
- Leveled Readers (TE pp. 337O–337R), Leveled Theme Paperbacks (TE pp. R2–R7), or book from Leveled Bibliography (TE pp. 296E–296F)

✔ Opportunity to informally assess oral reading rate

- Rereading: Lessons on Writer's Craft, Genre (TE pp. 325, 329)
- Comprehension Skill: Main lesson (TE pp. 337A–337B)

- Reading the Poetry Link (TE pp. 334–337): Skill lesson (TE p. 334)
- Rereading the Link: Genre lesson (TE p. 336)
- Comprehension Skill: First Comprehension Review lesson (TE p. 309)

- Responding: Select from Activities (TE pp. 332–333)
- Information and Study Skills (TE p. 337H)
- Comprehension Skill: Second Comprehension Review lesson (TE p. 311)

TEACHER-LED

- Reread, review Comprehension Check (Practice Book p. 169).
- Preview Leveled Reader: Below Level (TE p. 337O), or read book from Leveled Bibliography (TE pp. 296E–296F). ✔

Partner or Individual Work

- Reread the Poetry Link (TE pp. 334–337).
- Complete Leveled Reader: Below Level (TE p. 337O), or read book from Leveled Bibliography (TE pp. 296E–296F).

TEACHER-LED

- Comprehension Skill: Reteaching lesson (TE p. R8)
- Preview, begin Leveled Theme Paperback: Below Level (TE pp. R2–R3), or read book from Leveled Bibliography (TE pp. 296E–296F). ✔

TEACHER-LED

- Teacher check-in: Assess progress (Challenge Handbook p. 330).
- Preview Leveled Reader: Above Level (TE p. 337Q), or read book from Leveled Bibliography (TE pp. 296E–296F). ✔

Individual Work

- Complete activity (Challenge Handbook p. 330).
- Complete Leveled Reader: Above Level (TE p. 337Q), or read book from Leveled Bibliography (TE pp. 296E–296F).

TEACHER-LED

- Evaluate activity and plan format for sharing (Challenge Handbook p. 330).
- Read Leveled Theme Paperback: Above Level (TE pp. R6–R7), or read book from Leveled Bibliography (TE pp. 296E–296F). ✔

Partner or Individual Work

- Complete Comprehension Check (Practice Book p. 169).
- Begin Leveled Reader: Language Support (TE p. 337R), or read book from Leveled Bibliography (TE pp. 296E–296F).

TEACHER-LED

- Reread the Poetry Link (TE pp. 334–337) ✔ and review Link Skill (TE p. 334).
- Complete Leveled Reader: Language Support (TE p. 337R), or read book from Leveled Bibliography (TE pp. 296E–296F). ✔

Partner or Individual Work

- Preview, read book from Leveled Bibliography (TE pp. 296E–296F).

- Responding activities (TE pp. 332–333)
- Language Center activities (TE pp. 337M–337N)
- **Fluency Practice:** Reread *Pepita Talks Twice* ✔
- Activities relating to *Pepita Talks Twice* at Education Place www.eduplace.com

Turn the page for more independent activities.

FLEXIBLE GROUPS

Pepita Talks Twice

Classroom Management

Independent Activities

Assign these activities while you work with small groups.

Differentiated Instruction for Small Groups

- **Handbook for English Language Learners,** pp. 198–207

- **Extra Support Handbook,** pp. 194–203

Independent Activities

- Language Center, pp. 337M–337N

- Challenge/Extension Activities, Theme Resources, pp. R9, R15

- **Classroom Management Handbook,** Activity Masters CM6-1–CM6-4

- **Challenge Handbook,** pp. 46–47

Look for more activities in the Classroom Management Kit.

Art

Picture This

👤 Singles	🕐 30 minutes
Objective	Analyze illustrations.
Materials	Anthology

What do you think about the illustrations in *Pepita Talks Twice*? Write a paragraph that tells what you notice about the illustrations. Use details from the story and the pictures to support your opinion. Think about questions such as:

- How well do the pictures illustrate the story?

- How does the illustrator use colors, shapes, and lines?

- How does the illustrator show what is most important in the picture?

- How do the illustrations provide additional information that is not given in the story?

Language

Time to Talk Twice

👥 Pairs	🕐 15 minutes
Objective	Say words in English and Spanish.
Materials	Index cards, paper bag

Pepita decides that it's great to speak two languages. Now it's your turn! On your own, make a list of five words in English and the same five words in Spanish. Write each English word on one side of an index card. Write the Spanish word on the other side. Now get together with a partner.

- First, look carefully at both sides of each other's cards.

- Put all the cards in a paper bag and shake up the bag.

- Take turns picking out a card, reading the word on one side, and trying to remember the word on the other side.

- Keep playing until you each know how to say at least three words in both English and in Spanish.

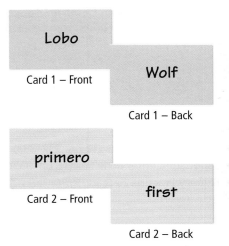

Lobo
Card 1 – Front

Wolf
Card 1 – Back

primero
Card 2 – Front

first
Card 2 – Back

Consider copying and laminating these activities for use in centers.

Social Studies

Aztec and Mayan Cultures

👤 Singles	🕐 45 minutes
Objective	Research and write about Aztec or Mayan culture.
Materials	Reference sources

Much of the food that Pepita's family eats comes from Mexico and Central America. Long ago, the Aztec and Mayan civilizations flourished in this part of the world.

Research to find out more about the Aztecs or the Maya and their civilizations. Think about

- where they lived
- when they lived
- what they ate
- what activities they did
- what special buildings they built

Organize the information you gather and write a paragraph about the people you chose. Draw a picture to go with your paragraph. Then post your paragraph and picture in the classroom.

Language Arts

Means the Same

👤👤👤 Groups	🕐 30 minutes
Objective	Identify synonyms for story words.
Materials	Slips of paper, a container, game pieces, dictionary

Play a game with synonyms. Each person picks four English words from the story that have familiar synonyms. Players write the four words on separate slips of paper, fold the papers, and put them into a container.

- Draw a game board with ten spaces in a row on a sheet of paper. Each player puts a game piece in the first square.

- The first player picks a word from the container and reads it aloud.

- The player names a synonym for the word and moves his or her game piece ahead one square. If necessary, use a dictionary to verify that the synonym is correct.

- If the player cannot name a synonym, then the next player gets a chance at the same word.

- Keep playing until one player reaches the last square.

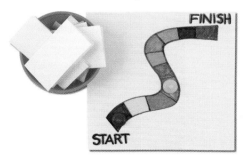

Career

Pepita the Translator

👤👤 Pairs	🕐 15 minutes
Objective	Make a list of situations in which a translator could help.

When Pepita walks by Mr. Hobbs's store, he calls her over to translate for him. Many people who know two or more languages work as translators. Translators are people who change words from one language into another language.

With a partner, brainstorm situations in which it would be helpful to have a translator on the job. Record your ideas in a web.

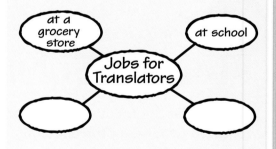

Listening Comprehension

OBJECTIVE

- Listen to solve a problem.

Building Background

Tell students that you are going to read aloud a story about a family in a dangerous situation.

- Ask students to share what they know about fire safety. Have volunteers describe what they do in a fire drill.

Fluency Modeling

Explain that as you read aloud, you will be modeling fluent oral reading. Ask students to listen carefully to your phrasing and your expression, or tone of voice and emphasis.

COMPREHENSION SKILL
Problem Solving

Explain that the following steps can be followed to solve a problem along with a character in a story:

- Find out what the problem is.
- Brainstorm possible solutions.
- Think about which solutions might work best.
- Choose and evaluate a solution.

Purpose Setting Read the selection aloud, asking students to think about the story problem and possible solutions as they listen. Then use the Guiding Comprehension questions to assess students' understanding. Reread the selection for clarification as needed.

Teacher Read Aloud

Run to the River
by Pamela Kuck

1 "Fire's somewhere close!" cried Margaret as she hurried up the hill to the house, lugging a pail of milk.

"Mama, I smell smoke," she shouted as she burst into the house, milk sloshing from the pail.

"Margaret, be careful," said Mama, frowning.

Margaret knew that the frown was more from worry than from spilled milk. "When will Papa be home?" she asked.

"He should be here already," said Mama. "I'm beginning to get anxious." Margaret followed her out to the porch.

To the south, the sky was red. No flames could be seen, but the heat was becoming unbearable.

"What shall we do, Mama?" asked Margaret. Her eyes stung from the smoke in the air. Her heart pounded in her chest like deer hooves hitting the ground.

2 "Wake your two brothers and stay with them," said Mama. "I'll be right back. I must run to the barn and let the animals loose."

Terrified, Margaret ran to the room where her little brothers lay sleeping. Their wet hair stuck to their foreheads.

"Paul . . . Anthony . . . wake up," said Margaret as she shook them. "It isn't safe to sleep. There's a fire, somewhere close."

3 Margaret led them outside. Daylight was fading. The winds had picked up, swirling dust about them. By now she could see flames leaping above the treetops, exploding in the air.

The roar of the fire sounded like cannons as it advanced, igniting the tops of the trees. Sparks scattered in every direction.

4 "Run to the river!" screamed Margaret, snatching the dish towels that hung drying on the railing. She grabbed her brothers' hands, and they raced through the fields toward the river, away from the advancing flames.

As she ran, she stole a look backward. Dry grass was burning everywhere. Pine needles ignited with the tiniest spark. Then she saw flames engulf the barn. "Mama!" she screamed. But she couldn't stop.

"Run faster! Run to the river!" she shouted.

Finally they reached the water, splashing into it with relief. Margaret quickly bent and soaked the dish towels. She draped one over each of her brothers' heads to protect them from the flying sparks and debris. The winds were violent now, blowing over them like a hurricane.

Margaret waded deeper into the river, dragging her brothers behind her. Hours passed as they watched the flames consume their land—first the barn, then the house, and finally the woods and fields. Mama's only chance would have been to run downriver behind the barn, away from them.

"Mama!" Margaret shouted desperately. "Mama!"

Suddenly she heard a shout from downriver. "Margaret! Paul! Anthony! Are you there?"

"Mama?" yelled Margaret. "Yes, Mama! We're here!"

Mama was splashing toward them through the water, screaming their names.

"Oh, Mama. We were so scared. I saw the barn burning and I thought . . . and I thought that maybe . . . "

"Hush, now, child," said Mama, holding her close. "We are safe, thanks to your quick thinking. I am so proud of you, Margaret. You will make Papa proud, too."

As if in answer to her words a sound came from the shore, rising above the smoke and charred remains, as welcome as rain. Papa was shouting their names.

As she followed Mama out of the muddy, dark river, Margaret's spirits soared. Her family was safe, and they were together.

CRITICAL THINKING
Guiding Comprehension

1 **PROBLEM SOLVING** What problem do Margaret and her mother have? (A fire has started nearby and it is getting closer.)

2 **PROBLEM SOLVING** What are the first things Mama does to protect the family? (She tells Margaret to wake her brothers so they will be ready to move if necessary. She lets their animals loose so they can run to safety.)

3 **PROBLEM SOLVING** Why does Margaret decide that she cannot wait at the house with her brothers as Mama has instructed? (The wind is blowing the fire closer to the house.)

4 **PROBLEM SOLVING** What solution does Margaret chose to solve the problem? Is it a good solution? (She tells her brothers to run for the river. It is a good solution because being in the river water should help to protect them from the fire.)

Discussion Options

Personal Response Point out that Margaret's family lost all their possessions in the fire, yet Margaret's spirits soar as the story ends. Ask students to tell whether they think they would feel as Margaret does in that situation and why.

⭐ **Connecting/Comparing** Have students discuss why *Run to the River* belongs in a theme called *Smart Solutions*.

 English Language Learners

Supporting Comprehension

Help students use pictures or gestures to explain the meanings of *smoke, flames, heat, sparks,* and *burning.* Invite students to draw pictures of key events in the story. Then help them write captions for their illustrations, using as many of the words they have just defined as possible.

Building Background

Key Concept: Speaking Two Languages

Tell students that in *Pepita Talks Twice,* they will read about a girl who uses her knowledge of two languages to help people who speak only one language.

Ask if any students speak languages other than English. Ask them if they can think of words from their language—food words, for example—that are used in English. Then use "Spanish Words" on Anthology pages 302–303 to point out some English words that come from Spanish.

- Have a student read aloud "Spanish Words."

- Have students discuss English words they know that come from Spanish.

Get Set to Read

Background and Vocabulary

Pepita Talks Twice

Read to find the meanings of these words.

e • Glossary

enchilada

languages

salsa

Spanish

taco

tamales

tortilla

Spanish Words

The girl in the story you are about to read speaks two **languages** — English and **Spanish**. You might be surprised to learn that many everyday words in English come from Spanish. Do you know the words *canyon,* *enchilada,* *plaza, rodeo,* *salsa,* or *tortilla*? If you do, then you know some Spanish. These are all Spanish words that have become part of the English language. Here are some other words that come from Spanish. Which ones do you know?

iguana

302

English Language Learners

Supporting Comprehension

Beginning/Preproduction Have students listen to the article. Ask students to point to the correct picture as you read aloud each caption.

Early Production and Speech Emergence Point out and explain the Key Vocabulary words. Ask volunteers to repeat each word after you and use it in a sentence.

Intermediate and Advanced Fluency Have partners take turns asking each other questions based on the article.

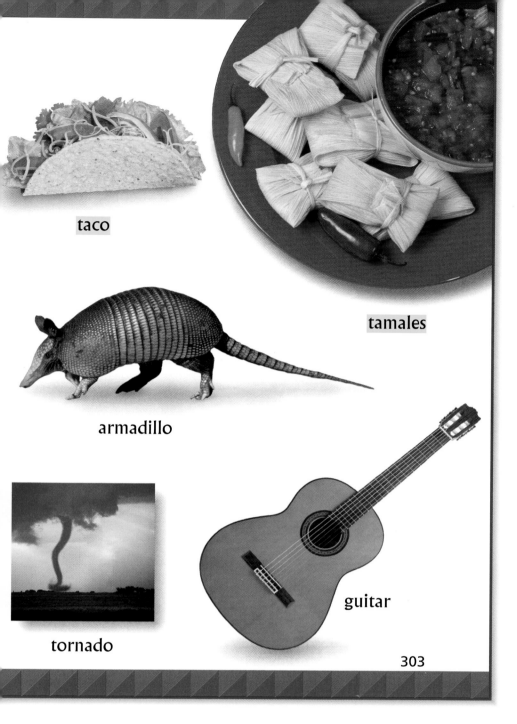

taco

tamales

armadillo

tornado

guitar

303

Introducing Vocabulary

Key Vocabulary

These words support the Key Concept and appear in the selection.

language spoken or written human speech

Spanish a language

enchiladas tortillas rolled around a filling, then covered with spicy sauce

salsa a spicy sauce usually made with tomatoes, onions, and peppers

tortilla a round, flat bread made of corn, from Mexico and Central America

tamales cornmeal dough wrapped in a corn husk or leaf around a filling and steamed

tacos tortillas folded around a filling such as ground meat or cheese

e • **Glossary**
e • **WordGame**

See Vocabulary notes on pages 306, 308, 310, 318, 328, and 330 for additional words to preview.

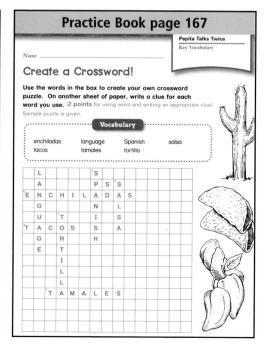

Transparency 6–1

Where Do These Words Belong?

Vocabulary Words		
tamales	salsa	tortilla
enchiladas	Spanish	tacos
language		

Food Words
tamales
enchiladas
salsa
tacos
tortilla

Words About Speaking and Writing
language
Spanish

TRANSPARENCY 6–1
TEACHER'S EDITION PAGE 303

ANNOTATED VERSION
SMART SOLUTIONS Pepita Talks Twice
Key Vocabulary

Practice Book page 167

Pepita Talks Twice
Key Vocabulary

Name

Create a Crossword!

Use the words in the box to create your own crossword puzzle. On another sheet of paper, write a clue for each word you use. (2 **points** for using word and writing an appropriate clue) Sample puzzle is given.

Vocabulary			
enchiladas	language	Spanish	salsa
tacos	tamales	tortilla	

Display Transparency 6–1.

- Model using what you know about the word *tamales* to fill it in the "Food Words" box.

- Have students read each remaining word and use what they know to insert the word in the correct box. Have students explain why they placed each word where they did.

- Ask students to look for these words as they read and use them as they discuss the story.

Practice/Homework Assign **Practice Book** page 167.

Introducing Vocabulary 303

COMPREHENSION STRATEGY

Evaluate

Teacher Modeling Ask a student to read the Strategy Focus aloud. Explain that a good evaluation of a story tells if the author has succeeded in his or her purpose. Ask students to read page 306. Then model the strategy.

Think Aloud *People ask Pepita to talk for them in Spanish and English. Today she doesn't want to help anyone, because she wants to get home and teach her dog a trick. That seems realistic. Sometimes I don't want to do my chores, because I want to do other, fun things.*

Test Prep Tell students that the Evaluate strategy will help them on tests. Encourage them to ask questions such as these as they read: What do I like about this passage? Why? Is it useful or entertaining? Why?

COMPREHENSION SKILL

Problem Solving

Introduce the Graphic Organizer. Tell students that a Problem-Solving Chart can help them use experience and knowledge from their own lives to evaluate Pepita's problem and how she tries to solve it. Explain that as they read, students will fill out the Problem-Solving Chart found on **Practice Book** page 168.

- Display **Transparency 6–2.** Have students read Anthology page 306.

- Model filling in the pros and cons for the first solution. Monitor students' work as needed.

Meet the Author
Ofelia Dumas Lachtman

Birthday: July 9
Where she lives: Los Angeles, California
Favorite author as a child: Louisa May Alcott, who wrote *Little Women*
Where she gets her ideas: "I get my best ideas from scribbling, sometimes while sitting under a tree."
Hobbies: walking, listening to music, taking care of her cats
Other books: *Pepita Thinks Pink/Pepita y el color rosado*

Meet the Illustrator
Mike Reed

Birthday: August 22
Where he grew up: Northville, Michigan
Where he lives now: Minneapolis, Minnesota
His sons: Alex and Joseph
His dog: named Mousse by his youngest son because "he's brown and sweet"

Other books:
Christopher (by Lauren Wohl)
Space Dogs from the Planet K-9 (by Joan Holub)
Taming the Wild Waiyuuzee (by Rita Williams-Garcia)

If you want to learn more about Ofelia Dumas Lachtman and Mike Reed, visit Education Place. www.eduplace.com/kids

304

Transparency 6–2

Problem-Solving Chart

Problem: Pepita does not like having to talk twice.	
Responses may vary.	
Possible Solutions	**Pros (+) and Cons (−)**
1. Stop speaking Spanish.	(+) You wouldn't have to talk twice for people anymore.
	(−) You wouldn't be able to talk with people who speak only Spanish.
2. Stop speaking English.	(+) You wouldn't have to talk twice for people anymore.
	(−) You wouldn't be able to talk with people who speak only English.
3. Get mad and point out that you don't have time to speak twice.	(+) People would stop asking you to talk twice.
	(−) You would probably lose a lot of friends.
4. Politely say that you can't speak twice when you don't have time.	(+) Most people would probably stop asking you to talk twice.
	(+) You could still talk with people who speak only Spanish or English.

SMART SOLUTIONS Pepita Talks Twice
Graphic Organizer Problem-Solving Chart

ANNOTATED VERSION

TRANSPARENCY 6–2
TEACHER'S EDITION PAGE 304

Practice Book page 168

Pepita Talks Twice
Graphic Organizer Problem-Solving Chart

Name _____

Problem-Solving Chart

Problem: Pepita does not like having to talk twice.	
Responses may vary.	
Possible Solutions	**Pros (+) and Cons (−)**
1. Stop speaking Spanish.	(+) You wouldn't have to talk twice for people anymore.
	(−) You wouldn't be able to talk with people who spoke only Spanish. **(2 points)**
2. Stop speaking English.	(+) You wouldn't have to talk twice for people anymore. **(2)**
	(−) You wouldn't be able to talk with people who spoke only English. **(2)**
3. Get mad and point out that you don't have time to speak twice.	(+) People would stop asking you to talk twice. **(2)**
	(−) You would probably lose a lot of friends. **(2)**
4. Politely say that you can't speak twice when you don't have time.	(+) Most people would probably stop asking you to talk twice. **(2)**
	(+) You could still talk with people who speak only Spanish or English. **(2)**

Strategy Focus

As you find out why Pepita has to talk twice, **evaluate** how the author makes Pepita and her problem seem real to you.

Extra Support/Intervention

Selection Preview

pages 305–311 Many people ask Pepita to help them by talking to someone in Spanish or English. Why might this bother Pepita after a while?

pages 312–315 Pepita decides that she will solve her problem by not speaking Spanish anymore. What problems do you think her decision might cause?

pages 316–319 Pepita's dog Lobo doesn't understand her English. In school, Pepita is asked to help a new girl who only speaks Spanish. Will Pepita help her?

pages 320–331 Pepita's decision causes other problems and makes her and her family unhappy. What can change Pepita's mind? Will Pepita talk twice again?

Purpose Setting

- Remind students that this story tells about a girl who is tired of talking in two languages.
- Have students preview the selection. Ask them to predict how Pepita will solve her problem.
- As they read, have students evaluate how well the author makes Pepita's problem seem real to them.
- Ask students to think about the solutions to Pepita's problem as they read.
- You may want to preview the Responding questions on Anthology page 332 with students.

Journal ▶ Students can record their personal feelings about the text and how well they think the author has portrayed Pepita's problem.

STRATEGY REVIEW
Phonics/Decoding

Remind students to use the Phonics/Decoding Strategy as they read.

Modeling Write this sentence from *Pepita Talks Twice* and point to *delivery*: *Come talk to the <u>delivery</u> man in English.*

Think Aloud *I know the first word part,* dih, *from words like* decide. *Then I see* live *and the* r-y. *I know that* y *at the end of a word can be pronounced* ee. *If I blend the sounds, I say* dih-lihv-ree. *That's close to* dih-LIHV-uh-ree. *A delivery man delivers packages. That makes sense.*

Guiding Comprehension

1 **PROBLEM SOLVING** How might Pepita help people by talking for them in English and Spanish? (She might help by translating, or repeating what one person says in the other person's language.)

2 **MAKING INFERENCES** What can you infer about the detail that, until today, Pepita helped people *without a grumble*? (Pepita is usually a helpful, patient person.)

3 **DRAWING CONCLUSIONS** Why would stopping to help people keep Pepita from doing what she planned after school today? (If Pepita stops to help people on her way home, Juan will get home first and will teach Lobo the trick she wants to teach him.)

1 Pepita was a little girl who spoke Spanish and English.

"Come, Pepita, please help us," people would say. Everybody called on Pepita to talk for them in Spanish and English. And she **2** did what they asked without a grumble. Until today.

Today she didn't want to help anyone. She wanted to get home **3** before her brother Juan [HWAN]. She wanted to teach their dog Lobo a new trick. She wanted to teach him to fetch a ball. But if she didn't hurry, Juan would teach Lobo first.

Pepita era una niña pequeña que hablaba español e inglés.

—Ven acá, Pepita. Ayúdanos, por favor —le decía la gente. Todo el mundo llamaba a Pepita para que hablara por ellos en español y en inglés. Y ella hacía lo que le pedían sin quejarse. Hasta hoy.

Hoy, Pepita no tenía ganas de ayudar a nadie. Quería llegar a casa antes que su hermano Juan. Quería enseñarle un nuevo truco a su perro Lobo. Quería enseñarle a recoger la pelota. Y si Pepita no se apuraba, Juan se lo iba a enseñar a Lobo primero.

306

English Language Learners

Supporting Comprehension

Before reading, show students how the story itself "speaks twice" because the very same story is written both in English and in Spanish. Ask a student who reads Spanish to read the text in Spanish on page 306. Alternatively, play the audio CD for the class.

Vocabulary

Spanish a language

grumble a complaint; to complain

307

Extra Support/Intervention

Strategy Modeling: Evaluate

Use this example to model the strategy.

I ask myself whether the author has succeeded in interesting me in the story. I think it's interesting that Pepita can speak two languages, and I want to find out how that works in the story. I also want to read more about Lobo, because I like dogs.

CRITICAL THINKING

Guiding Comprehension

4 MAKING INFERENCES Why does Pepita race by the grocery store? (She knows that Mr. Hobbs, who owns the store, might ask her for help.)

5 WRITER'S CRAFT What words does the author use to show that Pepita is trying to sneak past Aunt Rosa's house? *(tiptoed, softly)*

6 MAKING INFERENCES What do you think the author means when she says that *deep inside her,* Pepita's *grumble grew*? (Pepita wants to get home and is getting more and more annoyed with people who stop her for help.)

4 Pepita raced by the grocery store that belonged to Mr. Hobbs, but not fast enough. "Pepita," Mr. Hobbs called. "Come speak to this lady in Spanish. Tell me what she wants!"

Pepita did what Mr. Hobbs asked. But deep inside of her a grumble began.

5 She tiptoed by the house where her Aunt Rosa lived, but not softly enough. "Pepita," her aunt called in Spanish. "Come talk to the delivery man in English. Tell me what he wants!"

Pepita did what Aunt Rosa asked. But deep inside of her **6** the grumble grew.

Pepita salió corriendo por la tienda de Mr. Hobbs, pero no pudo escaparse a tiempo. —Pepita —Mr. Hobbs la llamó—. Ven para que le hables a esta señora en español. ¡Dime lo que quiere!

Pepita hizo lo que Mr. Hobbs le pedía, pero muy por dentro sintió el principio de una queja.

Pasó en puntillas por la casa donde vivía su Tía Rosa, pero no pasó sin hacer un poco de ruido. —Pepita, ven a hablarle al repartidor en inglés. ¡Mira a ver qué quiere!

Pepita hizo lo que su tía le pidió, pero muy por dentro la queja se fue haciendo más fuerte.

308

Vocabulary

tiptoed walked quietly

309

Author's Viewpoint

Teach

- Remind students that an author's viewpoint is the way he or she looks at, thinks of, or feels about a subject.
- Explain that viewpoint is revealed by
  - an author's purpose for writing (to inform, persuade, entertain, describe, or express)
  - the language used to describe different characters and events
  - the information included in, or left out of, a story

Practice/Apply

- Help students understand that the author shows the reader that Pepita is generally a patient, helpful person by showing that Pepita always helps people when they ask her.
- As they read, have students complete a word web to identify the author's viewpoint toward Pepita.

helpful — Pepita — smart

Review Skill Trace	
Teach	Theme 2, p. 185A
Reteach	Theme 2, p. R8
▶ Review	Theme 4, p. 61; p. 309

English Language Learners

Supporting Comprehension

Read the first few pages as a class and ask, What is special about Pepita? Have you ever helped someone by "speaking twice"? Would you like to speak twice? Why doesn't Pepita want to help anyone anymore?

CRITICAL THINKING
Guiding Comprehension

7 **CAUSE AND EFFECT** What happens each time Pepita agrees to help people when she doesn't really want to? (The grumble inside her grows; she gets more upset.)

8 **MAKING INFERENCES** Why does seeing Juan playing with Lobo make Pepita's grumble *explode*? (because Pepita wanted to get home first and teach Lobo to fetch a ball)

COMPREHENSION STRATEGY
Evaluate

Teacher/Student Modeling Model using the Evaluate strategy to think about the character and the way the author tells the story.

- *I understand why the grumble inside Pepita grows and finally bursts. Sometimes I get upset when I don't get to do something that is really important to me.*

- *The author is doing a good job describing Pepita's situation. Pepita seems real because she does things such as getting mad at her brother.*

Ask students to read page 312 and to evaluate how the author shows Pepita's relationship with her brother. (friendly but competitive; Juan says Pepita's solution is *pretty dumb.*)

Vocabulary

ducked lowered one's head and body quickly to avoid being seen by others

---

She ducked behind the fence as she went by her neighbors' house, but not low enough.

"Pepita," Miguel called and said in Spanish, "my mother wants you to talk on the telephone in English. Please tell her what the man wants."

7

Pepita did what Miguel asked. But deep inside of her the grumble grew larger.

8

And when she went into her own yard and found her brother Juan teaching Lobo to return a ball, the grumble grew so big that it exploded.

"If I didn't speak Spanish and English," she burst out, "I would have been here first!"

Se deslizó detrás de la cerca de sus vecinos con la cabeza agachada, pero no la bajó lo suficiente.

—Pepita —Miguel la llamó y le dijo en español— mi madre quiere que hables por teléfono en inglés. Por favor, ven a ver lo que el hombre quiere.

Pepita hizo lo que Miguel le pidió, pero muy por dentro la queja se hizo más fuerte todavía.

Y cuando entró en su propio jardín y encontró que su hermano Juan ya estaba enseñándole a Lobo a recoger la pelota, la queja se volvió tan fuerte que explotó.

—¡Si yo no hablara español e inglés —exclamó—, habría llegado aquí primero!

310

311

Making Inferences

Teach

- Remind students that to really understand stories, readers must often make inferences, or guesses, based on personal knowledge and the information an author gives.

Practice/Apply

- Guide students to use information in the second paragraph on page 310 plus personal knowledge to infer who Miguel is. (Miguel is a neighbor and friend of Pepita's.)

- Then have students complete a chart like the one below to make an inference about how many languages Miguel's mother knows.

What's in the Story		What I Know		Inference
Miguel's mother wants Pepita to talk on the telephone in English.	+	Grown-ups don't usually want children to talk for them on the telephone.	=	Miguel's mother doesn't speak English, only Spanish.

Review Skill Trace	
Teach	Theme 1, p. 89A; Theme 5, p. 183A
Reteach	Theme 1, p. R10; Theme 5, p. R8
▶ Review	Theme 2, p. 193; Theme 3, p. 351; p. 311

Guiding Comprehension

❾ DRAWING CONCLUSIONS Why do you think Pepita decided to stop speaking Spanish instead of telling people when she doesn't have time to talk twice? (Maybe she didn't think of this idea; maybe she was upset; maybe she feels uncomfortable telling people she doesn't have time to help.)

❿ MAKING INFERENCES Do Pepita's mother and brother seem to approve of her decision? What makes you think so? (No; Juan says Pepita's decision is dumb; Pepita's mother seems surprised; says *My, oh my* when Pepita tells her.)

⓫ MAKING JUDGMENTS Do you think you would you feel the same way as Pepita does about talking twice? What do you think of Pepita's decision? (Answers will vary.)

That night as Pepita lay in bed, she thought and thought. By morning she had decided what she would do. She slipped out of bed and tiptoed by Lobo, who was sleeping on the floor. She hurried into the kitchen, where her mother was cooking breakfast and Juan was eating.

❾ "I am never, ever going to speak Spanish anymore," Pepita said loudly.

❿ "That's pretty dumb," Juan said.

"My, oh my, Pepita. Why?" her mother asked.

"Because I'm tired of talking twice."

"Twice?" her mother asked.

⓫ "Yes! Once in Spanish and once in English. So I'm never going to speak Spanish anymore."

Esa noche, ya en cama Pepita se puso a pensar y pensar. Cuando amaneció, ya había decidido lo que iba a hacer. Deslizándose de la cama, pasó en puntillas junto a Lobo, que dormitaba en el piso. Entró rápidamente en la cocina, donde su madre estaba preparando el desayuno y Juan estaba comiendo.

—Nunca más voy a volver a hablar español —Pepita dijo en voz muy alta.

—Ésa es una gran tontería —Juan le dijo.

—¡Ay, ay, Pepita! ¿Por qué? —le dijo su mamá.

—Porque estoy cansada de hablar dos veces.

—¿Cómo dos veces? —su madre le preguntó.

—¡Sí! Primero en inglés y después en español. Así que no voy a hablar más en español.

312

ASSIGNMENT CARD 1

Picture This!

Word Choice

On page 312, words such as *slipped*, *tiptoed*, and *hurried* help the reader picture Pepita on the day that she announces her decision to never speak Spanish again. Where else in the story does the author's word choice help you picture what is happening? As you look back through the story, make a list of the vivid verbs that you find.

313

Challenge

Word Choice

Have students identify verbs on page 313 that help them picture Pepita the morning that she announces her decision. Have students find other places in the story where the author's word choice helps them picture what is happening.

Pepita slipped, tiptoed, hurried.

CRITICAL THINKING
Guiding Comprehension

⑫ MAKING JUDGMENTS Why do you think Juan points out a problem with Pepita's decision to stop speaking Spanish? (to annoy his sister; to support his earlier remark that it is dumb not to speak Spanish)

⑬ DRAWING CONCLUSIONS What conclusion can you draw from the fact that Pepita calls Lobo "Wolf"? ("Lobo" means "Wolf" in Spanish.)

⑭ MAKING INFERENCES Why does Lobo follow Pepita instead of obeying her command to go home? (Lobo has learned his name and commands in Spanish; he doesn't understand words in English.)

⑫ Juan took a bite of tortilla and grinned. "How will you ask for enchiladas and tamales . . . and tacos with salsa?" he asked. "They are all Spanish words, you know."

"I will find a way," Pepita said with a frown. She hadn't thought about that before.

After breakfast, Pepita kissed her mother, picked up her lunch box, and started to school. Outside, she put her lunch box down and closed the gate to the fence, but not tight enough. Lobo pushed the gate open and followed at her heels.

⑬ "Wolf," Pepita scolded, "go home!" But Lobo just wagged his

⑭ tail and followed her to the corner.

Juan mordió un pedazo de tortilla y se sonrió. —¿Cómo vas a pedir enchiladas y tamales . . . y tacos con salsa? —preguntó—. Todas ésas son palabras españolas, ¿sabes?

—Buscaré la forma —Pepita dijo arrugando la frente. No había pensado en eso antes.

Después de desayunar, Pepita besó a su madre, recogió la lonchera con su almuerzo y salió para la escuela. Afuera, bajó la lonchera al suelo y cerró la verja del jardín, pero no del todo. Lobo abrió la verja de un empujón y la siguió.

—Wolf —Pepita lo regañó—, go home!— Pero Lobo le meneó la cola y la siguió hasta la esquina.

314

Vocabulary

tortilla a round, flat bread made of corn, from Mexico and Central America

enchiladas tortillas rolled around a filling, then covered with spicy sauce

tamales cornmeal dough wrapped in a corn husk or leaf around a filling and steamed

tacos tortillas folded around a filling such as ground meat or cheese

salsa a spicy sauce usually made with tomatoes, onions, and peppers

REACHING ALL LEARNERS

Extra Support/ Intervention

Review (pages 305–315)

Before students join the whole class for Stop and Think on page 315, have them

- take turns modeling Evaluate and any other reading strategies they used
- add to **Transparency 6–2**
- check and revise their Problem-Solving Charts on **Practice Book** page 168, and use it to summarize

English Language Learners

Strategy Modeling: Phonics/Decoding

Use this example to model the strategy.

When I look at the word scolded, *I see the word part* cold *in the middle. With the* s *in front, I say* skohld. *When I add the* e-d *ending, I pronounce the word* SKOHLD-ehd. *That means* spoke angrily at someone for something they did. *That makes sense.*

315

Stop and Think

Critical Thinking Questions

1. **CAUSE AND EFFECT** So far, what are the effects of Pepita's decision to stop speaking Spanish? (Her brother calls her *dumb* and her mother is surprised; Pepita can't ask for foods that have Spanish names; her dog doesn't understand her anymore.)

2. **MAKING JUDGMENTS** Do you think Pepita's decision to stop speaking Spanish is a good one? Explain your opinion. (Answers will vary.)

Strategies in Action

Have students take turns modeling Evaluate and other strategies they used.

Discussion Options

You may want to bring the entire class together to do one or more of the activities below.

- **Review Predictions/Purpose** Discuss which predictions were accurate and which needed to be revised. Record any changes and new predictions. Ask students what they have learned about Pepita's attempt to solve her problem.

- **Share Group Discussions** Have students share their questions and literature discussions.

- **Summarize** Help students use their Problem-Solving Charts to summarize what has happened in the story so far.

ASSIGNMENT CARD 2

Literature Discussion

Form a small group with several other classmates. Discuss the following questions and any other questions or ideas you thought of while reading.

- How do you think Pepita's family feels when she stops speaking Spanish?

- Do you think Pepita's decision to stop speaking Spanish is a good one? Explain why you feel this way.

- What are some other ways Pepita might solve her problem?

Theme 6: Smart Solutions

Teacher's Resource BLM page 86

Monitoring Student Progress

If . . .	Then . . .
students have successfully completed the Extra Support activities on page 314,	have them read the rest of the selection cooperatively or independently.

CRITICAL THINKING

Guiding Comprehension

15 **PROBLEM SOLVING** What problem does Pepita have with Lobo? How does she solve it? (Lobo is trying to follow her to school. She asks the crossing guard to keep Lobo.)

16 **AUTHOR'S VIEWPOINT** What do you think Mr. Jones's reaction to Pepita's decision tells about the author's viewpoint? (Mr. Jones says what the author believes.)

15 "Mr. Jones," Pepita said to the crossing guard, "will you please keep Wolf for me? If I take him back home, I'll be late for school."

"I'll walk him home when I'm through," Mr. Jones said. "But I thought his name was Lobo?"

"No," Pepita said. "His name is Wolf now. I don't speak Spanish anymore."

"That's too bad," said Mr. Jones, picking up his red stop sign. **16** "I thought it was a good thing to speak two languages."

"It's not a good thing at all, Mr. Jones. Not when you have to speak twice!"

—Mr. Jones —Pepita le dijo al guardia de cruce—, ¿puede guardarme a Wolf? Si lo llevo a casa otra vez, voy a llegar tarde a la escuela.

—Yo te lo llevaré a casa cuando termine —Mr. Jones le dijo—. Pero yo creía que su nombre era Lobo.

—No —Pepita le dijo—. El se llama Wolf ahora. Yo ya no hablo español.

—¡Qué lástima! —dijo Mr. Jones tomando su letrero rojo de "Alto"—. Yo creía que era bueno hablar dos lenguas.

—No es nada bueno, Mr. Jones. No cuando uno tiene que hablar dos veces.

316

Vocabulary

language spoken or written human speech

Soy
Lobo.
¿Quién es Wolf?

317

 English Language Learners

Supporting Comprehension

Discuss the illustration on page 317 with students. Point out Lobo and the way he looks at Pepita. Ask, What might Lobo be thinking?

CRITICAL THINKING
Guiding Comprehension

17 MAKING JUDGMENTS Do you agree with Pepita's decision not to help Carmen? Why or why not? (Answers will vary.)

18 WRITER'S CRAFT Why do you think the author has Pepita mumble her thought about speaking two languages when she has Pepita express the same thought aloud on page 316? (to show that Pepita is starting to feel a little unsure of her decision to stop speaking Spanish)

COMPREHENSION STRATEGY
Evaluate

Student Modeling Ask students how the author changes the way the reader feels about Pepita on page 318. If necessary, use the following prompt: Right now, do you feel more sorry for Pepita or for Carmen?

At school her teacher, Miss García, smiled and said, "We have a new student starting today. Her name is Carmen and she speaks no English. We must all be as helpful as we can."

Miss García looked at Pepita and said, "Pepita, please tell Carmen where to put her lunch and show her where everything is."

17 Carmen smiled at Pepita and Pepita just wanted to run away and hide. Instead, she stood up and said, "I'm sorry, Miss García, but I can't. I don't speak Spanish anymore."

"That is really too bad," her teacher said. "It's such a wonderful thing to speak two languages."

18 Pepita mumbled to herself, "It is not a wonderful thing at all, not when you have to speak twice!"

En la escuela, la maestra, Miss García, se sonrió y dijo:
—Tenemos una nueva alumna comenzando hoy. Se llama Carmen y no habla inglés. Todos debemos de ayudarla lo más que podamos.

Miss García miró hacia Pepita y le dijo: —Pepita, por favor, dile a Carmen donde puede poner su almuerzo y donde está todo.

Carmen le sonrió a Pepita y Pepita tuvo ganas de salir corriendo y esconderse, pero se levantó y dijo en inglés: —Lo siento, Miss García, pero no puedo. Yo ya no hablo español.

—¡Qué lástima! —dijo la maestra—. Es tan maravilloso hablar dos lenguas.

Pepita murmuró entre dientes: —¡No es nada maravilloso, no cuando uno tiene que hablar dos veces!

318

English Language Learners

Supporting Comprehension

To help students recognize the range of consequences that Pepita's solution has, ask students, To whom does Pepita speak usually Spanish? Now that she speaks only English, what things can't she do? Do you think her solution is a good one? Why or why not? Can you think of a better one?

Vocabulary

mumbled said softly and unclearly

319

Problem Solving

Teach

- Remind students that problem-solving steps include
  - defining the problem
  - brainstorming possible solutions
  - studying the pros and cons of each solution
  - choosing the best solution

Practice

- Ask students what Pepita's problem is on page 318. (Pepita is not speaking Spanish anymore, and her teacher asks her to help a new student by speaking Spanish.)

- Use a chart like the one below to discuss the pros and cons of two solutions. Ask students to choose the better alternative.

Possible Solutions	Pros (+) and Cons (-)
1. Pepita sticks to her plan.	(+) Doesn't have to talk twice (-) Feels guilty (-) Carmen feels bad and has no help
2. Pepita speaks Spanish one more time to help Carmen.	(+) Feels good about helping (-) Has to talk twice

Apply

- Have students work in small groups to come up with a third solution and its pros and cons.

Target Skill Trace	
Preview; Teach	p. 301A; p. 304; p. 319; p. 337A
Reteach	p. R8
Review	pp. 413D–413E; Theme 3, p. 327; Theme 4, p. 89

Reading the Selection 319

CRITICAL THINKING

Guiding Comprehension

⑲ COMPARE AND CONTRAST How does Lobo respond to commands given in English and in Spanish? (Lobo doesn't respond at all when Pepita speaks to him in English, but responds immediately when Juan gives the same command in Spanish.)

⑳ DRAWING CONCLUSIONS What does the author mean when she says that Lobo came "like a streak" when Juan called him? (Lobo ran to Juan very quickly.)

㉑ MAKING INFERENCES How do you think Pepita feels when Lobo does not come to her when she calls him? (Sample answers: disappointed, angry, sad, frustrated, worried, annoyed)

⑲ When Pepita walked into her yard after school, she found Lobo sleeping on the front porch. "Wolf, come here!" she called. "Wolf, wake up!" But he didn't open an eye or even wiggle an ear.

⑳ From the sidewalk behind her, Juan shouted, "¡Lobo! ¡Ven acá!" Like a streak, Lobo raced to the gate and barked.

㉑ Juan laughed and said, "Hey, Pepita, how are you going to teach old Lobo tricks if you don't speak Spanish?"

"I'll find a way," Pepita said with a frown. She had not thought about this either.

Cuando Pepita entró en su jardín al regresar de la escuela, encontró a Lobo durmiendo en el portal. —¡Wolf, ven acá, despiértate! —le dijo en inglés. Pero el perro no abrió ni un ojo ni meneó una oreja.

Desde la acera, Juan gritó en español: —¡Lobo! ¡Ven acá! —Lobo salió disparado hacia la verja, ladrando.

Juan se rió y dijo: —Oye, Pepita, ¿cómo vas a enseñarle trucos a Lobo si tú no hablas español?

—Ya buscaré la forma —Pepita dijo arrugando la frente. No había pensado en esto tampoco.

320

Extra Support/Intervention

Strategy Modeling: Evaluate

Use this example to model the strategy.

Pepita's first problem was that talking twice for people made her get home late, so Juan played with Lobo first and taught him to fetch a ball. Now Pepita has a new problem. She has stopped speaking Spanish, but because Lobo doesn't understand English, Juan still gets to play with Lobo and teach him tricks. How can Pepita finally solve her problem?

321

CRITICAL THINKING
Guiding Comprehension

22 **PROBLEM SOLVING** Can you think of any way that Pepita could sing with Miguel's brothers and sisters without speaking Spanish? (Sample answers: She could sing softly in English as the others sing in Spanish, or she could hum along.)

23 **MAKING INFERENCES** Why does Pepita frown when she realizes things she didn't consider at the time she made her decision? (Maybe she realizes that giving up speaking Spanish also means giving up a lot of things she likes.)

24 **DRAWING CONCLUSIONS** What conclusion can you draw from the fact that Pepita keeps discovering things she hadn't thought about when she made her decision? (She didn't think about the effects her decision would have when she made it.)

Pepita's neighbor Miguel was on the sidewalk bouncing a rubber ball. His brothers and sisters were sitting on their front porch singing. When they saw her, they called, "Come, Pepita! Sing with us!"

22

"I can't," she called. "All of your songs are in Spanish, and I don't speak Spanish anymore."

"Too bad," they said. "How will you help us sing at the birthday parties?"

23

"I'll find a way," Pepita said with a frown. This was something

24 else she had not thought about.

El vecino de Pepita, Miguel, estaba en la acera jugando con una pelota de goma. Sus hermanos estaban sentados en el portal cantando. Cuando la vieron, la llamaron: —¡Ven, Pepita! ¡Ven a cantar con nosotros!

—No puedo —respondió—. Todas las canciones de ustedes son en español y yo ya no hablo español —dijo en inglés.

—¡Qué lástima! —dijeron—. ¿Cómo vas a poder cantar con nosotros en las fiestas de cumpleaños?

—Buscaré la forma —Pepita dijo arrugando la frente. Esto era algo más que no había pensado.

322

323

English Language Learners

Supporting Comprehension

Point out Pepita's frowning expression in the illustration on page 323. Have students draw two faces, one smiling and one frowning. Ask them whether they think Pepita might be smiling at the end of the story.

CRITICAL THINKING
Guiding Comprehension

25 **MAKING INFERENCES** Why do you think Pepita's mother announces at the dinner table that Abuelita has a new story for Pepita? (Maybe Pepita's mother thinks Pepita will speak Spanish with Abuelita.)

26 **PREDICTING OUTCOMES** How might Pepita's decision to stop speaking Spanish affect her visit with Abuelita? (If Abuelita doesn't speak English, Pepita won't be able to talk with her.)

27 **MAKING INFERENCES** Why do you think Pepita swallows hard before she tells her father about her decision? (She knows her father won't approve of her decision.)

---

25 At the supper table, Pepita's mother told everyone that Abuelita [ah-bweh-LEE-ta], their grandmother, was coming the next day. "Abuelita says she has a new story for Pepita."

26 Juan laughed. "Abuelita tells all her stories in Spanish. What are you going to do now?"

"Nothing," said Pepita. "I can listen in Spanish."

"¿Qué pasa? ¿Qué pasa?" Pepita's father said. "What is going on?"

27 Pepita swallowed hard. "I don't speak Spanish anymore, Papá," she said.

"Too bad," her father said. "It's a fine thing to know two languages."

"It's not a fine thing at all," Pepita said and then stopped. Her father was frowning at her.

En la mesa a la hora de comer, la madre de Pepita le dijo a todos que Abuelita iba a llegar al día siguiente. —Abuelita me dice que tiene un cuento nuevo para Pepita.

Juan se rió. —Abuelita cuenta todos sus cuentos en español. ¿Cómo te las vas a arreglar ahora?

—No importa —dijo Pepita en inglés—. Puedo escuchar en español.

—¿Qué pasa? ¿Qué pasa? —el padre de Pepita dijo en español—. What's going on? —dijo luego en inglés.

Pepita tragó con dificultad. —I don't speak Spanish anymore, Papá —dijo.

—¡Qué lástima! —dijo su padre—. Es muy bueno saber dos lenguas.

—No es nada bueno —Pepita dijo y luego se detuvo. Su papá la miraba, arrugando la frente.

324

English Language Learners

Supporting Comprehension

Pause on page 324 to help students pronounce the Spanish question "¿Qué pasa?" [KAY PAH-sah] Then, to help students evaluate the author's success in conveying a realistic situation, ask, Do you or people you know ever speak two languages in the same conversation? Ask students whether they think Pepita's father is upset at her decision and why or why not.

325

Writer's Craft

Mood

Teach

- Tell students that mood is the feeling in a scene or story.

- Explain that authors use words, details, and descriptive language to create a mood.

Practice/Apply

- Read the last three paragraphs on page 324 with students.

- Help students understand that the phrases *swallowed hard* and *said and then stopped,* along with the image of Pepita's father frowning, convey a mood of tension and uneasiness at the supper table, even though the author doesn't say this directly.

- Have students read page 326 and identify words or phrases that show how this mood deepens as the scene continues. (*his frown grew deeper; with a long sad sigh*)

CRITICAL THINKING

Guiding Comprehension

(28) MAKING INFERENCES Why might Pepita's father feel hurt or unhappy that Pepita has stopped speaking Spanish? (Sample answers: Spanish is a part of his family's tradition, and he wants her to be proud of it; he knows that speaking two languages is a useful skill; he knows that her decision will cause a lot of trouble for her.)

(29) DRAWING CONCLUSIONS What conclusions can you draw about Pepita's character from the fact that, even though her decision causes many problems, she refuses to change her mind? (Pepita is stubborn, determined to do things her own way.)

(30) MAKING JUDGMENTS Does Pepita have a good solution to the problem of saying *taco* in English? Explain. (No; the words she uses in English take too long to say and are confusing.)

(28) "She even calls Lobo 'Wolf'!" Juan said.

"Wolf?" her father said, and his frown grew deeper. "Well then, Pepita, we'll have to find a new name for you, won't we? How will you answer to Pepita if that is no longer your name?"

"I'll find a way," Pepita said with a long sad sigh. This was something she had never ever thought about before.

(29) That night when she went to bed, Pepita pulled the blankets up to her chin and made a stubborn face. "I'll find a way," she thought. "If I have to, I can call myself Pete. I can listen in Spanish. I can hum with the singing. I can call a taco a crispy, crunchy, folded-over, round corn sandwich! And Wolf will have to learn his name!" With that she turned over and went to sleep.

(30)

—¡Hasta le dice 'Wolf' a Lobo! —Juan dijo.

—¿'Wolf'? —dijo su padre con aún más arrugas en la frente. —Bueno, Pepita, entonces vamos a tener que encontrarte un nombre nuevo. ¿Cómo vas a responder a 'Pepita' si ése ya no es tu nombre?

—Ya buscaré la forma —Pepita dijo suspirando muy hondo. Esto era algo que nunca había pensado antes.

Esa noche cuando se acostó, Pepita estiró las cobijas hasta la barbilla y puso una cara de terca. —Buscaré la forma —dijo—. Si quiero, puedo ponerme el nombre de Pete. Puedo escuchar en español. Puedo tararear cuando canten. Puedo llamarle al taco sandwich redondo de maíz doblado, tostado y crujiente. ¡Y Wolf tendrá que aprenderse su nombre!— Con esto se dio la vuelta y se durmió.

326

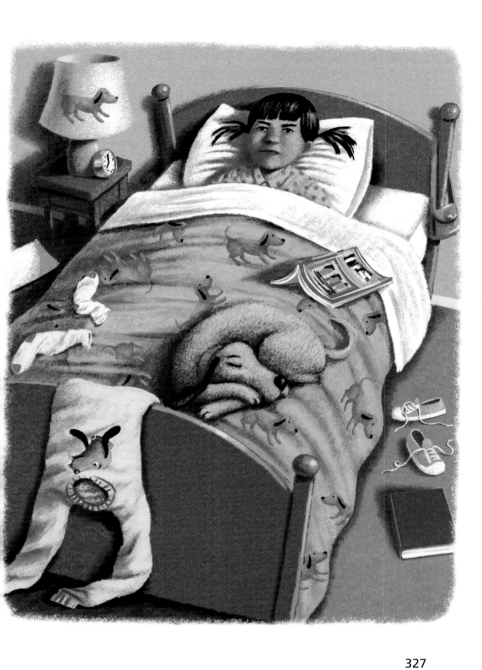

Fluency Practice

Rereading for Fluency Have students choose a favorite part of the story to reread to a partner, or suggest that they read page 326. Encourage students to read expressively.

Guiding Comprehension

31 **MAKING INFERENCES** Why do you think Pepita continues to call Lobo "Wolf" even though he doesn't understand her? (to make him learn his name in English)

32 **WRITER'S CRAFT** What does the author do to create suspense on this page? (She reveals what happens slowly: first, Lobo runs through the gate, then he runs into the street, and then the author says that a car is coming.)

33 **MAKING INFERENCES** How do you think Pepita feels at the end of page 328? (very scared that the car will hit Lobo)

In the morning, when Pepita was leaving for school, her friend Miguel threw his ball into her yard. Lobo fetched it and dropped it at Pepita's feet.

31

"You're a good dog, Wolf," she said.

She put her lunch box down and threw the ball back to Miguel. The little boy laughed and clapped his hands. Just as she was opening the gate, he threw the ball again. This time it went into the street. Like a flash, Lobo ran after it.

32

"Wolf!" Pepita yelled. But Lobo didn't listen and went through the gate.

"Wolf! Come here!" Pepita shouted. But Lobo darted right into the street.

33

A car was coming!

Por la mañana, cuando Pepita iba a salir para la escuela, su amigo Miguel tiró su pelota al jardín de Pepita. Lobo la recogió y la dejó caer a los pies de Pepita.

—Eres un buen perro, Wolf —dijo ella en inglés.

Pepita colocó la lonchera en el suelo y le tiró la pelota de vuelta a Miguel. El niñito se rió y aplaudió. En el mismo momento en que Pepita abría la verja, Miguel volvió a tirarle la pelota. Esta vez cayó en la calle. Lobo corrió disparado a buscarla.

—Wolf! —Pepita gritó. Pero Lobo no le prestó atención y salió por la verja.

—Wolf! Come here! —Pepita gritó. Pero Lobo corrió hasta la misma calle.

¡Un automóvil se aproximaba!

328

Vocabulary

darted moved suddenly and very quickly

ASSIGNMENT CARD 3

Searching for Clues

Foreshadowing

When a writer gives clues about what will happen later in a story, it is called **foreshadowing**. For example, on page 306 Pepita wants to get home first to teach Lobo to fetch. On page 314, Lobo gets out of the yard and follows Pepita to school. Both of these events foreshadow Lobo chasing the ball into the street on page 328.

Look through the story to find other examples of foreshadowing. What clues are there that Lobo will not listen to Pepita on page 328? What hints did the author give earlier in the story that Lobo would not listen to Pepita when she spoke English? Write your ideas on a piece of paper.

Theme 6: Smart Solutions

Teacher's Resource BLM page 86

329

Realistic Fiction

Teach

- Explain that realistic fiction is fiction in which the story events could happen in real life.

- Point out that the story characters in *Pepita Talks Twice* speak, think, feel, and act like real people do and have problems real people might have.

Practice/Apply

- Help students identify details from the story that make *Pepita Talks Twice* a piece of realistic fiction. (Sample answers: the way the characters talk to each other; the scene at supper; Lobo chasing the ball into the street)

- Have small groups create a chart that gives examples of ways in which Pepita behaves like a real girl.

Ways Pepita Seems Realistic
Thoughts:
Actions:
Problems:
Feelings:
Words:

Guiding Comprehension

34 **MAKING INFERENCES** Why does Pepita close her eyes before calling Lobo one last time in Spanish? (Sample answer: She's afraid the car will hit him, and she's scared to watch.)

35 **DRAWING CONCLUSIONS** Why is the driver of the car *red-faced* and why does he shout out the window? (He's upset because Lobo ran in front of his car; because he almost hit Lobo; he's angry that Pepita didn't call Lobo back sooner.)

36 **MAKING INFERENCES** What helps you figure out the meaning of the words that Pepita finally screams to Lobo in Spanish? (two paragraphs later, Pepita says, *Lobo, oh, Lobo, you came when I called in Spanish!*, the words Pepita called out to Lobo earlier in English.)

34   Pepita closed her eyes. "¡Lobo!" she screamed. "¡Lobo! ¡Ven acá!"

    Lobo turned back just before a loud screech of the car's brakes. Pepita opened her eyes in time to see the ball roll to the other side of the street. A red-faced man shouted out the window of the car, and **35** Lobo raced back into the yard!

36   Pepita shut the gate firmly behind Lobo and hugged him. "Lobo, oh, Lobo, you came when I called in Spanish!"

    She nuzzled her face in his warm fur. "I'll never call you Wolf again," she said. "Your name is Lobo. Just like mine is Pepita. And, oh, Lobo, I'm glad I talked twice! It's great to speak two languages!"

    Pepita cerró los ojos. —¡Lobo! —gritó en español—. ¡Lobo! ¡Ven acá!

    Lobo dio la vuelta un instante antes de que los frenos del automóvil chillaran. Cuando Pepita abrió los ojos, la pelota rodaba hacia el otro lado de la calle. Un hombre con la cara roja de furia gritaba por la ventanilla de su carro y Lobo regresaba corriendo al jardín.

    Pepita cerró la verja firmemente detrás de Lobo y lo abrazó. —¡Lobo, oh, Lobo, viniste cuando te llamé en español!

    Pepita escondió la cara en el pelaje caliente del perro. —Nunca más te llamaré Wolf —dijo—. Tu nombre es Lobo, como el mío es Pepita. Y ¡oh, Lobo, cómo me alegro de haber hablado dos veces! ¡Qué maravilloso es hablar dos lenguas!

330

Vocabulary

nuzzled rubbed gently

Extra Support/ Intervention	On Level	Challenge
Selection Review Before students join the whole class for Wrapping Up on page 331, have them • take turns modeling the reading strategies they used • complete **Transparency 6–2** with you and their Problem-Solving Charts • summarize the whole selection	**Literature Discussion** Have small groups of students discuss the story, using their own questions or the questions in Think About the Selection on page 331.	

331

Wrapping Up

Critical Thinking Questions

1. **DRAWING CONCLUSIONS** How does Lobo's near-accident change Pepita's attitude about speaking two languages? (Like her family, friends, teacher, and neighbors, she thinks it's good to speak two languages.)

2. **PREDICTING OUTCOMES** How do you think Pepita will react from now on when people ask her to talk twice? (Answers will vary.)

Strategies in Action

Have students take turns modeling how and where they used the Evaluate strategy.

Discussion Options

Bring the entire class together to do one or more of the activities below.

Review Predictions/Purpose Have students discuss the solutions they came up with for Pepita's problem while reading.

Share Group Discussions Have students share their literature discussions.

Summarize Have students use their Problem-Solving Charts to summarize the story.

Comprehension Check

Use **Practice Book** page 169 to assess students' comprehension of the selection.

Monitoring Student Progress

If . . .	Then . . .
students score 6 or below on **Practice Book** page 169,	guide them in reviewing the selection and discussing their answers.

Practice Book page 169

Pepita Talks Twice
Comprehension Check

Name _____

What Happened?

Mark a T if the sentence is true and an F if it is false.
If the sentence is false, rewrite it to make it correct.

1. Pepita's dog is a wolf.
   F Pepita's dog is named Lobo, which means wolf. (1 point)

2. Some adults in Pepita's neighborhood speak only Spanish.
   T (1)

3. Pepita loses her temper when Juan gets home first and teaches Lobo to fetch a ball.
   T (1)

4. Before she makes her decision, Pepita thinks about all the problems she might have if she stops speaking Spanish.
   F Pepita does not think about the problems she might have. (1)

5. Lobo does not understand Pepita when she speaks in English.
   T (1)

6. Pepita's father is happy when he learns that Pepita has stopped speaking Spanish.
   F Pepita's father is upset. (1)

Write a complete sentence to answer the question below.

What event finally convinces Pepita that it is a good thing to speak both English and Spanish?
She saves Lobo from getting hit when she calls to him in Spanish. (2)

Think About the Selection

Have students discuss or write their answers. Sample answers are provided; accept reasonable responses.

READ & COMPREHEND

1. **CAUSE AND EFFECT** People are always stopping Pepita and asking her to speak for them in Spanish or English. She wants to get home quickly so she can teach her dog a new trick before her brother does.

2. **NOTING DETAILS** People tell Pepita that it's good to be able to speak two languages; some point out problems she will face if she stops speaking Spanish.

3. **AUTHOR'S VIEWPOINT** The author uses the dog as Pepita's reason for deciding not to speak Spanish. Then the dog becomes Pepita's reason for speaking Spanish again. Also, by including Lobo in the story, the author helps readers relate to Pepita, her problems, and the story as a whole.

4. **MAKING GENERALIZATIONS** Answers will vary but may include the ability to speak with more people, have more friends, and be helpful to people who only speak one language.

5. **MAKING JUDGMENTS** Answers will vary.

6. **Connecting/Comparing** Answers will vary, but most will probably choose the decision to speak Spanish again. Encourage reasons beyond simply her being able to save Lobo.

Responding

Think About the Selection

1. What makes Pepita grumble at the beginning of the story?

2. In what ways do other people help Pepita change the way she thinks about her problem?

3. Why do you think the author made Lobo so important to the story?

4. After reading this story, what do you think is the best part of speaking two languages?

5. What new languages would you like to learn? Explain your answer.

6. **Connecting/Comparing** Which of Pepita's decisions do you think was a smart solution? Give reasons for your answer.

Persuading

Write an Opinion

What do you think of Pepita's actions? Did she do the right thing when she stopped speaking Spanish? What else could she have done to solve her problem? Write your opinion and then share it with a classmate.

Tips
- Focus on one or two of Pepita's decisions.
- State your opinion in a respectful way.
- Use phrases such as *I think* or *It seems to me*.

332

REACHING ALL LEARNERS

English Language Learners

Supporting Comprehension

Beginning/Preproduction Ask students to draw their favorite part of the story. Then help students label and describe what they have drawn.

Early Production and Speech Emergence Ask small groups to choose a scene from the story and practice the dialogue as a skit. Students can modify the conversation according to their English skills.

Intermediate and Advanced Fluency Ask students to discuss their own or Pepita's experiences with speaking twice.

Listening and Speaking

Perform a Reader's Theater

In a small group, choose two or three scenes from the story to read aloud. Plan who will play each part, including the narrator. Practice reading your parts with each other. Then present your scenes to the class.

Tips

- Speak slowly and clearly.
- Use expression in your face and voice.
- Let other readers finish their lines before you start yours.

Vocabulary

Label Your Classroom

Make Spanish labels for things in your classroom. On a self-stick note, write a Spanish word from the list below. Put the note near the item that it names. Do the same for the other words on the list.

Bonus Use a Spanish/English dictionary to create more labels for your classroom.

el libro

Spanish	English
el pizarrón	chalkboard
el escritorio	desk
la silla	chair
la ventana	window
el papel	paper
el lápiz	pencil
el libro	book
el almuerzo	lunch

Solve a Spanish Mystery Grid

Learn some Spanish counting words. Visit Education Place and solve a puzzle in Spanish and English! **www.eduplace.com/kids**

333

Additional Responses

Personal Response Invite students to share their personal responses to the selection.

Journal ▸ Ask students to write about Pepita's problem and how she solved it or about a problem they had to solve themselves.

Selection Connections Remind students to add to **Practice Book** page 166.

Responding 333

Extra Support/ Intervention

For the writing activity, suggest that students respond to the questions on Anthology page 332. If needed, simplify the questions: What did Pepita do? Do you think that was good or bad? Why? Assist students who are unaccustomed to stating their opinions.

Practice Book page 166

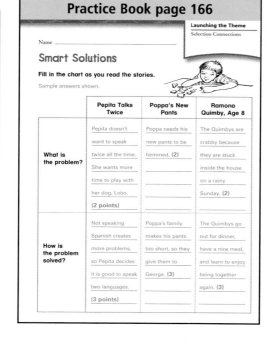

Name ____

Smart Solutions

Fill in the chart as you read the stories.

Sample answers shown.

Launching the Theme
Selection Connections

	Pepita Talks Twice	Poppa's New Pants	Ramona Quimby, Age 8
What is the problem?	Pepita doesn't want to speak twice all the time. She wants more time to play with her dog, Lobo. (2 points)	Poppa needs his new pants to be hemmed. (2)	The Quimbys are crabby because they are stuck inside the house on a rainy Sunday. (2)
How is the problem solved?	Not speaking Spanish creates more problems, so Pepita decides it is good to speak two languages. (3 points)	Poppa's family makes his pants too short, so they give them to George. (3)	The Quimbys go out for dinner, have a nice meal, and learn to enjoy being together again. (3)

Monitoring Student Progress

End-of-Selection Assessment

Selection Test Use the test on pages 141–142 in the **Teacher's Resource Blackline Masters** to assess selection comprehension and vocabulary.

Student Self-Assessment Have students assess their reading with additional questions such as

- Which parts of this selection were difficult? Why?
- Which strategies helped me understand the story better?
- Would I recommend this story to my friends? Why or why not?

Poetry Link

Skill: How to Read a Poem

- **Introduce** the poems, which are written in both English and Spanish.

- **Discuss** the Skill Lesson on Anthology page 334. Explain that a poet expresses an idea or feeling in a poem by using rhythm, rhyme, and word choice.

- **Model** reading a poem. Have volunteers read aloud the poem "Little Piece of Prickly Pear" in English on page 334, and "Pedacito de nopal" in Spanish, if possible.

- **Explain** that when a poem is written in two languages, one way to compare them is to look at the titles of the poems, the number of words in each one, and how the punctuation is the same or different in the two poems.

- **Set a purpose** for reading. Have students read each remaining poem several times and identify one idea or feeling they feel each poem expresses. Suggest that they use Evaluate and other strategies as they read.

Skill: How to Read a Poem

❶ **Read** the poem several times. Look for patterns, such as rhythm or rhyme, in the words.

❷ Sometimes the same poem is written in two languages. **Look** at the poem in both languages. **Compare** titles, number of words, and punctuation.

❸ **Think** about what idea or feeling the poet is trying to express.

334

Little Piece of Prickly Pear

Mama calls me her little piece of prickly pear
when I am sour, when I stamp my feet.

Mama calls me her little *tuna*, good enough to eat
when I am smiling, when I am sweet.

Pedacito de nopal

Mamá me dice "pedacito de nopal"
cuando me enojo, cuando pataleo.

Mamá me dice "tunita" y me comería a besos
cuando sonrío, cuando soy tierna.

Tony Johnston

Vocabulary

prickly pear a type of cactus you can eat

tuna the sweet, red fruit of the prickly pear cactus

I Like to Ride My Bike

I'm ready
for a bike ride. I wear
long blue shorts, my red helmet and
a white T-shirt hanging to my knees.
One pedal
spins
and then, I'm off!

Leaves blur into green air
people shout hello, be careful
stay on the sidewalk.

The wind cools my arms
and legs.
I feel free.

Me gusta montar mi bicicleta

Estoy lista para mi paseo en bicicleta. Llevo
mis largas bermudas azules, mi casco rojo y
una camiseta blanca colgando hasta las rodillas.
Un pedal
gira
y luego, ¡parto!

Las hojas se desvanecen en el verdor del aire
La gente grita ¡Hola! ten cuidado
quédate en la acera.

El viento refresca mis brazos
y piernas.
Me siento libre.

Lori Marie Carlson

335

Extra Support/Intervention

Identifying Metaphors

Help students understand the metaphoric use of *prickly pear* and *tuna* in "Little Piece of Prickly Pear" by discussing affectionate pet names that parents sometimes use with their children. Ask students to find two names in the poem that the speaker's mother uses for her child, one when the speaker is behaving well and the other when the speaker is behaving badly. (Good behavior: *little tuna*; bad behavior: *little piece of prickly pear*)

Poetry

Teach

Review these characteristics of poetry:

- Poems look different from other kinds of writing. Poems are written in stanzas made up of lines.

- Sounds are important to the meaning and enjoyment of a poem. Sound patterns may appear within the poem or as rhyming at the ends of lines.

- It is important to read a poem aloud.

- All poems have rhythm. Some poems have a regular rhythm that repeats from beginning to end. Other poems have the same rhythm as everyday speech.

Practice/Apply

- Guide students to identify the characteristics of poetry in "Little Piece of Prickly Pear" on page 334.

- Ask students to identify these characteristics in a poem of their choice from pages 335–337.

Las canciones de mi abuela

compartían
el ritmo
de la lavadora

transformaban
la cocina
en una pista de baile

consolaban
las sillas
patas arriba

alegraban
los retratos colgados
de la familia

arrullaban
las sábanas
en el tendedero

les daban sabor
a los frijoles
de olla

las canciones
que cantaba
mi abuela

eran capaces
de hacer salir
a las estrellas

convertir
a mi abuela
en una joven

que de nuevo
iba por agua
al río

y hacerla
reír y llorar
a la vez

336

English Language Learners

Supporting Comprehension

Read one of the poems aloud to the class, exaggerating the rhythm so students can hear it. Have students work in small mixed groups, and assign each group a poem. Encourage students to take turns reading their poem aloud a few times. Then have each group list the images in each stanza and illustrate each stanza. Make time for groups to share and discuss their illustrations, and for a volunteer from each group to read the poem aloud.

Vocabulary

consoling comforting

portraits pictures of people

My Grandma's Songs

would follow
the beat of
the washing machine

turning
our kitchen
into a dance floor

consoling
the chairs placed
upside down

delighting
the family portraits
on the walls

putting to sleep
the sheets
on the clothesline

giving flavor
to the boiling pot
of beans

the songs
my grandma
used to sing

could make
the stars
come out

could turn
my grandma
into a young girl

going back
to the river
for water

and make her
laugh and cry
at the same time

Francisco X. Alarcón

337

Wrapping Up

Critical Thinking Questions

Ask students to review the characteristics of each poem to answer these questions.

1. **MAKING INFERENCES** What is the speaker in the first poem feeling and doing when Mama calls the child *her little piece of prickly pear*? When she calls the child *her little tuna*? (feeling angry and stamping his or her feet; feeling happy and behaving well)

2. **NOTING DETAILS** Reread the second stanza of "I Like to Ride My Bike." What is unusual about the punctuation? (no quotation marks around the words the people shout)

3. **AUTHOR'S VIEWPOINT** What is the poet expressing in "My Grandma's Songs"? (Grandma sang songs as she did housework; her songs made everything seem joyful to the poet, and made Grandma remember the joys and sorrows of her childhood.)

4. **Connecting/Comparing** How are the three poems and *Pepita Talks Twice* alike? How are they different? (Both are written in English and Spanish. The poems are written in stanzas with short lines, sometimes without punctuation; the story is written in paragraphs with full punctuation.)

Challenge

Music

Have volunteers set one of the poems in the Link to music. Students may use a recorded piece of music (without words) or compose a tune of their own. Students who play musical instruments can accompany a classmate as he or she reads or sings the words of the poem.

COMPREHENSION SKILLS

OBJECTIVES

- Brainstorm possible solutions to a character's problem.
- List pros and cons to determine the best solution.
- Learn academic language: *pros, cons, solutions.*

Target Skill Trace

Preview, Teach	p. 301A; p. 302; p. 319; p. 337A
Reteach	p. R8
Review	pp. 413D–413E; Theme 3, p. 327; Theme 4, p. 87
See	*Extra Support Handbook,* pp. 196–197; pp. 202–203

Transparency 6–2

Problem-Solving Chart

Problem: Pepita does not like having to talk twice.

Responses may vary.

Possible Solutions	Pros (+) and Cons (−)
1. Stop speaking Spanish.	(+) You wouldn't have to talk twice for people anymore.
	(−) You wouldn't be able to talk with people who speak only Spanish.
2. Stop speaking English.	(+) You wouldn't have to talk twice for people anymore.
	(−) You wouldn't be able to talk with people who speak only English.
3. Get mad and point out that you don't have time to speak twice.	(+) People would stop asking you to talk twice.
	(−) You would probably lose a lot of friends.
4. Politely say that you can't speak twice when you don't have time.	(+) Most people would probably stop asking you to talk twice.
	(+) You could still talk with people who speak only Spanish or English.

TRANSPARENCY 6–2
TEACHER'S EDITION PAGE 304

SMART SOLUTIONS *Pepita Talks Twice*
Graphic Organizer Problem-Solving Chart

ANNOTATED VERSION

Practice Book page 168

Pepita Talks Twice
Graphic Organizer Problem-Solving Chart

Name _____

Problem-Solving Chart

Problem: Pepita does not like having to talk twice.

Responses may vary.

Possible Solutions	Pros (+) and Cons (−)
1. Stop speaking Spanish.	(+) You wouldn't have to talk twice for people anymore.
	(−) You wouldn't be able to talk with people who spoke only Spanish. **(2 points)**
2. Stop speaking English.	(+) You wouldn't have to talk twice for people anymore. (2)
	(−) You wouldn't be able to talk with people who spoke only English. (2)
3. Get mad and point out that you don't have time to speak twice.	(+) People would stop asking you to talk twice. (2)
	(−) You would probably lose a lot of friends. (2)
4. Politely say that you can't speak twice when you don't have time.	(+) Most people would probably stop asking you to talk twice. (2)
	(+) You could still talk with people who speak only Spanish or English. (2)

TARGET SKILL COMPREHENSION: Problem Solving and Decision Making

❶ Teach

Review the story problem in *Pepita Talks Twice*. Use **Transparency 6–2** to talk about Pepita's problem and to discuss the way in which she first tried to solve it. Students can refer to the selection and to **Practice Book** page 168. Discuss how students solve problems in their own lives. Use these prompts:

- Do you consider several possible solutions?
- Do you list pros and cons, or discuss them with someone?
- Do your decisions work out? Why or why not?

Model problem solving. Have students reread page 312 to verify how Pepita first decides to solve her problem in the story. (She decides to stop speaking Spanish.) Then model the skill.

Think Aloud *As I think about the decision Pepita makes, I see that the pro side to this solution is that she doesn't have to talk twice anymore. The con side is that Pepita can't talk with people who speak only Spanish. The real problem is that Pepita doesn't consider the cons of her solution or any other possible solutions before she makes her decision!*

❷ Guided Practice

Have students solve a problem. Point out another problem in the story: Both Pepita and Juan want their own time to play with Lobo. Have small groups brainstorm solutions. Have them list the pros and cons of each solution on a chart similar to the one below. Call on groups to model their work at the board.

Problem: Pepita and Juan each want time alone with Lobo.

Possible Solutions:	Pros (+) and Cons (−)
1. Juan plays with Lobo for the first 30 minutes after school, and Pepita plays with Lobo for the second 30 minutes.	(+) Both Pepita and Juan will get the same amount of time with Lobo.
2. Pepita and Juan agree to play with Lobo together.	(−) Lobo may get tired and not want to play during the second 30 minutes.

❸ Apply

Assign **Practice Book** pages 170–171. Also have students apply this skill as they read their **Leveled Readers** for this week. You may also select books from the Leveled Bibliography for this theme, pages 296E–296F.

 **Test Prep** Discuss test questions that ask students to write their own answer. Explain that these questions may ask students to evaluate the way a character solves a problem. Tell students to use their own thoughts and experiences, as well as details from the story, to support their answers.

Leveled Readers and Leveled Practice

Students at all levels apply the comprehension skill as they read their Leveled Readers. See lessons on pages 337O–337R.

● BELOW LEVEL   ▲ ON LEVEL   ■ ABOVE LEVEL   ◆ LANGUAGE SUPPORT

Tall Tony by Lucy Floyd illustrated by Diane Hearn

Talented Alex by Lee S. Justice illustrated by David Austin Clar

Paul the Artist by Floyd Messmer illustrated by Liz Callen

The Tallest Boy in the Class by Lucy Floyd illustrated by Diane Hearn

Reading Traits

Teaching students how to understand problem solving and decision making is one way of encouraging them to "read between the lines" of a selection. This comprehension skill supports the reading trait **Realizing Context**.

Practice Book page 170

Pepita Talks Twice
Comprehension Skill
Problem Solving

Name _____

A Homework Problem

Read the story. Then complete the chart on the next page.

The Volcano or Numberland

"Pakki! Help me in the kitchen! Now! Hurry!" I ran down to the kitchen, terrified. There sat my sister, Kayla, drinking milk and calmly reading the television listings in the newspaper.

"What's wrong?" I asked, out of breath from running to the kitchen.

"The science project I've been working on for two weeks is due tomorrow. Ms. Odenpak may give me a bad grade if I don't have my model volcano finished. But a TV show called *Niles in Numberland* is starting in twenty minutes. My math teacher, Mr. Browning, told us to watch it and be ready to talk about it tomorrow in class. What I should do? Help!"

"I have three ideas," I answered. "One, you finish your volcano while I watch the TV show and take notes. Of course, I'm not very good at taking notes," I reminded her. "Two, you can watch the TV show and ask Ms. Odenpak for an extra day to finish your volcano. Or three, you can work on your volcano in front of the television while you take notes on the show."

"Hmm," Kayla answered, thinking deeply. "Which one's the best solution?"

Practice Book page 171

Pepita Talks Twice
Comprehension Skill
Problem Solving

Name _____

A Homework Problem *continued*

Read the problem. Write one possible solution from the story in each box. Then give a pro and a con about the solution.

> **The Problem:** Kayla needs to finish her science project, and she also needs to watch TV for a math assignment.

Possible Solution: Kayla can finish the volcano while Pakki takes notes on the TV show. **(1 point)**

Pro: Kayla will be able to finish both assignments on time. **(1)**

Con: Pakki's notes might not be good enough for the discussion. **(1)**

Possible Solution: Kayla can watch the TV show and ask Ms. Odenpak for an extra day to finish her volcano. **(1)**

Pro: Kayla will take her own notes and be prepared to talk. **(1)**

Con: If she doesn't get an extra day, she might fail. **(1)**

Possible Solution: Kayla can finish the volcano in front of the television while she's taking notes on the TV show. **(1)**

Pro: Kayla will be able to finish both assignments on time. **(1)**

Con: Her attention will be split, so she may not do either well. **(1)**

Which of these solutions do you think is the best? Why? Answers will vary. The last solution seems best because she'll finish both. **(1)**

Monitoring Student Progress

If . . .	Then . . .
students score 7 or below on **Practice Book** page 171,	use the Reteaching lesson on Teacher's Edition page R8.
students have successfully met the lesson objectives,	have them do the Challenge/ Extension activities on Teacher's Edition page R9.

OBJECTIVES

- Read words with the VCCCV pattern.
- Apply the Phonics/Decoding Strategy.
- Learn academic language: *VCCCV pattern.*

Target Skill Trace

Teach	p. 337C
Reteach	p. R14
Review	pp. 413F–413G
See	*Handbook for English Language Learners,* p. 167; *Extra Support Handbook,* pp. 162–163; pp. 166–167

Practice Book page 172

Name _____

Playing with the Pattern

Read each word in dark type. Then follow the directions to make a new word. Write the new word on the line, and draw a picture in the box to show its meaning.

Example: single   Replace **si** with **ju.**
The new word is ___jungle___.

1. **bundle**   Replace **bu** with **ca.**
   The new word is _candle (1 point)_.

2. **dollar**   Replace **lar** with **phin.**
   The new word is _dolphin (1)_.

3. **twinkle**   Replace **twi** with **a.**
   The new word is _ankle (1)_.

4. **letter**   Replace **let** with **mons.**
   The new word is _monster (1)_.

5. **turtle**   Replace **tur** with **cas.**
   The new word is _castle (1)_.

(1 point for each picture)

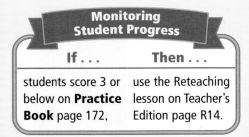

Pepita Talks Twice
Structural Analysis VCCCV Pattern

Monitoring Student Progress

If . . .	Then . . .
students score 3 or below on **Practice Book** page 172,	use the Reteaching lesson on Teacher's Edition page R14.

STRUCTURAL ANALYSIS/ VOCABULARY: VCCCV Pattern

❶ Teach

Introduce the VCCCV pattern. Write the word *English* but do not pronounce it.

- Label each vowel in the word *(E, i)* with a V. Remind students that each syllable has one vowel sound.
- Label each consonant between the vowels *(n, g, l)* with C.
- Explain that the word *English* follows the VCCCV pattern.

Explain consonant clusters with the VCCCV pattern. Point out that in words with three consonants between two vowels, two of the consonants are almost always a consonant cluster *(bl, sw, tr)* or digraph *(th, sh, ch).*

Model the Phonics/Decoding Strategy. Write *"I'm tired of talking twice,"* Pepita <u>complained</u>. Then model the process of decoding *complained.*

Think Aloud — *First, I'll mark the vowels* o, a, i, *and* e *with V. Next I'll mark each consonant between the vowels with C. That's* m, p, *and* l. *Complained has the VCCCV pattern. I see the consonant cluster* pl, *so I'll keep those letters together. I'll split the word between the* m *and the* p. *The first syllable is closed so it sounds like* kahm. *Next I'll decode the second syllable,* plain, *and the* -ed *ending. When I put it all together, I say* kahm-playnd. *It's* kuhm-PLAYND.

❷ Guided Practice

Have students decode words with the VCCCV pattern. Display the sentences below. Ask partners to copy the underlined words, divide them into syllables, decode the words, and give their meanings. Have students share their work with the class.

1. Pepita had a <u>simple</u> idea.
2. Lobo came running the <u>instant</u> he heard his name.
3. Pepita learned about the <u>Pilgrims</u> in school.

❸ Apply

Assign Practice Book page 172.

PHONICS REVIEW:
Word Endings -er and -le

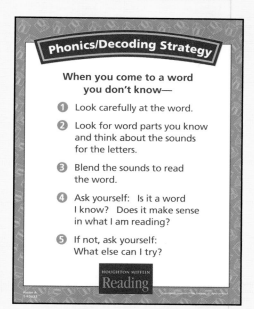

Phonics/Decoding Strategy

When you come to a word
you don't know—

1 Look carefully at the word.

2 Look for word parts you know
and think about the sounds
for the letters.

3 Blend the sounds to read
the word.

4 Ask yourself: Is it a word
I know? Does it make sense
in what I am reading?

5 If not, ask yourself:
What else can I try?

HOUGHTON MIFFLIN
Reading

❶ Teach

Review the word endings -er and -le. Explain that in words
with more than one syllable

- the *er* spelling pattern can have the final /ər/ sound
- the *le* spelling pattern can have the final /əl/ sound

Model the Phonics/Decoding Strategy. Write *But Lobo didn't
open an eye or even <u>wiggle</u> an ear.* Then model how to decode
wiggle.

Think Aloud — *When I look at this word, I notice the shorter word* wig. *In the
second part I see the word ending* -le, *which I know can have
the final* uhl *sound as in the word* middle. *When I blend that with the letter* g, *the
second part might sound like* guhl. *All together the word is* wihg-guhl. *Oh, it's*
WIHG-uhl. *I know that word and it makes sense.*

❷ Guided Practice

Have students pronounce -er and -le word endings. Display
the following phrases.

her <u>brother</u> Juan	at the <u>supper</u> <u>table</u>
<u>never ever</u> speak Spanish	how will you <u>answer</u>

- Have students copy the underlined words. Then help them circle
  the endings in the underlined words and decode the words.
- Call on individuals to model their work at the board.

❸ Apply

Have students decode words with -er and -le word endings.
Ask students to decode the words below from *Pepita Talks Twice*
and discuss their meanings.

people	page 306	corner	page 314
grumble	page 306	teacher	page 318
larger	page 310	either	page 320

SPELLING: Words Ending with *er/le*

OBJECTIVES

● Write Spelling Words that end with *er* or *le*.

SPELLING WORDS

Basic

summer	apple
winter	able
little*	November
October	ever*
travel	later*
color	purple

Review	**Challenge**
flower	thermometer
people*	mumble*

Forms of these words appear in the literature.

Extra Support/Intervention

Basic Word List Consider using only the left column of Basic Words with students who need extra support.

Challenge

Challenge Word Practice Students can use the Challenge Words to write a paragraph about a very cold day.

DAY 1 INSTRUCTION

Words Ending with *er/le*

Pretest Use the Day 5 Test sentences.

Teach Tell students that this lesson's words have two syllables and end with the /ər/ or /əl/ sounds.

● Write *summer* and *little* on the board, say each word, and have students repeat it. Explain these principles:

Final /ər/ sounds can be spelled *er*. (*summer*)

Final /əl/ sounds can be spelled *le*. (*little*)

● Add *color* and *travel* to the board, say each word, and have students repeat it. Explain that *or* and *el* are less common spelling patterns for final /ər/ and /əl/.

● List the remaining Basic Words, and have students say them. Choose students to underline the patterns that spell the final vowel and consonant sounds.

Practice/Homework Assign **Practice Book** page 243.

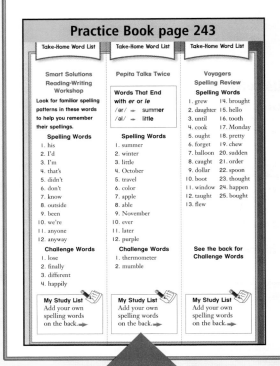

Practice Book page 243

Take-Home Word List

DAY 2 REVIEW & PRACTICE

Reviewing the Principle

Go over the spelling patterns for final /ər/ and /əl/ with students.

Practice/Homework Assign **Practice Book** page 173.

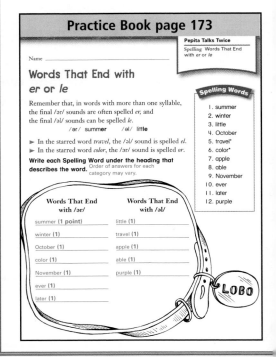

Practice Book page 173

Making Inferences

List the Basic Words on the board.

- Dictate the clues below and ask students to write the Basic Word that matches each clue.

    – People take suitcases when they do this. (travel)

    – You might see snow during this season. (winter)

    – Children might use crayons to do this. (color)

    – You might find one of these in your lunch box. (apple)

- Have students use each Basic Word from the board orally in a sentence. (Sentences will vary.)

Practice/Homework For spelling practice, assign **Practice Book** page 174.

Game: Spelling Ticktacktoe

Have students work in groups of 3: 2 players and 1 caller. Ask players to draw a ticktacktoe board. Give the caller a Basic Word list, and supply each player with a different colored pencil. Explain these game rules:

- The caller reads a Basic Word. The first player writes the word in any square, using his or her colored pencil.

- The caller reads another word. The second player writes that word in any remaining square, using the other colored pencil.

- If a player misspells a word, the word is erased. The first player to write 3 correct words across, down, or diagonally wins.

- For the next round, the caller and a player switch roles.

Practice/Homework For proofreading and writing practice, assign **Practice Book** page 175.

Spelling Test

Say each underlined word, read the sentence, and then repeat the word. Have students write only the underlined word.

Basic Words

1. It is hot in the **summer**.
2. How cold is it in **winter**?
3. My puppy is very **little**.
4. We took a trip last **October**.
5. We will **travel** far.
6. Blue is a **color** that I love.
7. He ate the **apple**.
8. Who is **able** to carry the box?
9. We will be busy in **November**.
10. How did you **ever** find me?
11. I will have to do it **later** on.
12. We ran out of **purple** paint.

Challenge Words

13. The **thermometer** is outside the house.
14. I can't understand you when you **mumble**.

Practice Book page 174

Pepita Talks Twice
Spelling Words That End with *er* or *le*

Name _____

Spelling Spree

Crossword Puzzle Write a Spelling Word in the puzzle that means the same as each clue.

Spelling Words
1. summer
2. winter
3. little
4. October
5. travel*
6. color*
7. apple
8. able
9. November
10. ever
11. later
12. purple

Across
3. the month before December (1)
4. not big (1)
6. the month after September (1)
7. red or yellow or green (1)

Down
1. the hottest season (1)
2. take a trip (1)
4. the opposite of *sooner* (1)
5. a mix of blue and red (1)

Word Search Write the Spelling Word that is hidden in each sentence.
Example: I myself lowered the flag. flower

9. When I take a nap, please be quiet. apple (1)
10. The cab lets two people out. able (1)
11. Lie very quietly here on the bed. ever (1)
12. We'll win terrific prizes! winter (1)

Practice Book page 175

Pepita Talks Twice
Spelling Words That End with *er* or *le*

Name _____

Proofreading and Writing

Proofreading Circle the five misspelled Spelling Words in this paragraph. Then write each word correctly.

Spelling Words
1. summer
2. winter
3. little
4. October
5. travel*
6. color*
7. apple
8. able
9. November
10. ever
11. later
12. purple

Sarah liked summir. It was her favorite time of year. The heat did not evir bother her. Her parents, however, did not like the heat. They often wished to travil someplace cool. When Sarah got hot, she rested in the cool kitchen. Later, she would eat a nice, juicy appel. She liked the fruit's pleasant red coler and smooth skin. It was too bad her parents weren't able to enjoy this season as much as she did.

1. summer (2 points)   4. apple (2)
2. ever (2)   5. color (2)
3. travel (2)

▶ **Write a Paragraph** What can Sarah do to help her parents stay cool? How can Sarah get her parents to like the summer as much as she does?
On a separate sheet of paper, write a paragraph about what Sarah might do or say to her parents to help them enjoy the summer. Use Spelling Words from the list. Responses will vary. (2)

OBJECTIVES

- Identify synonyms for specific words.
- Select synonyms.
- Learn academic language: *synonym*.

Target Skill Trace

Teach	p. 337G
Review	pp. 413H–413I
Extend	Challenge/Extension Activities, p. R15
See	*Handbook for English Language Learners*, p. 203

Transparency 6–3

Synonyms

1. Pepita **raced** by the grocery store.
2. Pepita <u>hurried</u> by the grocery store.
3. Pepita <u>crawled</u> by the grocery store.
4. Pepita <u>ran</u> by the grocery store.
5. Pepita <u>zoomed</u> by the grocery store.

Read the sentences below and answer the questions.

Pepita <u>answered</u> in English.
Juan <u>grinned</u> at her.
Pepita <u>closed</u> her eyes.

6. Which word is a synonym for *smiled*? grinned
7. Which word is a synonym for *shut*? closed
8. Which word is a synonym for *replied*? answered

SMART SOLUTIONS Pepita Talks Twice
Vocabulary Skill Synonyms
ANNOTATED VERSION

TRANSPARENCY 6–3
TEACHER'S EDITION PAGE 337G

Monitoring Student Progress

If . . .	Then . . .
students score 7 or below on **Practice Book** page 176,	have them work with partners to correct the items they missed.

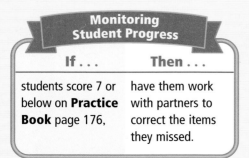

TARGET SKILL VOCABULARY: Synonyms

❶ Teach

Define synonyms. Tell students that two or more words that mean nearly the same thing are called synonyms. Authors use synonyms to add different shades of meaning to their writing.

Display Transparency 6–3. Show Sentences 1 through 5. Read aloud Sentence 1. Explain that *raced* has many synonyms.

- Read Sentence 2. Explain that *hurried* is a synonym for *raced* because both words refer to something moving very fast.
- Read Sentence 3. Explain that *crawled* is not a synonym for *raced* because it refers to something moving very slowly. It changes the meaning of the sentence.
- Repeat the steps for the underlined words in Sentences 4 and 5, *ran* and *zoomed*. Explain that both are synonyms of *raced*.

Model selecting a synonym. Display this sentence from Anthology page 308: *She tiptoed by the house where her Aunt Rosa lived, but not <u>softly</u> enough.* Model selecting a synonym for *softly*.

Think Aloud *I know that* soft *can mean "squishy," or "able to bend," or "quiet." In this sentence* softly *describes* tiptoed, *so I know that it has something to do with being quiet, not with feeling soft. I'll use that meaning to think of a synonym. I'll use* quietly *in the sentence instead of* softly. Pepita tiptoed, but not quietly enough. *The meaning stays the same.* Quietly *is a good synonym for* softly *in this sentence.*

❷ Guided Practice

Give students practice in selecting synonyms. Uncover the rest of the transparency. In pairs or small groups, have students answer questions 6 through 8. Ask groups to share their answers with the class.

❸ Apply

Assign Practice Book page 176.

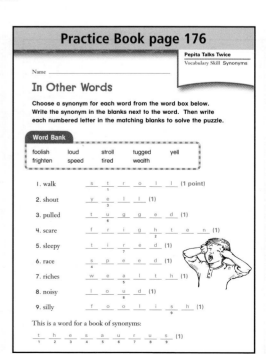

Practice Book page 176

Pepita Talks Twice
Vocabulary Skill Synonyms

Name _____

In Other Words

Choose a synonym for each word from the word box below. Write the synonym in the blanks next to the word. Then write each numbered letter in the matching blanks to solve the puzzle.

Word Bank

foolish	loud	stroll	tugged	yell
frighten	speed	tired	wealth	

1. walk   s t r o l l (1 point)
2. shout   y e l l (1)
3. pulled   t u g g e d (1)
4. scare   f r i g h t e n (1)
5. sleepy   t i r e d (1)
6. race   s p e e d (1)
7. riches   w e a l t h (1)
8. noisy   l o u d (1)
9. silly   f o o l i s h (1)

This is a word for a book of synonyms:

t h e s a u r u s (1)

STUDY SKILL:
Bilingual Dictionary

OBJECTIVES
- Compare and contrast bilingual dictionaries to single-language dictionaries.
- Use a bilingual dictionary to find the Spanish equivalents for English words.
- Learn academic language: *bilingual*.

❶ Teach

Introduce the bilingual dictionary.

- Bilingual dictionaries have two languages. Like single-language dictionaries, they contain:
    - entries arranged in alphabetical order,
    - guide words at the tops of the pages,
    - several meanings for one word,
    - pronunciation guides.
- Bilingual dictionaries include words in another language, such as Spanish, in addition to words in English. They have
    - one section in which you can look up a word in English and find the word in another language that has the same meaning;
    - one section in which you can look up a word in another language and find its meaning in English.

Model how to use a bilingual dictionary. Have students look at page 306 of *Pepita Talks Twice* as you think aloud.

Think Aloud *I wonder if the Spanish words say the same thing as the English words, so I look up some of the words in a bilingual dictionary for English and Spanish. To find the Spanish word for* girl, *I turn to the English-Spanish part of the dictionary. I look up* girl *and the entry says that* niña *is the Spanish word for* girl. *If I look up the word* niña *in the Spanish-English part of the dictionary, I will find* girl, *the word in English for* niña.

❷ Practice/Apply

Give students practice in using a bilingual dictionary.

- Have students select words from either the English or Spanish part of a page in the story. Have them tell which section of a bilingual dictionary they will use to look up the word.
- Have partners look up simple nouns, such as *mother, father, dog,* and *kitchen,* in a bilingual dictionary. Have them share their words with the class.

GRAMMAR: Adjectives

OBJECTIVES

- Identify adjectives, including articles.
- Use adjectives and articles in sentences.
- Proofread and correct sentences with grammar and spelling errors.
- Improve writing by expanding sentences with adjectives.
- Learn academic language: *articles.*

Transparency 6–4

Daily Language Practice

Correct two sentences each day.

1. pepita is abel to speak too languages.
   Pepita is able to speak two languages.
2. We found out latter that she knows an word for almost anything.
   We found out later that she knows a word for almost anything.
3. Even in Winnter, Pepita's mother made an enchiladas.
   Even in winter, Pepita's mother made the enchiladas.
4. Tomatoes, with their red cullar, are a important part of salsa.
   Tomatoes, with their red color, are an important part of salsa.
5. She takes a litel more than a hour to prepare the tamales.
   She takes a little more than an hour to prepare the tamales.
6. She also likes to use a aple in her cooking
   She also likes to use an apple in her cooking.
7. Last sumer, Pepita helps to prepare an spanish feast.
   Last summer, Pepita helped to prepare a Spanish feast.
8. In novembber, she made up a new recipe for Tortillas.
   In November, she made up a new recipe for tortillas.
9. Have you evver seen Lobo runs after an bouncing ball.
   Have you ever seen Lobo run after a bouncing ball?
10. Pepita learns an useful lesson when she travvells to school.
    Pepita learns a useful lesson when she travels to school.

TRANSPARENCY 6–4
TEACHER'S EDITION PAGE 337I

SMART SOLUTIONS Pepita Talks Twice
Grammar Skill Adjectives
Spelling Skill Words That End with *er* or *le*

ANNOTATED VERSION

Monitoring Student Progress

If . . .	Then . . .
students score 7 or below on **Practice Book** page 178,	use the Reteaching lesson on Teacher's Edition page R20.

DAY 1 INSTRUCTION

Adjectives

Teach Go over the following ideas:

– An **adjective** describes a noun.

– Some adjectives tell *what kind* or *how many.*

– *A, an,* and *the* are special adjectives called **articles.** Use *a* before a word beginning with a consonant sound. Use *an* before a word beginning with a vowel sound. Use *a* and *an* before singular nouns. Use *the* before singular and plural nouns.

- Display **Transparency 6–5.** Help students realize that the words *crisp* and *two* describe *tacos* in the two sentences at the top.

- Have students look at the adjectives and articles in the charts.

- Ask volunteers to find the adjectives in Sentences 1–4 and complete Sentences 5–8.

Daily Language Practice
Have students correct Sentences 1 and 2 on **Transparency 6–4.**

Transparency 6–5

Adjectives

Pepita enjoys *crisp* tacos.
Pepita eats *two* tacos.

What Kind?	How Many?
Miguel sings *beautiful* songs.	Miguel sings *many* songs.
Pepita learns *new* words.	Pepita learns *ten* words.

A	An	The
Pepita makes *a* decision.	Pepita has *an* angry feeling.	*The* dog learns quickly.
A neighbor asks for help.	It took *an* hour to get home.	Pepita talks to *the* neighbors.

1. Pepita takes a long walk. _____ a long
2. She helps some friendly neighbors. _____ some friendly
3. Mr. Hobbs asks an interesting question. _____ an interesting
4. The delivery man left a large package for me.
   The delivery; a large
5. Lobo fetches ____a____ rubber ball. (a, an)
6. Juan teaches Lobo ___the___ new tricks. (a, the)
7. Pepita gives ___an___ honest answer. (a, an)
8. Pepita loves to play ____a____ game with Lobo. (a, an)

TRANSPARENCY 6–5
TEACHER'S EDITION PAGE 337I

SMART SOLUTIONS Pepita Talks Twice
Grammar Skill Adjectives

ANNOTATED VERSION

DAY 2 PRACTICE

Independent Work

Practice/Homework Assign **Practice Book** page 177.

Daily Language Practice
Have students correct Sentences 3 and 4 on **Transparency 6–4.**

Practice Book page 177

Pepita Talks Twice
Grammar Skill Adjectives

Name _____

Writing with Adjectives

On the lines to the right of each sentence, list the adjectives. Then write each adjective in the chart below.

1. Pepita has one playful dog. one; playful (2 points)
2. She has many friendly neighbors. many; friendly (2)
3. Pepita has an unusual problem. an; unusual (2)
4. She speaks perfect Spanish and English. perfect (2)
5. She does not confuse the two languages. the; two (2)
6. Pepita gets an angry feeling. an; angry (2)
7. Juan teaches Lobo a new trick. a; new (2)
8. Mother makes a dozen tacos. a; dozen (2)
9. She also prepares some salsa. some (2)
10. Pepita learns an important lesson. an; important (2)

What Kind?	How Many?	Articles
playful	one	a
friendly	many	an
unusual	two	the
perfect	dozen	
angry	some	
new		
important		

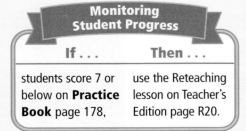

What Kind of Clusters?

Have students use word clusters to explore adjectives and find interesting nouns in *Pepita Talks Twice* for the center of a word cluster.

- Draw an example word cluster on the board, writing the noun *tacos* in the center circle and the following adjectives in circles around the center: *several, crisp, eight, two, tasty, folded, delicious, crunchy.* Draw a line from the center circle to each of the surrounding circles.

- Remind students to include adjectives that tell *what kind* and *how many* in their clusters.

- After students create several word clusters, have them use the words to write sentences.

- Ask volunteers to read their sentences aloud, and ask listeners to identify adjectives and articles.

Daily Language Practice
Have students correct Sentences 5 and 6 on **Transparency 6–4**.

Independent Work

Practice/Homework Assign **Practice Book** page 178.

Daily Language Practice
Have students correct Sentences 7 and 8 on **Transparency 6–4**.

Expanding Sentences

Teach Explain to students that good writers use adjectives to make their writing more descriptive and interesting.

- Show the three sentence pairs at the top of **Transparency 6–6** to model how adjectives can increase the interest in a sentence.

- In the third example, point out that the article *a* changed to *an* because the adjective *old-fashioned* begins with a vowel sound.

- Ask volunteers to suggest ways to add adjectives to Sentences 1–5.

- Have students review a piece of their own writing to see if they can improve it by expanding their sentences with adjectives.

Practice/Homework Assign **Practice Book** page 179.

Daily Language Practice
Have students correct Sentences 9 and 10 on **Transparency 6–4**.

Practice Book page 178

Pepita Talks Twice
Grammar Skill Adjectives

Name _____

Adjectives in Paragraphs

Read this paragraph about a neighborhood. Choose an adjective from the box to complete each sentence. Use the clues in parentheses to help you.

Word Bank

| an | beautiful | exciting | favorite | full |
| happy | hundred | long | several | the |

Carlos's neighborhood has an _exciting_ (1 point)

(what kind) block party. Almost a _hundred_ (1)

(how many) people are there. Many people help to prepare

an _(1)_ (article) excellent meal. Two _long_ (1)

(what kind) tables are covered with _full_ (1)

(what kind) plates. Carlos and _several_ (1)

(how many) neighbors sing their _favorite_ (1)

(what kind) songs. The _beautiful_ (1) _____ (what

kind) words are in Spanish. Soon, everyone joins _the_ (1)

(article) singers. Even the dog woofs a _happy_ (1)

(what kind) bark at the end of every song.

Transparency 6–6

SMART SOLUTIONS *Pepita Talks Twice*
Grammar Skill Improving Your Writing

ANNOTATED VERSION

Expanding Sentences with Adjectives

Pepita was in a mood.
Pepita was in a grouchy mood.

Lobo is a dog.
Lobo is a small black dog.

Miguel sings a song.
Miguel sings an old-fashioned song.

1. Pepita eats her lunch.
2. She makes a decision.
3. Lobo catches the ball.
4. Mr. Hobbs talks to his customer.
5. The customer asks Pepita a question.

TRANSPARENCY 6–6
TEACHER'S EDITION PAGE 337J

Practice Book page 179

Pepita Talks Twice
Grammar Skill Improving Your Writing

Name _____

Expanding Sentences with Adjectives

Rewrite each sentence. Add at least one adjective to each sentence. Remember that you may need to change a or an, too.
(Answers may vary. Sample answers are included.)

1. Pepita and Juan have a dog.
   Pepita and Juan have a **young** dog. **(1 point)**

2. Pepita goes to a picnic.
   Pepita goes to a **neighborhood** picnic. **(1)**

3. She helps prepare the food.
   She helps prepare the **delicious** food. **(1)**

4. The neighbors sing songs.
   The **friendly** neighbors sing **sweet** songs. **(1)**

5. Lobo almost runs into a truck.
   Lobo almost runs into an **enormous** truck. **(1)**

6. Pepita calls the dog.
   Pepita calls the **naughty** dog. **(1)**

7. The dog hears her shout.
   The **silly** dog hears her **loud** shout. **(1)**

8. She gives Lobo a hug.
   She gives Lobo a **big** hug. **(1)**

Grammar 337J

WRITING: Announcement

OBJECTIVES

- Identify the parts of an announcement.
- Write an announcement.
- Organize information by order of importance.

Writing Traits

Organization As you teach the lesson on Day 3, encourage students to think about their audience as they order information. Ask the following questions:

- What do your readers need to know right at the beginning?
- What can you wait to tell your readers? Where do your readers need to know these other details?

DAY 1 ACTIVITY

Introducing the Format

Define an announcement.

- An announcement tells important information about an event.
- It can be written or spoken. It can be broadcast live or recorded on tape or video.
- It answers the questions What? When? Where? Who? Why? How?

Start students thinking about writing an announcement.

- Have students list three special events. They can list births, weddings, concerts, fairs, or parades. They can also list sports events.
- Have students save their notes.

DAY 2 INSTRUCTION

Discussing the Model

Display Transparency 6–7. Ask:

- Who is making the announcement? (Pepita)
- What is she announcing? (that she will no longer speak Spanish)
- When will she stop speaking Spanish? (as of the date shown)
- Where will she no longer speak Spanish? (at home, at school, and in stores)
- Why will she no longer speak Spanish? (tired of saying everything twice)
- What other information does the announcement include? (will reply in English if spoken to in Spanish; will use English names; will call her dog Wolf.)

Display Transparency 6–8, and discuss the guidelines.

Have students write an announcement.

- Assign **Practice Book** page 180 to help students organize their writing.
- Have students use their notes from Day 1.
- Provide support as needed.

Transparency 6–7

An Announcement

SMART SOLUTIONS Pepita Talks Twice
Writing Skill An Announcement

ANNOTATED VERSION

Important Announcement

WHO?
I Pepita Alvarez announce to one and all that
WHEN?
starting today,
WHAT?
September 16, 200-, I will no longer speak Spanish. I will
WHERE?
speak only English at home, at school, in stores, and with my relatives, friends, and neighbors. If anyone asks me to speak
HOW?
Spanish, I will say no, and I will reply in English. I will use only English names for food, and my beloved dog Lobo I will now call Wolf. I would like everyone to know that
WHY?
I am making this change because I am tired of having to say everything twice, once in English and once in Spanish.

TRANSPARENCY 6–7
TEACHER'S EDITION PAGE 337K

Transparency 6–8

Guidelines for Writing an Announcement

SMART SOLUTIONS Pepita Talks Twice
Writing Skill An Announcement

ANNOTATED VERSION

- Have one main purpose. State it clearly at the beginning.
- Tell all important information. Answer the questions What? When? Where? Who? Why? How?
- Include exact dates, exact times, and exact places. Tell costs, if any.
- Leave out information that is not important.
- Organize information from most to least important.

TRANSPARENCY 6–8
TEACHER'S EDITION PAGE 337K

Practice Book page 180

Pepita Talks Twice
Writing Skill An Announcement

Name _____

Announcement Planner

Use this page to organize your ideas for an announcement. Write an announcement about a birth, wedding, concert, fair, parade, or other special event.

Who?	What?	Where?	When?	Why?	How?

ANNOUNCEMENT

Responses will vary. (12 points)

Improving Writing: Ordering Information

Discuss ordering important information.

- The order should be clear.

- Information can be presented in order of importance.

- The most important information is always first. The details that follow are in order of importance from most to least.

- See Writing Traits on page 337K.

Display Transparency 6–9.

- Display only the information at the top. Discuss each bullet.

- Uncover the announcement. Point out that the sentences are out of order.

- Have different volunteers read each sentence. Ask, Is the order clear? (no)

- Uncover the questions at the bottom of the transparency. Discuss each question.

- Work with students to renumber the sentences. (Sample answers are shown.)

Assign Practice Book page 181.

- Ask students to check the order of information in their announcements.

Writing Game

Have students write silly announcements.

- Distribute slips of paper to students.

- Have students write one event they have planned for later that day. Tell them to focus on ordinary, not special, activities. Give these examples:

  – Tasha: flute lesson

  – Lonnie: walking the dog

  – Ana: softball practice

  – Enzo: visiting Grandma

- Collect the slips of paper, mix them up, and have each student draw one.

- Have students write an announcement for the event they drew.

- Tell them to make their announcements sound silly by writing about the event by inventing colorful details that answer the questions Who? What? Where? When? and Why? about the event.

Sharing Writing

Consider these sharing options.

- Ask students to read a piece of their writing from the Author's Chair.

- Encourage students to record themselves reading their writing on audiotape.

Portfolio Opportunity

Save students' announcements as samples of their writing development.

Transparency 6–9

SMART SOLUTIONS Pepita Talks Twice
Writing Skill Improving Your Writing

ANNOTATED VERSION

Ordering Important Information

- When writing an announcement, first decide what information is most important. Put that information first.
- Put other information in order of importance from most important to least important.
- Be sure your announcement includes all the necessary information that answers some or all of these questions: Who? What? Where? When? How? Why?

Announcement

4	The party will be in Miss Garcia's classroom.
1	Come to a party!
3	The party is for new student Carmen Gutierrez, who just started in Miss Garcia's class this week.
2	Miss Garcia's students are giving the party.
5	The party will begin at 2:00 P.M. and end at 3:00 P.M.
6	Snacks will be served.

1. What information should be first? Place the number 1 next to it.
2. What information should be second? Third? Number the other information in order of importance.
3. What information is missing?
   the day of the party
4. Where should the missing information go?
   before or after the time of the party

TRANSPARENCY 6-9
TEACHER'S EDITION PAGE 337L

Practice Book page 181

Pepita Talks Twice
Writing Skill Improving Your Writing

Name _____

Ordering Important Information

▶ When writing an announcement, first decide what information is most important. Put that information first.
▶ Put other information in order of importance from most important to least important.
▶ Be sure your announcement includes all the necessary information that answers some or all of these questions: Who? What? Where? When? How? Why?

Number the information in the order it should go in the announcement. Write I for the first thing that should be in the announcement. Write 2 for the second thing.
(1 point each)

2 or 4 Practice will be at Jamal's house.

5 or 3 Practice will end at noon.

1 There will be band practice on Saturday.

4 or 2 Practice begins at 10:00 a.m.

3 or 5 Jamal's address is 32 Windsor Lane.

Rewrite the announcement in the order you marked.

(3 points)

_____
_____
_____
_____
_____

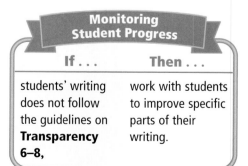

Monitoring Student Progress

If . . .	Then . . .
students' writing does not follow the guidelines on **Transparency 6–8,**	work with students to improve specific parts of their writing.

Language Center

VOCABULARY

Building Vocabulary

👤 Singles	🕐 15 minutes
Objective	Identify names of languages.

The selection *Pepita Talks Twice* mentions the words *English* and *Spanish* many times. These words are made from a country's name and can be used as proper nouns or proper adjectives.

Country	⇨	**Language**
England	⇨	English
Spain	⇨	Spanish

Think of other words that name languages. Record the languages in a web. If the language comes from the name of a country, record the country name if you know it.

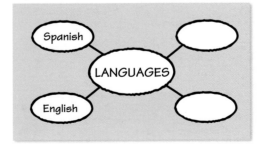

GRAMMAR

Use Adjectives to Describe

👥 Pairs	🕐 30 minutes
Objective	Use adjectives to describe nouns.
Materials	Index cards

Play a game called Guess My Word. With your partner, look through *Pepita Talks Twice* and choose ten different nouns, such as *mother, bed,* and *kitchen.* Choose nouns that you can easily describe using adjectives. Write each noun on a card.

To play the game:

- Mix up the cards and place them face-down in a pile.
- Take turns with your partner.
- The first player takes a card and reads it silently.
- That player names several adjectives that describe the noun.
- The partner tries to identify the noun on the card. The partner keeps the card if he or she guesses correctly.
- If the partner cannot name the noun, the first player reveals the card and then puts it at the bottom of the pile.
- Continue the game until all the cards are gone.

VOCABULARY

Vocabulary Game

👥👥 Groups	🕐 30 minutes
Objective	Use Key Vocabulary words in a restaurant role-playing game.
Materials	Several copies of Activity Master 6–1 on page R23

- Your group is in a restaurant. Pick someone to be the waiter or waitress.
- Cut out one menu with definitions for the waiter or waitress and a menu with prices for each customer.
- The waiter or waitress begins the game by reading the definition (but not the name) of the first item on the menu to the group.
- The first person to correctly guess the name of that item writes it on the first line of his or her menu.
- The waiter or waitress continues reading definitions until the customers have guessed each item.
- The customer with the most items filled in on his or her menu is the winner—and pays for everyone's meal!
- Pick a new waiter or waitress and play again. Try mixing up the menu items this time.

Consider copying and laminating these activities for use in centers.

LISTENING/SPEAKING

Resolve a Conflict

Pairs	⏱ 30 minutes
Objective	Work together to resolve a conflict.

Pepita and Juan have a disagreement about Lobo. Both want to be the first to teach Lobo new tricks. Work with your partner to resolve this conflict.

- Read the Tips below.
- Try to see the problem from both Pepita's and Juan's point of view.
- Think of several possible ways to solve it.
- Resolve the conflict in a way that both you and your partner can agree on.
- Write a paragraph that tells about the problem, some possible solutions, and why your solution works best.

Here are some steps you can use to resolve conflict:

Tips for Resolving Conflicts

- Identify the problem.
- Consider the causes of the problem.
- Brainstorm several solutions.
- Discuss each solution. Decide what is good and bad about each one.
- Pick the solution that is best for everyone.

PHONICS/SPELLING

Scrambled -er and -le Words

Pairs	⏱ 15 minutes
Objective	Unscramble and scramble words that end with -er and -le.

Read each sentence below. Figure out what the scrambled word is in each one. Hint: Each unscrambled word ends in -er or -le.

Juan is Pepita's robhtre.

Pepita eats at the supper ebtla.

On your own, brainstorm and list words with more than one syllable that end in -er and -le.

- Think of four sentences that include words from your list. Then write your sentences on a sheet of paper with the -er and -le words scrambled.
- Trade papers with your partner.
- Identify the scrambled words and write them correctly on the paper.

Leveled Readers

Tall Tony

Summary *Tony is a boy with a problem: He is the tallest person in his class. This means he is always being asked to reach up high to help other people. Tony tries to complain once, but is interrupted. Later in gym class, the coach has a problem to solve: he needs to pick a basketball captain. As everyone lists qualifications, a winner emerges—Tony, who suddenly doesn't mind being tall.*

Vocabulary

Introduce the Key Vocabulary and ask students to complete the BLM.

mural a large painting done on a wall, *p. 10*

coach a person who trains or teaches people to play sports, *p. 14*

captain the leader of a group, *p. 14*

super (informal) very, *p. 15*

Building Background and Vocabulary

Discuss the advantages of being tall, as well as the types of problems that being tall might present. Preview the story with students, using the story vocabulary when possible.

Comprehension Skill: Problem Solving

Have students read the Strategy Focus on the book flap. Remind students to use the strategy and to note how a character solves a problem as they read the book. (See the Leveled Readers Teacher's Guide for **Vocabulary and Comprehension Practice Masters**.)

Responding

Have partners discuss how to answer the questions on the inside back cover.

Think About the Selection Sample answers:

1. He likes being able to reach things that no one else can reach.
2. He is often asked to reach to high places. He is tired of always having to be the one to do those jobs.
3. Possible response: Hold a stepladder so a classmate could reach some of the high places safely.

Making Connections Responses will vary.

Building Fluency

Model Read aloud page 11. Explain that the reader knows to read the word *AND* with more emphasis than the other words because the letters in the word are all capitals.

Practice Have volunteers read the passage to the rest of the class, emphasizing the word *AND*. Then have students look for other passages with a word set in all capital letters. Students can then read aloud the passages they find.

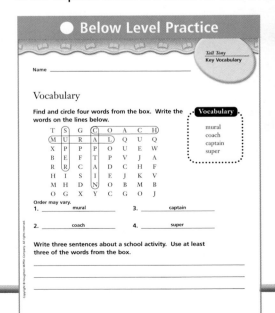

Leveled Readers

Talented Alex

Summary *Everyone in Alex's family seems to have a special talent. His father is a dancer, his mother is a dancer and a great cook, one sister is an artist, another is a musician, and his grandmother is a clothing designer. Alex seems to think that he is the only member of the family without a special talent. At dinner one night, he realizes that his family has known his special talent all along—he is a talented detective who solves all the family's mysteries.*

Vocabulary

Introduce the Key Vocabulary and ask students to complete the BLM.

talented skilled, *p. 4*

program a list of things to be performed in a show, *p. 5*

salsa* a spicy sauce usually made of tomatoes, onions, and peppers, *p. 7*

fashion current style, *p. 11*

Spanish having to do with Spain, *p. 15*

*Forms of these words are Anthology Key Vocabulary words.

▲ ON LEVEL

Building Background and Vocabulary

Discuss talents that people can have such as singing or drawing. Elicit that being observant and paying attention to details can also be special skills. Preview the story with students, using the story vocabulary when possible.

Comprehension Skill: Problem Solving

Have students read the Strategy Focus on the book flap. Remind students to use the strategy and to note how a character solves a problem as they read the book. (See the Leveled Readers Teacher's Guide for **Vocabulary and Comprehension Practice Masters**.)

Responding

Have partners discuss how to answer the questions on the inside back cover.

Think About the Selection Sample answers:

1. Possible response: They are all talented, busy people. They also seem to be somewhat forgetful.
2. He always knows where they can find the things they've misplaced.
3. Possible response: Alex doesn't know he is good at solving the household mysteries. It is just something he does naturally.
4. Responses will vary.

Making Connections Responses will vary.

Building Fluency

Model Read aloud page 5. Explain that the phrases following dialogue, like *Dad said in a puzzled voice,* can tell how something is said.

Practice Have students work in pairs to find other examples of phrases that tell how a character speaks. Have them read the dialogue to their partners.

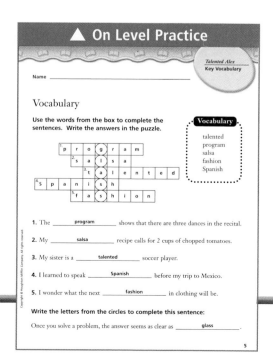

▲ On Level Practice

Talented Alex
Key Vocabulary

Name _____

Vocabulary

Use the words from the box to complete the sentences. Write the answers in the puzzle.

Vocabulary
talented
program
salsa
fashion
Spanish

1. The _____program_____ shows that there are three dances in the recital.
2. My _____salsa_____ recipe calls for 2 cups of chopped tomatoes.
3. My sister is a _____talented_____ soccer player.
4. I learned to speak _____Spanish_____ before my trip to Mexico.
5. I wonder what the next _____fashion_____ in clothing will be.

Write the letters from the circles to complete this sentence:

Once you solve a problem, the answer seems as clear as _____glass_____.

5

▲ On Level Practice

Talented Alex
Comprehension Skill
Problem Solving

Name _____

Comprehension

Read about Alex's problem. Write pros and cons for each solution. Then write your solution and write its pros and cons. Responses will vary. Possible responses are shown.

It is Saturday morning and Alex realizes he has a problem! His parent's dance recital is at 3 o'clock. He promised his dad that he would be there to hand out programs. But he forgot about that promise when he told his friend he could go to the movies at the very same time.

Possible Solutions	Pros (+) and Cons (–)
Alex could ask his friend to go to a later showing of the movie.	(+) Alex would be able to keep his promise to his father.
	(–) Alex's friend may not be able to go to a later showing of the movie.
Alex could ask his father to have someone else give out the programs.	(+) Alex would be able to join his friend at the movie.
	(–) Alex's father may get angry that Alex is breaking a promise.
My solution: Responses will vary.	(+) Responses will vary.
	(–) Responses will vary.

7

LEVELED READERS

Pepita Talks Twice

337P

LEVELED READERS

Paul the Artist

Summary *Paul, a third grader, becomes known as a talented artist after creating illustrations for his teacher. Soon, everyone—from friends to the school principal—is asking him to draw something. At first, Paul is flattered, but he soon realizes that he has no time for his own art projects. More importantly, he feels unappreciated. Paul decides to give up drawing altogether. However, at the end of the year, he decides to dust off his art supplies and make decorations for his teacher's retirement party.*

Vocabulary

Introduce the Key Vocabulary and ask students to complete the BLM.

presentation oral report, *p. 2*

intimidated nervous or frightened, *p. 5*

concentration undivided attention, *p. 5*

mascot person, animal, or object believed to bring good luck, *p. 8*

Building Background and Vocabulary

Ask students to discuss experiences they have had with art projects. Discuss the idea that art can be fun, but it can also be hard work. Preview the story with students, using the story vocabulary when possible.

Comprehension Skill: Problem Solving

Have students read the Strategy Focus on the book flap. Remind students to use the strategy and to note how a character solves a problem as they read the book. (See the Leveled Readers Teacher's Guide for **Vocabulary and Comprehension Practice Masters.**)

Responding

Have partners discuss how to answer the questions on the inside back cover.

Think About the Selection Sample answers:

1. She is impressed with Paul's work and thinks his drawings will be helpful with a lesson she is going to teach.
2. He is sad and feels hurt that Robby has ignored his story.
3. When Ms. Alvarez retires, Paul realizes that sharing his talent is important.
4. Responses will vary.

Making Connections Responses will vary.

Building Fluency

Model Read aloud page 4. Explain to the students that *After his presentation* is a transition phrase that indicates a change in time.

Practice Have students look for similar transition phrases in the book that show a change in time or place. If students have trouble, point them to page 9 where they will find the phrase *After he finished it.*

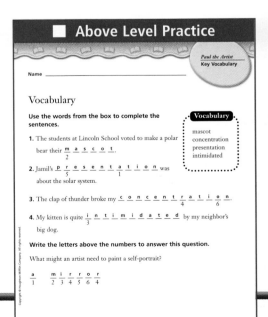

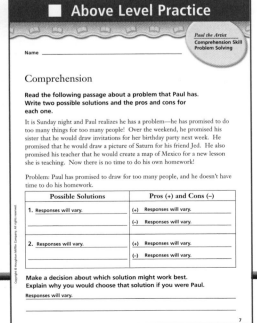

The Tallest Boy in the Class

Summary *Tony is the tallest boy in the class, even taller than his teacher. He ends up doing all the tasks that require someone tall. Just as he starts to get annoyed, it's time for gym class. The coach announces that the basketball team needs a captain. When Tony is made captain, he is happy to be tall.*

Vocabulary

Introduce the Key Vocabulary and ask students to complete the BLM.

reach to touch something, *p. 4*

measured found out how big something is, *p. 11*

coach a person who trains or teaches athletes and teams, *p. 14*

captain the person in command, *p. 14*

leader a person who guides others, *p. 15*

Building Background and Vocabulary

Have students try to reach things high up in the classroom. Decide who is *tall*, *taller*, and *tallest* in the classroom. Then distribute the **Build Background Practice Master**. Discuss the picture and what students know about basketball. Than have partners complete the page.

🎯 Comprehension Skill: Problem Solving

Have students read the Strategy Focus on the book flap. Remind students to use the strategy and to note how a character solves a problem as they read the book. (See the Leveled Readers Teacher's Guide for **Build Background, Vocabulary, and Graphic Organizer Masters**.)

Responding

Have partners discuss how to answer the questions on the inside back cover.

Think About the Selection Sample answers:

1. Tony can reach things that nobody else can.
2. Tony has to do everything for everybody because he is tall and can reach things.
3. Responses will vary.

Making Connections Tony was annoyed because everyone asked him to do too many things. At the end, Tony was proud. He stood up straight when he said he wanted to be the captain of the team.

🎯 Building Fluency

Model Read aloud pages 3–4 as students follow along in their books.

Practice Have students read the text on their own several times until they can read accurately and with expression.

◆ **Language Support Practice**

The Tallest Boy in the Class
Build Background

Name _____

Build Background

Use the picture to answer the questions.

1. To play this game, does it help to be tall? Why or why not?
yes; because you can reach the basket and hold the ball over other people's heads

2. What other things might help in this game?
running, jumping

3. Think of some other times it helps to be tall.
Answers will vary.

4. When might it help to be short?
Answers will vary.

5

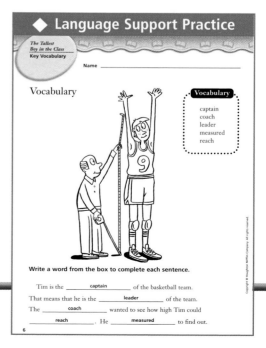

◆ **Language Support Practice**

The Tallest Boy in the Class
Key Vocabulary

Name _____

Vocabulary

Vocabulary
captain
coach
leader
measured
reach

Write a word from the box to complete each sentence.

Tim is the ___captain___ of the basketball team.
That means that he is the ___leader___ of the team.
The ___coach___ wanted to see how high Tim could
___reach___. He ___measured___ to find out.

6

337R

Reading-Writing Workshop

Persuasive Essay

In the Reading-Writing Workshop for Theme 6, *Smart Solutions,* students read Nancy's persuasive essay, "Working Together," on Anthology pages 338–339. Then they follow the five steps of the writing process to write a persuasive essay.

Meet the Author

Nancy A.
Grade: three
State: Michigan
Hobbies: writing stories and using the computer
What she wants to be when she grows up: a teacher

Theme Skill Trace

Writing
- Ordering Important Information, 337L
- Paraphrasing, 367L
- Using Exact Adverbs, 399L

Grammar
- Expanding Sentences with Adjectives, 337J
- Using *good* and *well*, 367J
- Expanding Sentences with Adverbs, 399J

Spelling
- Words That End with *-er* or *-le*, 337E
- Words That Begin with *a* or *be*, 367E
- Contractions, 399E

Pacing the Workshop

Here is a suggestion for how you might pace the workshop within one week or on five separate days across the theme.

DAY 1 PREWRITING

Students
- read the Student Writing Model, 338–339
- choose a topic for their persuasive essay, 339A
- organize and plan their essay, 339B

Spelling Frequently Misspelled Words, 339F; *Practice Book*, 243

DAY 2 DRAFTING

Students
- state a goal and give reasons for their persuasive essay, 339C
- draft their essay, giving facts and examples, 339D

Spelling *Practice Book*, 184

Focus on Writing Traits: Persuasive Essay

The workshop for this theme focuses on the traits of ideas and voice. However, students should think about all of the writing traits during the writing process.

IDEAS It is often easier for students to think of convincing reasons if they can talk about them during prewriting.

- Ask students to tell their goal and each reason that supports the goal. Praise convincing reasons. Ask questions about weak or unrelated reasons.

- Have students discuss their goal and reasons with a partner. Partners can identify convincing reasons and ask questions about unconvincing ones.

VOICE In working with students to develop voice in their persuasive essay, consider these points.

- During prewriting, encourage them to choose a topic that they care about deeply. Start them thinking about what their audience will find convincing.

- During drafting, encourage them to add plenty of confident, persuasive words such as *obviously, strongly,* and *definitely*.

- During revising, remind them to choose words that show they care about their topic.

Tips for Teaching the Writing Traits

- Teach one trait at a time.

- Discuss examples of the traits in the literature students are reading.

- Encourage students to talk about the traits during a writing conference.

- Encourage students to revise their writing for one trait at a time.

DAY 3 REVISING

Students

- evaluate their persuasive essay, 339E
- revise their essay, 339E
- have a writing conference, 339E

Spelling *Practice Book*, 185

DAY 4 PROOFREADING

Students

- proofread their persuasive essay, 339E
- improve their writing by correcting run-on sentences, 339E
- correct frequently misspelled words in their essay, 339F

Spelling *Practice Book*, 186

DAY 5 PUBLISHING

Students

- publish their persuasive essay, 339G
- reflect on their writing experience, 339G

Spelling *Assessment*, 339F

Persuasive Essay

Discussing the Guidelines

Display **Transparency RWW6–1,** and discuss what makes a great persuasive essay.

- Remember that students should think about all the writing traits as they write: ideas, organization, voice, word choice, sentence fluency, conventions, and presentation.

Discussing the Model

Have students read the Student Writing Model on Anthology pages 338–339.

- Discuss with students what the writer did to make her persuasive essay interesting to read.
- Use the Reading As a Writer questions on the next page.

A Persuasive Essay

The purpose of a persuasive essay is to convince someone to think or act in a certain way. Use this student's writing as a model when you write a persuasive essay of your own.

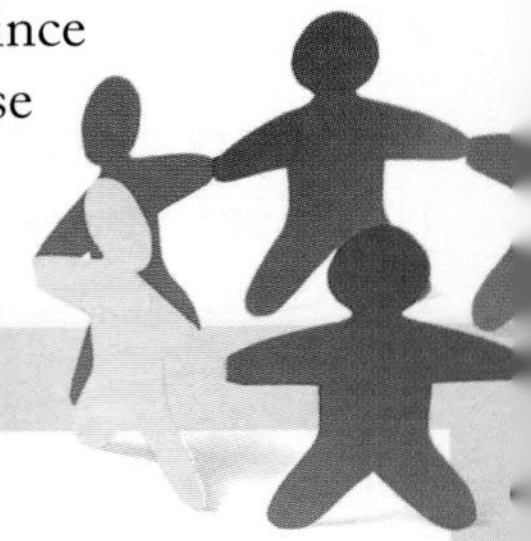

> A persuasive essay states a **goal** and gives **reasons**.

> It's important to support your reasons with **facts** and **examples**.

Working Together

I think that teamwork is important because it helps you learn more, it helps you make better choices at school, and it helps you make friends.

Teamwork helps you learn more because if you don't know something, you can learn it from your friends. One time at school, I didn't know how to do a map project. It was very hard. My friend Javier knew how to do the project, and he taught me how. We worked as a team. If you do this, you can help somebody learn something that they didn't know.

Another reason teamwork is important is because it helps you make better choices at school. Your friends on the team help you listen to the teacher. They tell you not to do something

338

---

dangerous. One time a girl in our class wasn't following the rules, and I helped her by showing her what the rules were and why they were important.

> Each fact and example needs a paragraph of its own.

The last reason that teamwork is important is that it helps you to make friends by working together. When you work on a team you learn about the other people on your team. You learn to talk with them and solve problems together.

I feel that everyone should work on a team because it teaches you to make good choices, it helps you to learn more than if you worked by yourself, and it helps you to make new friends. Working on a team is also lots of fun.

> The **ending** sums up a persuasive essay.

Meet the Author

Nancy A.
Grade: three
State: Michigan
Hobbies: writing stories and using the computer
What she wants to be when she grows up: a teacher

339

Reading As a Writer

1. What is the writer's goal? What does she want her readers to do? (convince readers to work in teams)

2. What reasons does the writer give to persuade readers to do what she asks? (Teamwork helps you learn; it helps you make better choices; it helps you make friends.)

3. What fact or example does the writer give to support her reason in the second paragraph? (the time Javier taught her how to do a map project)

4. What fact or example does the writer give to support her reason in the third paragraph? (the time a girl in her class learned it was important to follow the rules)

5. How does the writer sum up her reasons at the end of the essay? (She says that you should use teamwork because it helps you make good choices, it helps you learn more, and it helps you make friends.)

READING-WRITING WORKSHOP

Reading-Writing Workshop: Persuasive Essay **339**

Choosing a Topic

1 **Tell students they are going to write their own persuasive essay.** Tell them that they will start by choosing a goal, what they want their readers to think or do. Have students list at least three goals for a persuasive essay. Offer these prompts if students are having trouble getting started.

- What is your favorite book? Why should other people read it?
- What could be changed in your school? Why should this be changed
- What problem have you noticed in your neighborhood? How would you fix this problem? Why?

2 **Have students answer these questions** as they choose a goal, either in a writing journal or on a sheet of paper.

- Who will be your audience: friends? family? adults at your school?
- What is your purpose for writing? What do you want to persuade someone to think or do? Why do you care about this goal?
- How will you publish your persuasive essay: by making posters and leaflets? in a letter that you will send to the newspaper? in a speech

3 **Have students discuss their list of goals with a partner** an decide which topic would be the best one to write about. Encourage them to choose a goal that they feel strongly about. Then review thes tips with students.

Tips for Getting Started with a Topic

- Discuss with a partner the goal you chose. What reasons might you give to support your goal? Which reason does your partner like best? Why?

- What facts and examples might you use to support each reason? Which facts and examples does your partner find most convincing?

- Is your partner very interested in your goal? Does your partner agree or disagree with it?

Organizing and Planning

1 **Discuss the organization of a persuasive essay.**

- The essay begins by stating a goal.
- The goal is supported by at least three reasons.
- Each reason is supported by facts and examples.

2 **Discuss the difference between opinions and facts.** Explain that students should not use opinions to support a reason.

- A fact tells something that can be proved.
- An opinion tells what the writer believes.

3 **Display Transparency RWW6–2.** Work with students to brainstorm phrases that might introduce facts and phrases that might indicate opinions.

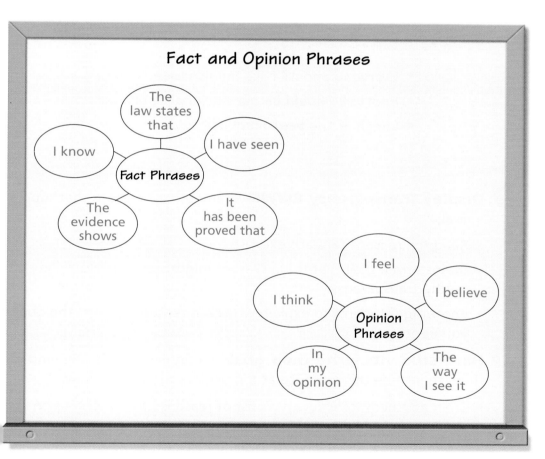

Fact and Opinion Phrases

4 **Ask students to brainstorm and organize their essay.**

- Have students list reasons that support their goal.
- Have them list facts and examples that support their reasons.

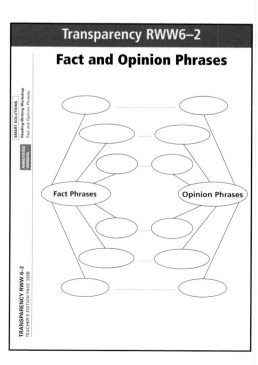

Stating Goals and Giving Reasons

Writing Traits

IDEAS Tell students that in a good persuasive essay a writer should do the following:

- State the goal clearly, explaining exactly what readers should think or do.
- Give reasons that explain why readers should think or do as he or she suggests.

1 **Tell students to state their goal in a single sentence.**
Explain that students should state their goal in the beginning of the essay. Share these examples of goal statements.

> - Everyone should take music class.
> - Football should be our national sport.
> - Lunch is the best meal of the day.

2 **Display Transparency RWW6–3,** and discuss reasons that support a goal.

- Read the reasons for each exercise.
- Brainstorm a goal that these reasons might support. Write the goal on the transparency.
- Encourage students to explain why each reason supports the goal you wrote.

3 **Have students write their goal** in a single sentence. Remind them to include this sentence at the beginning of their essay.

- Then ask them to review their list of reasons. Does each reason support their goal?
- Ask them to rephrase or replace any reasons that do not support their goal.
- Encourage them to think of words and phrases that show how they feel about their goal.

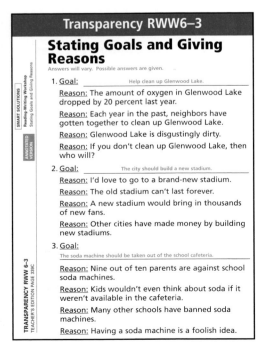

Transparency RWW6–3

Stating Goals and Giving Reasons

Answers will vary. Possible answers are given.

1. Goal: _____ Help clean up Glenwood Lake. _____

   Reason: The amount of oxygen in Glenwood Lake dropped by 20 percent last year.

   Reason: Each year in the past, neighbors have gotten together to clean up Glenwood Lake.

   Reason: Glenwood Lake is disgustingly dirty.

   Reason: If you don't clean up Glenwood Lake, then who will?

2. Goal: _____ The city should build a new stadium. _____

   Reason: I'd love to go to a brand-new stadium.

   Reason: The old stadium can't last forever.

   Reason: A new stadium would bring in thousands of new fans.

   Reason: Other cities have made money by building new stadiums.

3. Goal: _____
   The soda machine should be taken out of the school cafeteria.

   Reason: Nine out of ten parents are against school soda machines.

   Reason: Kids wouldn't even think about soda if it weren't available in the cafeteria.

   Reason: Many other schools have banned soda machines.

   Reason: Having a soda machine is a foolish idea.

Using Facts and Examples

1 Review these characteristics of facts and examples.

- Facts can be proved: *Hurricanes can knock down buildings.*
- Examples tell something that happened: *Last year our basement flooded.*

2 Explain that students should include facts and examples only if they support a reason. Remind them that a reason cannot be supported by an opinion.

3 Display Transparency RWW6–4, and discuss facts and examples.

- Point out that each numbered statement is a topic or goal. Explain that each of the statements after a letter (a, b, c, etc.) supports that topic or goal.
- Explain that some of the supporting statements are facts, some are examples, and some are neither.
- Model identifying 1a as a fact and 1b as an example. Model identifying 1c as neither because it tells an opinion.
- Work with students to complete the transparency.

4 Have students draft their persuasive essay.

- Remind them to group each fact or example in a paragraph with the reason it supports.
- Remind students that their sentences should flow smoothly.
- Tell them to use persuasive words such as *obviously* and *certainly*.
- Tell students to restate their goal in the ending.

Writing Traits

VOICE Tell students that their essay should show they care about their goal. Discuss which sentences are more persuasive.

- *The trash around Pleasant Lake should be taken away. It is ugly.*
- *The filthy garbage around Pleasant Lake should be cleaned up right away! It is ruining our beautiful lake.*

Transparency RWW6–4

Using Facts and Examples

1. **Topic:** Why you should join the Drama Club
   a. It's the most popular club in the school. ___Fact___
   b. Some famous actors started out in Drama Clubs. ___Example___
   c. I think you would like the Drama Club. ___Neither___
   d. Drama Club will help you understand acting and plays. ___Fact___
   e. Rhonda Biggs, a TV star, was in a Drama Club. ___Example___
   f. Everyone in the Drama Club will be popular. ___Neither___

2. **Topic:** Our town should build bike lanes.
   a. Bike lanes are a safe place to ride. ___Fact___
   b. I think bike lanes are popular. ___Neither___
   c. Bike lanes will save lives. ___Fact___
   d. Nearby towns have improved safety by building bike lanes. ___Example___
   e. I believe our town needs more bike shops. ___Neither___
   f. Holland has many bike lanes, and more people ride bikes there with fewer accidents. ___Example___

SMART SOLUTIONS
Reading-Writing Workshop
Using Facts and Examples

ANNOTATED VERSION

TRANSPARENCY RWW 6–4
TEACHER'S EDITION PAGE 339D

Practice Book page 182

Reading-Writing Workshop
Revising Your Persuasive Essay

Name _____

Revising Your Persuasive Essay

Reread your essay. Put a checkmark in the box for each sentence that describes your paper. Use this page to help you revise.

Rings the Bell
- [ ] My essay focuses on a goal supported by reasons.
- [ ] Each reason is supported by facts and examples.
- [ ] I told my goal in the beginning. I retold it in the end.
- [ ] I used persuasive words that show how I feel.
- [ ] My sentences flow well. There are few mistakes.

Getting Stronger
- [ ] The essay could be more focused. I need more reasons.
- [ ] There could be more facts and examples.
- [ ] I forgot to write a beginning or an ending.
- [ ] I need more persuasive words. It's not clear how I feel.
- [ ] Some sentences are choppy. There are some mistakes.

Try Harder
- [ ] The goal is not clear. There are almost no reasons.
- [ ] There are no facts or examples.
- [ ] Both the beginning and the ending are missing.
- [ ] I used no persuasive words. I don't seem to care.
- [ ] Most sentences are choppy. There are many mistakes.

Practice Book page 183

Reading-Writing Workshop
Improving Your Writing

Name _____

Correcting Run-On Sentences

Fix these run-on sentences. Write the sentences correctly on the lines provided. Answers will vary. Sample answers given.

1. Run-On: Jane Goodall is one of the world's great scientists, she studies chimpanzees.
   Corrected: Jane Goodall is one of the world's great scientists. She studies chimpanzees. (2 points)

2. Run-On: More than thirty years ago Goodall had an interesting idea, she would study chimps in their natural habitat.
   Corrected: More than thirty years ago Goodall had an interesting idea. She would study chimps in their natural habitat. (2)

3. Run-On: At first, the chimps were suspicious, gradually Goodall gained their trust.
   Corrected: At first, the chimps were suspicious. Gradually Goodall gained their trust. (2)

4. Run-On: Goodall got to know each chimp in the group, each chimp was given a name.
   Corrected: Goodall got to know each chimp in the group. Each chimp was given a name. (2)

5. Run-On: Goodall was the first to discover that chimps made tools, she also discovered that chimps could learn new ideas.
   Corrected: Goodall was the first to discover that chimps made tools. She also discovered that chimps could learn new ideas. (2)

Transparency RWW6-5

TRANSPARENCY RWW 6-5
TEACHER'S EDITION PAGE 339E

SMART SOLUTIONS
Reading-Writing Workshop
Correcting Run-On Sentences
ANNOTATED VERSION

Correcting Run-On Sentences

Answers will vary. Sample answers given.

1. Run-On: I think chimpanzees are smart animals, they can make tools and solve problems.
   Corrected: I think chimpanzees are smart animals. They can make tools and solve problems.

2. Run-On: One chimp named Washoe learned sign language, this chimp learned 130 sign language words.
   Corrected: One chimp named Washoe learned sign language. This chimp learned 130 sign language words.

3. Run-On: Washoe made up a new word in sign language to describe peanuts, she called the peanuts "rock berries."
   Corrected: Washoe made up a new word in sign language to describe peanuts. She called the peanuts "rock berries."

4. Run-On: Did Washoe remember words, she once recalled the name of a person she hadn't seen in more than ten years.
   Corrected: Did Washoe remember words? She once recalled the name of a person she hadn't seen in more than ten years.

5. Run-On: Washoe was visited by a baby chimp named Loulis, she taught Loulis some sign language words.
   Corrected: Washoe was visited by a baby chimp named Loulis. She taught Loulis some sign language words.

Revising

Have students use **Practice Book** page 182 to help them evaluate and then revise their persuasive essay. Students should also discuss their drafts in a writing conference with one or more classmates. (Distribute Conference Master, page R26. Discuss the sample thoughts and questions before students have their conferences.) Remind students to keep in mind their listeners' comments and questions when they revise.

Proofreading

Have students proofread their papers to correct capitalization, punctuation, spelling, and usage. They can use the proofreading checklist and proofreading marks on **Practice Book** pages 250 and 251.

Improving Writing: Correcting Run-On Sentences

Explain that good writers avoid run-on sentences. Run-on sentences are confusing because they have more than one subject, predicate, and complete thought.

Point out the following methods for finding and correcting run-on sentences.

- Reread the sentence. Ask, Does this sentence have more than one subject or predicate? Does it tell more than one complete thought?
- Correct run-on sentences by dividing them into two or more sentences or by joining them with *and* or *but*.
- Be sure to use a period at the end of the first new sentence you create and start the second sentence with a capital letter.

Display **Transparency RWW6–5.** Model the first example. Then have students complete the transparency.

Assign **Practice Book** page 183. Then encourage students to reread their persuasive essay and correct any run-on sentences.

Frequently Misspelled Words

Write the Spelling Words on the board, or distribute the list on **Practice Book** page 243. Help students identify the part of the word likely to be misspelled.

Spelling Pretest/Test

Basic Words

1. Simon loved **his** hamsters.
2. **I'd** see him petting them every day.
3. **I'm** not all that fond of hamsters.
4. **That's** just the way I feel.
5. I **didn't** want to pet his hamsters.
6. I **don't** have any pets of my own.
7. I **know** Simon loves his hamsters.
8. Sometimes, he takes them **outside**.
9. One has **been** lost for a long time.
10. **We're** not sure when it escaped.
11. If **anyone** sees it, let us know.
12. I'm sure it will be happy **anyway**.

Challenge Words

13. Simon will not **lose** more hamsters.
14. Another one **finally** escaped.
15. It ran around in **different** rooms.
16. It **happily** came back to its cage.

Practice Book page 184

Reading-Writing Workshop
Frequently Misspelled Words

Name _____

Spelling Words

Look for spelling patterns you have learned to help you remember the Spelling Words on this page. Think about the parts that you find hard to spell.

Write the missing letters and apostrophes in the Spelling Words below. Order of answers for 2–3 may vary.

1. h i___ s ___ (1 point)
2. I '___ d ___ (1)
3. I '___ m ___ (1)
4. th a___ t ___ s ___ (1)
5. did n___ '___ t (1)
6. do n___ '___ t (1)
7. k___ n___ ow (1)
8. o___ u___ tsid e___ (1)
9. b e___ e___ n (1)
10. we '___ r e___ (1)
11. a___ nyone (1)
12. a___ nyway (1)

Spelling Words

1. his
2. I'd
3. I'm
4. that's
5. didn't
6. don't
7. know
8. outside
9. been
10. we're
11. anyone
12. anyway

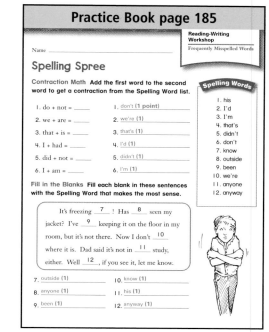

Study List On another sheet of paper, write each Spelling Word. Check the list to be sure you spelled each word correctly. Order of words may vary. (1 point each)

Practice Book page 185

Reading-Writing Workshop
Frequently Misspelled Words

Name _____

Spelling Spree

Contraction Math Add the first word to the second word to get a contraction from the Spelling Word list.

1. do + not = _____
2. we + are = _____
3. that + is = _____
4. I + had = _____
5. did + not = _____
6. I + am = _____

1. don't (1 point)
2. we're (1)
3. that's (1)
4. I'd (1)
5. didn't (1)
6. I'm (1)

Spelling Words

1. his
2. I'd
3. I'm
4. that's
5. didn't
6. don't
7. know
8. outside
9. been
10. we're
11. anyone
12. anyway

Fill in the Blanks Fill each blank in these sentences with the Spelling Word that makes the most sense.

It's freezing __7__ ! Has __8__ seen my jacket? I've __9__ keeping it on the floor in my room, but it's not there. Now I don't __10__ where it is. Dad said it's not in __11__ study, either. Well __12__, if you see it, let me know.

7. outside (1)   10. know (1)
8. anyone (1)   11. his (1)
9. been (1)   12. anyway (1)

Practice Book page 243

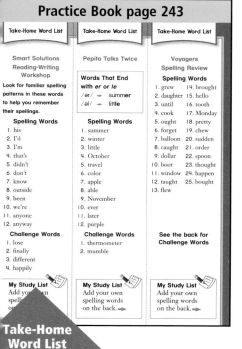

Take-Home Word List	Take-Home Word List	Take-Home Word List
Smart Solutions Reading-Writing Workshop	**Pepita Talks Twice**	**Voyagers** Spelling Review
Look for familiar spelling patterns in these words to help you remember their spellings.	**Words That End with er or le** /ər/ → summer /əl/ → little	**Spelling Words** 1. grew 14. brought 2. daughter 15. hello 3. until 16. tooth 4. cook 17. Monday
Spelling Words	**Spelling Words**	5. ought 18. pretty
1. his	1. summer	6. forget 19. chew
2. I'd	2. winter	7. balloon 20. sudden
3. I'm	3. little	8. caught 21. order
4. that's	4. October	9. dollar 22. spoon
5. didn't	5. travel	10. boot 23. thought
6. don't	6. color	11. window 24. happen
7. know	7. apple	12. taught 25. bought
8. outside	8. able	13. flew
9. been	9. November	
10. we're	10. ever	
11. anyone	11. later	
12. anyway	12. purple	
Challenge Words	**Challenge Words**	**See the back for Challenge Words**
1. lose	1. thermometer	
2. finally	2. mumble	
3. different		
4. happily		
My Study List Add your own spelling words on the back.	**My Study List** Add your own spelling words on the back.	**My Study List** Add your own spelling words on the back.

Take-Home Word List

Practice Book page 186

Reading-Writing Workshop
Frequently Misspelled Words

Name _____

Proofreading and Writing

Proofreading Circle the four misspelled Spelling Words in this advertisement. Then write each word correctly.

Do you have a problem that you don't (kno) how to solve? Then call us at Smart Solutions! We've (bin) solving people's problems for over twenty years. And (anywon) will tell you that our prices can't be beat. So give us a call at 555-1971 — (weare) waiting!

Spelling Words

1. his
2. I'd
3. I'm
4. that's
5. didn't
6. don't
7. know
8. outside
9. been
10. we're
11. anyone
12. anyway

1. know (1 point)   3. anyone (1)
2. been (1)   4. we're (1)

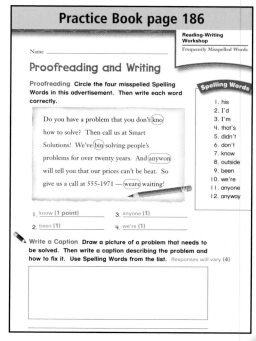

Write a Caption Draw a picture of a problem that needs to be solved. Then write a caption describing the problem and how to fix it. Use Spelling Words from the list. Responses will vary (4)

Publishing

📁 Portfolio Opportunity

Save students' final copy of their persuasive essay as an example of the development of their writing skills.

Have students publish their stories.

- Ask students to look back at the publishing ideas they noted when they chose a topic. Discuss the Ideas for Sharing box below.
- Then ask students to decide how they want to publish their writing.
- Tell them to make a neat final copy of their essay. Remind them to use good penmanship and to be sure that they have fixed all mistakes.

Ideas for Sharing

Write It
- Send your essay in a letter.
- Post it on your school Internet site.

Say It
- Present your essay as a speech.

Show It
- Make a photo essay. Use real photos or draw pictures.
- Make a poster.

Tips for Making a Speech

- Speak with expression. Raise your voice at the end of a question. Say exclamations with feeling. Speak so that your audience can hear you.
- Show your feelings with your face and hands. Use props to make your points clear.

Evaluating

Student Self-Assessment

- What did you think was the best part of your persuasive essay?
- How clearly did you state the goal of your persuasive essay? How convincing were the reasons you gave in support of that goal?
- What did you learn about writing a persuasive essay? How might you use what you learned in the next paper you write?

Have students write responses to the Student Self-Assessment questions.

Evaluate your students' writing, using the Writing Traits Scoring Rubric. The rubric is based on the criteria in this workshop and reflects the criteria student used in Revising Your Persuasive Essay on **Practice Book** page 182.

Persuasive Essay

Writing Traits Scoring Rubric

4

IDEAS	The essay focuses on a goal. The goal is supported by clear, strong reasons. Each reason is supported by facts and examples.
ORGANIZATION	An interesting beginning states the goal clearly. Each paragraph states a reason and includes supporting facts and examples. The ending restates the goal.
VOICE	The writer confidently expressed his or her feelings about the goal.
WORD CHOICE	The words chosen are persuasive.
SENTENCE FLUENCY	The writing flows well. Sentence length and structure vary.
CONVENTIONS	There are almost no errors in grammar, capitalization, spelling, or usage.
PRESENTATION	The final copy is neat and legible.

3

IDEAS	The essay focuses on a goal. Another reason may be needed. More facts and examples would make each reason more convincing.
ORGANIZATION	The beginning may be dull. Facts and examples may be misplaced. The ending may not restate the goal.
VOICE	The writer sometimes does not show his or her feelings about the goal.
WORD CHOICE	The writer could have used more persuasive words.
SENTENCE FLUENCY	The essay would benefit from greater sentence variety.
CONVENTIONS	There are a few mistakes, but they do not affect understanding.
PRESENTATION	The final copy is messy in a few places but still legible.

2

IDEAS	The essay expresses a goal but does not stay focused on it. The writer gave too few reasons, or the reasons are weak. Reasons are not supported by facts and examples.
ORGANIZATION	The goal may not be clearly stated in the beginning. The organization is inconsistent. The ending may be missing.
VOICE	The writer often does not show his or her feelings about the goal.
WORD CHOICE	Word choice is unpersuasive.
SENTENCE FLUENCY	The essay lacks sentence variety.
CONVENTIONS	Mistakes sometimes make the essay hard to understand.
PRESENTATION	The final copy is messy. It may be illegible in a few places.

1

IDEAS	The writer did not clearly state a goal. There are no convincing reasons. Facts and examples are weak or confusing.
ORGANIZATION	The goal may not be stated at all. Ideas may be presented just as a list.
VOICE	The writer does not seem to care about the goal.
WORD CHOICE	Word choice is vague or uninteresting. It may be confusing.
SENTENCE FLUENCY	Sentences are short, unclear, or repetitive.
CONVENTIONS	Many mistakes make the paper hard to understand.
PRESENTATION	The final copy is messy. It may be illegible in many places.

Lesson Overview

Literature

POPPA'S NEW PANTS

Angela Shelf Medearis

illustrated by John Ward

Selection Summary

When Poppa's family tries to help him by shortening his new pair of pants before church in the morning, both Poppa and his son George get a big surprise.

1 Background and Vocabulary

2 Main Selection

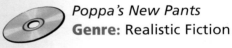

Poppa's New Pants
Genre: Realistic Fiction

3 Media Link

Instructional Support

Planning and Practice

Practice Book

- Planning and classroom management
- Reading instruction
- Skill lessons
- Materials for reaching all learners

- Independent practice for skills, Level 3.6

Teacher's Resource Blackline Masters

Instruction Transparencies/Masters and Strategy Posters

- Transparencies
- Strategy Posters
- Blackline Masters

- Newsletters
- Selection Summaries
- Assignment Cards
- Observation Checklists
- Selection Tests

Reaching All Learners

Intervention Strategies for Extra Support

Instructional Activities for Challenge

Instructional Strategies for English Language Learners

Independent Activities for Classroom Management

Coordinated lessons, activities, and projects for additional reading instruction

For
- Classroom teacher
- Extended day
- Pull out
- Resource teacher
- Reading specialist

Technology

Audio Selection

Poppa's New Pants

Get Set for Reading CD-ROM
- Background building
- Vocabulary support
- Selection Summary in English and Spanish

Accelerated Reader®
- Practice quizzes for the selection

www.eduplace.com

Log on to Education Place for more activities related to the selection, including vocabulary support—
e • Glossary
e • WordGame

Leveled Books for Reaching All Learners

Leveled Readers and Leveled Practice

- Independent reading for building fluency
- Topic, comprehension strategy, and vocabulary linked to main selection
- Lessons in Teacher's Edition, pages 367O–367R
- Leveled practice for every book

Technology

Leveled Readers
Audio available

Book Adventure®
- Practice quizzes for the Leveled Theme Paperbacks
www.bookadventure.org

● BELOW LEVEL

A Little Bit 'Hotter' Can't Hurt
by Joanna Korba
illustrated by Bethann Thornburgh
Leveled Readers

● Below Level Practice

A Little Bit Hotter Can't Hurt
Key Vocabulary

Name _____

Vocabulary

Use the clues to complete the puzzle. Choose your answers from the words in the box.

Vocabulary
mild
planted
mow
sweet potato

Across
2. gentle flavor, not at all hot
4. yellow or red root that is eaten as a vegetable

Down
1. put or placed firmly
3. to cut grass with a mower

5

● Below Level Practice

A Little Bit Hotter Can't Hurt
Comprehension Skill
Drawing Conclusions

Name _____

Comprehension

Carmen has a problem. Read this passage to find out what the problem is. Then draw conclusions by putting together story clues.

Carmen had a worried look on her face as she paced around the house. Then the phone rang. Carmen picked it up after the first ring and then listened. "Thank you so much, Mrs. Brooks!" Carmen said.
She listened again and then said, "My little sister left the back door open. By the time I saw that, Rufus had already escaped." Finally, Carmen said, "I'm going to get his leash. Then I'll come right over to get him."

1. Who is Rufus? Carmen's dog

2. What clues helped you draw this conclusion? She is going to get his leash.

3. What happened to Rufus? Rufus escaped the house.

4. What clues helped you draw this conclusion? Carmen says that her sister left the back door open and Rufus was gone.

5. Why does Mrs. Brooks call? She called to tell Carmen that she has Rufus.

6. What clues helped you draw this conclusion?
Carmen thanks her and says she'll go to Mrs. Brooks's house to get him.

7

▲ ON LEVEL

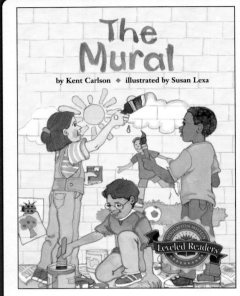

The Mural
by Kent Carlson ◆ illustrated by Susan Lexa
Leveled Readers

▲ On Level Practice

The Mural
Key Vocabulary

Name _____

Vocabulary

Use the words from the box to complete the sentences.

Vocabulary
mural
ballots
canvas
mascot
fierce-looking

1. The artist needed paint, two paintbrushes, and a new ___canvas___ to begin her next painting.

2. The ___fierce-looking___ tiger scared off his enemy with a loud growl.

3. The ___mascot___ of our school is a polar bear.

4. When the ___ballots___ were counted, Jana won the class election by five votes.

5. Everyone loved the ___mural___ that Paco painted on the wall of the community center!

Write three sentences about what you would like a school mural to look like. Use at least three words from the box.

_____

_____

_____

5

▲ On Level Practice

The Mural
Comprehension Skill
Drawing Conclusions

Name _____

Comprehension

Read this passage. Use the clues to help you draw a conclusion.

I remember all the sights and sounds from the big game! Coach Hu told the team that we had to be fierce-looking, like our mascot. He even had someone dressed up like an eagle outside the dugout. Just before the first pitch, there was total silence. The ball seemed like it took forever to reach my bat! But when it finally did, I heard a loud CRACK! The ball sailed over the field. It looked like it could be a home run. I ran like crazy to first base and that's when I heard the next sound—shattering glass.

1. What game is being played?
baseball

2. What clues helped you?
In the passage, I read words that had to do with baseball like dugout, pitch, ball, bat, and home run.

3. What has happened at the end of the passage?
The ball was hit through a window.

4. What clues helped you?
The ball sailed over the field, and they heard the sound of shattering glass.

7

Leveled Theme Paperbacks

- Extended independent reading in Theme-related trade books
- Lessons in Teacher's Edition, pages R2–R7

■ ABOVE LEVEL

Gampy's Lamps

by Lee S. Justice
illustrated by Alexandra Wallner

Leveled Readers

◆ LANGUAGE SUPPORT

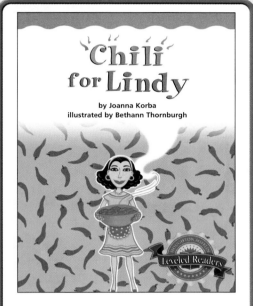

Chili for Lindy

by Joanna Korba
illustrated by Bethann Thornburgh

Leveled Readers

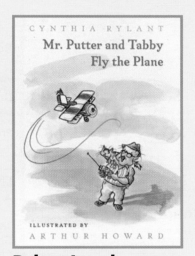

CYNTHIA RYLANT

Mr. Putter and Tabby
Fly the Plane

ILLUSTRATED BY
ARTHUR HOWARD

Below Level

■ Above Level Practice

Gampy's Lamps
Key Vocabulary

Name _____

Vocabulary

Draw a line from each word to its definition.

flea market	repairing
chimneys	an imaginary creature with extraordinary powers
mending	an outdoor market that sells secondhand items and antiques
genie	glass tubes around lamp flames
draped	hung

Vocabulary
flea market
chimneys
mending
genie
draped

Write three sentences about something you bought at a flea market. Use at least three words from the box.

_____
_____
_____

5

◆ Language Support Practice

Chili for Lindy
Build Background

Name _____

Build Background

Aunt Birdie is making a big pot of chili. Here are the steps she takes.

1. She chops an onion.

2. She cooks the onion with some oil in a pot.

3. She adds some meat.

4. She adds a can of tomatoes.

5. Aunt Birdie adds just one teaspoon of chili powder.

Use the pictures and sentences above to answer the questions.

1. What are three things that go in chili?
any three of the following: onion, oil, meat, tomatoes, chili powder

2. What do you cook chili in?
a pot

3. How much chili powder does Aunt Birdie put into the chili?
one teaspoon

5

WEST SIDE KIDS
Bank Street

THE BIG IDEA
ELLEN SCHECTER

On Level

■ Above Level Practice

Gampy's Lamps
Comprehension Skill
Drawing Conclusions

Name _____

Comprehension

Read the following passage. Then draw a conclusion by putting together clues from the information given by the teacher.

Brenda's alarm clock did not go off on the morning after the ice storm, and she is late for school. By the time she gets to class, her teacher is already giving information about an animal.

This is what she heard. "Most of them can pull their head, legs, and tail into their shells. The ones that live on land have a high, rounded shell. Those that live in water have a flatter shell. Like all reptiles, they are cold-blooded, which means their body temperature stays the same as the air or water they are in. They come in all sizes. The largest ones grow up to eight feet long, but most of them are much smaller. They can live almost anywhere—in deserts, forests, lakes, ponds, rivers, and in the sea. Most kinds eat both plants and animals."

1. What kind of animal was the teacher talking about? turtles

2. What clues helped you draw that conclusion? They are reptiles, can pull their head, legs, and tail into their shell, come in all sizes, and live almost everywhere.

3. What school subject is the class studying? science

4. What clues helped you draw that conclusion? The teacher is talking about animals, environments, and habitats. These are topics for a science class.

7

◆ Language Support Practice

Chili for Lindy
Key Vocabulary

Name _____

Vocabulary

Write in a word from the box to complete each sentence.

Vocabulary
chili
hotter
mild
pie
pretend
Texas

I have never been to the state of ___Texas___ before.

How do you like your ___chili___?

Mine is too ___mild___
Please make it ___hotter___

I just ___pretend___ to like chili. I really just want some ___pie___

6

MARY STOLZ
Stealing Home

The rules have changed. Is the game the same?

Challenge

Daily Lesson Plans

Technology
Lesson Planner CD-ROM allows you to customize the chart below to develop your own lesson plans.

T Skill tested on Theme Skills Test and/or Integrated Theme Test

	DAY 1	**DAY 2**
50–60 minutes **Reading** **Comprehension** 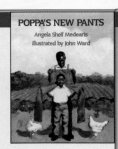 **Leveled Readers** • Fluency Practice • Independent Reading	**Teacher Read Aloud,** 339S–339T *Seven Foolish Fishermen:* *A Story from France* Building Background, 340 **Key Vocabulary,** 341 draped · mended · plaid fabric · pattern · rustling hem **Reading the Selection,** 342–361 **Comprehension Skill,** 342 Drawing Conclusions **T** **Comprehension Strategy,** 342 Predict/Infer **Leveled Readers** *A Little Bit Hotter Can't* *Hurt* *The Mural* *Gampy's Lamps* *Chili for Lindy* Lessons and Leveled Practice, 367O–367R	**Reading the Selection,** 342–361 Comprehension Check, 361 Responding, 362 Think About the Selection **Comprehension Skill Preview,** 359 Drawing Conclusions **T** **Leveled Readers** *A Little Bit Hotter Can't* *Hurt* *The Mural* *Gampy's Lamps* *Chili for Lindy* Lessons and Leveled Practice, 367O–367R
20–30 minutes **Word Work** **Phonics/Decoding** **Vocabulary** **Spelling**	**Phonics/Decoding,** 343 Phonics/Decoding Strategy **Vocabulary,** 342–361 Selection Vocabulary **Spelling,** 367E Words Beginning with *a/be* **T**	**Structural Analysis,** 367C VCV Pattern **T** **Vocabulary,** 342–361 Selection Vocabulary **Spelling,** 367E Words Beginning with *a/be* Review and Practice **T**
20–30 minutes **Writing and Oral Language** **Writing** **Grammar** **Listening/Speaking/Viewing**	**Writing,** 367K Prewriting a Summary **Grammar,** 367I Comparing with Adjectives **T** **Daily Language Practice** 1. The red and gray fabric is alliv with color and brightest than the brown fabric. (alive; brighter) 2. Poppa says it is abowt the sharper plaid he has ever seen. (about; sharpest) **Listening/Speaking/Viewing,** 339S–339T, 353 Teacher Read Aloud, Stop and Think	**Writing,** 367K Drafting a Summary **Grammar,** 367I Comparing with Adjectives Practice **T** **Daily Language Practice** 3. We looked agin and saw that the plaid pants had the bolder pattern in the shop. (again; boldest) 4. He begann to say the pants are longest than Poppa's pair. (began; longer) **Listening/Speaking/Viewing,** 361, 362 Wrapping Up, Responding

Target Skills of the Week

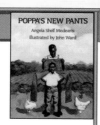

Comprehension	Predict/Infer; Drawing Conclusions
Vocabulary	Antonyms
Phonics/Decoding	VCV Pattern
Fluency	Leveled Readers

DAY 3

Rereading the Selection
Rereading for Writer's Craft, 357
Vivid Language

Comprehension Skill, 367A–367B
Drawing Conclusions **T**

Leveled Readers
A Little Bit Hotter Can't Hurt
The Mural
Gampy's Lamps
Chili for Lindy

Lessons and Leveled Practice, 367O–367R

Phonics Review, 367D
Words Beginning with *a-* and *be-*

Vocabulary, 367G
Antonyms **T**

Spelling, 367F
Vocabulary: Definitions; Words Beginning with *a/be* Practice **T**

Writing, 367L
Revising a Summary
Paraphrasing

Grammar, 367J
Adjective Game **T**

Daily Language Practice
5. Grandma Tiny went ahed and mended the pants fastest than Big Mama. (ahead; faster)
6. Betwene you and me, Aunt Viney was the faster of all three (Between; fastest; three.)

DAY 4

Reading the Media Link, 364–367
"No Problem!"

Skill: How to Read a Diagram

Rereading for Visual Literacy, 366
Comic Strips

Comprehension Skill Review, 349
Cause and Effect

Leveled Readers
A Little Bit Hotter Can't Hurt
The Mural
Gampy's Lamps
Chili for Lindy

Lessons and Leveled Practice, 367O–367R

Phonics/Decoding, 364–367
Apply Phonics/Decoding Strategy to Link

Vocabulary, 367M
Language Center: Building Vocabulary

Spelling, 367F
Spelling Game, Proofreading **T**

Writing, 367L
Proofreading a Summary

Grammar, 367J
Comparing with Adjectives Practice **T**

Daily Language Practice
7. The rustling noise behinde him was louderer than a mouse. (behind; louder)
8. He looked arond and saw Big Mama, the taller of the three. (around; tallest)

Listening/Speaking/Viewing, 367
Discuss the Link

DAY 5

Rereading for Fluency, 351

Responding Activities, 362–363
Write a Funny Story
Cross-Curricular Activities

Information and Study Skills, 367H
Following Directions **T**

Comprehension Skill Review, 355
Compare and Contrast

Leveled Readers
A Little Bit Hotter Can't Hurt
The Mural
Gampy's Lamps
Chili for Lindy

Lessons and Leveled Practice, 367O–367R

Structural Analysis, 367N
Language Center: VCV Syllable Puzzles

Vocabulary, 367M
Language Center: Vocabulary Game

Spelling, 367F
Test: Words Beginning with *a/be* **T**

Writing, 367L
Publishing a Summary

Grammar, 367J, 367M
Using *good* and *well*
Language Center: Comparative Adjective Poster

Daily Language Practice
9. Befour bed, Poppa draped his newestest pants on the chair. (Before; newest)
10. He liked the cloth becuz it was softest than an kitten. (because; softer; a)

Listening/Speaking/Viewing, 367N
Language Center: Give a Persuasive Speech

Managing Flexible Groups

	DAY 1	**DAY 2**
WHOLE CLASS	• Teacher Read Aloud (TE pp. 339S–339T) • Building Background, Introducing Vocabulary (TE pp. 340–341) • Comprehension Strategy: Introduce (TE p. 342) • Comprehension Skill: Introduce (TE p. 342) • Purpose Setting (TE p. 343) **After reading first half of** *Poppa's New Pants* • Stop and Think (TE p. 353)	**After reading** *Poppa's New Pants* • Wrapping Up (TE p. 361) • Comprehension Check (Practice Book p. 189) • Responding: Think About the Selection (TE p. 362) • Comprehension Skill: Preview (TE p. 359)
SMALL GROUPS		
Extra Support	**TEACHER-LED** • Preview *Poppa's New Pants* to Stop and Think (TE pp. 342–353). • Support reading with Extra Support/ Intervention notes (TE pp. 343, 347, 348, 352, 355, 357, 360).	**Partner or Individual Work** • Reread first half of *Poppa's New Pants* (TE pp. 342–353). • Preview, read second half (TE pp. 354–361). • Comprehension Check (Practice Book p. 189)
Challenge	**Individual Work** • Begin "It Was So Funny…" (Challenge Handbook p. 48). • Extend reading with Challenge notes (TE pp. 359, 360).	**Individual Work** • Continue work on activity (Challenge Handbook p. 48).
English Language Learners	**TEACHER-LED** • Preview vocabulary and *Poppa's New Pants* to Stop and Think (TE pp. 341–353). • Support reading with English Language Learners notes (TE pp. 340, 344, 346, 351, 356, 361, 362).	**TEACHER-LED** • Review first half of *Poppa's New Pants* (TE pp. 342–353). ✔ • Preview, read second half (TE pp. 354–361). • Begin Comprehension Check together (Practice Book p. 189).

Independent Activities

- Get Set for Reading CD-ROM
- Journals: selection notes, questions
- Complete, review Practice Book (pp. 187–191) and Leveled Readers Practice Blackline Masters (TE pp. 367O–367R).
- Assignment Cards (Teacher's Resource Blackline Masters pp. 87–88)
- Leveled Readers (TE pp. 367O–367R), Leveled Theme Paperbacks (TE pp. R2–R7), or book from Leveled Bibliography (TE pp. 296E–296F)

✔ Opportunity to informally assess oral reading rate

FLEXIBLE GROUPS

Leveled Instruction and Leveled Practice

- Rereading: Lesson on Writer's Craft, Visual Literacy (TE p. 357)

- Comprehension Skill: Main lesson (TE pp. 367A–367B)

- Reading the Media Link (TE pp. 364–367): Skill lesson (TE p. 364)

- Rereading the Link: Visual Literacy lesson (TE p. 366)

- Comprehension Skill: First Comprehension Review lesson (TE p. 349)

- Responding: Select from Activities (TE pp. 362–363)

- Information and Study Skills (TE p. 367H)

- Comprehension Skill: Second Comprehension Review lesson (TE p. 355)

TEACHER-LED

- Reread, review Comprehension Check (Practice Book p. 189).

- Preview Leveled Reader: Below Level (TE p. 367O), or read book from Leveled Bibliography (TE pp. 296E–296F). ✔

Partner or Individual Work

- Reread the Media Link (TE pp. 364–367).

- Complete Leveled Reader: Below Level (TE p. 367O), or read book from Leveled Bibliography (TE pp. 296E–296F).

TEACHER-LED

- Comprehension Skill: Reteaching lesson (TE p. R10)

- Reread Leveled Theme Paperback: Below Level (TE pp. R2–R3), or read book from Leveled Bibliography (TE pp. 296E–296F). ✔

TEACHER-LED

- Teacher check-in: Assess progress (Challenge Handbook p. 48).

- Preview Leveled Reader: Above Level (TE p. 367Q), or read book from Leveled Bibliography (TE pp. 296E–296F). ✔

Individual Work

- Complete activity (Challenge Handbook p. 48).

- Complete Leveled Reader: Above Level (TE p. 367Q), or read book from Leveled Bibliography (TE pp. 296E–296F).

TEACHER-LED

- Evaluate activity and plan format for sharing (Challenge Handbook p. 48).

- Reread Leveled Theme Paperback: Above Level (TE pp. R6–R7), or read book from Leveled Bibliography (TE pp. 296E–296F). ✔

Partner or Individual Work

- Complete Comprehension Check (Practice Book p. 189).

- Begin Leveled Reader: Language Support (TE p. 367R), or read book from Leveled Bibliography (TE pp. 296E–296F).

TEACHER-LED

- Reread the Media Link (TE pp. 364–367) ✔ and review Link Skill (TE p. 364).

- Complete Leveled Reader: Language Support (TE p. 367R), or read book from Leveled Bibliography (TE pp. 296E–296F). ✔

Partner or Individual Work

- Reread book from Leveled Bibliography (TE pp. 296E–296F).

- Responding activities (TE pp. 362–363)
- Language Center activities (TE pp. 367M–367N)
- **Fluency Practice:** Reread *Pepita Talks Twice; Poppa's New Pants* ✔
- Activities relating to *Poppa's New Pants* at Education Place www.eduplace.com

Turn the page for more independent activities.

Classroom Management

Independent Activities

Assign these activities while you work with small groups.

Differentiated Instruction for Small Groups

- **Handbook for English Language Learners,** pp. 208–217

- **Extra Support Handbook,** pp. 204–213

Independent Activities

- Language Center, pp. 367M–367N

- Challenge/Extension Activities, Theme Resources, pp. R11, R17

- **Classroom Management Handbook,** Activity Masters CM6-5–CM6-8

- **Challenge Handbook,** pp. 48–49

Look for more activities in the Classroom Management Kit.

Art

Colorful Expressions

👤 Singles	🕐 15 minutes
Objective	Illustrate colorful expressions.
Materials	Anthology, markers

George uses many colorful expressions to tell his story. He says that Grandma Tiny was running around like a "Texas tornado." Later he says that Grandma Tiny was "smiling fit to beat the band." Can you imagine what those scenes look like?

Choose one of George's expressions. Then draw a picture that shows what you imagine it looks like. Write the sentence with the expression below the picture. Underneath the expression, write a one-sentence explanation of the expression. Hang your drawing in the classroom.

Grandma Tiny had been tearing around all morning like a Texas tornado.

Poetry

An Ode to Clothing

👤 Singles	🕐 30 minutes
Objective	Write a poem.

George likes his new pants. Do you have any favorite clothes? Write a poem about your favorite article of clothing. You might make it rhyme, use vivid words, or use similes. Draw a picture to go with your poem. Share your poem and drawing with the class.

Consider copying and laminating these activities for use in centers.

Language Arts

Like Father, Like Son?

Pairs	🕐 15 minutes
Objective	Use a Venn diagram to compare and contrast.
Materials	Anthology

On your own, compare and contrast Poppa and George.

- Review the story.
- Look at the pictures.
- Make a Venn diagram like the one begun below. Label one circle **George** and the other **Poppa**. Label the overlapping area **Both**.

In the outer parts of the two circles, list the things about Poppa and George that are different. Then, where the circles overlap each other, write how these two characters are alike.

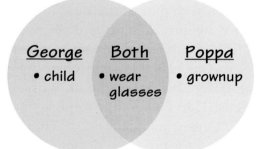

George
- child

Both
- wear glasses

Poppa
- grownup

Now get together with your partner. Compare your Venn diagrams to see whether you listed any of the same details.

Social Studies

Life in the Country

👤 Singles	🕐 15 minutes
Objective	Make a word web with details of life in the country.
Materials	Anthology

The illustrations and the text in *Poppa's New Pants* help the reader know that this story is set in the country, not in the city. Look through the selection to find details of life in the country. Record the details in a word web.

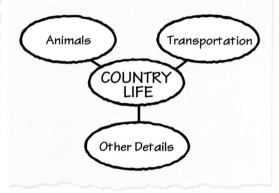

Animals

Transportation

COUNTRY LIFE

Other Details

Career

Making Clothes

Pairs	🕐 30 minutes
Objective	Research clothing design and manufacture.
Materials	Reference resources

Grandma Tiny, Big Mama, and Aunt Viney all know how to sew and make clothes. With a partner, research what kind of jobs there are in designing and making clothing.

- Create a jobs poster that lists the names and descriptions of the jobs.
- Add pictures to your descriptions.
- Display your poster in the classroom.

Listening Comprehension

Building Background

Tell students that you are going to read aloud a story about seven brothers.

- Ask students to describe group or school trips they have taken. Have students tell how chaperones keep track of the students, pointing out if necessary that they take a roll call or count heads periodically.

Fluency Modeling

Explain that as you read aloud, you will be modeling fluent oral reading. Ask students to listen carefully to your phrasing and your expression, or tone of voice and emphasis.

COMPREHENSION SKILL

Drawing Conclusions

Explain that sometimes authors don't tell everything they want their readers to know. Then it is necessary to

- use story details to figure out what the author has not stated.

Purpose Setting Read the story aloud, asking students to note details that will help them draw conclusions as they listen. Then use the Guiding Comprehension questions to assess students' understanding. Reread the story for clarification as needed.

Teacher Read Aloud

Seven Foolish Fishermen
A STORY FROM FRANCE
retold by Martha Hamilton and Mitch Weiss

❶ Long ago, in a small village in France, there lived seven brothers. They were known not only for their great skill as fishermen but also for their complete lack of sense.

One day they decided to take a trip to Paris. None of them had ever left his little village before. Their mother was worried. She warned them, "It's easy to get lost in such a big city. Be sure to watch out for each other."

It was a three-day walk to Paris, so they set out early. The brothers made good time as they talked of all the sights they would see. At midday, they came upon a large well. They took a drink, ate their lunch, and rested for a while.

When it was time to continue on their way, the oldest brother remembered what his mother had said. He decided they had better count to make sure no one had gotten lost so far. He lined his brothers up and counted, "One, two, three, four, five, six. What? Only six? I must have counted wrong. Someone else try." But when the second oldest brother counted, he, too, came up with only six. All the brothers tried, and all got the same result.

"Oh, no!" they cried. "One of us is missing!" They began to call and look around for their lost brother. They looked up in the trees and behind the bushes, but he was nowhere to be found.

❷ One of them happened to look over the edge of the well, into the water at the bottom. He called to the others, "I've found him! He's fallen in the well, but he seems to be fine."

"Don't be scared," he called to his brother down in the well. "We'll have you out of there in no time."

The other brothers came running. They couldn't figure out how to rescue the lost brother without a rope or a ladder. Then the youngest had an idea. "I've got it," he said. "We must form a chain down into the well so that our brother can climb up and make his escape."

They agreed this was a brilliant idea. The eldest brother held on to the top of the well, and the next brother climbed down and got hold of his ankles. It wasn't long before the brothers hung from each other's ankles.

But just then, the oldest brother felt a big sneeze coming on. *"Ah-ah-ah-choo!"* When he sneezed, he let go of the top of the well and tumbled in along with all his brothers. Now they were stuck at the bottom of the well. At least, they reasoned, they were all together again.

The brothers noticed that there were gaps between the stones, just big enough so they could use their hands and feet to climb out. Before long, they were all out of the well. Since their clothes were dripping wet, they took them off and hung them in a tree to dry. When a stranger passed by and saw them all standing there wearing only their underwear, he asked them what had happened. They explained about losing their brother and rescuing him from the well. "Sir," said the oldest brother. "We'd like to be absolutely sure we're all here. Would you please count us?"

3 "I have a better idea," said the stranger, who was doing his best not to laugh. "Since you all hung your pants up to dry, why don't you count how many pairs of pants are hanging in the tree?"

The brothers knew a good idea when they heard one. They counted and were pleased to find there were *seven* pairs of pants! They thanked the stranger again and again for his cleverness.

When the clothes were dry, the brothers decided to go home. If one of them had almost gotten lost on the *way* to Paris, surely one of them would get lost *in* Paris. They returned home, thankful they were all safe and sound.

CRITICAL THINKING
Guiding Comprehension

1 **DRAWING CONCLUSIONS** Why is the mother worried about her sons? (They have never left the village before and they have no sense.)

2 **DRAWING CONCLUSIONS** Why do you think the brother who has fallen into the well doesn't speak? (Sample answer: because he is only a reflection of the brother who is looking at himself.)

3 **DRAWING CONCLUSIONS** What does the stranger realize when the brothers tell him their story? (No one was ever really lost. Each brother forgot to count himself when counting the others. One brother saw his own reflection in the well water and thought a brother had fallen in.)

Discussion Options

Personal Response Ask students to tell whether they found this story funny or not and why.

⭐ **Connecting/Comparing** Have students compare the relationship of the brothers in *Seven Foolish Fishermen* to that of Pepita and Juan in *Pepita Talks Twice*.

 English Language Learners

Language Development

Ask students to explain what a "brilliant" idea is and if it is better than a "good" idea or not. Point out that the author refers to a "good" idea, a "better" idea, and a "brilliant" idea. Then explain that the superlative of *good* is *best*. Help students to place the words *good, better,* and *best* on a continuum from left to right. You might also want to make another continuum with the comparative adjectives *bad, worse,* and *worst.* Point out that the comparative and superlative forms of these adjectives are not formed in the usual way.

Building Background

Key Concept: Helping Out

Remind students that this theme is called *Smart Solutions*. Explain that in the next story, *Poppa's New Pants,* family members work too hard to solve a problem.

Have students tell what they know about sewing, especially shortening pants or skirts. Use "Sewing Clothes" on pages 340–341 to help students learn about sewing and fabric.

- Have a student read aloud "Sewing Clothes."

- Have students read the captions, study the photos, and discuss sewing or repairing clothes.

Background and Vocabulary

Sewing Clothes

POPPA'S NEW PANTS
Angela Shelf Medearis
illustrated by John Ward

Poppa's New Pants

Read to find the meanings of these words.

e • Glossary

fabric
hem
mended
patterns
plaid

Have you ever ripped your shirt by accident or had a pair of pants that was too long? If you have, then you probably know what it's like to have your clothes **mended**. After you have mended your clothes, they'll fit well and you'll look great.

To fix a hole, you often have to find another piece of **fabric**. Then you must sew a patch of the fabric over the hole.

For clothes that are too long, like the pants in the story you are about to read, you'll need to **hem** the fabric. Fold the fabric under and sew it in place.

340

REACHING ALL LEARNERS

English Language Learners

Supporting Comprehension

Beginning/Preproduction Have students listen to the article. List and explain the Key Vocabulary words: *mended, fabric, hem, patterns, plaid.* Have students demonstrate the meaning of each by drawing or pantomiming.

Early Production and Speech Emergence Point out and explain the Key Vocabulary words. Have students use these frame sentences to point out examples of the words: This is (a) (mended; fabric; hem; plaid.) These are (patterns.)

Intermediate and Advanced Fluency Ask students to state the main idea of each paragraph in their own words. Invite them to explain how each illustration adds to what they know about sewing.

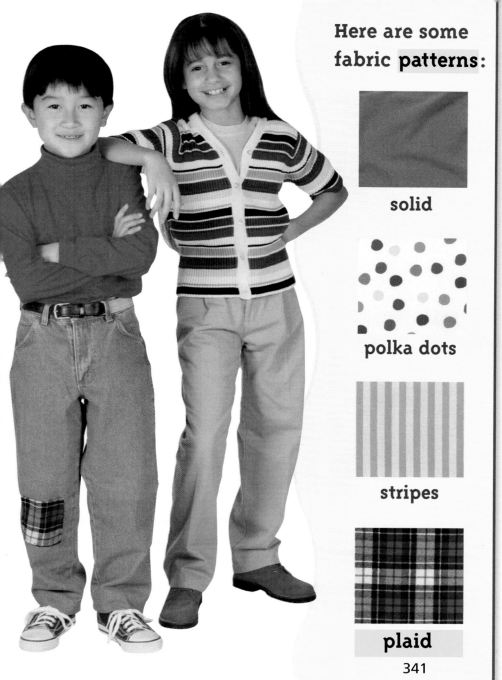

Here are some fabric patterns:

solid

polka dots

stripes

plaid

Introducing Vocabulary

Key Vocabulary

These words support the Key Concept and appear in the selection.

draped hung loosely in folds

fabric cloth

hem to fold back and sew down the edges

mended repaired by sewing

pattern a repeated design or decoration

plaid a pattern of stripes that cross each other

rustling quick, soft, fluttering sound

 e • Glossary
e • WordGame

See Vocabulary notes on pages 344, 346, 348, 350, 352, 354, 356, 358, 360, 364, and 366 for additional words to preview.

Display Transparency 6–10.

- Model how to use context clues to figure out the meaning of *pattern*.

- Have students figure out the meaning of each remaining word, following your example.

- Ask students to look for these words as they read and use them as they discuss the story.

Practice/Homework Assign **Practice Book** page 187.

Transparency 6–10

Mending Words

Date: 01/18/2002 2:27:50 P.M. Pacific Standard Time
From: crramirez@email.com
To: vrramirez@email.com

Dear Vicki,

    I'm so glad we chose the polka dot pattern for your new dress. I know you liked the plaid cloth with the crossing blue and green lines, but the pink dots on a yellow background are much more cheerful. I also like to hear the rustling of the stiff fabric when you brush up against something. I have your finished dress draped over the back of the chair next to my computer. I'm looking at it as I type this e-mail. It is on top of a pile of clothes that are waiting to be mended. Time to go! I need to patch the hole in Poppa's favorite jeans and hem your dress so it's not as long.

Love,
Grandma Carmina

pattern	a. large patches	b. repeated design	c. colored paper
plaid	a. crossing stripes	b. wild circles	c. solid shapes
rustling	a. fake fighting	b. fluttering sound	c. steady dripping
fabric	a. plastic	b. heavy cardboard	c. cloth
draped	a. folded	b. pinned	c. dropped
mended	a. painted	b. repaired	c. thrown out
hem	a. shorten	b. stretch	c. loosen

Practice Book page 187

Name _____

Poppa's New Pants
Key Vocabulary

Sewing Words

Fill in the blanks with the correct word from the Word Bank. (Hint: Not every word will be used.) Then find and circle all the Word Bank words in the puzzle.

Word Bank

fabric	hem	mended	pattern
rustling	plaid	draped	

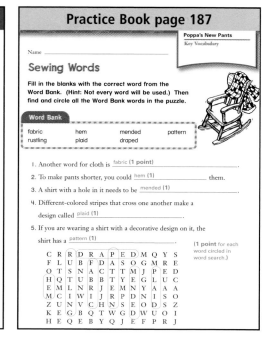

1. Another word for cloth is fabric **(1 point)**

2. To make pants shorter, you could hem **(1)** _____ them.

3. A shirt with a hole in it needs to be mended **(1)**

4. Different-colored stripes that cross one another make a
    design called plaid **(1)** _____.

5. If you are wearing a shirt with a decorative design on it, the
    shirt has a pattern **(1)** _____.

(1 point for each word circled in word search.)

```
C R R D R A P E D M Q Y S
F L U B F D A S O G M R E
O T S N A C T T M J P E D
H Q T U B B T Y E G L U C
E M L N R J E M N Y A A A
M C I W I J R P D N I S O
Z U N V C H N S E O D S Z
K E G B Q T W G D W U O I
H E Q E B Y Q J E F P R J
```

COMPREHENSION STRATEGY
Predict/Infer

Teacher Modeling Ask a student to read the title, the author's and illustrator's names, and the Strategy Focus aloud. Remind students that to predict is to make a sensible guess about what will happen based on story clues and information they already know. Ask students to read page 344. Then model the strategy.

Think Aloud *On page 344 I learn that Grandma Tiny is excited about a visit from relatives. She sends Poppa and George, the narrator, to the store. Since the title is* Poppa's New Pants *and I know that people like to look their best when visitors come, I predict that Poppa will buy some new pants to wear for the visit.*

Test Prep Tell students to use the Predict/Infer strategy before reading each test passage. Suggest that they use the title and any illustrations to predict whether the passage is fiction or nonfiction. Then they should predict what will happen.

COMPREHENSION SKILL
Drawing Conclusions

Introduce the Graphic Organizer.
Tell students that a Conclusions Chart can help them put together story clues to figure out information that is not stated directly. Explain that, as they read, students will fill out the Conclusions Chart found on **Practice Book** page 188.

- Display **Transparency 6–11**. Have students read Anthology page 344 and the first paragraph on page 346.
- Model how to answer the first question. Then monitor students' work as needed.

Meet the Author
Angela Shelf Medearis

Where she lives: Austin, Texas
Fun fact: One day she started counting all the picture books she owns. She counted 500 and had to stop because she was too tired!
Her books: She writes funny stories because she thinks laughter is one of the happiest sounds in the world.
Other books: *Annie's Gifts, Too Much Talk, Princess of the Press, The Singing Man*

Meet the Illustrator
John Ward

Where he lives: He lives in Freeport, New York, with his wife, Olympia, and his cat, Pumpkin.
Fun fact: He teamed up with Angela Shelf Medearis once again to create *Poppa's Itchy Christmas*, another funny story starring the characters in *Poppa's New Pants*.
Other books: *Fireflies for Nathan* (by Shulamith Levey Oppenheim), *The Bus Ride* (by William Miller)

Stop by Education Place to learn more about Angela Shelf Medearis and John Ward. **www.eduplace.com/kids**

342

Transparency 6–11

Conclusions Chart
Some answers may vary. Examples are given.

Pages	Question
284–286	1. What is the narrator's name? George Which story clues helped you? Poppa and the narrator go to the store. The storekeeper says, "Howdy, Poppa. Howdy, George."
286	2. How does Poppa feel about plaid pants? He likes them better than plain ones. Which story clues helped you? Poppa thinks the plain ones are "poor pickings"; he whistles when he sees the plaid ones.
288	3. How does George feel about being kissed by Big Mama and Aunt Viney? He doesn't like it. Which story clues helped you? George says that they covered his face with lipstick; he "almost drowned in a sea of sloppy wet kisses."
292	4. Who is the first shape? Grandma Tiny Which story clues helped you? The first shape is small and white; her name is Tiny.

SMART SOLUTIONS Poppa's New Pants
Graphic Organizer Conclusion Chart

ANNOTATED VERSION

TRANSPARENCY 6–11
TEACHER'S EDITION PAGES 342 AND 367A

Practice Book page 188

Poppa's New Pants
Graphic Organizer
Conclusions Chart

Name _____

Conclusions Chart
Some answers may vary. Examples are given.

Pages	Questions
284–286	1. What is the narrator's name? George (1 point) Which story clues helped you? Poppa and the narrator go to the store. The storekeeper says, "Howdy, Poppa. Howdy, George." (2)
286	2. How does Poppa feel about plaid pants? He likes them better than plain ones. (1) Which story clues helped you? Poppa thinks the plain ones are "poor pickings"; he whistles when he sees the plaid ones. (2)
288	3. How does George feel about being kissed by Big Mama and Aunt Viney? He doesn't like it. (1) Which story clues helped you? George says that they covered his face with lipstick; he "almost drowned in a sea of sloppy wet kisses." (2)
292	4. Who is the first shape? Grandma Tiny (1) Which story clues helped you? The first shape is small and white; her name is Tiny. (2)

Purpose Setting

- Remind students that in this selection Poppa buys new pants.
- Have students preview the selection. Then ask them to predict what else might happen in the story.
- Remind students to use Predict/Infer and other strategies as they read.
- Ask students to draw conclusions as they read.
- You may want to preview the Responding questions on Anthology page 362 with students.

Journal ▶ Students can use their journals to record their original predictions and to add new ones. They can also note conclusions they draw about the characters or events.

STRATEGY REVIEW

Phonics/Decoding

Remind students to use the Phonics/Decoding Strategy as they read.

Modeling Write this sentence from *Poppa's New Pants*: *We were all so tired that there wasn't much* conversation *at dinner.* Point to *conversation*.

Think Aloud *When I look at this word, I see the word part* con-, *as in* confuse, *and the* -tion *ending, as in the words* action *and* motion. *I'll look for spelling patterns that can help me break the rest of the word into syllables. I see a* v *and then* -e-r-s-a. *That's a VCCV pattern, so I'll break it between the* r *and the* s. *That gives me the syllables* ver *and* say *or* sah. *Maybe I can say the word,* kahn-ver-SAY-shun. *Oh, I know that word. It means "talking." That makes sense.*

POPPA'S NEW PANTS

Angela Shelf Medearis

illustrated by John Ward

Strategy Focus

When Poppa buys new pants, his whole family gets involved. As you read, use what you find out about the characters to **predict** what will happen next.

343

Extra Support/Intervention

Selection Preview

pages 344–349 Visitors are coming. At the store, Poppa buys pants that are too long. Will Big Mama or one of the visitors hem the pants for him?

pages 350–353 Everyone is too tired to hem the pants. George sleeps in the kitchen to make room for the visitors. In the dark, he sees a white shape and hears strange noises. What might that be?

pages 354–355 In the night, George sees two other shapes and hears the strange noises each time. He hides under the covers. How do you think he feels?

pages 356–360 The next morning, the women surprise Poppa. What has happened to Poppa's pants? Who gets to wear the pants now?

CRITICAL THINKING
Guiding Comprehension

❶ MAKING INFERENCES What does the author mean about the house being *in an uproar*? (Everyone is busily cleaning the house, which means that their daily routines are changed.)

❷ MAKING INFERENCES Why do you think Grandma Tiny wants everything to look nice when the visitors arrive? (She wants to show them what a good housekeeper she is.)

❸ DRAWING CONCLUSIONS Who is the narrator? How can you tell? (Probably the boy in the illustration; it can't be Grandma Tiny, and Poppa must be older than the narrator.)

❶ The house was in an uproar. Grandma Tiny had been tearing around all morning like a Texas tornado. Big Mama and Aunt Viney were coming for a visit. Grandma Tiny wanted everything and **❷** everyone to look nice when her mother and sister arrived. Poppa and I had beaten so many rugs, washed so many windows, and moved around so much furniture that we'd sweated a bucketful.

We were both glad when Grandma Tiny told us to hitch up old Buck and go to the store.

344

English Language Learners

Supporting Comprehension

Before beginning, assign roles to be read (narrator, George, Poppa . . .). Read the story aloud as a class, pausing for the dialogue sections to be read by individuals.

Vocabulary

uproar noisy excitement and confusion

345

ASSIGNMENT CARD 4

Playing with Personality

Character Development

You can learn a lot about a character's personality through the character's words, actions, and thoughts. For example, Poppa cleans, runs errands, and buys groceries. These actions show that Poppa is kind and helpful.

Work with a partner to identify some of George's personality traits based on details from the story. Then discuss whether you think the author was successful in making George seem like a real boy.

Theme 6: Smart Solutions

Teacher's Resource BLM page 87

Guiding Comprehension

4 MAKING INFERENCES Why does Poppa let out a long whistle? (He sees a pair of pants he really likes.)

5 MAKING JUDGMENTS Do you think the author has succeeded in making George and Poppa likable? Explain. (Answers will vary. Sample answers: Yes; George says funny things, Poppa likes the plaid pants, and gets his grandson candy.)

COMPREHENSION STRATEGY
Predict/Infer

Teacher/Student Modeling Discuss story clues on page 346 that help students predict what Poppa will do after he first sees the pants. (Sample answer: When he finds the pants, he whistles. He probably wants to buy them.)

Ask students to predict what Poppa will do when he gets home with his new pants. (Sample answer: Poppa will probably ask his wife to shorten the pants.)

Vocabulary

bust a gusset to be excited or upset enough to burst

plaid having a pattern of stripes that cross each other

pattern a repeated design or decoration

fabric cloth

draped hung loosely in folds

hem to fold back and sew down the edges

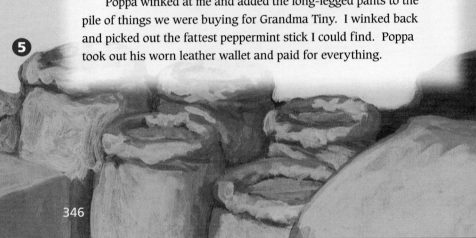

"Howdy, Poppa. Howdy, George," said Mr. Owens, the storekeeper, when we arrived. "What can I do for y'all today?"

"I've got a list of things to get for Tiny," said Poppa. "Her mama and sister are coming up from Kansas City. She's about to bust a gusset making sure everything's just right."

Mr. Owens laughed as Poppa handed him the list. Poppa and I wandered around the store while Mr. Owens filled our order. We were having a good time looking at the shiny new farm equipment when Poppa spied a pile of pants stacked on a table. Most of them were plain black or brown corduroy.

"Mighty poor pickings here," Poppa said. But when he reached the bottom of the pile, he let out a long whistle.

"George," he said, holding up a pair for me to see. "What do you think about these?"

They were gray pants with a red plaid pattern. The fabric was as velvety soft as old Buck's nose.

"They look real nice, Poppa," I said, "but they must have been made for a giant! They're way too long for you."

Poppa held the pants against his waist. The extra fabric was so long, it draped onto the floor.

"Well," said Poppa, "so they are. But I bet your Grandma Tiny could hem them before church in the morning."

Poppa winked at me and added the long-legged pants to the pile of things we were buying for Grandma Tiny. I winked back and picked out the fattest peppermint stick I could find. Poppa took out his worn leather wallet and paid for everything.

346

English Language Learners

Supporting Comprehension

Pause at the end of page 346 to discuss the similes *like a Texas tornado* and *soft as Buck's nose.* First, ask students what a *tornado* is and who Buck is. (a strong wind storm; the family horse) Ask if anyone has ever seen a tornado or touched a horse's nose. If they have, ask them to describe what it was like. Then ask students to restate the similes in their own words.

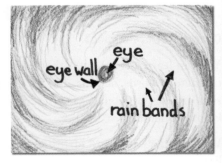

347

REACHING ALL LEARNERS

Extra Support/Intervention

Family Relationships

You may want to make the family relationships in this story clear for students.
Explain the following details:

- Grandma Tiny is married to Poppa.
- George, the narrator, is their grandson.
- Big Mama is Tiny's mother.
- Aunt Viney is Tiny's sister.

Also point out that, in some regions, Poppa is a common reference to a person's
grandfather.

Guiding Comprehension

6 **MAKING INFERENCES** Why do you think the author uses the phrases *snatched me out of the wagon like I was a rag doll* and *almost drowned in a sea of sloppy wet kisses?* (to be funny; to express how embarrassed George is by the attention)

7 **WRITER'S CRAFT** How does the author communicate Poppa's feelings about his new pants? (He shows them proudly to his relatives. He seems eager to wear them, because he asks to have them hemmed that night.)

8 **WRITER'S CRAFT** How does the author show the family's warm feelings for each other? (Aunt Viney and Big Mama hug and kiss George; everyone speaks pleasantly; they call each other *honey* and *dear*.)

6 Big Mama and Aunt Viney had arrived by the time we got home. They must have been mighty glad to see me because they snatched me from the wagon like I was a rag doll. Big Mama hugged me so hard that she squeezed the breath right out of my body. Then Aunt Viney and Big Mama took turns covering my face with red lipstick. I almost drowned in a sea of sloppy wet kisses.

"Come on in, y'all," Grandma Tiny finally said. "Supper's just about ready."

Grandma hustled Poppa inside so she could get the groceries put away. I ran after them as fast as I could.

Poppa set down a bag of groceries and unwrapped his new pants. He proudly stretched them across the table for Grandma Tiny, Big Mama, and Aunt Viney to see.

"Nice fabric," said Big Mama.

"What a beautiful pattern," said Aunt Viney.

348

Extra Support/Intervention

Strategy Modeling: Predict/Infer

Use this example to model the strategy.

On these pages, Poppa seems quite eager to wear his new pants, because he asks his wife and then each of his guests to hem them. I predict that if Big Mama won't hem the pants, Poppa will try to hem them himself.

Vocabulary

plum worn out very tired

brother-in-law the man who is married to your sister

"Yes, they're mighty pretty pants," said Grandma Tiny. "But they're way yonder too big for a tee-ninchy little man like you, Poppa. Looky here! They're almost long enough to use as a tablecloth."

"Well, honey," said Poppa, "I was hoping you could cut off about six inches and hem them tonight so I could wear them to church tomorrow."

❼

"Oh, honey," said Grandma Tiny, "I'm plum worn out! I've been cooking and cleaning since sunrise. As soon as supper's finished and Mama and Viney get settled in, I'm going to bed!"

"Okay," said Poppa. He turned to Aunt Viney. "Do you think you could hem my pants for me, Viney?"

"Oh Brother-in-law, dear," Aunt Viney said, "I'd love to, really I would, but my eyes are troubling me from driving so long. I need to get some sleep."

❽

"I understand," Poppa said. He looked hopefully at Big Mama and held up his new pants.

349

Cause and Effect

Review

- Remind students that some story events are related. To figure out such cause-and-effect relationships, students should ask themselves:
  – What happens? *(effect)*
  – Why does it happen? *(cause)*
- Explain that sometimes a whole series of events can be related.

Practice/Apply

- Have a student read aloud the second sentence on page 348. Ask what causes Big Mama and Aunt Viney to snatch George from the wagon. (They are glad to see him.) Guide students to see that words such as *because*, *since*, and *so* often signal two related events.
- Then work with students to create a cause-effect chain similar to the following.

1. Poppa asks Tiny to hem the pants.
   ↓
2. Tiny says she's too tired.
   ↓
3. Poppa asks Viney to hem the pants.
   ↓
4. Viney says she's too tired, too.
   ↓
5. Poppa looks hopefully at Big Mama.

Review Skill Trace	
Teach	Theme 1, p. 49A
Reteach	Theme 1, p. R8
▶ Review	p. 349; Theme 3, p. 377; Theme 5, p. 205

CRITICAL THINKING

Guiding Comprehension

9 **MAKING INFERENCES** Why do you think Poppa says *That's all right,* even though he's really disappointed? (to show that he understands that the women feel tired)

10 **DRAWING CONCLUSIONS** How do you think each woman feels about refusing to hem the pants? How can you tell? (Answers will vary. Sample answer: Each feels bad about disappointing him. There's not much dinner conversation, and they don't have their usual long talk afterward.)

11 **NOTING DETAILS** Why is George sleeping in the kitchen? (Big Mama and Aunt Viney are sleeping in his room.)

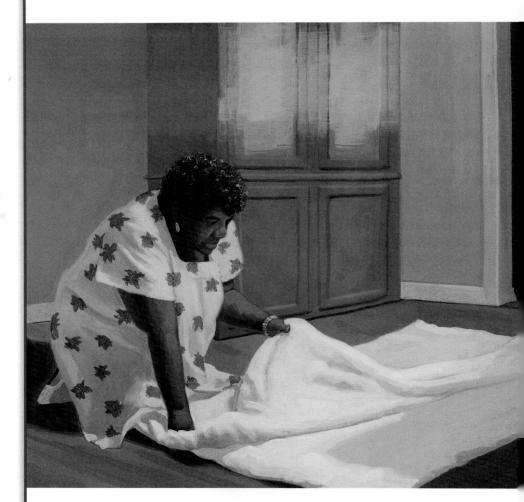

350

Vocabulary

arthritis soreness and swelling in the body

mended repaired by sewing; fixed

pallet narrow, hard bed or mattress

"Sorry, son," Big Mama said. "I've got arthritis in my knee joints so bad I can hardly move. I'm looking forward to just resting this evening."

"That's all right, y'all," Poppa said sadly. He put his new pants across the rocker to be mended. Then he went out on the back porch to wash up for supper. **9**

Grandma Tiny called everyone to dinner. She'd cooked everything from chicken and dressing to chocolate cake. The table looked like it was going to buckle in the middle. Supper was delicious, but we were all so tired, conversation was mighty poor. As soon as Poppa was finished eating, he said good night all around and got ready for bed.

Grandma Tiny, Big Mama, and Aunt Viney **10** usually have a good long gossip spell when they get together. But this time, the three women quietly finished their chores and turned in for the night. Big Mama and Aunt Viney had taken over my room. Grandma Tiny made **11** a pallet for me on the kitchen floor while I changed into my pajamas. I took my glasses off and put them on the kitchen table.

351

Fluency Practice

Rereading for Fluency Have students choose a favorite part of the story to reread to a partner, or suggest that they read page 351. Encourage students to read expressively.

English Language Learners

Supporting Comprehension

Review the plot to help students prepare for the "ghosts." Ask: What does Poppa want? Why won't the women help him? What do you think will happen next?

I wonder what will happen next?

CRITICAL THINKING
Guiding Comprehension

12 **MAKING INFERENCES** Why do you think George says that the house is *moaning*? (to show that he feels scared)

13 **DRAWING CONCLUSIONS** What do you think the white shape is doing in the kitchen? (Answers will vary.)

14 **WRITER'S CRAFT** Why does the author put ellipses, or the series of periods, between the words *closer . . . and closer . . . and closer?* (to show how slowly the shape moves; to add suspense)

12 I kicked the covers around until I found a soft spot to snuggle into. I could hear Poppa snoring gently and the dark house moaning softly as everyone settled down for the night.

I wasn't used to sleeping in the kitchen. It was kind of spooky. The huge wooden china cabinet and big, black woodburning stove crouched in the corners. The grandfather clock wheezed awake every hour and rang out the time. After awhile, the moon crept into the room, making a big pool of bright, white light by the rocking chair. I jumped when a tree limb scraped against the window screen. I was just drifting off to sleep when I spotted something out of the corner of my eye.

13 A small, white shape was moving slowly into the kitchen. I was so scared that at first, I forgot to breathe. I squeezed my eyes closed and pulled the covers over my head.

14 I told myself over and over that there were no such things as ghosts. But I didn't believe it. I could hear whatever it was slowly coming closer . . . and closer . . . and closer. It must have brushed up against the rocking chair because the chair creaked softly back and forth, back and forth. I held my breath until I thought I'd burst. I heard a snip, snip, snip and a funny rustling. Then all was quiet.

It was too quiet! After an hour that seemed like days, I pulled the covers off my head. I finally made my eyes open so I could peek over the edge of the quilt. The ghost-thing was gone! I was tempted to go and sleep on the floor by Poppa and Grandma Tiny.

352

Vocabulary

crouched sat low to the ground

wheezed breathed hard with a whistling sound

rustling a quick, soft, fluttering sound

Extra Support/Intervention

Review (pages 344–353)

Before students join the whole class for Stop and Think on page 353, have them

- take turns modeling Predict/Infer and other strategies they used
- add to **Transparency 6–11** with you
- check and revise their Inference Chart on **Practice Book** page 188, and use it to summarize

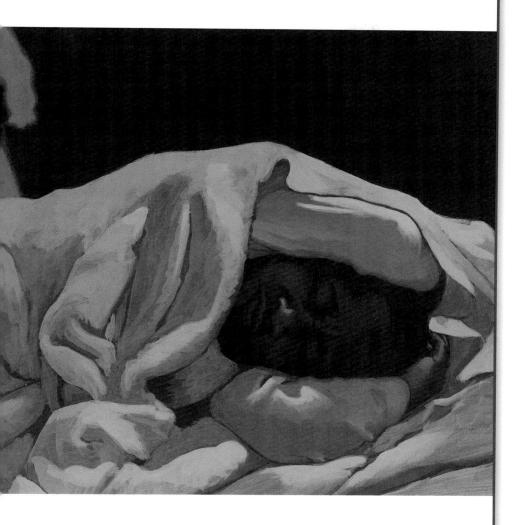

353

Stop and Think

Critical Thinking Questions

1. **MAKING INFERENCES** How would you describe Poppa? Why? (Answers will vary. Sample answers: He's kind and caring; he helps clean, run errands, and carry groceries. He's understanding; he doesn't get angry when the women won't hem his pants.)

2. **COMPARE AND CONTRAST** How is this story similar to other scary stories you've read? How is it different? (Answers will vary.)

Strategies in Action

Have students take turns modeling Predict/Infer and other strategies they used.

Discussion Options

You may want to bring the entire class together to do one or more of the activities below.

- **Review Predictions/Purpose** Discuss which predictions were accurate and which needed to be revised. Record story clues and inferences that lead to predictions.

- **Share Group Discussions** Have students share their questions and literature discussions.

- **Summarize** Help students use their Conclusions Charts to summarize what has happened in the story so far.

ASSIGNMENT CARD 5

Literature Discussion

In a small group, discuss your answers to these questions.

- Why do you think the author has George use so many exaggerations and special expressions? Which are your favorites?

- How well does the author succeed in making the characters seem real? Give examples.

- How does the author show the family's warm feelings for each other?

- How is this story similar to other scary stories you've read? How is it different?

Theme 6: Smart Solutions

Teacher's Resource BLM page 88

Monitoring Student Progress

If . . .	Then . . .
students have successfully completed the Extra Support activities on page 352,	have them read the rest of the selection cooperatively or independently.

Reading the Selection 353

CRITICAL THINKING

Guiding Comprehension

15 **MAKING INFERENCES** Why does George give up on going to Poppa and Grandma Tiny's room? (He's afraid the ghostly figure will see him if he gets up from the pallet.)

16 **NOTING DETAILS** How does the author show that George is scared? (He curls up into a ball, shakes all over, and his teeth rattle.)

354

Vocabulary

mustering gathering together

dozed off fell into a light sleep

armadillo an animal with a hard shell that may roll up into a ball if attacked

I lay quietly for awhile, mustering up my courage. Just when I thought it was safe to make a run for it, I spied a tall, thin, ghostly white figure drifting into the room. I threw the covers back over my head. My heart was thumping like old Buck's after a long, hard run. I heard the rocking chair creak back and forth, back and forth. Then I heard that funny snip, snip, snip, rustle, rustle sound. After awhile, all was quiet again.

I gave up on the idea of going into Poppa and Grandma Tiny's room. I kept the covers over my head and prayed for morning to come. I must have dozed off because when I opened my eyes, I couldn't figure out where I was. It was so hot, I started to throw the quilt off my head, but then I remembered about the ghosts.

I pulled the covers down inch by inch. I pried open my eyes and slowly looked around the room. A big, white ghost was drifting through the doorway, and it was coming toward me!

I dove down to the foot of the pallet and curled up into a ball. I was shaking all over like a wet dog. I felt something brush past me heavily. Then the rocking chair moaned loudly as it creaked back and forth, back and forth. I heard that snip, snip, snip, rustle, rustle sound and all was quiet again. My teeth were rattling so loud, I thought some of them were going to fall out! I stayed balled up under those blankets like an armadillo for the rest of the night.

15

16

355

Compare and Contrast

Review

- Remind students that
  - comparing two or more things means finding ways they are alike.
  - contrasting things means finding ways they are different.

- Explain that comparing and contrasting characters and events will help readers better understand and summarize what they read.

Practice/Apply

- Ask how many ghostly figures George saw. (three) Have students scan pages 352 and 355 for details about the figures and the sounds George hears.

- Guide students to use a chart like the one below to compare and contrast the three figures.

Ways They Are Alike
white; ghostly; creaking rocking chair; snipping and rustling sounds

Ways They Are Different
first shape—small second shape—tall, thin third shape—big

Review Skill Trace	
Teach	Theme 4, p. 69A
Reteach	Theme 4, p. R10
Review	p. 355

Guiding Comprehension

17 **WRITER'S CRAFT** Why do you think the author mentions George's glasses?
(to remind readers that George cannot see very well)

18 **MAKING INFERENCES** How does George convince himself that he might have been dreaming?
(Everything seems so normal in the morning; he's never heard of seeing three ghosts in one night.)

COMPREHENSION STRATEGY

Predict/Infer

Student Modeling Ask students to model the Predict/Infer strategy. If necessary, use the following prompt:

What will George discover about the ghostly figures he thinks he sees?

"George! George!" The sound of Grandma Tiny's voice woke me the next morning as she whipped the covers off my head.

"Boy, why in the world are you sleeping under all those blankets as hot as it is?" Before I could answer she said, "Go get washed up. We need to hurry if we're going to make it to church on time."

17

Bright yellow sunlight filled the room. It was morning and I was still alive. I checked to make sure all my limbs were in place. Everything was where it should be. I put on my glasses and stumbled sleepily through the door. Poppa was already on the back porch shaving. I didn't want to say anything about last night. Three ghosts in one evening! I'd never heard a story like that! Besides,

18 maybe I was dreaming. The rocking chair and everything else in the room looked just like they always did.

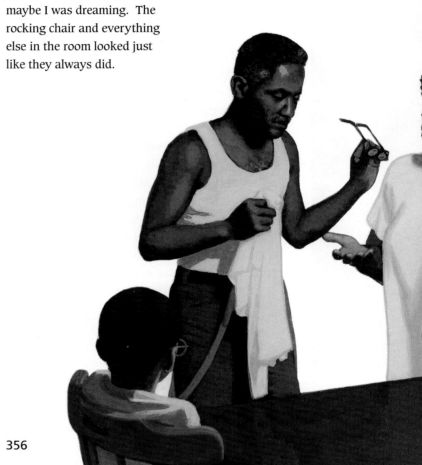

356

English Language Learners

Supporting Comprehension

Pause at the end of page 356 to ask students what they think about the *ghost:*
What is the ghost? What clues are given in the passage? What does the ghost do?
If students don't know, ask them to guess or make predictions.

Vocabulary

limbs arms and legs

smiling fit to beat the band
smiling very happily

I mumbled good morning to Poppa and splashed cold water on my face. I'd just finished brushing my teeth when Grandma Tiny came out on the porch.

"Poppa," she said, "hurry up and come inside. There's a surprise for you!" As Poppa went into the kitchen, I followed behind, wondering what all the fuss was about.

Grandma Tiny, Big Mama, and Aunt Viney were gathered around the table. I said good morning and quickly sat down. I didn't want to give Big Mama and Aunt Viney a chance to hug and kiss the life out of me again. Besides, I had had a hard time getting that red lipstick off my face. Grandma Tiny was smiling fit to beat the band. She had Poppa's new pants folded across her arm.

357

Extra Support/Intervention

Strategy Modeling: Predict/Infer

If students need help modeling the strategy, use this example to model it.

In the morning George wonders if he really saw ghosts or if he was just dreaming. He also mentions putting on his glasses. I know that people who wear glasses can't see very well without them. This helps me predict that the ghosts George thought he saw will turn out to be something else.

Writer's Craft

Vivid Language

Teach

- Explain that in *Poppa's New Pants*, Angela Shelf Medearis has created a memorable story by using distinct, vivid language, including

  – words and descriptions that appeal to the senses

  – exaggerations, or the overstating of events to make them seem more important than they are

  – comparisons of unlike things (similes, metaphors, personification)

  – idioms and other expressions with special meanings

Practice/Apply

- Display this sentence from page 348: *I almost drowned in a sea of sloppy wet kisses.* Ask how the author's vivid language helps readers picture the scene and experience what George must have felt. (Examples: He exaggerates his feelings by claiming he's drowning; the words *wet* and *sloppy* help readers understand how the kisses feel.)

- Have students find and discuss other phrases and story passages that use vivid language.

CRITICAL THINKING

Guiding Comprehension

19 **WRITER'S CRAFT** Why do you think the author has each of the three women tell about hemming the pants? (to make it clear to readers why the pants will be too short)

20 **CAUSE AND EFFECT** Why is George surprised to learn who the ghosts were and what they were doing? (He wasn't wearing his glasses, so he didn't realize the shapes were the three women.)

21 **WRITER'S CRAFT** Why do you think the author has Poppa say, "*Well, these pants aren't too long now!*"? (to further explain the funny situation; to show that Poppa isn't angry)

"Honey," said Grandma Tiny, "I got to thinking about what a wonderful husband you are and about how much you wanted to wear these pants. So I got up last night, cut off six inches, and hemmed them for you."

Poppa's smile lit up the room.

"Oh no," said Aunt Viney. "I got to thinking about what a sweet brother-in-law he is, so I got up last night, cut off six inches, and hemmed them up, too!" Poppa stopped smiling and looked at Aunt Viney.

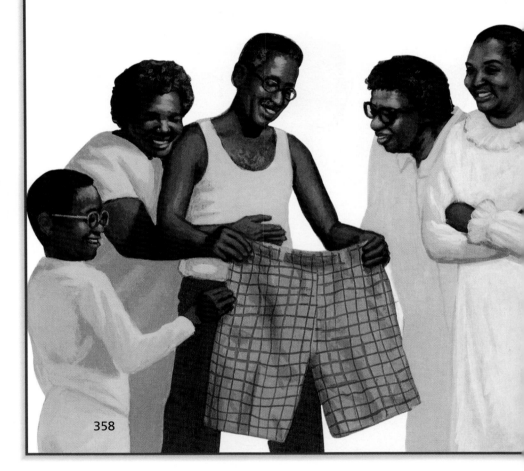

358

Vocabulary

haunting visiting; appearing to someone

"Well sir, would you listen to this," said Big Mama. "I couldn't rest for thinking about what a good son-in-law he is. So I got up last night, cut six inches off those pants, and hemmed them up, too!"

My mouth dropped open. So these were the ghosts that were haunting me last night!

Poppa grabbed his new pants from Grandma Tiny and held them up to his waist. The beautiful, soft gray pants with the red plaid gently unfolded to his knees.

We all stared at what was left of Poppa's new pants. Poppa hung his head and clutched the pants to his chest. His thin shoulders started to shake. Then all of a sudden, Poppa burst out laughing.

"Well, these pants aren't too long now!" he said.

He put them on and smiled at us. Then he danced around the room in the cut-off pants. He looked so funny we couldn't help laughing. After a long while he wheezed to a stop. Grandma Tiny hugged Poppa around the waist.

19

20

21

359

ASSIGNMENT CARD 6

Funny Business

Humor

An author often uses one or more of the following elements to create humor in a story:

- **Exaggeration** For example, George says he is drowning in "a sea of sloppy wet kisses."

- **Unexpected events** For example, when Poppa holds up his pants, it's a surprise when they only reach to his knees.

Look back through the story for more examples of these types of humor. Discuss your ideas with a partner.

Theme 6: Smart Solutions

Teacher's Resource BLM page 88

Drawing Conclusions

Teach

- Explain that authors don't always state everything about characters or events.
- Tell students that sometimes readers must put together details to figure out a sensible idea about something in the story.

Practice

- Point out that each woman confesses to cutting off six inches from the pants.
- Guide students to conclude that the pants were about eighteen inches shorter.
- Ask what other conclusion can be drawn. (They'll be too short for Poppa.)

Apply

- Have students use story clues to draw a conclusion about how George and Poppa are related. (Answers will vary. Sample answer: Grandma Tiny is George's grandma; Grandma Tiny is Poppa's wife. Therefore, Poppa must be George's grandfather.)

Target Skill Trace	
Preview; Teach	p. 339S, p. 342, p. 359; p. 367A
Reteach	p. R10
Review	pp. 413D–413E

Reading the Selection 359

CRITICAL THINKING
Guiding Comprehension

22 **MAKING INFERENCES** Why do you think Grandma Tiny speaks gently to Poppa? (She knows he's disappointed about the pants and wants to find a way to apologize for the mix-up.)

23 **DRAWING CONCLUSIONS** Who benefits from the mix-up? Why? (George; the pants are now short enough for him to wear.)

24 **MAKING INFERENCES** How does George feel about his new knickers? How do you know? (Happy; he says he looks *mighty sharp* and they are *just right*.)

"Honey," said Grandma Tiny gently, "don't you worry about those old pants. Next time we go to the store, I'll help you pick out some pants that fit." Poppa hugged her back.

"Come on, y'all," said Big Mama, looking at the clock. "We'll miss Sunday School but we can still make it to church." We scurried around getting ready.

We pulled up in front of Rock Hill Church just in time for the eleven o'clock service. Grandma Tiny, Aunt Viney, and Big Mama looked real pretty in their Sunday going-to-meeting hats. They rustled through the wooden doors of the sanctuary like walking flower gardens. Poppa looked nice too, although he was wearing the same black pants he wears every Sunday. And I must say, I looked mighty sharp in my brand new gray knickers with the red plaid.

360

Vocabulary

scurried moved around hurriedly

sanctuary the main room of a place of worship

knickers short, loose pants gathered below the knee; the shortened form of the word *knickerbockers*

REACHING ALL LEARNERS	Extra Support/ Intervention	On Level Challenge

Selection Review

Before students join the whole class for Wrapping Up on page 361, have them

- take turns modeling the reading strategies they used
- complete **Transparency 6–11** with you and finish their Conclusions Charts
- summarize the whole story

Literature Discussion

Have small groups of students discuss the story, using their own questions or the questions in Think About the Selection on page 362.

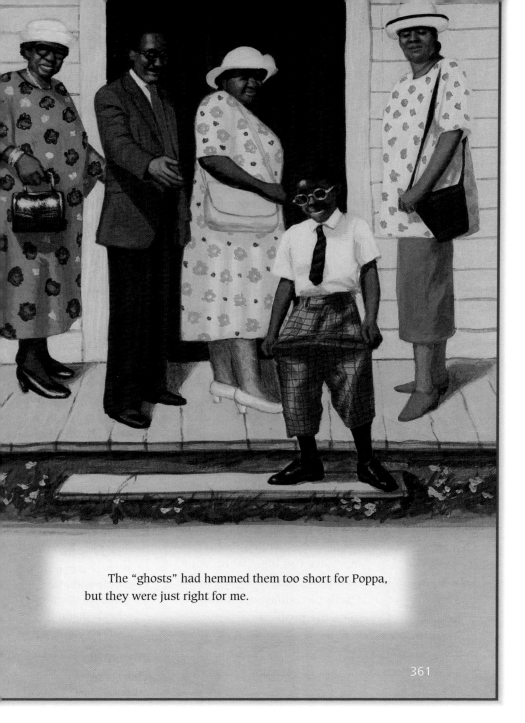

The "ghosts" had hemmed them too short for Poppa,
but they were just right for me.

361

Wrapping Up

Critical Thinking Questions

1. **AUTHOR'S VIEWPOINT** Why do you think the author chose to tell the story from George's perspective? (An older character would be more likely to find out who the shapes were, so there wouldn't have been a humorous misunderstanding.)

2. **MAKING JUDGMENTS** Would you like to be friends with the family in the story? Why or why not? (Answers will vary. Sample answer: Yes; they all seem cheerful, helpful, and loving.)

Strategies in Action

Have students model how they used the Predict/Infer strategy.

Discussion Options

Bring the entire class together to do one or more of the activities below.

Review Predictions/Purpose Discuss the accuracy of students' predictions.

Share Group Discussions Have students discuss how they feel about the story characters and the story's outcome.

Summarize Have students use their Conclusions Charts to summarize the story.

Comprehension Check

Use **Practice Book** page 189 to assess students' comprehension of the selection.

English Language Learners

Language Development

Remind students that most verbs show past and present progressive tenses by adding *-ed* and *-ing* respectively, but one-syllable words with a vowel followed by a single consonant need to double the consonant. Have partners scan pages 358–360 and create a list of such verbs. (hemmed, dropped, grabbed . . .)

Practice Book page 189

Poppa's New Pants
Comprehension Check

Name _____

Who, What, and Why?

Use complete sentences to answer the questions about *Poppa's New Pants*.

Who comes to visit Grandma Tiny, Poppa, and George?
Aunt Viney and Big Mama come to visit. **(1 point)**

What is wrong with the pants Poppa buys?
They are too long. **(1)**

Why won't the women hem Poppa's pants?
They are too tired. **(1)**

Why does George have trouble getting to sleep?
He is not used to sleeping in the kitchen; the furniture looks scary and makes

scary noises. **(1)**

What weird sights does George see?
He sees three white shapes: one small; one tall, thin, and ghostly; and one big one. **(1)**

What is Grandma Tiny's surprise?
She has hemmed Poppa's pants. **(1)**

Why do the women surprise each other?
They did not know that the others had hemmed the pants too, so now the pants

are too short. **(1)**

Why does George feel lucky about the mix-up?
The pants are the right size for knickers for him. **(1)**

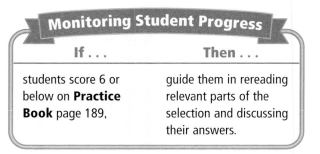

Monitoring Student Progress

If . . .	Then . . .
students score 6 or below on **Practice Book** page 189,	guide them in rereading relevant parts of the selection and discussing their answers.

Think About the Selection

Have students discuss or write their answers. Sample answers are provided; accept reasonable responses.

1. **MAKING INFERENCES** He thinks what happens to his pants is very funny.

2. **CAUSE AND EFFECT** Because George cannot see very well, the women in their long, white nightgowns look like ghosts to him.

3. **DRAWING CONCLUSIONS** George takes off his glasses, which suggests that he may make mistakes about things he sees; George is scared about sleeping in the kitchen, so he may expect to see scary things; the sizes and shapes of the ghosts match the women's sizes and shapes.

4. **PROBLEM SOLVING** He could have realized that the snipping sound was the sound of scissors cutting; he could have put his glasses on or turned on the lights.

5. **NOTING DETAILS** Grandma Tiny works very hard to get ready for her relatives' visit; the women all get up in the middle of the night to hem Poppa's pants; they help each other and laugh together.

6. **Connecting/Comparing** Answers will vary. Sample answers: In both stories, the characters' decisions cause unexpected events. When Pepita realizes that Spanish can be useful, she changes her mind in time to save her dog. Each woman in *Poppa's New Pants* is sorry about her decision, changes her mind, and hems Poppa's pants. This results in too-short pants for Poppa.

READ & COMPREHEND

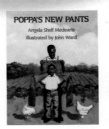

Think About the Selection

1. Why isn't Poppa angry that his pants are now too short for him?

2. George wears glasses. How does this affect what happens in the story?

3. What clues do the author and illustrator give about what really happens during George's restless night?

4. How do you think George could have figured out who the mysterious night visitors were?

5. How do George, Poppa, and the rest of the family show that they care about each other?

6. ★ **Connecting/Comparing** In both *Pepita Talks Twice* and *Poppa's New Pants*, one problem creates others. Tell how each character's decision affects what happens.

Write a Funny Story

What other things could happen to Poppa? Maybe his new shirt needs to be mended or his new shoes are too big. Write your own funny story about Poppa. Think of a smart solution to solve the problem.

Tips
- To begin, make a story map.
- Write a beginning that will make people want to keep reading.
- Give your story a clever title.

362

English Language Learners

Supporting Comprehension

Beginning/Preproduction Have students take turns asking one another to find objects in the illustrations in the story.

Early Production and Speech Emergence Ask students to describe what occurs in each illustration. Each student can describe the event in one illustration.

Intermediate and Advanced Fluency Read the Think About the Selection questions aloud, asking students to explain them in their own words.

Math

Make Poppa's Pants

Cut pants like Poppa's out of butcher paper. They should be 48 inches long from the waist to the hem. Then, using information from the story, mark three lines to show where each person hems the pants. Measure carefully! If you have time, decorate your pants with a plaid design.

Social Studies

Compare Community Stores

In a small group, discuss where you would buy groceries, pants, and farm equipment in your community. If possible, use the alphabetical list in the yellow pages of a phone book to help you. Then talk about how these stores compare to the store that Poppa and George visit.

Additional Responses

Personal Response Invite students to share their personal responses to the selection with a partner.

Journal ▸ Ask students to write in their journals about something funny that happened in their own family.

Selection Connections Remind students to add to **Practice Book** page 166.

Solve a Web Logic Puzzle

Collect clues to help Poppa and George fix another crazy mix-up when you visit Education Place. **www.eduplace.com/kids**

363

Extra Support/ Intervention

Funny Stories

For the writing activity, ask students to write a paragraph story about Poppa's New Shirt or New Shoes. Remind them to have a strong beginning, middle, and end. Reread the beginning and end of *Poppa's New Pants* to reinforce examples of a strong beginning and a strong end.

Practice Book page 166

Name _____

Launching the Theme
Selection Connections

Smart Solutions

Fill in the chart as you read the stories.

Sample answers shown.

	Pepita Talks Twice	Poppa's New Pants	Ramona Quimby, Age 8
What is the problem?	Pepita doesn't want to speak twice all the time. She wants more time to play with her dog, Lobo. (2 points)	Poppa needs his new pants to be hemmed. (2)	The Quimbys are crabby because they are stuck inside the house on a rainy Sunday. (2)
How is the problem solved?	Not speaking Spanish creates more problems, so Pepita decides it is good to speak two languages. (3 points)	Poppa's family makes his pants too short, so they give them to George. (3)	The Quimbys go out for dinner, have a nice meal, and learn to enjoy being together again. (3)

Monitoring Student Progress

End-of-Selection Assessment

Selection Test Use the test on pages 143–144 in the **Teacher's Resource Blackline Masters** to assess selection comprehension and vocabulary.

Student Self-Assessment Have students assess their reading with additional questions such as

- Which parts of this selection were difficult? Why?
- Which strategies helped me understand the story better?
- Would I like to read another story by the same author? Why or why not?

Media Link

Skill: How to Read a Diagram

- **Introduce** "No Problem!" a nonfiction article about comic strips.

- **Discuss** the Skill Lesson on Anthology page 364. Tell students that a comic strip combines words and pictures to tell a short, funny story or joke.

- **Model** reading a comic strip. Read aloud the *Peanuts* strip on page 364.

- **Explain** how to use a chart to show the humorous problems and solutions explored in the *Peanuts* strip.

  – Display the Problem/Solution Chart. Have students help you fill in the problems and solutions.

  – Before filling in the last column, ask why it is funny that in the last frame the birds are standing on the brim of Snoopy's hat. (The birds look funny; the solution only helps the birds, not Snoopy.)

- **Set a purpose** for reading. Tell students to use a Problem/Solution Chart as they read each remaining comic strip in the Link. Remind students to use Predict/Infer and other strategies as they read.

Comic Strip	Problem	Solution	Why This Is Funny
Peanuts comic strip #1	There are dangerous snakes around.	Birds stand on Snoopy's hat.	The birds look funny. Also, the solution only helps the birds, not Snoopy.

Vocabulary

wilderness a wild area where no people live

inhabited lived in

leaf blower a tool used to blow leaves into a pile

Media Link

Skill: How to Read a Comic Strip

1. Read the comic strip from left to right.

2. Read the words inside each speech balloon. The tail of each balloon points to the character who is talking.

3. Look carefully at the faces and the details in each picture.

4. Laugh!

364

No Problem!

Just like in a book, the characters in comic strips sometimes have problems to solve. Whatever the problem is, they're sure to solve it in a creative and silly way. So enjoy these smart solutions that will tickle your funny bone too!

PEANUTS
BY CHARLES M. SCHULZ

365

Extra Support/Intervention

Problem/Solution Chart

Some students may have trouble understanding the jokes in the cartoons and using the Problem/Solution Chart on their own. You may want to team these students with more proficient partners. Alternatively, you might have students study each comic strip in small groups, filling in the chart as they go.

Comic Strips

Teach

- Remind students that details in the artists' drawings help to create the humor of each comic strip.

- Ask students to describe the expressions on Snoopy's face in the first comic strip. (In the first two frames, Snoopy looks very serious and knowledgeable. In the last frame he appears annoyed as he looks up at the birds on his hat.)

- Point out that these details make the strip funny by emphasizing how the birds have solved their own problem, but not Snoopy's.

Practice/Apply

- Ask students to identify visual details in the other strips.

- Have students tell how the visual details help to create the humor in each strip.

366

English Language Learners

Supporting Comprehension

Have students complete the activities with partners or in small groups. Then ask: What is the problem? How did the characters solve it? Why is that funny? These questions should help students who don't understand the joke on the first read-through. Then they will be better prepared to fill in the Problem/Solution Chart.

Vocabulary

hopeless having no hope

PEANUTS

BY CHARLES M. SCHULZ

367

Challenge

Original Comics

Have students create their own comic strip that presents a problem and a solution in a funny way. Alternatively, they can draw a new final frame for each of the strips in "No Problem!" Post their work in a bulletin board display entitled *Funny Solutions*. To help students think of ideas, ask them to bring their favorite comic strips from newspapers or books to share with the class.

Wrapping Up

Critical Thinking Questions

Ask students to read aloud the parts of the selection that support their answers.

1. **PROBLEM SOLVING** Think about the solution presented in each comic strip. Which solutions would actually work and which would not? (Strip #1: The birds' solution might work for them but not for most other creatures. Strip #2: You could not fly a kite using a leaf blower. Strip #3: You can't clean your body with a vacuum cleaner. Strip #4: You could melt snow using a hairdryer, but it would be dangerous and would take a long time. Strip #5: If a person feels sad, it probably would help for someone to give him or her a kiss.)

2. **COMPARE AND CONTRAST** What do the two *Calvin and Hobbes* strips have in common with the *FoxTrot* strip? (In all three, an electrical appliance is used in a funny way.)

3. **COMPARE AND CONTRAST** How are the two *Peanuts* strips alike and different? (Alike: Snoopy is in both of them; they both present problems and their solutions. Different: The first strip is silly while the second is amusing but thoughtful and not silly.)

4. **Connecting/Comparing** Give examples of odd combinations of things or ideas from *Poppa's New Pants* and from two of the comic strips. (*Poppa's New Pants:* ghosts and a rocking chair; *FoxTrot:* a kite and a leaf blower; the second *Calvin and Hobbes:* a lost quarter and an electric hairdryer)

Media Link 367

OBJECTIVES

- Draw conclusions about story characters and events.
- Learn academic language: *drawing conclusions*.

Target Skill Trace

Preview, Teach	p. 339T; p. 340; p. 359; p. 367A
Reteach	p. R10
Review	pp. 413D–413E; Theme 2, p. 199; Theme 3, p. 361; Theme 6, p. 331
See	*Extra Support Handbook*, pp. 206–207; pp. 212–213

Transparency 6–11

SMART SOLUTIONS Poppa's New Pants
Graphic Organizer Conclusions Chart

ANNOTATED VERSION

Conclusions Chart

Some answers may vary. Examples are given.

Pages	Question
284–286	1. What is the narrator's name? George Which story clues helped you? Poppa and the narrator go to the store. The storekeeper says, "Howdy, Poppa. Howdy, George."
286	2. How does Poppa feel about plaid pants? He likes them better than plain ones. Which story clues helped you? Poppa thinks the plain ones are "poor pickings"; he whistles when he sees the plaid ones.
288	3. How does George feel about being kissed by Big Mama and Aunt Viney? He doesn't like it. Which story clues helped you? George says that they covered his face with lipstick; he "almost drowned in a sea of sloppy wet kisses."
292	4. Who is the first shape? Grandma Tiny Which story clues helped you? The first shape is small and white; her name is Tiny.

TRANSPARENCY 6–11
TEACHER'S EDITION PAGES 342 AND 367A

Practice Book page 188

Poppa's New Pants
Graphic Organizer
Conclusions Chart

Name _____

Conclusions Chart

Some answers may vary. Examples are given.

Pages	Questions
284–286	1. What is the narrator's name? George **(1 point)** Which story clues helped you? Poppa and the narrator go to the store. The storekeeper says, "Howdy, Poppa. Howdy, George." **(2)**
286	2. How does Poppa feel about plaid pants? He likes them better than plain ones. **(1)** Which story clues helped you? Poppa thinks the plain ones are "poor pickings"; he whistles when he sees the plaid ones. **(2)**
288	3. How does George feel about being kissed by Big Mama and Aunt Viney? He doesn't like it. **(1)** Which story clues helped you? George says that they covered his face with lipstick; he "almost drowned in a sea of sloppy wet kisses." **(2)**
292	4. Who is the first shape? Grandma Tiny **(1)** Which story clues helped you? The first shape is small and white; her name is Tiny. **(2)**

TARGET SKILL
COMPREHENSION: Drawing Conclusions

1 Teach

Review conclusions about *Poppa's New Pants*. Remind students that drawing conclusions means putting together story details to figure out ideas that the author doesn't explain directly. Complete the Graphic Organizer on **Transparency 6–11** with students. Have them refer to the selection and to **Practice Book** page 188. Discuss these ideas:

- Sometimes it is necessary to add up several story clues to draw a conclusion.
- Readers should monitor their reading to confirm or revise their conclusions, based on new story information.

Model drawing a conclusion. Read aloud page 346, starting at the third paragraph. Have students think about Poppa's reaction to the plain black and brown pants and the plaid pants as you think aloud.

Think Aloud *When Poppa looks at the black and brown pants, he says, "Mighty poor pickings." That means, "This isn't a very good selection." This tells me that he doesn't like the black and brown pants. But when he sees the plaid pants, he whistles, which usually means, "I like what I see." Adding up these story clues helps me conclude that Poppa likes pants with a bright pattern better than plain ones. The pants are too long, but Poppa decides to buy them anyway. That confirms my conclusion that he really likes the pants.*

2 Guided Practice

Have students practice drawing conclusions. Have students work in pairs to draw a conclusion about the story, based on more than two story clues. Ask them to record their work in a graphic organizer. Sample answers are shown.

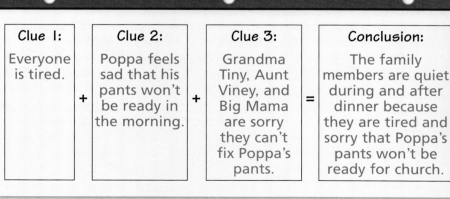

Clue 1:		Clue 2:		Clue 3:		Conclusion:
Everyone is tired.	+	Poppa feels sad that his pants won't be ready in the morning.	+	Grandma Tiny, Aunt Viney, and Big Mama are sorry they can't fix Poppa's pants.	=	The family members are quiet during and after dinner because they are tired and sorry that Poppa's pants won't be ready for church.

❸ Apply

Assign **Practice Book** pages 190–191. Also have students apply this skill as they read their **Leveled Readers** for this week. You may also select books from the Leveled Bibliography for this theme, pages 296E–296F.

Test Prep Open-response questions about drawing conclusions may make some students anxious. Emphasize that open-response questions have more than one right answer. Explain that students will be scored on how clearly they state their conclusion and how well they support it with details from the passage.

Leveled Readers and Leveled Practice

Students at all levels apply the comprehension skill as they read their Leveled Readers. See lessons on pages 367O–367R.

● BELOW LEVEL — A Little Bit Hotter Can't Hurt by Joanna Korba
▲ ON LEVEL — The Mural by Kent Carlson • illustrated by Susan Lexa
■ ABOVE LEVEL — Gampy's Lamps by Lee S. Justice illustrated by Alexandra Wallner
◆ LANGUAGE SUPPORT — Chili for Lindy by Joanna Korba illustrated by Bethann Thornburgh

Reading Traits

Teaching students how to draw conclusions is one way of encouraging them to "read between the lines" of a selection. This comprehension skill supports the reading trait **Developing Interpretations**.

Practice Book page 190

Poppa's New Pants
Comprehension Skill
Drawing Conclusions

Name _____

Drawing Conclusions

Read the story. Then complete the chart on the next page.

The Pink Sweatshirt

"But Mom, I need a *pink* sweatshirt for our play!" I argued. "I'm the pig who builds with bricks! We need pink sweatshirts with hoods so we can sew on pink felt ears."

"Linda, I just bought you a white sweatshirt," said Mom. "You'll have to spend your own money if you want a pink one."

I was saving all my money for a new bike. "Oh, Mom! Tina's and Ali's parents are buying them pink ones," I whined.

This did not convince my mother. "Lots of pigs aren't pink," she said firmly. "You can be a white pig in a white sweatshirt."

But Tina, Ali, and I wanted our costumes to match. So, I got my new pair of red shorts, the ones labeled, "Wash in COLD WATER only." I dumped those and my white sweatshirt into the washing machine. Then I punched the button marked HOT WATER. Too bad I didn't look in the washer first! The load of white laundry left in there got washed again (in hot water) with my sweatshirt and red shorts.

So, today I'm spending my savings on new white socks for my brother, a white shirt for Dad, and four white towels. Luckily, Dad likes the new color of his bathrobe. It reminds him of a strawberry milkshake.

Practice Book page 191

Poppa's New Pants
Comprehension Skill
Drawing Conclusions

Name _____

Drawing Conclusions continued

Answer each question about "The Pink Sweatshirt." Then tell which story clues helped you to draw that conclusion.

1. Who is the girl telling the story?
Linda (1 point)
Story Clues: She is talking to her mom; her mom calls her Linda. (2)

2. What happens when you wash red and white laundry together in hot water?
Some clothes are dyed pink. (1)
Story Clues: Linda wanted to dye her white sweatshirt pink, so she washed it in hot water with her red shorts; the new color of Dad's bathrobe reminds him of a strawberry milkshake. (2)

3. What other laundry was already in the washing machine?
There were white socks, a shirt, towels, and a bathrobe. (1)
Story Clues: Linda must buy new socks, shirt, and towels; her dad's bathrobe is now pink. (2)

4. Why must Linda spend the money she is trying to save?
Linda must replace the other laundry that turned pink. (1)
Story Clues: A load of laundry was washed again when she washed her clothes; Linda has to buy new white socks, shirt, and towels. (2)

Monitoring Student Progress

If . . .	Then . . .
students score 8 or below on **Practice Book** page 191,	use the Reteaching lesson on Teacher's Edition page R10.
students have successfully met the lesson objectives,	have them do the Challenge/Extension activities on Teacher's Edition page R11.

OBJECTIVES

- Read words with the VCV pattern.
- Apply the Phonics/Decoding Strategy.
- Learn academic language: VCV *pattern*.

Target Skill Trace

Teach	p. 367C
Reteach	p. R16
Review	pp. 413F–413G
See	*Handbook for English Language Learners,* p. 209; *Extra Support Handbook,* pp. 204–205; pp. 208–209

Practice Book page 192

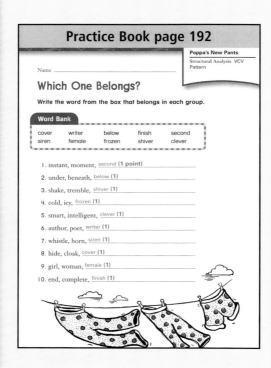

Poppa's New Pants
Structural Analysis VCV Pattern

Name _____

Which One Belongs?

Write the word from the box that belongs in each group.

Word Bank

cover	writer	below	finish	second
siren	female	frozen	shiver	clever

1. instant, moment, second **(1 point)** _____
2. under, beneath, below **(1)** _____
3. shake, tremble, shiver **(1)** _____
4. cold, icy, frozen **(1)** _____
5. smart, intelligent, clever **(1)** _____
6. author, poet, writer **(1)** _____
7. whistle, horn, siren **(1)** _____
8. hide, cloak, cover **(1)** _____
9. girl, woman, female **(1)** _____
10. end, complete, finish **(1)** _____

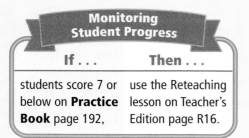

Monitoring Student Progress

If . . .	Then . . .
students score 7 or below on **Practice Book** page 192,	use the Reteaching lesson on Teacher's Edition page R16.

STRUCTURAL ANALYSIS/ VOCABULARY: VCV Pattern

❶ Teach

Introduce the VCV pattern.

- Some words with a VCV pattern divide before the consonant and others divide after the consonant.
- Open syllables end in a vowel and the vowel sound is often long.
- Remind students that marking the pattern of vowels and consonants can help readers figure out how to pronounce a word.

Model the Phonics/Decoding Strategy. Write *moment* and model the process of decoding it.

Think Aloud *When I look at this word I see the* VCV *pattern* o-m-e. *I'll try dividing the word between the first vowel and the consonant:* mo-ment. *This makes the first syllable open, so I'll pronounce the* o *with a long vowel sound. The word might sound like* moh-ment. *That sounds right.*

- Many VCV words divide after the consonant, so the first syllable has a short vowel sound. Decode *cover* and *visit*, following the same process.

❷ Guided Practice

Have students decode words with the VCV pattern. Display the sentences below. Ask partners to copy the underlined words, divide the words into syllables, decode the words, and give their meaning. Have students share their work with the class.

1. The cafeteria <u>opens</u> at eleven thirty.
2. I need a <u>topic</u> for my report.
3. I spied a thin, white <u>figure</u> drifting into the room.

❸ Apply

Assign Practice Book page 192.

PHONICS REVIEW: Words Beginning with *a-* and *be-*

❶ Teach

Review word beginnings *a-* and *be-*. Tell students that understanding the word beginnings *a-* and *be-* can help them decode unfamiliar words.

- The letter *a* can have the unstressed /ə/ sound at the beginning of a two-syllable word.

- The *be* spelling pattern can have the unstressed /bih/ sound at the beginning of a two-syllable word.

Model the Phonics/Decoding Strategy. Write *The grandfather clock wheezed* <u>awake</u> *every hour and rang out the time.* Then model how to decode *awake*.

Think Aloud *I know that the letter* a *at the beginning of a word can have the* uh *sound, and I also see the shorter word* wake. *Maybe this word is* uh-WAYK. *I know that word, and it makes sense here.*

❷ Guided Practice

Have students pronounce words beginning with *a-* and *be-*. Write the following phrases:

> I knew they were glad to see me <u>because</u>
>
> I didn't <u>believe</u> it
>
> a tree limb scraped <u>against</u> the screen

- Have students copy the underlined words. Then help them circle the word part that begins each word, pronounce the word, and see if it makes sense.

- Call on individuals to model their work at the board.

❸ Apply

Have students decode words beginning with *a-* and *be-*. Ask students to decode the words below from *Poppa's New Pants* and discuss their meanings.

awhile	page 352	besides	page 356
again	page 355	across	page 357
alive	page 356	behind	page 357

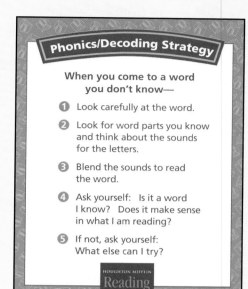

OBJECTIVES

- Read words with the beginnings *a-* and *be-*.
- Apply the Phonics/Decoding Strategy.

Phonics/Decoding Strategy

When you come to a word you don't know—

❶ Look carefully at the word.

❷ Look for word parts you know and think about the sounds for the letters.

❸ Blend the sounds to read the word.

❹ Ask yourself: Is it a word I know? Does it make sense in what I am reading?

❺ If not, ask yourself: What else can I try?

HOUGHTON MIFFLIN
Reading

SPELLING: Words Beginning with *a/be*

OBJECTIVES

- Write Spelling Words that begin with *a* or *be*.

SPELLING WORDS

Basic

begin	alive*
again*	because*
around*	ahead
before*	between
away*	behind*
about*	ago

Review†	**Challenge**
they*†	awhile*
want*†	beyond

*Forms of these words appear in the literature.

†*Because this lesson presents these spelling patterns for the first time, the Review Words do not contain the lesson's patterns.*

REACHING ALL LEARNERS

Extra Support/ Intervention

Basic Word List Consider using only the left column of Basic Words with students who need extra support.

Challenge

Challenge Word Practice Students can use the Challenge Words to write directions telling someone how to get from one place to another.

DAY 1 INSTRUCTION

Words Beginning with *a/be*

Pretest Use the Day 5 Test sentences.

Teach Write *again* in syllables on the board. *(a/gain)* Say the word slowly, and ask students to repeat it.

- Underline the first syllable's *a*, and explain that it spells the schwa sound. Note that the unstressed /ə/ sound at the beginning of a two-syllable word may be spelled *a*.

- Write *before* in syllables on the board, and repeat the process above. *(be/fore)* Explain that the unstressed /bĭ/ sound at the beginning of a two-syllable word may be spelled *be*.

- Add the remaining Basic Words to the board, and repeat the process. Select students to identify the spelling patterns for the /ə/ and /bĭ/ sounds.

Practice/Homework Assign **Practice Book** page 245.

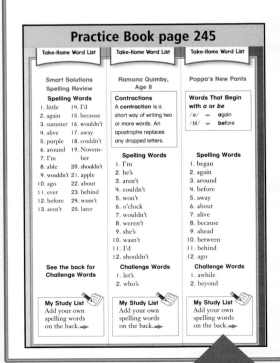

Practice Book page 245

Take-Home Word List	Take-Home Word List	Take-Home Word List
Smart Solutions Spelling Review **Spelling Words**	**Ramona Quimby, Age 8**	**Poppa's New Pants**
1. little 14. I'd	**Contractions** A **contraction** is a short way of writing two or more words. An apostrophe replaces any dropped letters.	**Words That Begin with *a* or *be***
2. again 15. because		/ə/ → again
3. summer 16. wouldn't		/bĭ/ → before
4. alive 17. away		
5. purple 18. couldn't		
6. around 19. November	**Spelling Words**	**Spelling Words**
7. I'm	1. I'm	1. began
8. able 20. shouldn't	2. he's	2. again
9. wouldn't 21. apple	3. aren't	3. around
10. ago 22. about	4. couldn't	4. before
11. ever 23. behind	5. won't	5. away
12. before 24. wasn't	6. o'clock	6. about
13. aren't 25. later	7. wouldn't	7. alive
	8. weren't	8. because
	9. she's	9. ahead
	10. wasn't	10. between
	11. I'd	11. behind
	12. shouldn't	12. ago
See the back for Challenge Words	**Challenge Words** 1. let's 2. who's	**Challenge Words** 1. awhile 2. beyond
My Study List Add your own spelling words on the back.→	**My Study List** Add your own spelling words on the back.→	**My Study List** Add your own spelling words on the back.→

DAY 2 REVIEW & PRACTICE

Reviewing the Principle

Go over the spelling principle for words that begin with *a* or *be* with students.

Practice/Homework Assign **Practice Book** page 193.

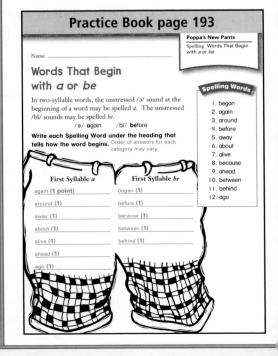

Practice Book page 193

Poppa's New Pants
Spelling Words That Begin with *a* or *be*

Name _____

Words That Begin with *a* or *be*

In two-syllable words, the unstressed /ə/ sound at the beginning of a word may be spelled *a*. The unstressed /bĭ/ sounds may be spelled *be*.

Write each Spelling Word under the heading that tells how the word begins. Order of answers for each category may vary.

First Syllable *a*	First Syllable *be*
again (1 point)	began (1)
around (1)	before (1)
away (1)	because (1)
about (1)	between (1)
alive (1)	behind (1)
ahead (1)	
ago (1)	

Spelling Words
1. began
2. again
3. around
4. before
5. away
6. about
7. alive
8. because
9. ahead
10. between
11. behind
12. ago

Take-Home Word List

Definitions

Write the Basic Words on the board.

- Dictate each definition below and ask students to write the Basic Word that fits each meaning.

  "in, to, or toward the rear" (behind)

  "once more" (again)

  "living" (alive)

  "earlier in time" (before)

- Have students use each Basic Word from the board orally in a sentence. (Sentences will vary.)

Practice/Homework For spelling practice, assign **Practice Book** page 194.

Game: Guess a Letter

Have students play in groups of 4. Give each group a list of Basic and Review Words and a set of letter tiles or cards. Explain these rules:

- Player 1 chooses a list word. The other 3 players cover their eyes as Player 1 arranges the tiles or cards to spell the word. Player 1 then turns the letters face-down and gives a clue about the word. For example, "the opposite of dead" might be a clue for *alive*.

- The other 3 students, without using the word list, take turns guessing a letter. If a student guesses a letter in the word, Player 1 must turn over all tiles or cards with that letter.

- Students can guess the word only on their turn. The student who guesses the word earns a point and gets to choose the next word.

Practice/Homework For proofreading and writing practice, assign **Practice Book** page 195.

Spelling Test

Say each underlined word, read the sentence, and then repeat the word. Have students write only the underlined word.

Basic Words

1. Class will **begin** soon.
2. I will read this book **again**.
3. We will run **around** the park.
4. Please call **before** you come.
5. The fox ran **away**.
6. The book is **about** two friends.
7. The old tree was still **alive**.
8. We cheered **because** we won.
9. Who is in line **ahead** of me?
10. Draw a line **between** the dots.
11. The dog hid **behind** the chair.
12. We ate an hour **ago**.

Challenge Words

13. I had to wait **awhile** for my turn.
14. The road is **beyond** the trees.

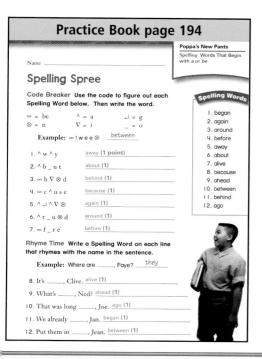

Practice Book page 194

Poppa's New Pants
Spelling Words That Begin with *a* or *be*

Name _____

Spelling Spree

Code Breaker Use the code to figure out each Spelling Word below. Then write the word.

∞ = be   ^ = a   ⌐ = g
⊗ = n   ∇ = i   _ = o

Example: ∞twee⊗   between

1. ^w^y   away (1 point)
2. ^b_ut   about (1)
3. ∞h∇⊗d   behind (1)
4. ∞c^use   because (1)
5. ^⌐^∇∇⊗   again (1)
6. ^r_u⊗d   around (1)
7. ∞f_re   before (1)

Spelling Words
1. began
2. again
3. around
4. before
5. away
6. about
7. alive
8. because
9. ahead
10. between
11. behind
12. ago

Rhyme Time Write a Spelling Word on each line that rhymes with the name in the sentence.

Example: Where are ____, Faye?   they

8. It's ____, Clive.   alive (1)
9. What's ____, Ned?   ahead (1)
10. That was long ____, Joe.   ago (1)
11. We already ____, Jan.   began (1)
12. Put them in ____, Jean.   between (1)

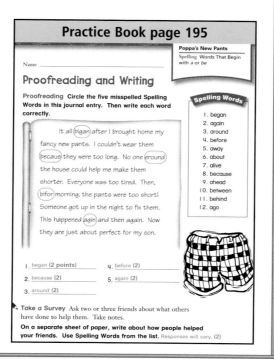

Practice Book page 195

Poppa's New Pants
Spelling Words That Begin with *a* or *be*

Name _____

Proofreading and Writing

Proofreading Circle the five misspelled Spelling Words in this journal entry. Then write each word correctly.

It all (bigan) after I brought home my fancy new pants. I couldn't wear them (becaue) they were too long. No one (around) the house could help me make them shorter. Everyone was too tired. Then, (bifor) morning, the pants were too short! Someone got up in the night to fix them. This happened (agin) and then again. Now they are just about perfect for my son.

Spelling Words
1. began
2. again
3. around
4. before
5. away
6. about
7. alive
8. because
9. ahead
10. between
11. behind
12. ago

1. began (2 points)   4. before (2)
2. because (2)   5. again (2)
3. around (2)

Take a Survey Ask two or three friends about what others have done to help them. Take notes.

On a separate sheet of paper, write about how people helped your friends. Use Spelling Words from the list. Responses will vary. (2)

OBJECTIVES

- Identify pairs of antonyms.
- Select antonyms for given words.
- Learn academic language: *antonym*.

Target Skill Trace

Teach	p. 367G
Review	pp. 413H–413I
Extend	Challenge/Extension Activities, p. R17
See	*Handbook for English Language Learners*, p. 213

Transparency 6–12

Antonyms

1. The windows used to be dirty.
2. Now the windows are clean.
3. Poppa's old pants were black.
4. His new pants are gray and red.
5. At first George was asleep.
6. When he heard the strange sounds, he was awake.
7. George hid under the blankets all night.
8. Grandma Tiny's voice woke him the next day.
9. At first Poppa's pants were too long.
10. Now they are too short!

SMART SOLUTIONS: Poppa's New Pants
Vocabulary Skill Antonyms
ANNOTATED VERSION

TRANSPARENCY 6–12
TEACHER'S EDITION PAGE 367G

Monitoring Student Progress

If . . .	Then . . .
students score 7 or below on **Practice Book** page 196,	have them work with partners to correct the items they missed.

VOCABULARY: Antonyms

TARGET SKILL

❶ Teach

Define antonyms. Tell students that words that have opposite meanings are called antonyms.

Display **Transparency 6–12**. Cover all but Sentences 1 and 2. Explain:

- Authors use antonyms to help readers see differences.
- The words *dirty* and *clean* are antonyms because they mean the opposite of each other.

Model how to identify antonyms. Display Sentences 3 through 10 of **Transparency 6–12**. Have students follow as you think aloud.

> **Think Aloud** *When I read Sentence 3, I learn that Poppa's old pants were black. Sentence 4 mentions that Poppa's new pants are red and gray. I know that* old *and* new *have opposite meanings, so I know that they are antonyms. Let me check the other words, just to be sure.* Black *is different from* red *and different from* gray, *but it is not the opposite of either red or gray. So* old *and* new *are the antonyms in these sentences.*

❷ Guided Practice

Give students practice in selecting antonyms. Uncover the rest of the transparency. Guide student pairs or groups to find the antonyms in Sentences 5 through 10. Afterward, have students suggest other antonyms for the sentences. Ask groups to share their answers with the class.

❸ Apply

Assign Practice Book page 196.

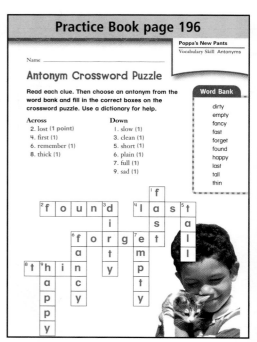

Practice Book page 196

Poppa's New Pants
Vocabulary Skill Antonyms

Name _____

Antonym Crossword Puzzle

Read each clue. Then choose an antonym from the word bank and fill in the correct boxes on the crossword puzzle. Use a dictionary for help.

Word Bank
dirty
empty
fancy
fast
forget
found
happy
last
tall
thin

Across
2. lost (1 point)
4. first (1)
6. remember (1)
8. thick (1)

Down
1. slow (1)
3. clean (1)
5. short (1)
6. plain (1)
7. full (1)
9. sad (1)

STUDY SKILL: Following Directions

❶ Teach

Introduce the steps in following directions.

- First, read or listen carefully to all the directions.
- Then imagine how to follow each of the steps.
- Ask for clarification if necessary.
- Then follow each step carefully and completely.

Model how to follow directions. Have students look at the "Make Poppa's Pants" activity on page 363 as you think aloud.

Think Aloud *First, I will read all the directions to make sure I understand them. I see the term* butcher paper. *I'm not sure what that is, so I find out. Then I look for action verbs that will tell me what I will be doing—* cut, mark, show, measure, *and* decorate. *I know what all of these verbs mean. When I do the activity, I will follow the directions in the order in which I read them. I will do each step completely and then go on to the next one, until I'm finished.*

❷ Practice/Apply

Give students practice in following directions. Write this series of letters:

CAYBOBUADIBDACICT

Read aloud the following directions. Allow time for all students to complete each step before reading the next one. Provide support as needed.

1. Copy these letters onto a sheet of paper.
2. Copy them in the same order in which you see them.
3. Cross out every letter A.
4. Cross out every letter B.
5. Cross out every letter C.
6. Write the remaining letters in a new row.
7. Divide them into three words.
8. Say what they spell. (YOU DID IT)

GRAMMAR: Comparing with Adjectives

OBJECTIVES

- Form common comparative and superlative adjectives.
- Use comparison of adjectives in sentences.
- Proofread and correct sentences with grammar and spelling errors.
- Use *good* and *well* correctly to improve writing.

DAY 1 INSTRUCTION

Comparing with Adjectives

Teach Display **Transparency 6–14**, and discuss how the word *long* is used in each of the three sentences at the top.

- Point out that *long* is an adjective that describes the noun *pants* in the first sentence. After students identify the endings added to *long* (-er, -est) when comparing, go over the bulleted rules below the sentences.

- Have students complete the chart below the rules with the correct forms of each adjective.

- Ask volunteers to read Sentences 1–4 and select the correct adjective form to complete each sentence.

Daily Language Practice

Have students correct Sentences 1 and 2 on **Transparency 6–13**.

DAY 2 PRACTICE

Independent Work

Practice/Homework Assign **Practice Book** page 197.

Daily Language Practice

Have students correct Sentences 3 and 4 on **Transparency 6–13**.

Transparency 6–13

Daily Language Practice

Correct two sentences each day.

1. The red and gray fabric is alliv with color and brightest than the brown fabric.
   The red and gray fabric is alive with color and brighter than the brown fabric.
2. Poppa says it is abowt the sharper plaid he has ever seen.
   Poppa says it is about the sharpest plaid he has ever seen.
3. We looked agin and saw that the plaid pants had the bolder pattern in the shop.
   We looked again and saw that the plaid pants had the boldest pattern in the shop.
4. He begann to say the pants are longest than Poppa's pair.
   He began to say the pants are longer than Poppa's pair.
5. Grandma Tiny went ahed and mended the pants fastest than Big Mama.
   Grandma Tiny went ahead and mended the pants faster than Big Mama.
6. Betwene you and me, Aunt Viney was the faster of all three
   Between you and me, Aunt Viney was the fastest of all three.
7. The rustling noise behinde him was louderer than a mouse.
   The rustling noise behind him was louder than a mouse.
8. He looked arond and saw Big Mama, the taller of the three.
   He looked around and saw Big Mama, the tallest of the three.
9. Befour bed, Poppa draped his newestest pants on the chair.
   Before bed, Poppa draped his newest pants on the chair.
10. He liked the cloth becuz it was softest than a kitten.
    He liked the cloth because it was softer than a kitten.

Monitoring Student Progress

If . . .	Then . . .
students score 7 or below on **Practice Book** page 198,	use the Reteaching lesson on Teacher's Edition page R21.

Transparency 6–14

Comparing with Adjectives

The brown pants are long.
The black pair is longer than the brown pair.
The gray pair is the longest of all.

- Add -er to most adjectives to compare two people, places, or things.
- Add -est to most adjectives to compare more than two people, places, or things.

Adjective	Compare Two Things	Compare More Than Two Things
long	longer	longest
short	shorter	shortest
clean	cleaner	cleanest
strong	stronger	strongest
small	smaller	smallest
green	greener	greenest

1. Poppa is _____ than I. (taller, tallest)
   taller
2. Poppa is the _____ person in our family. (taller, tallest)
   tallest
3. Poppa's new pants are _____ than his old pants. (shortest, shorter)
   shorter
4. Poppa's new pants are the _____ pants I have ever seen. (shortest, shorter)
   shortest

Practice Book page 197

Poppa's New Pants
Grammar Skill Comparing with Adjectives

Name _____

Writing Comparisons

Complete this chart with the correct forms of the adjective.

Adjective	Compare Two Things	Compare More Than Two Things
short	shorter	shortest
loud	1. louder (1 point)	2. loudest (1)
soft	3. softer (1)	4. softest (1)
bold	5. bolder (1)	6. boldest (1)
quiet	7. quieter (1)	8. quietest (1)
sharp	9. sharper (1)	10. sharpest (1)

Choose a word from the chart to complete each sentence.
Answers may vary. Sample answers are included.

11. The gray fabric is _softer (1)_ than the red fabric.
12. Big Mama is the _quietest (1)_ ghost.
13. The _loudest (1)_ sound came right after midnight.
14. Aunt Viney is a _softer (1)_ speaker than Grandma Tiny.
15. Big Mama takes the _sharpest (1)_ needle from her sewing kit.

DAY
3
ADJECTIVE GAME

The Greatest Match

Have each student use 3 note cards and draw a set of 3 similar items inspired by *Poppa's New Pants*. For example, a student might draw 3 pairs of pants—1 short, 1 medium, and 1 long. Alternatively, a student might draw the 3 *"ghosts,"* making sure that each one looks a little different.

- Ask students to swap cards and write 3 sentences about the cards. Students should use an adjective ending in *-er* or *-est* to compare 2 or more things in each sentence.

- Ask volunteers to read their sentences aloud to the class.

Daily Language Practice
Have students correct Sentences 5 and 6 on **Transparency 6–13**.

DAY
4
PRACTICE

Independent Work

Practice/Homework Assign **Practice Book** page 198.

Daily Language Practice
Have students correct Sentences 7 and 8 on **Transparency 6–13**.

DAY
5
IMPROVING WRITING

Using *good* and *well*

Teach Tell students that *good* and *well* are sometimes confused.

– *Good* is an adjective. It always describes a noun.

– *Well* is an adverb. It tells how something is done and modifies a verb.

- Display **Transparency 6–15.** Read the first two sentences.

- Point out that *good* describes *what kind* of pants Poppa buys, and *well* tells *how* Big Mama sews.

- Ask volunteers to complete Sentences 1–5.

- Have students proofread their own writing for *good* and *well*.

Practice/Homework Assign **Practice Book** page 199.

Daily Language Practice
Have students correct Sentences 9 and 10 on **Transparency 6–13**.

Practice Book page 198

Poppa's New Pants
Grammar Skill Comparing with Adjectives

Name _____

Writing the Correct Form

Write the correct form of the adjective in parentheses to complete each sentence.

1. Poppa's new pants are _longer (1 point)_ than his old pants. (long)

2. Big Mama is _older (1)_ than her sister. (old)

3. Aunt Viney is the _fastest (1)_ sewer of the three ghosts. (fast)

4. The snipping sound is _louder (1)_ than a whisper. (loud)

5. Grandma Tiny is the _loudest (1)_ of all. (loud)

6. Poppa is _taller (1)_ than George. (tall)

7. George thinks the second ghost is _odder (1)_ than the first. (odd)

8. Now Poppa's pants are the _shortest (1)_ pants in the house. (short)

9. George has _shorter (1)_ legs than Poppa. (short)

10. This story is the _weirdest (1)_ story I know. (weird)

Transparency 6–15

Using *good* and *well*

Poppa buys a good pair of pants.
Big Mama sews well.

- *Good* is an adjective. It always describes a noun.
- *Well* is an adverb. It tells how something is done and modifies a verb.

1. George tells his father a _____good_____ story.
   (good, well)

2. Big Mama wishes George a _____good_____ night.
   (good, well)

3. Aunt Viney sings very _____well_____.
   (good, well)

4. George's pants bring him _____good_____ luck.
   (good, well)

5. When he wears the pants, he always runs _____well_____.
   (good, well)

SMART SOLUTIONS Poppa's New Pants
ANNOTATED VERSION Grammar Skill Improving Your Writing

TRANSPARENCY 6–15
TEACHER'S EDITION PAGE 367J

Practice Book page 199

Poppa's New Pants
Grammar Skill Improving Your Writing

Name _____

A Good Story, Well Told

Using *good* and *well* Suppose George wrote a letter. Proofread the letter. Check that *good* and *well* are used correctly. Check for spelling errors too. Rewrite the letter below.

Dear Cousin,

Poppa bought a well new pair of pants last week. But they did not fit him good, so Poppa asked Big Mama, Grandma Tiny, and Aunt Viney to hemm the pants. They said no. Poppa was a little sad, but he is a good man. He didn't complain. Guess what happened next! All three women got up in the middle of the night. They each mennded the pants!

When Poppa woke up, he got a well shock. His new pants had turned into shorts. Luckily, the pants fit me good.

Your cousin,
George

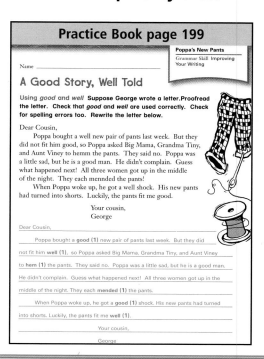

Dear Cousin,

Poppa bought a **good (1)** new pair of pants last week. But they did not fit him **well (1)**, so Poppa asked Big Mama, Grandma Tiny, and Aunt Viney to **hem (1)** the pants. They said no. Poppa was a little sad, but he is a good man. He didn't complain. Guess what happened next! All three women got up in the middle of the night. They each **mended (1)** the pants.

When Poppa woke up, he got a **good (1)** shock. His new pants had turned into shorts. Luckily, the pants fit me **well (1)**.

Your cousin,
George

WRITING: Summary

OBJECTIVES

- Identify the characteristics of a good summary.
- Write a summary.
- Paraphrase sentences without changing meaning.
- Learn academic language: *summary, paraphrase.*

Writing Traits

Sentence Fluency As students begin drafting on Day 2, emphasize the importance of combining short sentences to avoid choppy writing. Share these examples.

Choppy: Guests are coming. Grandma Tiny wants everything to be just right. Poppa buys pants at the store. The pants are plaid.

Smoother: Guests are coming, and Grandma Tiny wants everything to be just right. Poppa buys plaid pants at the store.

DAY 1 — PREWRITING

Introducing the Format

Define a summary.

- A summary is a brief account of a story or nonfiction selection.
- Writing a summary is a good way to share what a selection is about.
- Writing a summary also helps you recall the main events and characters in a story or the main ideas in a nonfiction selection.

Start students thinking about writing a summary.

- Ask students to decide on a story or nonfiction selection to summarize.
- They might choose a story they have read recently, such as *Yunmi and Halmoni's Trip, Pepita Talks Twice,* or another selection.
- Ask them to discuss with a partner who the story is about, what the problem is, what happens, and how the story ends.

DAY 2 — DRAFTING

Discussing the Model

Display Transparency 6–16.

- Explain that this is a graphic organizer students can use to plan a summary.
- Remind students that a summary is written using sentences and paragraphs.

Discuss Transparency 6–16. Ask:

- Who is the main character? (Poppa)
- What problem does Poppa have? (bought new pants that are too large and wants someone to shorten them)
- What happens? (First, Grandma, Aunt Viney, and Big Mama won't fix the pants for him; then they each get up secretly in the night and shorten the pants.)
- How does it end? (The pants end up too short; Poppa's grandson wears them as knickers.)

Display Transparency 6–17, and discuss the guidelines.

Have students draft a summary.

- Assign **Practice Book** page 200.
- Students can use their notes from Day 1.
- See Writing Traits on this page.

Transparency 6–16

Story Map

Who?

Poppa

↓

Problem

Poppa has bought new pants that are too large. He wants someone in the family to fix them.

↓

What happens?

Grandma, Aunt Viney, and Big Mama won't fix the pants for him because they say they are too tired. But then each of the women gets up secretly in the middle of the night and fixes the pants.

↓

How does it end?

As a result of the women's work, the pants are much shorter than they should be. Poppa's son gets to wear them as shorts.

TRANSPARENCY 6-16
TEACHER'S EDITION PAGE 367K

Transparency 6–17

Guidelines for Writing a Summary

- Use your own words.
- Make a story map to help you write the summary.
- For nonfiction, tell what the main idea is.
- For fiction, tell the main character's problem and the most important events.
- Describe the main events as briefly as possible.
- Tell the ending and how the main character feels about it.

TRANSPARENCY 6-17
TEACHER'S EDITION PAGE 367K

Practice Book page 200

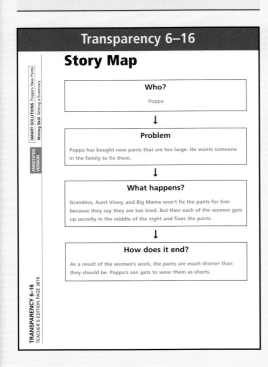

Poppa's New Pants
Writing Skill A Summary

Name _____

Story Map

Use this Story Map to plan a summary of a story you have read recently. Remember to tell who the story is about. Then tell the main things that happened in the story.

Who is the story about?
(2 points)

Problem
(2)

What happens?
(2)

How does it end?
(2)

Improving Writing: Paraphrasing

Introduce paraphrasing.

- When you paraphrase, you restate what you have read in your own words, without changing the author's meaning.
- Writing a summary and taking notes are examples of paraphrasing.

Display Transparency 6–18.

- Discuss the bullets at the top.
- Have volunteers read the sentence from the selection and the paraphrases below it.
- Ask: Which paraphrase does the best job of restating the quotation? Why? (A; B changes the author's meaning.)
- Have students paraphrase Sentences 1–5.

Assign Practice Book page 201.

Have students revise their drafts.

- Display **Transparency 6–17** again. Ask students to use it to revise their summaries.
- Have partners hold writing conferences.
- Ask them to revise any parts of their summary that still need work, making sure that they used their own words.

Checking for Errors

Have students proofread for errors in grammar, spelling, punctuation, and usage.

- Students can use the proofreading checklist on **Practice Book** page 250 to help them proofread their summaries.
- Students can also use the chart of proofreading marks on **Practice Book** page 251.

Sharing a Summary

Consider these publishing options.

- Ask students to read their summary or some other piece of writing from the Author's Chair.
- Some students might enjoy turning their summary of a story into a comic book, with a different frame for each important event.

Portfolio Opportunity

 Save students' summaries as samples of their writing development.

Transparency 6–18

Paraphrasing

- Paraphrasing is restating something in your own words, without changing the author's meaning.
- Writers use paraphrasing when they write a summary or notes for a report.

The grandfather clock wheezed awake every hour and rang out the time.

Which paraphrasing does not change the author's meaning?

A. The grandfather clock chimed every hour.

B. The grandfather clock was in the hall.

Paraphrase each sentence.

1. Big Mama hugged me so hard that she squeezed the breath right out of my body.
   Sample answer: Big Mama hugged me so tightly I couldn't breathe.

2. I could hear Poppa snoring gently and the dark house moaning softly as everyone settled down for the night.
   Sample answer: I could hear Poppa snoring and the house creaking as everyone went to sleep.

3. After a while, the moon crept into the room, making a big pool of bright, white light by the rocking chair.
   Sample answer: After a while, moonlight came shining brightly into the room.

4. The rocking chair moaned loudly as it creaked back and forth, back and forth.
   Sample answer: The rocking chair creaked loudly as it rocked.

5. Just when I thought it was safe to make a run for it, I spied a tall, thin, ghostly white figure drifting into the room.
   Sample answer: Just when I was about to run away, I saw what seemed to be a ghost.

TRANSPARENCY 6–18 TEACHER'S EDITION PAGE 367L
SMART SOLUTIONS Poppa's New Pants Writing Skill: Improving Your Writing
ANNOTATED VERSION

Practice Book page 201

Poppa's New Pants
Writing Skill: Improving Your Writing

Name _____

Paraphrasing

▶ Paraphrasing is restating something in your own words, without changing the author's meaning.
▶ Writers use paraphrasing when they write a summary or notes for a report.

Circle the letter of the paraphrasing that does not change the author's meaning in the following sentence.

"Grandma Tiny's about to bust a gusset making sure everything's just right."

A. "Grandma Tiny is working hard to make sure everything is just right."
B. "Grandma Tiny is working so hard that she broke something."

Paraphrase each sentence: Answers may vary.

1. Aunt Viney and Big Mama took turns covering my face with red lipstick.
   Aunt Viney and Big Mama took turns kissing me. (2 points)

2. Grandma Tiny, Big Mama, and Aunt Viney usually have a good long gossip spell when they get together.
   Grandma Tiny, Big Mama, and Aunt Viney usually gossip a lot when they get together. (2)

3. I stayed balled up under those blankets like an armadillo for the rest of the night.
   I stayed curled up under the blankets for the rest of the night. (2)

4. Grandma Tiny was smiling fit to beat the band.
   Grandma Tiny was beaming. (2)

Monitoring Student Progress

If . . .	Then . . .
students' writing does not follow the guidelines on **Transparency 6–17,**	work with students to improve specific parts of their writing.

Independent Activities

Language Center

VOCABULARY

Building Vocabulary

👤 Singles	🕐 15 minutes
Objective	Identify words that describe night noises.

In the selection *Poppa's New Pants,* George hears many different noises at night. Look through the selection and identify the words that name these noises. Record these words in a web.

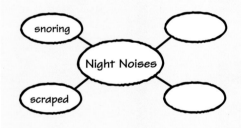

Now think of additional words to describe noises that you might hear at night. Add these words to your web.

GRAMMAR

Comparative Adjective Poster

👤 Singles	🕐 30 minutes
Objective	Make a comparative adjective poster.
Materials	Old magazines, scissors, glue, drawing materials

Create a poster illustrating how to compare with adjectives.

- Cut out magazine photos of similar things or draw your own pictures.
- Cut out or draw two similar things to compare. Label the first one with an adjective such as *small, long, high, dark, wide, young,* and so on. Label the second one with the *-er* form of the word.
- Next, cut out or draw three other similar things. Label the first two as you did before. Then label the third with the *-est* form of the word.
- Display your poster.

VOCABULARY

Vocabulary Game

👥 Pairs	🕐 30 minutes
Objective	Use Key Vocabulary words in sentences.
Materials	Activity Master 6–2 on page R24, art materials

- Make a spinner by cutting out the spinner face and the arrow. Glue each to a piece of cardboard cut in the same shape.
- Make a hole in the small end of the arrow and attach it to the center of the spinner face with a paper fastener. Make sure the arrow spins easily.

To play the game:

- Player 1 spins the arrow, reads aloud the word it lands on, and uses the word in a sentence.
- If Player 1 uses the word correctly, he or she gets a point. If not, he or she gets no point.
- Then Player 2 takes a turn. If the arrow points to a word that has been used already, Player 2 loses the turn, and Player 1 goes again.
- Continue until all of the Key Vocabulary words have been used correctly in sentences.
- The player with the most points wins.

Consider copying and laminating these activities for use in centers.

LISTENING/SPEAKING

Give a Persuasive Speech

👥👥👥 Groups	🕐 45 minutes
Objective	Give a persuasive speech to a group.
Materials	Anthology

Look through all the stories and poems that you have read so far in class. Choose your favorite. Now think of at least two reasons why it is your favorite. Try to support your ideas with examples from the story or poem.

Take turns trying to convince the others in your group to agree with your choice. Here are some strategies you can use to speak persuasively:

Tips for Speaking Persuasively

- State your goal or opinion clearly.

- Support it with several reasons.

- Choose reasons that will appeal to your audience.

- Speak with confidence and enthusiasm.

- Tell your audience what you want them to do or think.

STRUCTURAL ANALYSIS

VCV Syllable Puzzles

👥 Pairs	🕐 30 minutes
Objective	Make puzzles with VCV words.
Materials	Dictionary, self-stick notes, 2 paper clips

Each partner writes 5 words from the list below on a piece of paper. **Don't reveal your words.** Choose at least one word from each column. Draw a vertical line to divide each word into syllables. Check your work. Write your initials on your paper.

cover	below	woman
finish	writer	moment
siren	clever	opens
second	frozen	topic
female	shiver	figure

- For each word on your list, write the first syllable on one self-stick note and the second syllable on another self-stick note.

- Write your initials on the back of each note so the pieces don't get mixed up.

- Mix up your notes and put them in a pile. Fold up your list and use a paper clip to attach it to your pile of notes.

- **Important:** Cover up the columns of words above with a piece of paper.

- Trade piles with your partner.

- Match the syllables to make words.

When you've matched all the syllables, check your words against the list your partner made.

re   mind   cov   er

**A Little Bit Hotter
Can't Hurt**

Summary *Lindy and her mother visit her aunt and uncle in Texas. Knowing that Lindy likes chili, Aunt Birdie makes chili in her honor. But Lindy loves hot chili, not the mild kind Aunt Birdie makes. As the family sits outside visiting, everyone but Uncle Buster sneaks inside to add more chili powder to the chili. When they sit down to eat the surprisingly hot chili, family members laugh about what happened and decide they all like it that way.*

Vocabulary

Introduce the Key Vocabulary and ask students to complete the BLM.

mild gentle flavor, not at all hot, *p. 5*

planted put or placed firmly, *p. 6*

mow to cut grass with a lawn mower, *p. 10*

sweet potato a thick, sweet, yellow or red root that is cooked and eaten as a vegetable, *p. 11*

● BELOW LEVEL

Building Background and Vocabulary

Discuss what it is like to try new foods or foods that are prepared in an unusual way. Preview the story with students, using the story vocabulary when possible.

Comprehension Skill: Drawing Conclusions

Have students read the Strategy Focus on the book flap. Remind students to use the strategy and to draw conclusions as they read the book. (See the Leveled Readers Teacher's Guide for **Vocabulary and Comprehension Practice Masters.**)

Responding

Have partners discuss how to answer the questions on the inside back cover.

Think About the Selection Sample answers:

1. She made chili.
2. Three people add chili powder to the chili.
3. Possible response: She will make it hotter to begin with. She may ask people who are going to be eating the chili to try it to see if it is hot enough.

Making Connections Responses will vary.

Building Fluency

Model Read aloud page 5. Explain that italic text shows emphasis and that the italicized word *love* should be stressed.

Practice Have students work in pairs to find other examples of sentences with italic text. Then they can take turns reading the sentences until they read them accurately and with expression.

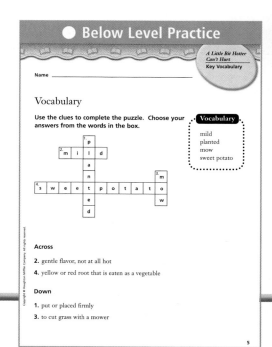

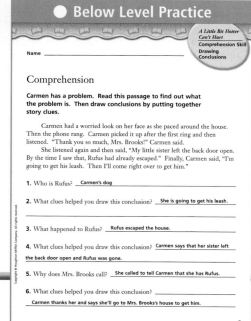

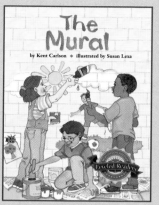

The Mural

Summary *Three students paint a mural depicting life at Marshall Elementary School. When the principal views the artwork, she is very pleased, but feels that something is missing. Without consulting each other, all three students add paintings of eagles. At first, the principal thinks there are too many eagles in the picture, but after hearing the reactions of several viewers, she believes the mural is perfect.*

Vocabulary

Introduce the Key Vocabulary and ask students to complete the BLM.

mural a scene painted on a wall, *p. 3*

ballots pieces of paper with votes written on them, *p. 5*

canvas fabric used to paint on, *p. 7*

mascot a person, animal, or object used to bring good luck, *p. 12*

fierce-looking scary-looking, *p. 14*

▲ ON LEVEL

Building Background and Vocabulary

Talk with students about a typical day at your school and invite them to suggest what might be included in your school mural. Preview the story with students, using the story vocabulary when possible.

Comprehension Skill: Drawing Conclusions

Have students read the Strategy Focus on the book flap. Remind students to use the strategy and to draw conclusions as they read the book. (See the Leveled Readers Teacher's Guide for **Vocabulary and Comprehension Practice Masters.**)

Responding

Have partners discuss how to answer the questions on the inside back cover.

Think About the Selection Sample answers:

1. The students voted after seeing a display of school artwork.
2. Possible response: They are worried that they painted too many eagles.
3. At first, Ms. Danzler thinks the students may have painted too many eagles, but she changes her mind when she sees Coach Hu and the bird-watching club admire the eagles as they walk by the mural.
4. Responses will vary.

Making Connections Responses will vary.

Building Fluency

Model Read aloud page 4, emphasizing the exclamations. Explain that sentences that end in exclamation points should be read with great feeling.

Practice Have partners look for other sentences in the story that end in exclamation points. Have them take turns reading aloud the sentences they find until they are able to read them accurately and with expression.

▲ On Level Practice

The Mural
Key Vocabulary

Name _____

Vocabulary

Use the words from the box to complete the sentences.

Vocabulary
mural
ballots
canvas
mascot
fierce-looking

1. The artist needed paint, two paintbrushes, and a new _____canvas_____ to begin her next painting.
2. The ____fierce-looking____ tiger scared off his enemy with a loud growl.
3. The ____mascot____ of our school is a polar bear.
4. When the ____ballots____ were counted, Jana won the class election by five votes.
5. Everyone loved the ____mural____ that Paco painted on the wall of the community center!

Write three sentences about what you would like a school mural to look like. Use at least three words from the box.

_____
_____
_____

5

▲ On Level Practice

The Mural
Comprehension Skill
Drawing Conclusions

Name _____

Comprehension

Read this passage. Use the clues to help you draw a conclusion.

I remember all the sights and sounds from the big game! Coach Hu told the team that we had to be fierce-looking, like our mascot. He even had someone dressed up like an eagle outside the dugout. Just before the first pitch, there was total silence. The ball seemed like it took forever to reach my bat! But when it finally did, I heard a loud CRACK! The ball sailed over the field. It looked like it could be a home run. I ran like crazy to first base and that's when I heard the next sound—shattering glass.

1. What game is being played?
baseball

2. What clues helped you?
In the passage, I read words that had to do with baseball like dugout, pitch, ball, bat, and home run.

3. What has happened at the end of the passage?
The ball was hit through a window.

4. What clues helped you?
The ball sailed over the field, and they heard the sound of shattering glass.

7

Leveled Readers

LEVELED READERS

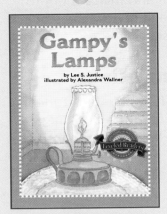

Gampy's Lamps

Summary *Brenda's great-grandfather, Gampy, has a hobby of collecting old oil lamps. Brenda likes the collection and loves to hear tales about the years before electricity was used in homes. Brenda's mother, however, believes the oil lamps are useless. When an ice storm causes a two-day power outage, Gampy's lamps become useful once again as they light the whole neighborhood at night.*

Vocabulary

Introduce the Key Vocabulary and ask students to complete the BLM.

flea market an outdoor market that sells secondhand items and antiques, *p. 2*

chimneys glass tubes around lamp flames, *p. 6*

mending* repairing, *p. 6*

genie an imaginary creature with extraordinary powers, *p. 9*

draped* hung loosely in folds, *p. 12*

*Forms of these words are Anthology Key Vocabulary words.

■ ABOVE LEVEL

Building Background and Vocabulary

Discuss antiques and ask students to suggest ways an antique could be useful. Preview the story with students, using the story vocabulary.

ⓖ Comprehension Skill: Drawing Conclusions

Have students read the Strategy Focus on the book flap. Remind students to use the strategy and to draw conclusions as they read the book. (See the Leveled Readers Teacher's Guide for **Vocabulary and Comprehension Practice Masters**.)

Responding

Have partners discuss how to answer the questions on the inside back cover.

Think About the Selection   Sample answers:

1. They are hand lamps that use oil. They were used for lighting homes before there was electricity.

2. Possible response: because they remind him of when he was young

3. Brenda's mother thinks the lamps are just old junk. Brenda seems to understand why her great-grandfather enjoys collecting them.

4. Responses will vary.

Making Connections   Responses will vary.

ⓖ Building Fluency

Model Explain that the sentences around dialogue often give us clues about how the dialogue should be read. Point out that when someone's eyes light up, the person is probably excited about something. Then read aloud the dialogue on page 3 appropriately.

Practice Have students read page 8 with a partner, looking for clues on how to read Gampy's dialogue in the last paragraph.

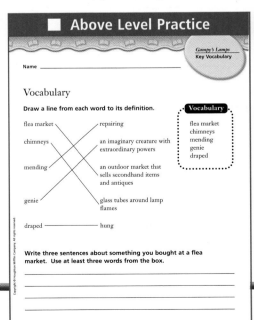

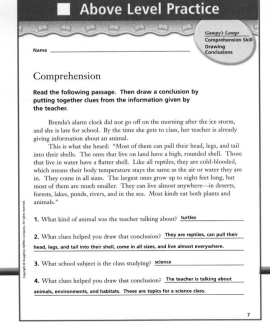

Leveled Readers

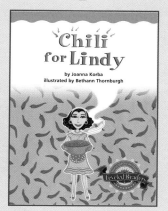

Chili for Lindy

Summary *Lindy and her mother go to visit family in Texas. When they arrive, Aunt Birdie has a pot of chili simmering on the stove. Lindy's mother, Aunt Birdie, and Lindy all add a little bit more chili powder to the pot. The result is a chili that's hotter than hot, but everyone enjoys it!*

Vocabulary

Introduce the Key Vocabulary and ask students to complete the BLM.

Texas a south-central state, *p. 4*

chili a spicy dish usually made with chili powder, meat, and beans, *p. 4*

mild not spicy or hot, *p. 5*

pretend to make-believe, *p. 5*

hotter spicier; causing a burning sensation in the mouth, *p. 7*

pie a dessert baked in a pastry shell, often with fruit filling, *p. 11*

◆ LANGUAGE SUPPORT

Building Background and Vocabulary

Have students pretend to order food in a restaurant. Customers should say whether they want their food hot and spicy or mild. Distribute the **Build Background Practice Master** and read aloud the directions and steps for making chili. Guide students in completing the page.

Comprehension Skill: Drawing Conclusions

Have students read the Strategy Focus on the book flap. Remind students to use the strategy and to draw conclusions as they read the book. (See the Leveled Readers Teacher's Guide for **Build Background, Vocabulary, and Graphic Organizer Masters.**)

Responding

Have partners discuss how to answer the questions on the inside back cover.

Think About the Selection Sample answers:

1. Lindy likes hot chili.
2. Aunt Birdie, Lindy, and Lindy's mother all add chili powder to the chili. Everyone's eyes open wide when they eat the chili.
3. Responses will vary.

Making Connections Responses will vary.

Building Fluency

Model Have students follow along in their books as they listen to pages 3–5 of the recording on audio CD.

Practice Have students read along with the recording until they can read the text on their own accurately and with expression.

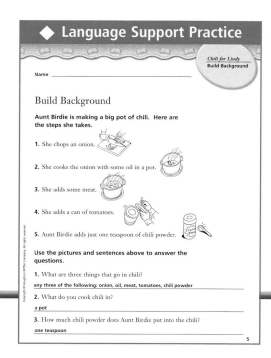

Literature

NEWBERY HONOR BOOK

BEVERLY CLEARY

Ramona Quimby, Age 8

ILLUSTRATED BY ALAN TIEGREEN

⭐ Selection Summary

Ramona and her family are struggling to make it through a rainy Sunday. Beezus is moody, Ramona is sulky, and Mr. and Mrs. Quimby seem tired and discouraged. The day turns around when a trip to Whopperburger gives the Quimbys something to smile about.

❶ Background and Vocabulary

❷ Main Selection

Ramona Quimby, Age 8
Genre: Realistic Fiction

❸ Drama Link

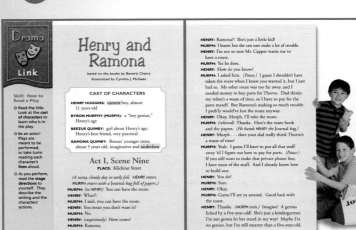

Instructional Support

Planning and Practice

- Planning and classroom management
- Reading instruction
- Skill lessons
- Materials for reaching all learners

- Independent practice for skills, Level 3.6

- Newsletters
- Selection Summaries
- Assignment Cards
- Observation Checklists
- Selection Tests

- Transparencies
- Strategy Posters
- Blackline Masters

Reaching All Learners

Coordinated lessons, activities, and projects for additional reading instruction

For
- Classroom teacher
- Extended day
- Pull out
- Resource teacher
- Reading specialist

Technology

Audio Selection

Ramona Quimby, Age 8

Get Set for Reading CD-ROM
- Background building
- Vocabulary support
- Selection Summary in English and Spanish

Accelerated Reader®
- Practice quizzes for the selection

www.eduplace.com

Log on to Education Place for more activities related to the selection, including vocabulary support—
  *e•*Glossary
  *e•*WordGame

Leveled Books for Reaching All Learners

Leveled Readers and Leveled Practice

- Independent reading for building fluency
- Topic, comprehension strategy, and vocabulary linked to main selection
- Lessons in Teacher's Edition, pages 399O–399R
- Leveled practice for every book

Technology

Leveled Readers
Audio available

Book Adventure®
- Practice quizzes for the Leveled Theme Paperbacks
  www.bookadventure.org

● BELOW LEVEL

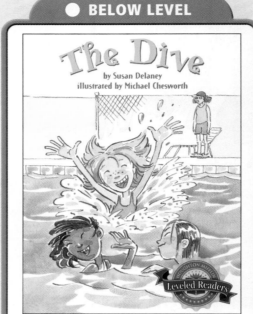

The Dive
by Susan Delaney
illustrated by Michael Chesworth

● Below Level Practice

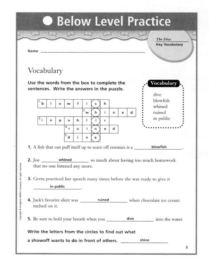

The Dive
Key Vocabulary

Name _____

Vocabulary

Use the words from the box to complete the sentences. Write the answers in the puzzle.

Vocabulary
dive
blowfish
whined
ruined
in public

1. A fish that can puff itself up to scare off enemies is a _____ blowfish

2. Joe ____whined____ so much about having too much homework that no one listened any more.

3. Greta practiced her speech many times before she was ready to give it in public _____ .

4. Jack's favorite shirt was ____ruined____ when chocolate ice cream melted on it.

5. Be sure to hold your breath when you ____dive____ into the water.

Write the letters from the circles to find out what a showoff wants to do in front of others. ____shine____

● Below Level Practice

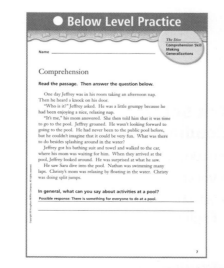

The Dive
Comprehension Skill
Making
Generalizations

Name _____

Comprehension

Read the passage. Then answer the question below.

One day Jeffrey was in his room taking an afternoon nap. Then he heard a knock on his door.
"Who is it?" Jeffrey asked. He was a little grumpy because he had been enjoying a nice, relaxing nap.
"It's me," his mom answered. She then told him that it was time to go to the pool. Jeffrey groaned. He wasn't looking forward to going to the pool. He had never been to the public pool before, but he couldn't imagine that it could be very fun. What was there to do besides splashing around in the water?
Jeffrey got his bathing suit and towel and walked to the car, where his mom was waiting for him. When they arrived at the pool, Jeffrey looked around. He was surprised at what he saw.
He saw Sara dive into the pool. Nathan was swimming many laps. Christy's mom was relaxing by floating in the water. Christy was doing split jumps.

In general, what can you say about activities at a pool?
Possible response: There is something for everyone to do at a pool.

▲ ON LEVEL

First Day For CARLOS

by Amanda Ferguson
illustrated by
Kristen Goeters

▲ On Level Practice

First Day for Carlos
Key Vocabulary

Name _____

Vocabulary

Use the clues to complete the puzzle. Choose your answers from the words in the box.

Vocabulary
discouraged
hall monitor
pelting
sullenly
transfer

Across
2. a person who checks students' behavior in a school hallway (two words)
5. not happily

Down
1. change from one place to another
3. hitting hard
4. not hopeful

▲ On Level Practice

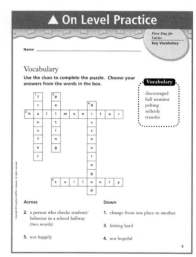

First Day for Carlos
Comprehension Skill
Making
Generalizations

Name _____

Comprehension

Read each sentence below. Use them to make a generalization about how Carlos makes friends in his new school.

Carlos met Nicki, Wendy, and Gregg when Ms. Mertens told students to work together to write a paragraph.

Carlos got to know Gregg when Ms. Mertens told students to interview a partner.

Carlos got to know Wendy when Ms. Mertens told them to pair up to pass out art supplies.

Carlos got to know Nicki when Ms. Mertens asked them to work together on a book report.

In general, what statement can you make about how Carlos got to know his classmates?
Possible response: Carlos got to know his classmates by doing school assignments with them.

Leveled Theme Paperbacks

- Extended independent reading in Theme-related trade books
- Lessons in Teacher's Edition, pages R2–R7

Below Level

On Level

Challenge

■ ABOVE LEVEL

■ Above Level Practice

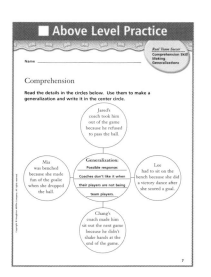

◆ LANGUAGE SUPPORT

◆ Language Support Practice

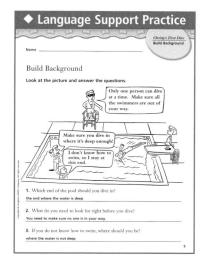

◆ Language Support Practice

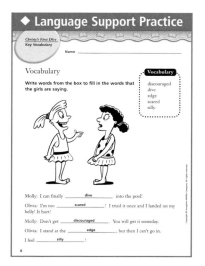

Daily Lesson Plans

Technology
Lesson Planner CD-ROM allows you to customize the chart below to develop your own lesson plans.

T Skill tested on Theme Skills Test and/or Integrated Theme Test

	DAY 1	**DAY 2**
⏱ 50–60 minutes  **Reading** **Comprehension** 	**Teacher Read Aloud,** 367CC–367DD *The Fastest Cat on Earth* **Building Background,** 368 **Key Vocabulary,** 369 ceaseless dismal pelting companionable dreary sullenly discouraged exhausted **Reading the Selection,** 370–393 **Comprehension Skill,** 370 Making Generalizations **T** **Comprehension Strategy,** 370 Summarize **T** **Leveled Readers** *The Dive* *First Day for Carlos* *Real Team Soccer* *Christy's First Dive* Lessons and Leveled Practice, 399O–399R	**Reading the Selection,** 370–393 Comprehension Check, 393 Responding, 394 Think About the Selection **Comprehension Skill Preview,** 385 Making Generalizations **T** **Leveled Readers** *The Dive* *First Day for Carlos* *Real Team Soccer* *Christy's First Dive* Lessons and Leveled Practice, 399O–399R
⏱ 20–30 minutes **Word Work** **Phonics/Decoding** **Vocabulary** **Spelling**	**Phonics/Decoding,** 371 Phonics/Decoding Strategy **Vocabulary,** 370–393 Selection Vocabulary **Spelling,** 399E Contractions **T**	**Structural Analysis,** 399C Contractions **T** **Vocabulary,** 370–393 Selection Vocabulary **Spelling,** 399E Contractions Review and Practice **T**
⏱ 20–30 minutes **Writing and Oral Language** **Writing** **Grammar** **Listening/Speaking/Viewing**	**✏ Writing,** 399K Prewriting an Essay **Grammar,** 399I Adverbs **T** **Daily Language Practice** 1. Ramona says shes total discouraged. (she's; totally) 2. The dreary rain at ten aclok quick ruined her plans. (o'clock; quickly) **Listening/Speaking/Viewing,** 367CC–367DD, 381 Teacher Read Aloud, Stop and Think	**✏ Writing,** 399K Drafting an Essay **Grammar,** 399I Adverbs Practice **T** **Daily Language Practice** 3. The soft rain wont pound heavy the roof. (won't; heavily; on) 4. Wuzent it strange that Ramona stared sullen out the window. (Wasn't; sullenly; window?) **Listening/Speaking/Viewing,** 393, 394 Wrapping Up, Responding

Leveled Readers
- Fluency Practice
- Independent Reading

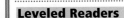

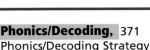

Target Skills of the Week

Comprehension	Summarize; Making Generalizations
Vocabulary	The Spelling Table in a Dictionary
Phonics/Decoding	Contractions
Fluency	Leveled Readers

DAY 3

Rereading the Selection
Rereading for Writer's Craft, 387
Imagery

Comprehension Skill, 399A–399B
Making Generalizations T

Leveled Readers
The Dive
First Day for Carlos
Real Team Soccer
Christy's First Dive

Lessons and Leveled Practice, 399O–399R

Phonics Review, 399D
Soft *c* and Soft *g*

Vocabulary, 399G
The Spelling Table in a Dictionary T

Spelling, 399F
Vocabulary: Multiple Meanings; Contractions
Practice T

Writing, 399L
Revising an Essay
Using Exact Adverbs T

Grammar, 399J
Adverb Game T

Daily Language Practice
5. Woodent you know that Mr. Quimby sudden made a decision. (Wouldn't; suddenly; decision?)
6. Ide say that he certain changed the dismal day. (I'd; certainly)

DAY 4

Reading the Drama Link,
396–399
"Henry and Ramona"

Skill: How to Read a Play

Rereading for Genre, 398
Play

Comprehension Skill Review, 383
Making Judgments

Leveled Readers
The Dive
First Day for Carlos
Real Team Soccer
Christy's First Dive

Lessons and Leveled Practice, 399O–399R

Phonics/Decoding, 396–399
Apply Phonics/Decoding Strategy to Link

Vocabulary, 399M
Language Center: Building Vocabulary

Spelling, 399F
Contractions Game, Proofreading T

Writing, 399L
Proofreading an Essay

Grammar, 399J
Adverbs Practice T

Daily Language Practice
7. Beezus shoodent have sobbed so loud.
(shouldn't; loudly)
8. Coodent you say that her mothers decision was complete unfair? (Couldn't; mother's; completely)

Listening/Speaking/Viewing, 399
Discuss the Link

DAY 5

Rereading for Fluency,
379

Responding Activities, 394–395
Write a Thank-You Note
Cross-Curricular Activities

Information and Study Skills, 399H
Real-Life Reading (menus, signs, etc.)

Comprehension Skill Review, 391
Drawing Conclusions

Leveled Readers
The Dive
First Day for Carlos
Real Team Soccer
Christy's First Dive

Lessons and Leveled Practice, 399O–399R

Structural Analysis, 399N
Language Center: Contraction Poster

Vocabulary, 399M
Language Center: Vocabulary Game

Spelling, 399F
Test: Contractions T

Writing, 399L
Publishing an Essay

Grammar, 399J, 399M
Expanding Sentences
Language Center: Adverb Game

Daily Language Practice
9. Im certain that the ceaseless rain near ruined Ramona's day. (I'm; nearly)
10. Wernt they saying that the stranger's gift real cheered everyone? (Weren't; really)

Listening/Speaking/Viewing, 399N
Language Center: Dramatize a Story

Managing Flexible Groups

Leveled Instruction and Leveled Practice

	DAY 1	**DAY 2**
WHOLE CLASS	• Teacher Read Aloud (TE pp. 367CC–367DD) • Building Background, Introducing Vocabulary (TE pp. 368–369) • Comprehension Strategy: Introduce (TE p. 370) • Comprehension Skill: Introduce (TE p. 370) • Purpose Setting (TE p. 371) **After reading first half of _Ramona Quimby, Age 8_** • Stop and Think (TE p. 381)	**After reading _Ramona Quimby, Age 8_** • Wrapping Up (TE p. 393) • Comprehension Check (Practice Book p. 204) • Responding: Think About the Selection (TE p. 394) • Comprehension Skill: Preview (TE p. 385)
SMALL GROUPS **Extra Support**	**TEACHER-LED** • Preview _Ramona Quimby, Age 8_ to Stop and Think (TE pp. 370–381). • Support reading with Extra Support/Intervention notes (TE pp. 371, 274, 377, 380, 385, 392).	**Partner or Individual Work** • Reread first half of _Ramona Quimby, Age 8_ (TE pp. 370–381). • Preview, read second half (TE pp. 382–393). • Comprehension Check (Practice Book p. 204)
Challenge	**Individual Work** • Begin "Another Sunday" (Challenge Handbook p. 50). • Extend reading with Challenge notes (TE pp. 379, 392).	**Individual Work** • Continue work on activity (Challenge Handbook p. 50).
English Language Learners	**TEACHER-LED** • Preview vocabulary and _Ramona Quimby, Age 8_ to Stop and Think (TE pp. 369–381). • Support reading with English Language Learners notes (TE pp. 368, 372, 375, 376, 380, 383, 386, 389, 390, 391).	**TEACHER-LED** • Review first half of _Ramona Quimby, Age 8_ (TE pp. 370–381). ✔ • Preview, read second half (TE pp. 382–393). • Begin Comprehension Check together (Practice Book p. 204).

Independent Activities

- Get Set for Reading CD-ROM
- Journals: selection notes, questions
- Complete, review Practice Book (pp. 202–206) and Leveled Readers Practice Blackline Masters (TE pp. 399O–399R).
- Assignment Cards (Teacher's Resource Blackline Masters pp. 89–90)
- Leveled Readers (TE pp. 399O–399R), Leveled Theme Paperbacks (TE pp. R2–R7), or book from Leveled Bibliography (TE pp. 296E–296F).

✔ Opportunity to informally assess oral reading rate

DAY **3**	DAY **4**	DAY **5**
• Rereading: Lessons on Writer's Craft (TE pp. 387) • Comprehension Skill: Main lesson (TE pp. 399A–399B)	• Reading the Drama Link (TE pp. 396–399): Skill lesson (TE p. 396) • Rereading the Link: Genre Lesson (TE p. 398) • Comprehension Skill: First Comprehension Review lesson (TE p. 383)	• Responding: Select from Activities (TE pp. 394–395) • Information and Study Skills (TE p. 399H) • Comprehension Skill: Second Comprehension Review lesson (TE p. 391)
TEACHER-LED • Reread, review Comprehension Check (Practice Book p. 204). • Preview Leveled Reader: Below Level (TE p. 399O), or read book from Leveled Bibliography (TE pp. 296E–296F). ✔	**Partner or Individual Work** • Reread the Drama Link (TE pp. 396–399). • Complete Leveled Reader: Below Level (TE p. 399O), or read book from Leveled Bibliography (TE pp. 296E–296F).	**TEACHER-LED** • Comprehension Skill: Reteaching lesson (TE p. R12) • Reread Leveled Theme Paperback: Below Level (TE pp. R2–R3), or read book from Leveled Bibliography (TE pp. 296E–296F). ✔
TEACHER-LED • Teacher check-in: Assess progress (Challenge Handbook p. 50). • Preview Leveled Reader: Above Level (TE p. 399Q), or read book from Leveled Bibliography (TE pp. 296E–296F). ✔	**Individual Work** • Complete activity (Challenge Handbook p. 50). • Complete Leveled Reader: Above Level (TE p. 399Q), or read book from Leveled Bibliography (TE pp. 296E–296F).	**TEACHER-LED** • Evaluate activity and plan format for sharing (Challenge Handbook p. 50). • Reread Leveled Theme Paperback: Above Level (TE pp. R6–R7), or read book from Leveled Bibliography (TE pp. 296E–296F). ✔
Partner or Individual Work • Complete Comprehension Check (Practice Book p. 204). • Begin Leveled Reader: Language Support (TE p. 399R), or read book from Leveled Bibliography (TE pp. 296E–296F).	**TEACHER-LED** • Reread the Drama Link (TE pp. 396–399) ✔ and review Link Skill (TE p. 396). • Complete Leveled Reader: Language Support (TE p. 399R), or read book from Leveled Bibliography (TE pp. 296E–296F). ✔	**Partner or Individual Work** • Reread book from Leveled Bibliography (TE pp. 296E–296F).

- Responding activities (TE pp. 394–395)
- Language Center activities (TE pp. 399M–399N)
- **Fluency Practice:** Reread *Pepita Talks Twice; Poppa's New Pants; Ramona Quimby, Age 8* ✔
- Activities relating to *Ramona Quimby, Age 8* at Education Place www.eduplace.com

Turn the page for more independent activities.

Ramona Quimby, Age 8

FLEXIBLE GROUPS

Managing Flexible Groups 367Z

Classroom Management

Independent Activities

Assign these activities while you work with small groups.

Differentiated Instruction for Small Groups

- **Handbook for English Language Learners,** pp. 218–227

- **Extra Support Handbook,** pp. 214–223

Independent Activities

- Language Center, pp. 399M–399N

- Challenge/Extension Activities, Theme Resources, pp. R13, R19

- **Classroom Management Handbook,** Activity Masters CM6-9–CM6-12

- **Challenge Handbook,** pp. 50–51

Look for more activities in the Classroom Management Kit.

Science

Cats

👤 Singles	🕐 30 minutes
Objective	Research and write about cats.
Materials	Research sources, markers

In *Ramona Quimby, Age 8,* Picky-picky can't make up his mind. Should he go out or stay in? He's a typical cat. What do you know about cats? Do research and write a paragraph about cats. Think about the following topics, or come up with your own:

- types of cats
- what cats need
- cat behavior

Draw a picture and write a caption for it to help readers understand more about cats.

All cats scratch. It helps them sharpen their claws.

Writing

What If . . .

👤 Singles	🕐 30 minutes
Objective	Write a new ending for a scene.

When the old man salutes Ramona in the restaurant and asks her a question, she is stunned. Then their hostess calls the Quimbys to their table, and Ramona is saved from having to answer him. What if the hostess hadn't seated them right away? Write a new ending for this scene. Think about these questions:

- What do you think Ramona would have done or said?
- How do you think the man would have responded?

Be sure to include dialogue in your story.

Consider copying and laminating these activities for use in centers.

Career

All About Ms. Cleary

👤 Singles	🕐 30 minutes
Objective	Find out about Beverly Cleary and write her a letter.
Materials	A computer with Internet access

Beverly Cleary has written many books for children. Learn more about her. The Education Place website at http://www.eduplace.com/kids/hmr/3/6 is a good place to start.

Think about what it would be like to be a children's author. Write a letter to Ms. Cleary to find out more about this career. Consider asking things such as

- where she gets her ideas
- how she knows what children want to read about
- how long it takes to write a book

In your letter, remember to be polite and to mention books of Ms. Cleary's that you have read and liked.

Dear Ms. Cleary,

    I like all your books, but my favorite is Henry and Ribsy. I think I could be a writer some day. What I would like to know

Art

Picture a Mood

👤 Singles	🕐 45 minutes
Objective	Create drawings of three different moods.
Materials	Anthology, drawing materials

The *mood* of a story is the general feeling you get from reading it. To create a mood, authors use words, details, and descriptive language.

In *Ramona Quimby, Age 8,* the mood changes as you read. Create three drawings that show the mood at three different points in the story.

- Use your imagination as you draw.
- Think about how different colors express different feelings.
- Your drawings do not have to have recognizable shapes or forms.

Write a caption for each drawing to name the mood and the part of the story it illustrates.

Language Arts

What to Do on a Rainy Sunday

👥 Pairs	🕐 30 minutes
Objective	Make a list of activities to do on a rainy Sunday.
Materials	Anthology

In the story, Ramona decides she cannot live through another rainy Sunday. Help her make a plan to survive the next rainy day.

List specific things she can do and places she can go. Remember that the Quimbys don't have much money. Look again at page 374 to see some of Ramona's ideas. Now think about

- fun things she can do inside
- places she can go on rainy days
- people she can call or visit

Get together with a partner and compare your lists. Choose the four best ideas and draw them in the sections of a piece of drawing paper you have folded into fourths. Write a caption for each picture.

Visit a museum.

Listening Comprehension

Building Background

Tell students that you are going to read aloud a folktale about a boastful cat and a fast-thinking crab.

• Ask students if it is more important to be fast or to be smart when running a race. Have students share stories in which the fastest runner does not win.

Fluency Modeling

Explain that as you read aloud, you will be modeling fluent oral reading. Ask students to listen carefully to your phrasing and your expression, or tone of voice and emphasis.

COMPREHENSION SKILL

Making Generalizations

Explain that a generalization is a statement that

• is true most of the time

• is based on facts

• may include words such as *usually*, *most*, *often*, *many*, or *few*

Purpose Setting Read the folktale aloud, asking students to note details they might use to state a generalization as they listen. Then use the Guiding Comprehension questions to assess students' understanding. Reread the folktale as needed.

Teacher Read Aloud

The Fastest Cat on Earth
by Alvin Schwartz

The cat we are about to meet is the fastest cat on earth. He is a regular whirlwind. He is so fast he can outrun anyone or anything. At least that is what he says.

The fastest cat on earth was lying in a meadow, half dozing in the hot sun. He was waiting for a mouse or a young rabbit to go by, or even a butterfly—anything he could chase and catch and eat. But nothing stirred. It was very boring.

❶ Then he saw a crab scurrying toward the beach in that weird way in which crabs move, its ten skinny legs all going like crazy.

"I *hate* crabmeat," the cat thought. "But maybe that crab and I could have a race. I would win, of course, but at least it would be something to do.

"Hey, crab," he called. "Do you want to race? It would be fun."

❷ "It would be fun for you," the crab said in its tiny voice. "You're faster than me." It paused. "Of course, I'm smarter than you. Okay. I'll do it."

"We'll race down the path to that tree," the cat said. "On your mark, get set—go!"

When the fastest cat on earth leaped forward, the crab grabbed the cat's tail and hung on tight. He weighed so little, the cat didn't even know he was there. The cat tore down the path as quickly as he could, with the crab dangling behind him.

Just before the cat reached the tree, he stopped, turned around, and looked back. The crab was nowhere in sight. But while the cat was peering back down the path, the crab quietly dropped to the ground and scurried across the finish line.

"I knew I would beat him," the cat thought. "But not this easily. Of course, I *am* the fastest cat on earth. Yet he does have *ten* legs." Then he heard a tiny voice.

3 "Hey, cat," the voice called. "I win!"

When the cat saw the crab, he could not believe his eyes. "You win?" he said. "When did you pass me? I didn't see you anywhere."

"You didn't?" said the crab. "Why, I was right behind you the whole way."

Guiding Comprehension

1 **MAKING GENERALIZATIONS** What generalizations can be made about cats based on the details you've heard? (Most cats are fast; most cats like to chase things.)

2 **MAKING GENERALIZATIONS** What could you say about crabs or cats in general, based on the details you've heard? (Most crabs move in a weird way; crabs usually have ten legs; most crabs don't weigh a lot; most cats have a tail; few cats actually eat crabs.)

3 **MAKING GENERALIZATIONS** What can you say in general about folktales, based on this tale and others you know? (Sample answers: Many folktales have a tricky ending; many folktales have animal characters; boastful folktale characters often get tricked; in folktales, small animals often outwit larger ones.)

Discussion Options

Personal Response Ask students to tell which character they liked better and why.

⭐ **Connecting/Comparing** Ask students to discuss why they think this story belongs in the theme *Smart Solutions*.

 English Language Learners

Language Development

Write the base words *fast* and *smart* on the board, and show how to build new words using *-er* and *-est* as endings. Reread the cat's conversation with the crab, and explain that the *-er* ending is used when comparing two things. Tell students that the *-est* ending is used when comparing three or more things. Invite students to use forms of these words in sentences of their own.

READ ALOUD

Ramona Quimby, Age 8

Building Background

Key Concept: Rainy-Day Moods

Remind students that this theme introduces characters who find unique ways to solve their problems. Now they will read a chapter from *Ramona Quimby, Age 8,* in which the Quimbys deal with rainy-day feelings.

Ask students what they usually do on a rainy weekend day. Do they play with brothers and sisters? friends? Then use "Rain, Rain, Go Away!" on pages 368–369 to discuss fun things to do on a rainy day.

- Have a student read aloud "Rain, Rain, Go Away!"
- Have students take turns reading the captions and commenting on the photos.

Background and Vocabulary

Ramona Quimby, Age 8

Read to find the meanings of these words.

e • Glossary

ceaseless
companionable
discouraged
dismal
dreary
exhausted
pelting
sullenly

368

Rain, Rain, Go Away!

What can you do on a rainy day, when everything outside looks gray and **dreary**? Inside, you can hear the **ceaseless** sound of raindrops **pelting** against the window. Such **dismal** weather can make you feel bored and even sad. Wandering **sullenly** around the house makes you feel **exhausted** and crabby. If you want company but no one else is feeling **companionable**, finding someone to play with or talk to can be hard.

Don't get **discouraged**. Rainy days don't have to be bad days. In the next story, you'll learn what happens when one family spends a cold and rainy Sunday afternoon indoors.

Here are some things you can do for fun on a rainy day.

◀ Bake some goodies.

REACHING ALL LEARNERS

English Language Learners

Supporting Comprehension

Beginning/Preproduction Have students listen to the article. Ask them to draw a picture of the outdoors on a rainy day. Help students label their pictures with the Key Vocabulary words *dreary, dismal, ceaseless,* and *pelting.*

Early Production and Speech Emergence Have students repeat these Key Vocabulary words after you: *companionable, discouraged, exhausted.* Explain that *sullenly* describes how you might act if you feel angry and resentful about something. Then have students act out each word for partners to guess.

Intermediate and Advanced Fluency Ask students to describe each photograph in their own words and then tell why these are good rainy-day activities.

▶ Build a tent and go camping *inside* your house.

◀ Do an art project you've always wanted to try.

▶ Play a favorite game or learn a new one.

◀ Read a book!

369

Introducing Vocabulary

Key Vocabulary

These words support the Key Concept and appear in the selection.

ceaseless not stopping; constant

companionable friendly

discouraged having little hope or enthusiasm

dismal gloomy; miserable

dreary gloomy; bleak; dull

exhausted very tired

pelting beating against again and again

sullenly in a bad-humored way; not happily; gloomily

e • Glossary
e • WordGame

See Vocabulary notes on pages 372, 374, 376, 378, 380, 382, 384, 386, 388, 390, and 392 for additional words to preview.

Display Transparency 6–19.

- Model how to figure out that *ceaseless* and the other words in the first line of the box mean roughly the same thing.

- Have students figure out the meaning of each of the remaining underlined words, following your example.

- Then have a different student read each question aloud and answer with the appropriate Key Vocabulary word or words.

- Ask students to look for these words as they read and to use them as they discuss rainy days.

Practice/Homework Assign **Practice Book** page 202.

Transparency 6–19

Rainy Day Words

SMART SOLUTIONS *Ramona Quimby, Age 8*
Key Vocabulary

ANNOTATED VERSION

ceaseless, unending, nonstop
friendly, companionable, chummy, social
discouraged, without hope, loss of heart
dismal, gloomy, cheerless, dreary, joyless
exhausted, tired, weary, drained, worn-out
beating, drumming, pelting, pouring
angrily, sullenly, sourly, unhappily

1. Which word describes how you might feel if you kept trying to hit the baseball and missed?
   discouraged

2. Which word describes a heavy rain? _pelting_

3. Which word might describe a thunderstorm that seems to go on forever? _ceaseless_

4. Which word might tell how you'd feel after carrying a heavy bag of books on a long hike?
   exhausted

5. Which two words might describe a gray, cloudy day when you are feeling sad and bored? _dismal, dreary_

6. Which word might describe how you would speak and act if you felt cranky about the weather?
   sullenly

7. Which word might describe how you'd feel if you and your friends are sitting around a warm fire?
   companionable

TRANSPARENCY 6–19
TEACHER'S EDITION PAGE 369

Practice Book page 202

Ramona Quimby, Age 8
Key Vocabulary

Name _____

A Rainy-Day Survey!

Write sentences to answer the following questions.

Answers will vary. Sample answers are provided.

1. Do you think rainy days are **dismal** and **dreary**? Why or why not?
   Yes, because I like to play outside, but not when it rains. **(2 points)**

2. On days when the rain is **ceaseless**, what do you do?
   I stay inside and read. **(2)**

3. Do you like the sound of rain **pelting** against your window?
   Yes, because it helps me fall asleep. **(2)**

4. What do you do when you feel **companionable**?
   I play with my friends. **(2)**

5. What advice would you give to a friend who feels **discouraged**?
   I would tell her to cheer up! **(2)**

6. What activity makes you feel **exhausted**?
   I feel exhausted after I play a game of soccer. **(2)**

TARGET SKILL
COMPREHENSION STRATEGY
Summarize

Teacher Modeling Ask a student to read the Strategy Focus aloud. Explain that summarizing what has happened so far is a good way to make sure you understand the story. Ask students to read page 372. Then model the strategy.

Think Aloud *One rainy Sunday afternoon in November, Ramona stands by the window thinking about how her family's mood matches the dismal day outside. She longs for sunshine and a happier family. Then her mother reminds her to clean her room and tells her not to smudge the window.*

✔ **Test Prep** Students can use the Summarize strategy as they read a test passage by stopping periodically to retell key facts or events in their own words. Encourage them to pay attention to the order of facts or events.

TARGET SKILL
COMPREHENSION SKILL
Making Generalizations

Introduce the Graphic Organizer. Tell students that using a Generalizations Chart to collect details will help them make accurate generalizations, or broad statements that are true most of the time. Explain that as they read, students will fill out the Generalizations Chart found on **Practice Book** page 203.

- Display **Transparency 6–20.** Have students turn to Anthology page 372.
- Model how to write the details about the rainy day in the first box.

THEME 6: Smart Solutions

MEET THE AUTHOR
Beverly Cleary

One rainy Sunday afternoon, when Beverly Cleary was in third grade, she was feeling bored. She decided to try to read a book. Cleary had never really enjoyed reading before, but this book was so exciting that she couldn't put it down! She read two whole books before bedtime. On that rainy day, Cleary realized that "grown-ups were right after all. Reading was fun!"

Other books: *Ramona's World, Beezus and Ramona, Ramona the Pest, The Mouse and the Motorcycle, Henry and Ribsy*

MEET THE ILLUSTRATOR
Alan Tiegreen

Alan Tiegreen has illustrated almost all of Beverly Cleary's books about Ramona Quimby. By now, he feels like the Quimbys are real friends of his. Sitting down to draw them is like inviting them over for a visit. As he starts to draw, he says, "Hey Ramona! Hey Beezus! Good to see you again!"

Internet

Discover more about Beverly Cleary and Alan Tiegreen at Education Place. **www.eduplace.com/kids**

370

Transparency 6–20
Generalizations Chart
Answers will vary. Examples are given.

Rainy Days	Older Sisters
unending rain pelting down family members cross and grouchy cleaning her room a boring chore for Ramona	Beezus mysteriously moody doesn't have to clean her room when Ramona does stalks around the house not speaking to anyone

Parents	Restaurants
mother and father nag Ramona to clean room mother's tone of voice hurts Ramona's feelings father jokes about price of fuel oil father decides to treat family to dinner at Whopperburger	wait to be seated order from menu served by waitress leave tip

In general, what statement can you make about people's feelings on rainy days?
Example: A rainy day often makes people feel grumpy.

SMART SOLUTIONS Ramona Quimby, Age 8
Graphic Organizer Generalizations Chart
ANNOTATED VERSION

TRANSPARENCY 6–20
TEACHER'S EDITION PAGES 370 AND 399A

Practice Book page 203

Ramona Quimby, Age 8
Graphic Organizer
Generalizations Chart

Name _____

Generalizations Chart
Answers will vary. Examples are given.

Rainy Days	Older Sisters
unending rain pelting down (1 point) family members are cross and grouchy (1) cleaning her room is a boring chore for Ramona (1)	Beezus mysteriously moody (1) doesn't have to clean her room when Ramona does (1) stalks around the house not speaking to anyone (1)

Parents	Restaurants
mother and father nag Ramona to clean her room (1) mother's tone of voice hurts Ramona's feelings (1) father jokes about price of fuel oil (1) father decides to treat family to dinner at Whopperburger (1)	wait to be seated (1) order from menu (1) served by waitress (1) leave tip (1)

In general, what statement can you make about people's feelings on rainy days?

Example: A rainy day often makes people feel grumpy. (1)

Selection 3

BEVERLY CLEARY

Ramona Quimby, Age 8

ILLUSTRATED BY ALAN TIEGREEN

Strategy Focus

As you read, **summarize** how Ramona feels at the beginning of the rainy Sunday and how her feelings change during the day.

371

Extra Support/Intervention

Selection Preview

pages 372–377 It's a dreary, rainy Sunday and everyone in the Quimby house is in a bad mood. Ramona doesn't want to clean her room. Mrs. Quimby refuses to let Beezus go on a sleepover, causing Beezus to retreat to her room, sobbing. How do you think this makes Mrs. Quimby feel?

pages 378–381 Mr. Quimby is trying to study for a class he's taking. How do you think he feels about being interrupted by Ramona? How can the Quimby family improve their bad moods?

pages 382–385 Mr. Quimby suggests they all go out to dinner. At the Whopperburger, an old man asks Ramona if she's been good to her mother. How do you think Ramona will react to this teasing?

pages 386–393 During dinner, everyone's mood improves. The old man pays for the Quimbys' dinner because he thinks they're a nice family. They are all much happier on the way home. Do you agree that the Quimbys are a nice family?

Purpose Setting

- Remind students that this selection tells about a rainy Sunday.

- Have students preview the selection by looking at the illustrations. Ask students to predict how Ramona will spend the day and how her feelings might change.

- Remind students to pause regularly and summarize story facts and details as they read.

- Ask students to think about the generalizations they can make.

- You may want to preview the Responding questions on Anthology page 394 with students.

Journal ▸ Students can record their predictions and summaries. They can also write down ideas about generalizations they might make.

STRATEGY REVIEW

Phonics/Decoding

Remind students to use the Phonics/Decoding Strategy as they read.

Modeling Write this sentence from *Ramona Quimby, Age 8: The old man <u>saluted</u> Ramona as if she were a soldier.* Point to *saluted*.

Think Aloud *I see the VCV spelling pattern a-l-u and an -ed ending. First, I'll try breaking the word after the letter a and pronouncing the a with a long vowel sound—say-luht-ehd. That doesn't sound right. I'll try breaking the word after the letter l—sal-uht-ehd. I know, the word is suh-LOOT-ehd. That makes sense here.*

CRITICAL THINKING
Guiding Comprehension

❶ COMPARE AND CONTRAST How does the mood inside the Quimby house match the weather outside when the story begins? (Outside it's dismal and dreary; inside, everyone feels tired and discouraged. It seems as if the family's mood—like the day itself—will never brighten.)

❷ WRITER'S CRAFT How does the author make ordinary household objects and even the cat contribute to the dismal mood? (The leftovers are *dreary*; the cat is *cross*; Mr. Quimby's pencil scratches *angrily*; the television is *blank and mute*; a log *sullenly* refuses to burn.)

Rainy Sunday

Rainy Sunday afternoons in November were always dismal, but Ramona felt this Sunday was the most dismal of all. She pressed her nose against the living-room window, watching the ceaseless rain pelting down as bare black branches clawed at the electric wires in front of the house. Even lunch, leftovers Mrs. Quimby had wanted to clear out of the refrigerator, had been dreary, with her parents, who seemed tired or discouraged or both, having little to say and Beezus mysteriously moody. Ramona longed for sunshine, sidewalks dry enough for roller-skating, a smiling, happy family.

"Ramona, you haven't cleaned up your room this weekend," said Mrs. Quimby, who was sitting on the couch, sorting through a stack of bills. "And don't press your nose against the window. It leaves a smudge."

372

Vocabulary

dismal gloomy; miserable

ceaseless not stopping; constant

pelting beating against again and again

dreary gloomy; dull

discouraged having little hope or enthusiasm

cross in a bad mood; grumpy

stalked walked in a stiff or angry manner

mute silent

sullenly in a bad-humored way

English Language Learners

Supporting Comprehension

Read aloud the subtitle on page 372. Ask, How do you feel when it rains? Do you feel happy or sad? What things do you like to do when it rains?

Ramona felt as if everything she did was wrong. The whole family seemed cross today, even Picky-picky who meowed at the front door. With a sigh, Mrs. Quimby got up to let him out. Beezus, carrying a towel and shampoo, stalked through the living room into the kitchen, where she began to wash her hair at the sink. Mr. Quimby, studying at the dining-room table as usual, made his pencil scratch angrily across a pad of paper. The television set sat blank and mute, and in the fireplace a log sullenly refused to burn.

373

ASSIGNMENT CARD 7

Sunny Sunday

Changing the Mood

Think about how this opening scene might be different if the chapter were called "Sunny Sunday" instead. What would the Quimbys and Picky-picky be doing on a sunny day? How might Ramona feel? How would household objects be different? Use your ideas to rewrite the opening scene.

Theme 6: Smart Solutions

Teacher's Resource BLM page 89

CRITICAL THINKING
Guiding Comprehension

3 **DRAWING CONCLUSIONS** Why do you think Ramona tells her mother that Beezus hasn't cleaned her room? (She wants to get Beezus in trouble; if she has to clean her room, she thinks Beezus should do the same.)

4 **COMPARE AND CONTRAST** Compare the things Ramona wishes she could do on this rainy day with the things she has to do. (She wishes she could do interesting, active, exciting things, but she must do boring, ordinary things.)

5 **WRITER'S CRAFT** How does the author make Ramona seem like a real-life girl? (Ramona has a good imagination; she doesn't like to clean her room; her feelings are hurt when she is yelled at.)

Mrs. Quimby sat down and then got up again as Picky-picky, indignant at the wet world outdoors, yowled to come in. "Ramona, clean up your room," she ordered, as she let the cat and a gust of cold air into the house.

3 "Beezus hasn't cleaned up her room." Ramona could not resist pointing this omission out to her mother.

"I'm not talking about Beezus," said Mrs. Quimby. "I'm talking about you."

Still Ramona did not move from the window. Cleaning up her room seemed such a boring thing to do, no fun at all on a rainy afternoon. She thought vaguely of all the exciting things

4 she would like to do — learn to twirl a lariat, play a musical saw,

374

Vocabulary

indignant angry because something is unfair

omission something left out

vaguely not clearly

lariat a rope that cowboys use

sulkily in an angry but silent way

  Extra Support/Intervention

Strategy Modeling: Summarize

Use this example to model the strategy.

When I summarize the story up to this point, I try not to mention every little thing —just the most important events or details. It's a rainy, dreary day. Everyone in the Quimby house is in a bad mood. Ramona and her mother argue when she doesn't want to clean her room.

flip around and over bars in a gymnastic competition while crowds cheered.

"Ramona, *clean up your room*!" Mrs. Quimby raised her voice.

"Well, you don't have to yell at me." Ramona's feelings were hurt by the tone of her mother's voice. The log in the fireplace settled, sending a puff of smoke into the living room.

"Then do it," snapped Mrs. Quimby. "Your room is a disaster area."

Mr. Quimby threw down his pencil. "Young lady, you do what your mother says, and you do it now. She shouldn't have to tell you three times."

"Well, all right, but you don't have to be so cross," said Ramona. To herself she thought, Nag, nag, nag.

5

Sulkily Ramona took her hurt feelings off to her room, where she pulled a week's collection of dirty socks from under her bed. On her way to the bathroom hamper, she looked down the hall and saw her sister standing in the living room, rubbing her hair with a towel.

"Mother, I think you're mean," said Beezus from under the towel.

Ramona stopped to listen.

375

English Language Learners

Supporting Comprehension

Pause after reading page 374 and ask students what each character is doing and why these things may be unpleasant. (Ramona isn't doing anything and she's bored. Her mother is sorting bills, which can be stressful if the family doesn't have much money. Mr. Quimby is studying, which is difficult when there are other people around.)

CRITICAL THINKING
Guiding Comprehension

6 **MAKING INFERENCES** Why is Ramona so interested in the discussion between Beezus and her parents? (She's a curious girl; she wonders how the outcome of the argument will affect her.)

7 **NOTING DETAILS** How does the author show that both Mr. and Mrs. Quimby are in a bad mood? (Mr. Quimby slams his pencil down; Mrs. Quimby pushes Picky-picky out the door, and she doesn't laugh when Mr. Quimby jokes that they can't afford to let the cat out.)

COMPREHENSION STRATEGY
Summarize

Teacher/Student Modeling Ask students to briefly tell the main points of the story and note Ramona's feelings after each event to see how they change. (Sample answer: On this rainy Sunday, Ramona is really bored and wishes she had something fun to do. Then she overhears an argument between her sister and her parents, and she suddenly becomes very curious. She's not so bored anymore.)

Vocabulary

protested	complained
flounced	walked in an angry way
vexed	bothered by
exhausted	very tired

"I don't care how mean you think I am," answered Mrs. Quimby. "You are not going to go, and that is that."

"But all the other girls are going," protested Beezus.

"I don't care if they are," said Mrs. Quimby. "You are not."

Ramona heard the sound of a pencil being slammed on the table and her father saying, "Your mother is right. Now would you kindly give me a little peace and quiet so I can get on with my work."

Beezus flounced past Ramona into her room and slammed the door. Sobs were heard, loud, angry sobs.

Where can't she go? Ramona wondered, as she dumped her socks into the hamper. Then, because she had been so good about picking up her room, Ramona returned to the living room, where Picky-picky, as cross and bored as the rest of the family, was once again meowing at the front door. "Where can't Beezus go?" she asked.

376

English Language Learners

Supporting Comprehension

Students may be unfamiliar with the family dynamics presented on page 377. To help students understand this situation, ask: What does Beezus want to do? Why does Ramona decide to defend her this time? Why doesn't Mrs. Quimby allow Beezus to go? How does Beezus react?

Mrs. Quimby opened the front door, and when Picky-picky hesitated, vexed by the cold wind that swept into the room, assisted him out with her toe. "She can't sleep over at Mary Jane's house with a bunch of girls from her class."

A year ago Ramona would have agreed with her mother so that her mother would love her more than Beezus, but this year she knew that she too might want to spend the night at someone's house someday. "Why can't Beezus sleep at Mary Jane's?" she asked.

"Because she comes home exhausted and grouchy." Mrs. Quimby stood by the door, waiting. Picky-picky's yowl was twisted by the wind, and when she opened the door, another cold gust swept through the house.

"With the price of fuel oil being what it is, we can't afford to let the cat out," remarked Mr. Quimby.

"Would you like to take the responsibility if I don't let him out?" asked Mrs. Quimby, before she continued with her answer to Ramona. "There are four people in the family, and she has no right to make the whole day disagreeable for the rest of us because she has been up half the night giggling with a bunch of silly girls. Besides, a growing girl needs her rest."

7

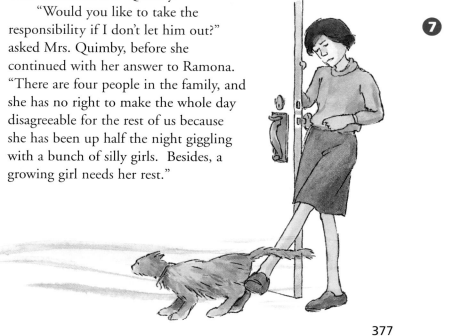

377

Extra Support/Intervention

Strategy Modeling: Phonics/Decoding

Use this example to model the strategy for *disagreeable.*

I recognize the prefix dis- *and the shorter words* agree *and* able. *When I put it all together, I say* dihs-uh-gree-ay-buhl. *I've got it. It's* dihs-uh-GREE-uh-buhl. *I know that the prefix* dis- *means "not." Someone who does not agree is probably grouchy. That sure makes sense here!*

CRITICAL THINKING
Guiding Comprehension

❽ DRAWING CONCLUSIONS What does Ramona mean when she says *the sort of books people who [do] not know anything about children so often [give] them*? (Ramona's probably talking about books that adults think are interesting but that children find boring.) **Do you think the books Beverly Cleary writes are like this?** (Answers will vary.)

❾ MAKING INFERENCES Why does Ramona feel *sorry for herself, misunderstood and unappreciated*? (Going to the Kemps' house after school and playing with Willa Jean isn't easy; her mother doesn't seem to understand her situation.) **Do you understand how she feels?** (Answers will vary.)

Ramona silently agreed with her mother about Beezus' coming home cross after such a party. At the same time, she wanted to make things easier for herself when she was in junior high school. "Maybe this time they would go to sleep earlier," she suggested.

"Fat chance," said Mrs. Quimby, who rarely spoke so rudely. "And furthermore, Ramona, Mrs. Kemp did not come right out and say so, but she did drop a hint that you are not playing as nicely with Willa Jean as you might."

Ramona heaved a sigh that seemed to come from the soles of her feet. In the bedroom, Beezus, who had run out of real sobs, was working hard to force out fake sobs to show her parents how mean they were to her.

Mrs. Quimby ignored the sighs and the sobs and continued. "Ramona, you know that getting along at the Kemps' is your job in this family. I've told you that before."

❽ How could Ramona explain to her mother that Willa Jean had finally caught on that Sustained Silent Reading was just plain reading a book? For a while, Willa Jean wanted Ramona to read aloud a few boring books the Kemps owned, the sort of books people who did not know anything about children so often gave them. Willa Jean listened to them several times, grew bored, and now insisted on playing beauty shop. Ramona did not want her fingernails painted by Willa Jean and knew she would be blamed if Willa Jean spilled nail polish. Instead of Mrs. Kemp's taking care of Ramona, Ramona was taking care of Willa Jean.

❾ Ramona looked at the carpet, sighed again, and said, "I try." She felt sorry for herself, misunderstood and unappreciated. Nobody in the whole world understood how hard it was to go to the Kemps' house after school when she did not have a bicycle.

378

Vocabulary

sustained continued

unappreciated not valued or thought to be important

relented softened in attitude

cognitive having to do with how the mind acquires knowledge

Fluency Practice

Rereading for Fluency Have students choose a favorite part of the story to reread orally in small groups, or suggest that they read from the fourth paragraph of page 378 to the end of the page. Encourage students to read expressively.

Mrs. Quimby relented. "I know it isn't easy," she said with a half smile, "but don't give up." She gathered up the bills and checkbook and went into the kitchen, where she began to write checks at the kitchen table.

Ramona wandered into the dining room to seek comfort from her father. She laid her cheek against the sleeve of his plaid shirt and asked, "Daddy, what are you studying?"

Once again Mr. Quimby threw down his pencil. "I am studying the cognitive processes of children," he answered.

Ramona raised her head to look at him. "What does that mean?" she asked.

"How kids think," her father told her.

379

Challenge

Word Study

Discuss with students the fact that Ramona feels sorry for herself. Have them write a short story about someone who feels this way and learns how to get over it. Students may write about themselves or make up a character.

> I'll never forget the day that I...

Ramona Quimby, Age 8

CRITICAL THINKING
Guiding Comprehension

10 **MAKING INFERENCES** Why doesn't Ramona like what her father is studying? (She believes that by studying how children think, he will be able to read her secret thoughts.)

11 **MAKING INFERENCES** Why do you think Beezus bothers to come out of her room if she isn't going to speak to anyone? (Maybe she wants everyone to see how angry she still is; or she wants to make everyone else as miserable as she is.)

---

10 Ramona did not like the sound of this subject at all. "Why are you studying *that*?" she demanded. Some things should be private, and how children thought was one of them. She did not like the idea of grown-ups snooping around in thick books trying to find out.

"That is exactly what I have been asking myself." Mr. Quimby was serious. "Why am I studying this stuff when we have bills to pay?"

"Well, I don't think you should," said Ramona. "It's none of your business how kids think." Then she quickly added, because she did not want her father to drop out of school and be a checker again, "There are lots of other things you could study. Things like fruit flies."

Mr. Quimby smiled at Ramona and rumpled her hair. "I doubt if anyone could figure out how you think," he said, which made Ramona feel better, as if her secret thoughts were still safe.

11 Mr. Quimby sat gnawing his pencil and staring out the window at the rain. Beezus, who had run out of fake sobs, emerged from her room, red-eyed and damp-haired, to stalk about the house not speaking to anyone.

380

Vocabulary

snooping looking in a sneaky way

checker someone who works the cash register at a store

rumpled messed up

emerged came out of

 Extra Support/ Intervention

Review (pages 372–381)
Before students join the whole class for Stop and Think on page 381, have them

- check predictions
- take turns modeling Summarize and other strategies they used
- add to **Transparency 6–20** with you
- check and revise their Generalizations Chart on **Practice Book** page 203 and use it to summarize

English Language Learners

Supporting Comprehension
After reading page 381, ask students to list Ramona's worries. (father being locked in a freezer, father not finishing school and not getting a job he likes) If students cannot list them all, reread sentences that give clues. Ask students if they think these are realistic worries.

Ramona flopped down on the couch. She hated rainy Sundays, especially this one, and longed for Monday when she could escape to school. The Quimbys' house seemed to have grown smaller during the day until it was no longer big enough to hold her family and all its problems. She tried not to think of the half-overheard conversations of her parents after the girls had gone to bed, grown-up talk that Ramona understood just enough to know her parents were concerned about their future.

Ramona had deep, secret worries of her own. She worried that her father might accidentally be locked in the frozen-food warehouse, where it was so cold it sometimes snowed indoors. What if he was filling a big order, and the men who were lucky enough to get small orders to fill left work ahead of him and forgot and locked the warehouse, and he couldn't get out and froze to death? Of course that wouldn't happen. "But it might," insisted a tiny voice in the back of her mind. Don't be silly, she told the little voice. "Yes, but —" began the little voice. And despite the worry that would not go away Ramona wanted her father to go on working so he could stay in school and someday get a job he liked.

381

ASSIGNMENT CARD 8

Literature Discussion

With some classmates, discuss these questions and any other questions or ideas you have.

- How does the author show that each member of the Quimby family is in a bad mood?

- If you could give Ramona any advice about how to cope with a rainy Sunday, what would you say?

- Do you think the author understands children? Why or why not?

- Do you think the members of the Quimby family have a good reason to be so crabby? Why or why not?

Theme 6: Smart Solutions

Teacher's Resource BLM page 90

Stop and Think

Critical Thinking Questions

1. **COMPARE AND CONTRAST** In what ways do the Quimbys seem like a real-life family? (Sample answer: They argue with one another; they have problems; they show how they feel.) In what ways are they different? (Ramona's feelings are hurt too easily; she worries a lot.)

2. **MAKING JUDGMENTS** Do you think the members of the Quimby family have good reasons to be crabby? Why or why not? (Sample answers: Yes; they're bored and tired of being inside. No; there are many ways to have fun on a rainy Sunday.)

Strategies in Action

Have students take turns modeling Summarize and other strategies they used.

Discussion Options

You may want to bring the entire class together to do one or more of the activities below.

- **Review Predictions/Purpose** Discuss which predictions were accurate and which needed to be revised. Record any changes and new predictions.

- **Share Group Discussions** Have students share their questions and literature discussions.

- **Summarize** Help students use their Generalizations Charts to summarize the story so far.

Monitoring Student Progress

If . . .	Then . . .
students have successfully completed the Extra Support activities on page 380,	have them read the rest of the selection cooperatively or independently.

Reading the Selection 381

CRITICAL THINKING
Guiding Comprehension

12 DRAWING CONCLUSIONS Why do you think Mr. Quimby decides to take everyone out to dinner? (to cheer everyone up)

13 NOTING DETAILS How does the author show that the Quimbys don't have much money to spare? (The girls wonder if they can afford to go out; Mrs. Quimby worries about the bills she is paying; Mr. Quimby will work extra hours to pay for the treat; the car is old.)

While Ramona worried, the house was silent except for the sound of rain and the scratch of her father's pencil. The smoking log settled in the fireplace, sending up a few feeble sparks. The day grew darker, Ramona was beginning to feel hungry, but there was no comfortable bustle of cooking in the kitchen.

Suddenly Mr. Quimby slammed shut his book and threw down his pencil so hard it bounced onto the floor. Ramona sat up. Now what was wrong?

12 "Come on, everybody," said her father. "Get cleaned up. Let's stop this grumping around. We are going out for dinner, and we are going to smile and be pleasant if it kills us. That's an order!"

382

Vocabulary

feeble weak

bustle busy activity

overtime payment for working extra hours

gourmet serving fancy and expensive food

transmission the system in a car by which power is carried from the engine to the wheels

balked stopped short and refused to go

The girls stared at their father and then at one another. What was going on? They had not gone out to dinner for months, so how could they afford to go now?

"To the Whopperburger?" asked Ramona.

"Sure," said Mr. Quimby, who appeared cheerful for the first time that day. "Why not? The sky's the limit."

Mrs. Quimby came into the living room with a handful of stamped envelopes. "But Bob —" she began.

"Now don't worry," her husband said. "We'll manage. During Thanksgiving I'll be putting in more hours in the warehouse and getting more overtime. There's no reason why we can't have a treat once in a while. And the Whopperburger isn't exactly your four-star gourmet restaurant."

Ramona was afraid her mother might give a lecture on the evils of junk food, but she did not. Gloom and anger were forgotten. Clothes were changed, hair combed, Picky-picky was shut in the basement, and the family was on its way in the old car with the new transmission that never balked at backing down the driveway. Off the Quimbys sped to the nearest Whopperburger, where they discovered other families must have wanted to get out of the house on a rainy day, for the restaurant was crowded, and they had to wait for a table.

13

383

English Language Learners

Supporting Comprehension

Pause at the end of page 383. Ask questions to help students see the shift in mood: What does Ramona's dad suggest? What do the other characters think about it? How do you think they feel? How can you tell?

Making Judgments

Teach

- Review the process of making judgments.
  - Ask yourself questions such as, Do I agree with this action? Is it fair? Is it right?
  - Consider facts from the story as well as personal beliefs and values as you think about each side of the issue.
  - Weigh both sides to arrive at the best judgment.

Practice/Apply

- Have students consider this question: Is it a good idea for the Quimbys to go to the Whopperburger? Begin a list of pros and cons on a chart. Ask students to suggest others.

- Have students discuss their opinions after carefully looking at both sides.

Yes	No
It's a change of pace.	It's expensive.
They can do it together.	Mr. Quimby has to study.
It's fun to eat out.	Wet roads are dangerous.

Review Skill Trace	
Teach	Theme 4, p. 99A
Reteach	Theme 4, p. R12
▶ Review	p. 383; Theme 1, p. 63; Theme 5, p. 171

CRITICAL THINKING

Guiding Comprehension

⑭ MAKING INFERENCES Why do you think Ramona gets so annoyed when the older gentleman asks if she has been good to her mother? (She feels guilty because earlier her mother had to tell her several times to clean her room.)

⑮ WRITER'S CRAFT In the restaurant, Mr. Quimby repeats what he said before they left home: *We are all going to smile and enjoy ourselves if it kills us.* Why do you think the author has him say this twice? (to show he is very determined that the family will get out of their grumpy moods)

Vocabulary

vending machine a machine you can buy small items from, such as candy

Muzak background music played in elevators, offices, malls

rummage a sale of used items, such as clothing

scowled made an angry face at; frowned

party [in this case] a group of people

upholstered covered with material, as a sofa is

seething in a state of turmoil

pry to snoop; to try to find out something

There were enough chairs for the grown-ups and Beezus, but Ramona, who had the youngest legs, had to stand up. She amused herself by punching the buttons on the vending machine in time to the Muzak, which was playing "Tie a Yellow Ribbon 'Round the Old Oak Tree." She even danced a little to the music, and, when the tune came to an end, she turned around and found herself face to face with an old man with neatly trimmed gray hair and a moustache that turned up at the ends. He was dressed as if everything he wore — a flowered shirt, striped tie, tweed coat and plaid slacks — had come from different stores or from a rummage sale, except that the crease in his trousers was sharp and his shoes were shined.

The old man, whose back was very straight, saluted Ramona as if she were a soldier and said, "Well, young lady, have you been good to your mother?"

Ramona was stunned. She felt her face turn red to the tips of her ears. She did not know how to answer such a question. Had she been good to her mother? Well . . . not always, but why was this stranger asking? It was none of his business. He had no right to ask such a question.

⑭

Ramona looked to her parents for help and discovered they were waiting with amusement for her answer. So were the rest of the people who were waiting for tables. Ramona scowled at the man. She did not have to answer him if she did not want to.

The hostess saved Ramona by calling out, "Quimby, party of four," and leading the family to a plastic-upholstered booth.

"Why didn't you answer the man?" Beezus was as amused as everyone else.

"I'm not supposed to talk to strangers," was Ramona's dignified answer.

"But Mother and Daddy are with us," Beezus pointed out, rather meanly, Ramona thought.

384

"Remember," said Mr. Quimby, as he opened his menu, "we are all going to smile and enjoy ourselves if it kills us."

As Ramona picked up her menu, she was still seething inside. Maybe she hadn't always been good to her mother, but that man had no right to pry. When she discovered he was seated in a single booth across the aisle, she gave him an indignant look, which he answered with a merry wink. So he had been teasing. Well, Ramona didn't like it.

15

385

Extra Support/Intervention

Strategy Modeling: Summarize

Use this example to model the strategy.

At this point in the story, Ramona and her family are in the restaurant, waiting to be seated. An older man with a mustache asks Ramona a question that embarrasses her—and she doesn't like it one bit.

Making Generalizations

Teach

- Remind students that a generalization is a statement that is based on fact and that is true most of the time.

- Explain that in a realistic fiction story, you are not dealing with facts, but you can still make generalizations based on story information and personal experience.

Practice/Apply

- Read aloud this detail from page 383: *Ramona was afraid her mother might give a lecture on the evils of junk food. . . .*

- Help students use this detail to make a generalization about Mrs. Quimby.

- Ask students to gather story details about what eating in a restaurant was like for the Quimbys.

- Have them use those details to make a generalization about eating in restaurants.

Details from Story
- wait to be seated
- listen to Muzak
- sit in booths
- order from menu
- are served by waitress
- leave tip

Target Skill Trace	
Preview; Teach	p. 367CC; p. 370; p. 385; p. 399A
Reteach	p. R12
Review	pp. 413D–413E; Theme 4, p. 29; Theme 5, p. 197

CRITICAL THINKING
Guiding Comprehension

16 **MAKING INFERENCES** What do you think Mrs. Quimby was about to say as Ramona was taking her first bite of hamburger? (She was probably going to tell Ramona to wipe her chin.) Why does Mrs. Quimby stop herself? (She doesn't want to ruin Ramona's happy mood by scolding her.)

17 **DRAWING CONCLUSIONS** Do you think the French fries really taste better than anything else Ramona has ever eaten? (They probably don't, but compared with the rest of the day, they are wonderful.)

386

English Language Learners

Language Development

Beverly Cleary uses many participles. Explain to students that sometimes action words can be used as adjectives. Give them some examples from page 387 *(colored, dreaded, understanding)* and then ask students to find others as they read.

Vocabulary

dreaded greatly feared

bliss complete happiness

tart sharp-tasting

dribbled dripped, trickled

386 **THEME 6: Smart Solutions**

When Ramona opened her menu, she made an exciting discovery. She no longer had to depend on colored pictures of hamburgers, French fries, chili, and steak to help her make up her mind. She could now read what was offered. She studied carefully, and when she came to the bottom of the menu, she read the dreaded words, "Child's Plate for Children Under Twelve." Then came the list of choices: fish sticks, chicken drumsticks, hot dogs. None of them, to Ramona, food for a treat. They were food for a school cafeteria.

"Daddy," Ramona whispered, "do I have to have a child's plate?"

"Not if you don't want to." Her father's smile was understanding. Ramona ordered the smallest adult item on the menu.

Whopperburger was noted for fast service, and in a few minutes the waitress set down the Quimbys' dinners: a hamburger and French fries for Ramona, a cheeseburger and French fries for Beezus and her mother, and hamburgers with chili for her father.

Ramona bit into her hamburger. Bliss. Warm, soft, juicy, tart with relish. Juice dribbled down her chin. She noticed her mother start to say something and change her mind. Ramona caught the dribble **16** with her paper napkin before it reached her collar. The French fries — crisp on the outside, mealy on the inside — tasted better than anything Ramona had ever eaten. **17**

387

Writer's Craft

Imagery

Teach

- Explain that imagery is the use of descriptive words that appeal to the senses.

- Writers use imagery to paint vivid pictures that linger in their readers' minds.

Practice/Apply

- Have students reread the last paragraph on page 387.

- Guide students to find the imagery Cleary uses to say that the hamburger is good. (*Warm, soft, juicy, tart with relish.*)

- Ask students to identify the imagery Cleary uses to say that the French fries are delicious. (*crisp on the outside, mealy on the inside*)

- Have students discuss other examples of imagery in the story:
  - the way the fireplace burns (pages 373 and 382)
  - the way Beezus looks and acts when she comes out of her room (page 380)
  - the way the older gentleman looks and dresses (page 384)

ASSIGNMENT CARD 9

Eating Smart

Health

It's okay to have a special treat once in a while, but the Quimby dinner isn't a meal you should eat everyday. Think about what you know about healthy eating. Plan a more balanced meal for the Quimbys that includes more fruits, vegetables, and grains, and less fat and sugar. Draw a picture of your meal or cut out pictures from magazines to show what foods and drinks the dinner would include. Label each item in your meal.

Theme 6: Smart Solutions

Teacher's Resource BLM page 90

Reading the Selection 387

CRITICAL THINKING
Guiding Comprehension

18 DRAWING CONCLUSIONS Do you agree with Mrs. Quimby when she says *A little change once in a while does make a difference*? Explain. (Sample answer: Yes, doing something out of your ordinary routine can brighten your day.)

19 WRITER'S CRAFT How does the author show that Ramona and Beezus are trying hard not to spoil the family's dinner? (They both stop themselves from saying something mean; they smile and laugh.)

COMPREHENSION STRATEGY
Summarize

Student Modeling Ask students to model the strategy by sharing their summaries of the story up to this point, especially focusing on how Ramona's feelings have changed since the beginning.

The family ate in companionable silence for a few moments until the edge was taken off their hunger. "A little change once in a while does make a difference," said Mrs. Quimby. "It does us all good."

18

"Especially after the way —" Ramona stopped herself from finishing with, "— after the way Beezus acted this afternoon." Instead she sat up straight and smiled.

19

"Well, I wasn't the only one who —" Beezus also stopped in midsentence and smiled. The parents looked stern, but they managed to smile. Suddenly everyone relaxed and laughed.

The old man, Ramona noticed, was eating a steak. She wished her father could afford a steak.

As much as she enjoyed her hamburger, Ramona was unable to finish. It was too much. She was happy when her mother did not say, "Someone's eyes are bigger than her stomach." Her father, without commenting on the unfinished hamburger, included her in the orders of apple pie with hot cinnamon sauce and ice cream.

Ramona ate what she could, and after watching the ice cream melt into the cinnamon sauce, she glanced over at the old man, who was having a serious discussion with the waitress. She seemed surprised and upset about something. The Muzak, conversation of other customers, and rattle of dishes made eavesdropping impossible. The waitress left. Ramona saw

388

Vocabulary

companionable friendly

stern serious; strict

eavesdropping listening secretly to a private conversation

tip extra money left in a restaurant for the person who served you

her speak to the manager, who listened and then nodded. For a moment Ramona thought the man might not have enough money to pay for the steak he had eaten. Apparently he did, however, for after listening to what the waitress had to say, he left a tip under the edge of his plate and picked up his check. To Ramona's embarrassment, he stood up, winked, and saluted her again. Then he left. Ramona did not know what to make of him.

389

English Language Learners

Supporting Comprehension

Make sure students understand what *tip* in this instance means. Explain that leaving a tip, or tipping, for services rendered is an old custom that is followed in many parts of the world. Although leaving a tip is usually voluntary, some workers, such as taxi drivers and waiters, often depend on tips for their livelihood.

CRITICAL THINKING

Guiding Comprehension

20 **CAUSE AND EFFECT** How does the sight of her family's smiles give Ramona the courage to ask her father about her worry that he won't finish college? (Everyone is in a good mood, so Ramona isn't afraid that her question will make anyone angry.)

21 **MAKING INFERENCES** Why do you think the older gentleman considers the Quimbys a nice family even though he really doesn't know anything about them? (In the restaurant, they are laughing and smiling and apparently having a good time together.)

20 She turned back to her family, whose smiles were now genuine rather than determined. The sight of them gave her courage to ask the question that had been nibbling at the back of her mind, "Daddy, you aren't going to be a college dropout, are you?"

Mr. Quimby finished a mouthful of pie before he answered, "Nope."

Ramona wanted to make sure. "And you won't ever be a checker and come home cross again?"

"Well," said her father, "I can't promise I won't come home cross, but if I do, it won't be from standing at the cash register trying to remember forty-two price changes in the produce section while a long line of customers, all in a hurry, wait to pay for their groceries."

Ramona was reassured.

When the waitress descended on the Quimbys to offer the grown-ups a second cup of coffee, Mr. Quimby said, "Check, please."

The waitress looked embarrassed. "Well . . . a . . ." She hesitated. "This has never happened before, but your meals have already been paid for."

The Quimbys looked at her in astonishment. "But who paid for them?" demanded Mr. Quimby.

"A lonely gentleman who left a little while ago," answered the waitress.

"He must have been the man who sat across the aisle," said Mrs. Quimby. "But why would he pay for our dinners? We never saw him before in our lives."

21 The waitress smiled. "Because he said you are such a nice family, and because he misses his children and grandchildren." She dashed off with her pot of coffee, leaving the Quimbys in

390

Vocabulary

genuine not false; real

determined trying really hard

descended arrived suddenly

astonishment sudden great surprise

wraps outer clothes; coats

obediently willingly

rhythmic in time to a beat

English Language Learners

Supporting Comprehension

After reading page 390, ask students to begin to think about the theme of this story. Ask: Why does the stranger pay for the Quimbys' meals? What does the family mean to him and to each other? What is the author trying to tell us about families?

surprised, even shocked, silence. A nice family? After the way
they had behaved on a rainy Sunday.

"A mysterious stranger just like in a book," said Beezus.
"I never thought I'd meet one."

"Poor lonely man," said Mrs. Quimby at last, as Mr. Quimby
shoved a tip under his saucer. Still stunned into silence, the family
struggled into their wraps and splashed across the parking lot to
their car, which started promptly and backed obediently out of
its parking space. As the windshield wipers began their rhythmic
exercise, the family rode in silence, each thinking of the events
of the day.

391

English Language Learners

Supporting Comprehension

Brainstorm with the class to create a two-column chart, comparing and contrasting
the family before they go out to eat and after. As a class, write a compare and
contrast paragraph with a topic sentence, detail sentences, and a conclusion.

Drawing Conclusions

Teach

- Remind students that authors may purposely leave out information in a story to make readers pay close attention to details.

- Readers can add up clues to draw conclusions about what the author doesn't say directly.

Practice/Apply

- Point out that Beverly Cleary doesn't actually say that the old man with the mustache pays for the Quimbys' dinner. Help students find clues in the text that lead readers to draw this conclusion. (He spoke to Ramona and winked at her later; he sat near the Quimbys; Ramona saw him talking with the waitress; the waitress referred to *a lonely gentleman*.)

- Have students cover the illustration on page 391. Ask, What is the weather like when the Quimbys leave the restaurant? (It's still raining.) What clues tell you this? (they splashed across the parking lot; the windshield wipers began their rhythmic exercise)

Review Skill Trace	
Teach	p. 367A
Reteach	p. R10
▶ Review	p. 391

CRITICAL THINKING

Guiding Comprehension

22 MAKING INFERENCES What does Ramona mean when she thinks to herself that *sometimes on the outside her niceness sort of—well, curdled*? (She usually intends to be nice and wants to do the right thing, but somehow it doesn't always come out that way.)

23 WRITER'S CRAFT How does the author show that Ramona has matured a little? (Ramona realizes that she has an important role in her family; she's determined to get along with Willa Jean.)

24 MAKING INFERENCES What does Ramona mean when she thinks to herself, *Tomorrow they would begin all over again*? (Right at that moment, the family members are happy, but tomorrow they will face new situations and have to find new ways of dealing with them.)

"You know," said Mrs. Quimby thoughtfully, as the car left the parking lot and headed down the street, "I think he was right. We are a nice family."

"Not all the time," said Ramona, as usual demanding accuracy.

"Nobody is nice all the time," answered her father. "Or if they are, they are boring."

"Not even your parents are nice all the time," added Mrs. Quimby.

Ramona secretly agreed, but she had not expected her parents to admit it. Deep down inside, she felt she herself was nice all the time, but sometimes on the outside her niceness **22** sort of — well, curdled. Then people did not understand how nice she really was. Maybe other people curdled too.

"We have our ups and downs," said Mrs. Quimby, "but we manage to get along, and we stick together."

"We are nicer than some families I know," said Beezus. "Some families don't even eat dinner together." After a moment she made a confession. "I don't really like sleeping on someone's floor in a sleeping bag."

"I didn't think you did." Mrs. Quimby reached back and patted Beezus on the knee. "That's one reason I said you couldn't go. You didn't want to go, but didn't want to admit it."

Ramona snuggled inside her car coat, feeling cozy enclosed in the car with the heater breathing warm air on her nice family. She was a member of a nice sticking-together family, and she was old enough to be depended upon, so she could ignore — or at least try to ignore — a lot of things. Willa Jean — she would try reading her Sustained Silent Reading books aloud because Willa Jean was old enough to

392

Extra Support/ Intervention	**On Level**	**Challenge**
Selection Review Before students join the whole class for Wrapping Up on page 393, have them ● take turns modeling the reading strategies they used ● complete **Transparency 6–20** with you ● finish their Generalizations Charts ● summarize the whole selection	**Literature Discussion** Have small groups of students discuss the story, using their own questions or the questions in Think About the Selection on Anthology page 394.	

Vocabulary

accuracy exactness

curdled spoiled, like milk

confession the act of admitting something

understand most of them. That should work for a little while. Mrs. Whaley — some things were nice about her and some were not. Ramona could get along.

"That man paying for our dinner was sort of like a happy ending," remarked Beezus, as the family, snug in their car, drove through the rain and the dark toward Klickitat Street.

"A happy ending for today," corrected Ramona. **24**
Tomorrow they would begin all over again.

393

Wrapping Up

Critical Thinking Questions

1. **PROBLEM SOLVING** How does the kindness and generosity of a stranger help the Quimby family see themselves in a different light? (They realize that although they have problems, they are a family that sticks together— indeed, they are "a nice family.")

2. **PREDICTING OUTCOMES** What do you think will happen to the Quimbys the next time they are stuck in the house together on a rainy Sunday? (Answers will vary.)

Strategies in Action

Have students take turns modeling how and where they used the Summarize strategy.

Discussion Options

Bring the entire class together to do one or more of the activities below.

Review Predictions/Purpose Discuss reasons why students' predictions were or were not accurate. Have students share any generalizations they made in their journals.

Share Group Discussions Have students talk about what Ramona learns about herself and her family.

Summarize Ask students to summarize the story, using their Generalizations Charts.

Comprehension Check

Use **Practice Book** page 204 to assess students' comprehension of the selection.

READ & COMPREHEND

Ramona Quimby, Age 8

Practice Book page 204

Ramona Quimby, Age 8
Comprehension Check

Name _____

Ramona's Diary

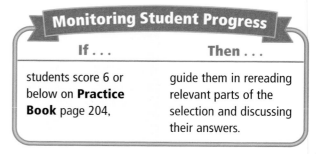

Suppose Ramona kept a diary. Finish this entry with details from *Ramona Quimby, Age 8*. Answers may vary. Examples are given.

Dear Diary,

Sunday afternoon was dismal and rainy (1 point) .

Mom and Dad were sorting bills and studying; tired, cross, grouchy (1) .

Mom kept reminding me to clean my room (1) .

Then Beezus asked Mom to let her sleep over at Mary Jane's house (1)
. But Mom and Dad
said no, so Beezus was upset.

Then Dad decided that we should go to the Whopperburger.
He wanted us to stop grumping around; have a treat (1) .

While we were waiting for our seats, I didn't like being teased by an
old man (1) . Dinner was really tasty
and fun too!

Before the man left, he paid for our dinners without telling us (1)
. On the way home, all
of us were happier; in better moods (1)

Monitoring Student Progress

If . . .	Then . . .
students score 6 or below on **Practice Book** page 204,	guide them in rereading relevant parts of the selection and discussing their answers.

Responding

Think About the Selection

READ & COMPREHEND

Have students discuss or write their answers. Sample answers are provided; accept reasonable responses.

1. **MAKING INFERENCES** Everyone is bored and cranky. A treat will make everyone feel better.

2. **WRITER'S CRAFT** Answers will vary. Sample answers: Ramona's feelings are easily hurt. She worries about her father.

3. **MAKING JUDGMENTS** Answers and explanations will vary.

4. **DRAWING CONCLUSIONS** Answers will vary but should include Mr. Quimby's reassurance that he plans to finish college and get a better job. Students might also note that having been told that they are a nice family should make them all feel happier.

5. **MAKING INFERENCES** Knowing how the family has squabbled in the past, it is safe to predict that tomorrow all the little annoyances will pop up again.

6. **Connecting/Comparing** Answers will vary. Sample answers: In *Pepita Talks Twice*, family members point out the things Pepita won't be able to do without speaking Spanish. In *Poppa's New Pants*, all the women try to help Poppa by shortening his new pants. In *Ramona Quimby, Age 8*, Mr. Quimby helps by taking the family out to dinner, and the girls help by not fighting at the table.

Think About the Selection

1. Why does Mr. Quimby decide that the family needs to go out to dinner?

2. How does Beverly Cleary make Ramona think and act like a real person? Find examples from the story.

3. Do you agree that the Quimbys are a nice family? Explain your answer.

4. Why do you think Ramona feels happier at the end of the story?

5. What does Cleary mean by the last sentence, "Tomorrow they would begin all over again"?

6. **Connecting/Comparing** In each story in this theme, how does a family help each other find a smart solution to a problem?

 Expressing

Write a Thank-You Note

 When someone does something kind for you, you should always thank them. Write a thank-you note that Ramona might have written to the man who paid for the Quimbys' dinner.

Tips
- Write the date at the top of the note.
- Begin with a greeting.
- End with a closing and a signature.

394

REACHING ALL LEARNERS

English Language Learners

Supporting Comprehension

Beginning/Preproduction As a group, use old magazines to make a collage demonstrating the story themes.

Early Production and Speech Emergence Ask: How did you know how the Quimbys felt? How do you know when members of your family are in a bad mood? Ask more proficient students to assist with vocabulary.

Intermediate and Advanced Fluency Ask students in what ways the Quimbys are similar to or different from their own family.

Math

Add Up a Restaurant Check

Look on page 387 to find out what kind of hamburger each of the Quimbys ate for dinner. Add up the prices from the menu below.

Bonus Add on four pieces of apple pie, four sodas, and two cups of coffee to find the total cost of the Quimbys' dinner.

Whopperburger Menu	
Hamburger with French fries	$5.75
Cheeseburger with French fries	$6.25
Hamburgers with chili	$7.50
Soda	$1.00
Cup of coffee	$1.25
Apple pie	$2.50

Listening and Speaking

Role-Play Ordering Food

With a partner, take turns playing a customer and a server in a restaurant. When you play the role of the customer, tell the server what you'd like to eat and drink. When you play the role of the server, listen carefully and write down the order. For fun, make up a menu for the customer to use.

Tips

- The server should start by asking, "May I take your order?"
- Speak clearly and be polite to one another.

Internet

Take an Online Poll

Ramona loves her Whopperburger dinner. If you could pick your perfect meal, what would it be? Come to Education Place and vote for your food favorites. **www.eduplace.com/kids**

395

Additional Responses

Personal Response Invite students to share their personal responses to the selection with a partner.

Journal ▸ Ask students to write in their journals about rainy-day activities.

Selection Connections Remind students to add to **Practice Book** page 166.

 Extra Support/ Intervention

Discuss Thank-You Notes

For the writing activity, ask students to share ways they thank others. Present the thank-you note as one way people thank each other. Then write a sample note on the board, encouraging students to use a similar format.

Practice Book page 166

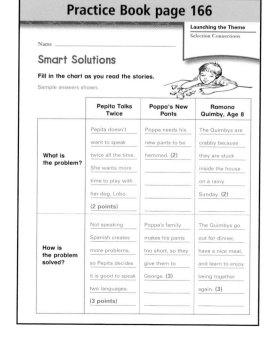

Launching the Theme
Selection Connections

Name _____

Smart Solutions

Fill in the chart as you read the stories.
Sample answers shown.

	Pepita Talks Twice	Poppa's New Pants	Ramona Quimby, Age 8
What is the problem?	Pepita doesn't want to speak twice all the time. She wants more time to play with her dog, Lobo. (2 points)	Poppa needs his new pants to be hemmed. (2)	The Quimbys are crabby because they are stuck inside the house on a rainy Sunday. (2)
How is the problem solved?	Not speaking Spanish creates more problems, so Pepita decides it is good to speak two languages. (3 points)	Poppa's family makes his pants too short, so they give them to George. (3)	The Quimbys go out for dinner, have a nice meal, and learn to enjoy being together again. (3)

End-of-Selection Assessment

Selection Test Use the test on pages 145–146 in the **Teacher's Resource Blackline Masters** to assess selection comprehension and vocabulary.

Student Self-Assessment Have students assess their reading with additional questions such as

- Which parts of this selection were difficult? Why?
- Which strategies helped me understand the story better?
- Would I read other books by Beverly Cleary? Why or why not?

Responding 395

Drama Link

Skill: How to Read a Play

- **Introduce** "Henry and Ramona," an excerpt from a play based on some of Beverly Cleary's characters.

- **Discuss** the Skill Lesson on Anthology page 396. Point out the title and the cast of characters. Make sure students understand what stage directions are.

- **Model** reading a play. Assign the role of Murph to a student and take the role of Henry. Read aloud the dialogue on Anthology page 396.

- **Explain** that plays, like stories, are often based on characters who are trying to solve a problem. Using a Problem-Solution Frame is a good way to understand what happens in a play. Have students copy the chart below and help you fill in the characters and setting. Then have them read Anthology page 397 and fill in the problem.

- **Set a purpose** for reading. Tell students to read the rest of the play excerpt to identify the solution. Then have them enter the solution on their charts. Remind students to use Predict/ Infer and other strategies as they read.

Main characters: Henry, Murph, Beezus, Ramona

....

Setting: Klickitat Street

....

Problem Facing Henry: Henry finally gets the paper route he's wanted, but Ramona prevents him from doing his job.

....

Solution: Henry makes Ramona pretend to be a robot that moves very slowly. Meanwhile, he sets off on his route.

Vocabulary

earnest not playful; sincere

underfoot in the way

Skill: How to Read a Play

❶ Read the title. Look at the **cast of characters** to learn who is in the play.

❷ Be an actor! Plays are meant to be performed, so take turns reading each character's **lines** aloud.

❸ As you perform, read the **stage directions** to yourself. They describe the setting and the characters' actions.

396

Henry and Ramona

based on the books by Beverly Cleary
dramatized by Cynthia J. McGean

CAST OF CHARACTERS

HENRY HUGGINS: earnest boy, almost 11 years old

BYRON MURPHY (MURPH): a "boy genius," Henry's age

BEEZUS QUIMBY: girl about Henry's age, Henry's best friend, very practical

RAMONA QUIMBY: Beezus' younger sister, about 5 years old, imaginative and underfoot

---

Act I, Scene Nine

PLACE: Klickitat Street

(A rainy, cloudy day in early fall. HENRY enters. MURPH enters with a Journal bag full of papers.)

MURPH: *(to HENRY)* You can have the route.

HENRY: What?!

MURPH: I said, you can have the route.

HENRY: You mean you don't want it?

MURPH: No.

HENRY: *(suspiciously)* How come?

MURPH: Ramona.

HENRY: Ramona?! She's just a little kid!

MURPH: I know, but she can sure make a lot of trouble.

HENRY: I'm not so sure Mr. Capper wants me to have a route.

MURPH: Yes he does.

HENRY: How do you know?

MURPH: I asked him. *(Pause.)* I guess I shouldn't have taken the route when I knew you wanted it, but I just had to. My other route was too far away, and I needed money to buy parts for Thorvo. Dad thinks my robot's a waste of time, so I have to pay for the parts myself. But Ramona's making so much trouble I prob'ly would've lost the route anyway.

HENRY: Okay, Murph, I'll take the route.

MURPH: *(relieved)* Thanks. Here's the route book and the papers. *(He hands HENRY the Journal bag.)*

HENRY: Murph . . . does your dad really think Thorvo's a waste of time?

MURPH: Yeah. I guess I'll have to put all that stuff away 'til I figure out how to pay for parts. *(Pause.)* If you still want to make that private phone line, I have most of the stuff. And I already know how to build one.

HENRY: You do?

MURPH: Sure.

HENRY: Okay.

MURPH: Guess I'll see ya around. Good luck with the route.

HENRY: Thanks. *(MURPH exits.)* Imagine! A genius licked by a five-year-old! She's just a kindergartner. I'm not gonna let her stand in my way! Maybe I'm no genius, but I'm still smarter than a five-year-old.

397

Extra Support/Intervention

Understanding Stage Directions

Point out that stage directions tell a reader or actor what action a character is carrying out or how a line should be read. Sometimes, they explain a character's feelings. Stage directions appear in brackets or parentheses. Using page 397, guide students to identify examples of stage directions that describe actions. Then have them find a stage direction that expresses a feeling.

Play

Teach

Review the elements of a play:

- A play may be divided into parts called acts or scenes.

- The character list—the cast—tells who the characters are.

- The setting describes where and when the action takes place.

- The dialogue is what the actors say on stage. The characters' names appear before the lines the actors speak.

- Stage directions, often shown in parentheses, tell the actors what to do and how to say their lines.

  – *Enter* means the characters come onto the stage; *exit* means they leave.

Practice/Apply

- Have students find examples of the elements listed above in the play excerpt.

(HENRY goes to get his bike. RAMONA enters and sits down

RAMONA: Hello.

HENRY: Hello, Ramona. *(He begins to deliver papers. RAMONA follows after him, picking up all his papers. HENRY spots her.)* Hey, cut that out! Give me those!

RAMONA: No! I'm going to deliver them!
(She and HENRY have a tug of war. He grabs the papers, and she begins a tantrum. BEEZUS enters.)

BEEZUS: Ramona! You're supposed to be in the house!

RAMONA: *(grabbing HENRY in an attempt to get the papers back)* I'm a paperboy — like Henry and Murph!

HENRY: Get off me, will ya?

BEEZUS: *(prying RAMONA free from HENRY)* I'm sorry, Henry. *(RAMONA is wailing.)* Ramona, be *quiet!* *(To HENRY)* Mom says she has to stay in her room 'til the papers are delivered, but she keeps getting out.

HENRY: We've got to do something, or I'll lose my route.

BEEZUS: We've tried, but when we don't want her to do something, she just wants to do it even more. The only way I can ever get her to do what I want is by getting her to pretend . . . wait a minute — !
(BEEZUS and HENRY look at each other and get an idea. They whisper together. RAMONA is now trying to listen in pleased to be the center of attention.)

HENRY: I know just the thing. Hang on to Ramona, Beezus.

BEEZUS: Gotcha. *(HENRY exits behind his house.)*

RAMONA: Where's Henry going?

BEEZUS: You'll see.

RAMONA: I want to go TOO!

398

Vocabulary

prying forcing apart

wailing protesting loudly; crying

BEEZUS: Ramona, how do you know you want to go if you don't know where he's going?!

RAMONA: But I WANT to go!

BEEZUS: Let's pretend that we're waiting for a bus. When Henry comes back, that means the bus is here. Okay?

RAMONA: Henry's not a bus, he's a paperboy. *(HENRY returns with a big cardboard box made into a makeshift robot head.)*

HENRY: Hey, Ramona — how would you like to be a robot like Thorvo? *(RAMONA nods excitedly.)* Now, remember. A robot can't move very fast, and it jerks along when it walks. *(He places the cardboard box over RAMONA's head.)*

RAMONA: Clank, clank. *(She begins walking, slowly and jerkily, like a robot.)*

BEEZUS: And a robot can't bend at the waist because it doesn't have any waist!

RAMONA: Clank.

BEEZUS: Henry, you're a genius!

HENRY: You're the one who thought of pretending.

BEEZUS: That's true. Well, guess you've got some papers to deliver.

HENRY: Yup. I better get going. *(He begins to leave. RAMONA waves at him as a robot.)*

RAMONA: Clank, clank!

HENRY: Clank, clank, Ramona! *(HENRY exits. RAMONA clanks out with BEEZUS.)*

399

Wrapping Up

Critical Thinking Questions

Ask students to read aloud the parts of the selection that support their answers.

1. **CAUSE AND EFFECT** Why did Murph want the paper route in the first place? Why does he give it up? (He wanted to earn money to buy parts for his robot, Thorvo. He gives it up because Ramona is making too much trouble.)

2. **MAKING GENERALIZATIONS** What word could you use to describe Ramona? What word could you use to describe Henry? (Sample answers: pesky; clever)

3. **PROBLEM SOLVING** Why is Henry's solution such a good one? (It challenges Ramona to use her active imagination and stops her from bothering him.)

4. **TEXT ORGANIZATION** How would your understanding of the solution to the main problem be affected if there were no stage directions on that page? (We would not know that Henry returned with the robot head, so nothing would make sense after that.)

Challenge

Perform a Play

Have interested students act out the scene using props. You may wish to have several performances, instructing students to pay attention to the different ways in which the actors interpret their lines. Other students may wish to write short reviews of the performances.

OBJECTIVES

- Make generalizations based on story information and personal experience.
- Learn academic language: *generalization*.

Target Skill Trace

Preview; Teach	p. 367CC; p. 368; p. 389; p. 399A
Reteach	p. R12
Review	pp. 413D–413E; Theme 4, p. 29; Theme 5, p. 197
See	*Extra Support Handbook,* pp. 216–217; pp. 222–223

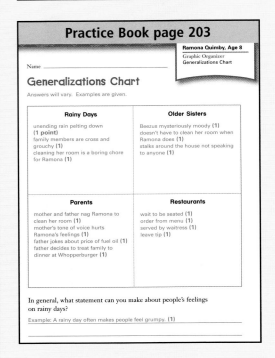

Transparency 6–20

SMART SOLUTIONS Ramona Quimby, Age 8
Graphic Organizer Generalizations Chart

ANNOTATED VERSION

Generalizations Chart
Answers will vary. Examples are given.

Rainy Days	Older Sisters
unending rain pelting down family members cross and grouchy cleaning her room a boring chore for Ramona	Beezus mysteriously moody doesn't have to clean her room when Ramona does stalks around the house not speaking to anyone

Parents	Restaurants
mother and father nag Ramona to clean room mother's tone of voice hurts Ramona's feelings father jokes about price of fuel oil father decides to treat family to dinner at Whopperburger	wait to be seated order from menu served by waitress leave tip

In general, what statement can you make about people's feelings on rainy days?
Example: A rainy day often makes people feel grumpy.

TRANSPARENCY 6–20
TEACHER'S EDITION PAGES 370 AND 399A

Practice Book page 203

Ramona Quimby, Age 8
Graphic Organizer
Generalizations Chart

Name _____

Generalizations Chart
Answers will vary. Examples are given.

Rainy Days	Older Sisters
unending rain pelting down **(1 point)** family members are cross and grouchy **(1)** cleaning her room is a boring chore for Ramona **(1)**	Beezus mysteriously moody **(1)** doesn't have to clean her room when Ramona does **(1)** stalks around the house not speaking to anyone **(1)**

Parents	Restaurants
mother and father nag Ramona to clean her room **(1)** mother's tone of voice hurts Ramona's feelings **(1)** father jokes about price of fuel oil **(1)** father decides to treat family to dinner at Whopperburger **(1)**	wait to be seated **(1)** order from menu **(1)** served by waitress **(1)** leave tip **(1)**

In general, what statement can you make about people's feelings on rainy days?
Example: A rainy day often makes people feel grumpy. **(1)**

TARGET SKILL COMPREHENSION: Making Generalizations

❶ Teach

Review generalizations about *Ramona Quimby, Age 8*. Remind students that a generalization is a broad statement that is true about most people or things in a group most of the time. Display the Graphic Organizer on **Transparency 6–20** and review details in *Ramona Quimby, Age 8* with students. (Sample answers are shown.) Students can refer to the selection and to **Practice Book** page 203. Discuss the question below the chart.

Model making a generalization. Have students reread the first paragraphs of page 372. Point out Ramona's generalization in the first sentence. Then model the skill.

Think Aloud *Rainy days in other months can seem gloomy, too, so I don't think Ramona's generalization is a very good one. But as I read, I note details about the ceaseless rain pelting down, the fussy cat, Ramona's nagging mother, and Ramona's gloomy mood. I've felt that way, too, on a rainy day. So, I'll say: In general, rainy days make some people feel gloomy.*

❷ Guided Practice

Have students practice making generalizations. Give students questions that require them to make generalizations, like the ones below. Guide students to use story details and personal observations to figure out answers that are generally true. Have them record their answer statements on a chart similar to the one shown on the transparency.

- What can you say about parents' reactions to the way kids keep their rooms?
- What can you say about the way sisters (or brothers) act when another sister or brother gets in trouble?
- What can you say about how the mood of one family member can influence everyone else?

❸ Apply

Assign **Practice Book** pages 205–206. Also have students apply this skill as they read their **Leveled Readers** for this week. You may also select books from the Leveled Bibliography for this theme on pages 296E–296F.

Test Prep Explain that reading tests often have multiple-choice questions that ask about generalizations. Caution students that the answer choices for these questions may be general statements that all sound true. Encourage students to choose the answer that is best supported by details in the test passage.

Leveled Readers and Leveled Practice

Students at all levels apply the comprehension skill as they read their Leveled Readers. See lessons on pages 399O–399R.

● BELOW LEVEL   ▲ ON LEVEL   ■ ABOVE LEVEL   ◆ LANGUAGE SUPPORT

The Dive — First Day For CARLOS — REAL TEAM SOCCER — Christy's First Dive

Reading Traits

As students develop the ability to make generalizations, they are learning to "read between the lines" of a selection. This comprehension skill supports the reading trait **Developing Interpretations**.

Practice Book page 205

Ramona Quimby, Age 8
Comprehension Skill
Making Generalizations

Name _____

Making Cafeteria Food

Read the story below. Then answer the questions on the next page.

Ms. Mallard and Meatloaf

Luis dropped his lunch tray on the table next to his friend Joey and sat down. "Can you believe this? They call this meatloaf!" Luis said. "And they just served it two weeks ago! I can't stand it."

"Then why don't you ask someone why it's always on the menu, Luis?" Joey replied. "All you do is complain."

"You're right. I will." Luis stood up and walked directly back to the serving line where the lunch lady was cleaning up. "Um, Ms. Mallard? Can I ask you something?"

Ms. Mallard turned around. "Ah, yes, of course, Luis. What is it? Enjoying your meatloaf?"

"Not really. That's why I'm here. How come you serve it every two weeks and why does it taste so strange?"

"Well, Luis, schools have rules about the kinds of food we serve," Ms. Mallard responded. "We need to make food that fits in the basic food groups. Meatloaf fits most of them, it's easy to make a lot of, and it doesn't cost much to make. That's why many schools put it on their menus."

"Okay, I get it. But how come it tastes so funny?"

"I can tell you, Luis, that you're not alone on this one. Last summer I went to a national meeting about cafeteria food. Almost everybody I talked to said how much the kids dislike the taste of meatloaf. It probably has something to do with the onions and the peppers in it. Not to mention the dry bread that goes in it. Some people just look at its color and think it can't taste good. That's why. Just try putting ketchup on it."

Practice Book page 206

Ramona Quimby, Age 8
Comprehension Skill
Making Generalizations

Name _____

Making Cafeteria Food *continued*

Answer the following questions based on the story "Ms. Mallard and Meatloaf." Answers will vary. Examples are given.

What broad statement can you make about schools and meatloaf?
Many schools serve meatloaf. **(2 points)**

What details support your generalization?
Schools have to serve food that fits into the food groups.
Meatloaf fits many of the food groups.
It's easy to make a lot of it.
It's cheap to make. **(4)**

In general, what can you say about kids and the school meatloaf?
Many kids don't like eating the school meatloaf. **(2)**

What details support your generalization?
Everybody from all over the country said that kids don't like its taste.
Meatloaf has onions and peppers in it.
It has dry bread in it.
The color of it makes some people think it doesn't taste good. **(4)**

Monitoring Student Progress

If . . .	Then . . .
students score 8 or below on **Practice Book** page 206,	use the Reteaching lesson on Teacher's Edition page R12.
students have successfully met the lesson objectives,	have them do the Challenge/ Extension activities on Teacher's Edition page R13.

OBJECTIVES

- Read contractions and identify their meanings.
- Apply the Phonics/Decoding Strategy.
- Learn academic language: *contraction*.

Target Skill Trace

Teach	p. 399C
Reteach	p. R18
Review	pp. 413F–413G
See	*Handbook for English Language Learners*, p. 219; *Extra Support Handbook*, pp. 214–215; pp. 218–219

Practice Book page 207

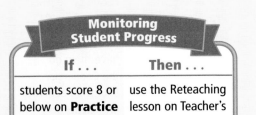

Name _____

Contraction Puzzler

What did Ramona learn on that rainy Sunday? Solve the puzzle to find out. Write the two words that each contraction is made from. Write only one letter on each line. Then write each numbered letter on the line with the matching number below.

1. we're   w e   a r e   (1 point)
2. she's   s h e   i s   (1)
3. wasn't   w a s   n o t   (1)
4. you're   y o u   a r e   (1)
5. he'll   h e   w i l l   (1)
6. they've   t h e y   h a v e   (1)
7. couldn't   c o u l d   n o t   (1)
8. I'm   a m   (1)
9. they'd   t h e y   w o u l d   (1)
10. aren't   a r e   n o t   (1)

What Ramona learned:

w e   a r e   a   n i c e
f a m i l y   (2)

Monitoring Student Progress

If . . .	Then . . .
students score 8 or below on **Practice Book** page 207,	use the Reteaching lesson on Teacher's Edition page R18.

STRUCTURAL ANALYSIS/ VOCABULARY: Contractions

① Teach

Define contractions. Explain that a contraction is a combination of two words in which an apostrophe stands for missing letters.

Analyze contractions. Tell students that analyzing contractions will help them recognize and understand contractions in their reading. Write *Ramona, you haven't cleaned up your room this weekend. Mother, I think you're mean.* Point out the apostrophes in the underlined contractions. Then write:

> haven't = have not
>
> you're = you are

Ask students what letters have been left out of each contraction. (haven't—the *o* in *not*; you're—the *a* in *are*)

Model the Phonics/Decoding Strategy. Write *During Thanksgiving I'll be putting in more hours in the warehouse and getting more overtime.* Model decoding *I'll.*

Think Aloud *I see the contraction* I'll. *I recognize the first word part, the word* I. *Then I see* apostrophe-l-l. *The apostrophe might be taking the place of the letters* w-i *in the word* will. *If I substitute* I will *in the sentence—*I will *be putting in more hours—that makes sense.*

② Guided Practice

Have students decode contractions. Display the sentences below. Ask partners to copy the underlined words, decode each contraction, and name the smaller words each contraction represents. Have students share their work with the class.

<u>Don't</u> press your nose.

<u>It's</u> none of your business.

<u>There's</u> no reason why we <u>can't</u> have a treat.

Ramona <u>didn't</u> like it.

<u>I'm</u> trying to study.

<u>I'd</u> like a hamburger.

③ Apply

Assign Practice Book page 207.

PHONICS REVIEW:
Soft *c* and Soft *g*

❶ Teach

Review the soft *c* and soft *g* sounds. Tell students that understanding the soft *c* and soft *g* sounds can help them decode unfamiliar words.

- The spelling patterns *ge*, *gi*, *gy*, and *dge* can have the /j/ sound.
- The spelling patterns *ce* and *ci* can have the /s/ sound.

Model the Phonics/Decoding Strategy. Write *She thought of all the exciting things she would like to do.* Model decoding *exciting*.

Think Aloud *When I look at this word, I recognize the word part ex- from words such as* extra *and* excellent. *Next I see c-i-t followed by the -ing ending. I know the c-i spelling pattern usually has the s sound as in* circle, *so this middle part probably sounds like* siht. *When I put it all together, I say* ehks-SIHT-ihng. *I know. The word is* ehks-SY-tihng. *That makes sense here.*

❷ Guided Practice

Have students identify soft *c* and soft *g* sounds. Write:

leaves a <u>smudge</u>

<u>cinnamon</u> sauce

speak to the <u>manager</u>

cash <u>register</u>

- Have students copy the underlined words. Then help them circle the soft *c* and soft *g* sounds they find in the underlined words and decode the words.
- Call on individuals to model their work at the board.

❸ Apply

Have students decode words with soft *c* and soft *g* sounds. Ask students to decode the words below and discuss their meanings.

refrigerator	gymnastic	dodged
pencil	emerged	accidentally
fireplace	concerned	genuine

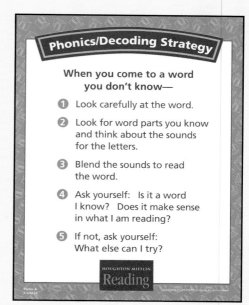

OBJECTIVES
- Read words and syllables with soft *c* and soft *g* sounds.
- Apply the Phonics/Decoding Strategy.

Phonics/Decoding Strategy

When you come to a word you don't know—
1. Look carefully at the word.
2. Look for word parts you know and think about the sounds for the letters.
3. Blend the sounds to read the word.
4. Ask yourself: Is it a word I know? Does it make sense in what I am reading?
5. If not, ask yourself: What else can I try?

HOUGHTON MIFFLIN
Reading

SPELLING: Contractions

OBJECTIVES

- Write Spelling Words that are contractions.
- Learn academic language: *contractions.*

SPELLING WORDS

Basic

I'm*	wouldn't*
he's	weren't
aren't*	she's
couldn't*	wasn't*
won't*	I'd*
o'clock	shouldn't*

Review	**Challenge**
can't*	let's*
isn't*	who's

Forms of these words appear in the literature.

Extra Support/ Intervention

Basic Word List Consider using only the left column of Basic Words with students who need extra support.

Challenge

Challenge Word Practice Students can use the Challenge Words to write an ad or a poster for a school event that is happening soon.

Contractions

Pretest Use the Day 5 Test sentences.

Teach Write the following on the board: *I am → I'm; are not → aren't.* Have students say each contraction after you.

- Explain that each word is a contraction, a short way of saying or writing two or more words. Tell students that an apostrophe takes the place of dropped letters. Point out that *a* was dropped to form *I'm,* and *o* was dropped to form *aren't.*

- Add *won't* and *o'clock* to the board; have students say them. Note that these contractions were formed in unusual ways: *won't* was made from *will not, o'clock* from *of the clock.*

- Write the remaining contractions on the board; have students say them. Ask students to identify the letter or letters dropped.

Practice/Homework Assign **Practice Book** page 245.

Reviewing the Principle

Go over the formation of contractions with students.

Practice/Homework Assign **Practice Book** page 208.

Practice Book page 245

Take-Home Word List | **Take-Home Word List** | **Take-Home Word List**

Smart Solutions Spelling Review

Spelling Words

1. little	14. I'd
2. again	15. because
3. summer	16. wouldn't
4. alive	17. away
5. purple	18. couldn't
6. around	19. November
7. I'm	ber
8. able	20. shouldn't
9. wouldn't	21. apple
10. ago	22. about
11. ever	23. behind
12. before	24. wasn't
13. aren't	25. later

See the back for Challenge Words

Ramona Quimby, Age 8

Contractions
A **contraction** is a short way of writing two or more words. An apostrophe replaces any dropped letters.

Spelling Words
1. I'm
2. he's
3. aren't
4. couldn't
5. won't
6. o'clock
7. wouldn't
8. weren't
9. she's
10. wasn't
11. I'd
12. shouldn't

Challenge Words
1. let's
2. who's

Poppa's New Pants

Words That Begin with *a* or *be*
/ə/ → again
/bi/ → before

Spelling Words
1. began
2. again
3. around
4. before
5. away
6. about
7. alive
8. because
9. ahead
10. between
11. behind
12. ago

Challenge Words
1. awhile
2. beyond

My Study List Add your own spelling words on the back. ➔

My Study List Add your own spelling words on the back. ➔

My Study List Add your own spelling words on the back. ➔

Take-Home Word List

Practice Book page 208

Ramona Quimby, Age 8
Spelling Contractions

Name _____

Contractions

A contraction is a short way of saying or writing two or more words. An apostrophe takes the place of one or more letters.

I am → **I'm**   are not → **aren't**

► The starred words use different patterns.

will not → **won't**   of the clock → **o'clock**

Write each Spelling Word under the heading that tells about it. Order of answers for each category may vary.

Spelling Words
1. I'm
2. he's
3. aren't
4. couldn't
5. won't*
6. o'clock*
7. wouldn't
8. weren't
9. she's
10. wasn't
11. I'd
12. shouldn't

Contractions with *not*	Other Contractions
aren't (1 point)	I'm (1)
couldn't (1)	he's (1)
won't (1)	o'clock (1)
wouldn't (1)	she's (1)
weren't (1)	I'd (1)
wasn't (1)	
shouldn't (1)	

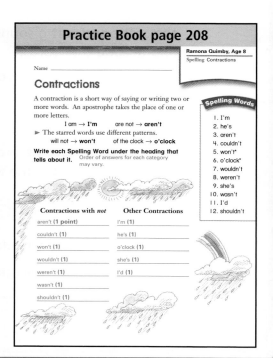

Multiple Meanings

Tell students that *he's, she's,* and *I'd* have more than one meaning.

- Write these meanings on the board: *he's:* "he is," "he has"; *she's:* "she is," "she has"; *I'd:* "I had," "I would."

- Select students to supply a sample sentence for each meaning. (Sentences will vary.)

- List the Basic Words on the board. Have students use each word orally in a sentence. (Sentences will vary.)

Practice/Homework For spelling practice, assign **Practice Book** page 209.

Game: Contraction Detection

Have students work in pairs, and tell each student to choose 6 different Basic Words.

- Ask individuals to write a sentence for each of his or her contractions, but to replace the contraction with the words from which it was formed. For example, a student who chose the contraction *aren't* might write this sentence: "Those gloves are not mine."

- Have partners exchange papers, search for the words that can be made into contractions, and write the contractions. Students who write all 6 contractions correctly are the winners.

Practice/Homework For proofreading and writing practice, assign **Practice Book** page 210.

Spelling Test

Say each underlined word, read the sentence, and then repeat the word. Have students write only the underlined word.

Basic Words

1. I hope that **I'm** right.
2. Tell Scott that **he's** funny.
3. We **aren't** saving these boxes.
4. The puppy **couldn't** jump high.
5. The knife **won't** cut the rope.
6. The show ends at one **o'clock**.
7. I **wouldn't** walk up there.
8. The trains **weren't** on time.
9. Ask Emma if **she's** warm.
10. I **wasn't** the last to leave.
11. I think **I'd** like some help.
12. The dog **shouldn't** be in here.

Challenge Words

13. Get your ball, and **let's** start the game.
14. Do you know **who's** in the play?

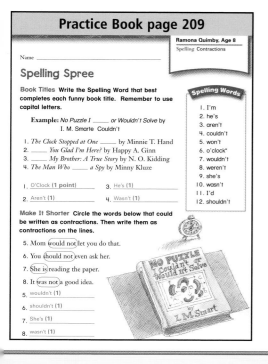

Practice Book page 209

Ramona Quimby, Age 8
Spelling Contractions

Name _____

Spelling Spree

Book Titles Write the Spelling Word that best completes each funny book title. Remember to use capital letters.

Example: *No Puzzle I ____ or Wouldn't Solve* by I. M. Smarte Couldn't

1. *The Clock Stopped at One ____* by Minnie T. Hand
2. *____ You Glad I'm Here?* by Happy A. Ginn
3. *____ My Brother: A True Story* by N. O. Kidding
4. *The Man Who ____ a Spy* by Minny Kluze

1. O'Clock **(1 point)**   3. He's **(1)**
2. Aren't **(1)**   4. Wasn't **(1)**

Make It Shorter Circle the words below that could be written as contractions. Then write them as contractions on the lines.

5. Mom would not let you do that.
6. You should not even ask her.
7. She is reading the paper.
8. It was not a good idea.

5. wouldn't **(1)**
6. shouldn't **(1)**
7. She's **(1)**
8. wasn't **(1)**

Spelling Words
1. I'm
2. he's
3. aren't
4. couldn't
5. won't
6. o'clock*
7. wouldn't
8. weren't
9. she's
10. wasn't
11. I'd
12. shouldn't

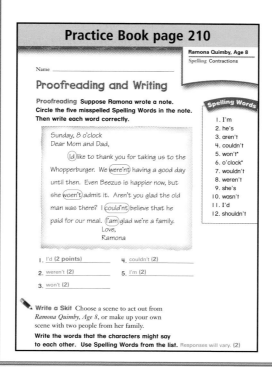

Practice Book page 210

Ramona Quimby, Age 8
Spelling Contractions

Name _____

Proofreading and Writing

Proofreading Suppose Ramona wrote a note. Circle the five misspelled Spelling Words in the note. Then write each word correctly.

Sunday, 8 o'clock
Dear Mom and Dad,

Id like to thank you for taking us to the Whopperburger. We weren't having a good day until then. Even Beezus is happier now, but she wo'nt admit it. Aren't you glad the old man was there? I could'nt believe that he paid for our meal. I'am glad we're a family.
Love,
Ramona

1. I'd **(2 points)**   4. couldn't **(2)**
2. weren't **(2)**   5. I'm **(2)**
3. won't **(2)**

Spelling Words
1. I'm
2. he's
3. aren't
4. couldn't
5. won't
6. o'clock*
7. wouldn't
8. weren't
9. she's
10. wasn't
11. I'd
12. shouldn't

Write a Skit Choose a scene to act out from *Ramona Quimby, Age 8,* or make up your own scene with two people from her family.

Write the words that the characters might say to each other. Use Spelling Words from the list. Responses will vary. **(2)**

Target Skill Trace

Teach	p. 399G
Review	pp. 413H–413I
Extend	Challenge/Extension Activities, p. R19
See	*Handbook for English Language Learners*, p. 223

Transparency 6–21

Dictionary: Spelling Table

A **spelling table** in a dictionary shows letters that spell the same sound in different words. Use a spelling table to look up a word you do not know how to pronounce or spell.

Sound	Spellings	Sample Words
/ă/	a, au	bat, have, laugh
/ā/	a, ai	made, later, rain
	ay, ea	play, great
/â/	air, ar, are	fair, scarce, care,
	eir, ere	their, where
/ä/	a, al	father, calm

SMART SOLUTIONS Ramona Quimby, Age 8
Vocabulary Skill Dictionary: Spelling Table

ANNOTATED VERSION

TRANSPARENCY 6–21
TEACHER'S EDITION PAGE 399G

Monitoring Student Progress

If . . .	Then . . .
students score 4 or below on **Practice Book** page 211,	have them work with partners to correct the items they missed.

VOCABULARY: The Spelling Table in a Dictionary

TARGET SKILL

❶ Teach

Introduce the spelling table. Explain that a spelling table is a useful feature in a dictionary. It can help readers look up words they don't know how to spell.

Display Transparency 6–21. Cover all but the description of *spelling table*. Read aloud the description. Then uncover the top row of the spelling table. Point out that a spelling table is broken into three sections, *Sound*, *Spellings*, and *Sample Words*.

- Point to the /ă/ sound in the first column.
- Then point to the spelling in the second column and explain that these are some different spellings for the sound /ă/.
- Finally, point to the third column and tell students that these are some words containing the sound /ă/ and the letters *a, au*.

Repeat the steps for each row of the spelling table.

Model how to use the spelling table. Using the transparency and the Think Aloud, model how to use the spelling table to spell the word *glanced*.

Think Aloud *I want to spell the word* glanced. *I'll look at the Sample Words column of the spelling table. I see that* bat, have, *and* laugh *have the same* a *sound as* glanced. *I see that this sound is spelled* a *or* au *in the Spellings column. Only the* a *seems right to me:* glanced. *I look it up in the dictionary and find that I made the right choice.*

❷ Guided Practice

Give students practice using the dictionary spelling table. Have partners model for each other how they use the spelling table to spell the words *square* and *wander*. Help students as needed.

❸ Apply

Assign Practice Book page 211.

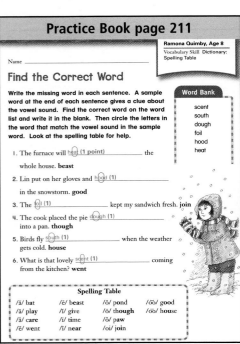

Practice Book page 211

Ramona Quimby, Age 8
Vocabulary Skill Dictionary: Spelling Table

Name _____

Find the Correct Word

Write the missing word in each sentence. A sample word at the end of each sentence gives a clue about the vowel sound. Find the correct word on the word list and write it in the blank. Then circle the letters in the word that match the vowel sound in the sample word. Look at the spelling table for help.

Word Bank

scent
south
dough
foil
hood
heat

1. The furnace will heat (1 point) _____ the whole house. **beast**

2. Lin put on her gloves and hood (1) _____ in the snowstorm. **good**

3. The foil (1) _____ kept my sandwich fresh. **join**

4. The cook placed the pie dough (1) _____ into a pan. **though**

5. Birds fly south (1) _____ when the weather gets cold. **house**

6. What is that lovely scent (1) _____ coming from the kitchen? **went**

Spelling Table

/ă/ bat	/ē/ beast	/ŏ/ pond	/ōō/ good
/ā/ play	/ĭ/ give	/ō/ though	/ōō/ house
/â/ care	/ī/ time	/ô/ paw	
/ĕ/ went	/ĭ/ near	/oi/ join	

STUDY SKILL:
Real-Life Reading (menus, signs, etc.)

❶ Teach

Introduce real-life reading. Point out that being able to read a menu helps people order exactly what they want—and what they can afford—in a restaurant.

- Headings in special type may divide menus into separate Breakfast, Lunch, and Dinner sections. Hours for ordering from each section may be listed.

- Menu headings also tell what kind of food is listed.

- Main sections may include ordering options or choices.

- The cost of each item usually appears directly beside it.

- Sometimes each dish will have a creative name and a short description giving details about what it is like.

Model how to read a menu. Use **Transparency 6–22** and the Think Aloud to model how to use the menu.

Think Aloud *It's 1:00 P.M., so I'll look at the* Lunch *section. I'll skip the* Soup *section because I want a sandwich. Under* Sandwiches, *the* Luckyburger *sounds like too much food, and it's pretty expensive. I only have $10.00. I think I'll order a Turkey Club. It says above that I get a choice of chips or fries. I'll choose fries. The* Beverages *section doesn't say what kinds of juices they have, so I'll have to ask. I'll skip dessert. Then I'll have enough money left over for a tip.*

❷ Practice/Apply

Give students practice in real-life reading.

- Have pairs or small groups study the classroom walls and school corridors for real-life reading opportunities. Then have them share the information they found with another pair or group.

- Have students keep a log for a week of real-life reading that they encounter in the community. Then have them share the kinds of information they found and discuss reading strategies they found helpful.

OBJECTIVES

- Learn menu-reading strategies.
- Identify real-life reading situations.
- Use real-life reading examples as sources of information.

Transparency 6–22

Real-Life Reading
(menus, signs, etc.)

Whopperburger Menu

Lunch
(served from 11:30 to 3:30)
Soups
(cup, $2.50; bowl, $3.50)
Clam Chowder, Chicken Noodle, Lentil
Sandwiches
(come with choice of French fries or chips)

Hamburger	$5.75
Cheeseburger	$6.25
Luckyburger (double-cheeseburger served with lettuce, tomato, and chili topping)	$7.00
BLT	$5.00
Roast Beef	$6.00
Veggie-Burger	$6.00
Turkey Club	$6.00

Salads

Garden	$2.50
Caesar	$3.50

Beverages

Soda	$1.00
Juice	$1.00
Coffee	$1.25
Iced Tea	$1.25

Dessert

Apple Pie	$2.50
Ice Cream Sundae	$3.25

SMART SOLUTIONS Ramona Quimby, Age 8
Information and Study Skills Real-Life Reading
ANNOTATED VERSION

TRANSPARENCY 6–22
TEACHER'S EDITION PAGE 399H

GRAMMAR: Adverbs

GRAMMAR

OBJECTIVES

- Identify adverbs.
- Use adverbs in sentences.
- Proofread and correct sentences with grammar and spelling errors.
- Improve writing by expanding sentences with adverbs.
- Learn academic language: *adverb*.

DAY 1 INSTRUCTION

Adverbs

Teach Display **Transparency 6–24,** and read aloud the three sentences at the top.

- Have students find the words that tell *how, when,* or *where* Beezus walks. Students should identify *sulkily, always,* and *away.* Explain that these words are adverbs.

- Go over the bulleted definitions and rules below the sentences.

- Point out examples of adverbs that tell *how, when,* or *where* on the chart below the rules.

- Have students suggest other examples of adverbs that end in *-ly.* If students suggest words that are not adverbs, tell them that not all words that end in *-ly* are adverbs.

- Ask volunteers to identify the adverbs in Sentences 1–5 and tell whether each adverb tells *how, when,* or *where.*

Daily Language Practice
Have students correct Sentences 1 and 2 on **Transparency 6–23.**

DAY 2 PRACTICE

Independent Work

Practice/Homework Assign **Practice Book** page 212.

Daily Language Practice
Have students correct Sentences 3 and 4 on **Transparency 6–23.**

Transparency 6–23

SMART SOLUTIONS Ramona Quimby, Age 8
Grammar Skill Adverbs
Spelling Skill Contractions

ANNOTATED VERSION

Daily Language Practice

Correct two sentences each day.

1. Ramona says shes total discouraged.
   Ramona says she's totally discouraged.
2. The dreary rain at ten aclok quick ruined her plans.
   The dreary rain at ten o'clock quickly ruined her plans.
3. The soft rain wont pound heavy the roof.
   The soft rain won't pound heavily on the roof.
4. Wuzent it strange that Ramona stared sullen out the window.
   Wasn't it strange that Ramona stared sullenly out the window?
5. Woodent you know that Mr. Quimby sudden made a decision.
   Wouldn't you know that Mr. Quimby suddenly made a decision?
6. Ide say that he certain changed the dismal day.
   I'd say that he certainly changed the dismal day.
7. Beezus shoodent have sobbed so loud.
   Beezus shouldn't have sobbed so loudly.
8. Coodent you say that her mothers decision was complete unfair?
   Couldn't you say that her mother's decision was completely unfair?
9. Im certain that the ceaseless rain near ruined Ramona's day.
   I'm certain that the ceaseless rain nearly ruined Ramona's day.
10. Wernt they saying that the stranger's gift real cheered everyone?
    Weren't they saying that the stranger's gift really cheered everyone?

TRANSPARENCY 6–23
TEACHER'S EDITION PAGE 399I

Monitoring Student Progress

If . . .	Then . . .
students score 7 or below on **Practice Book** page 213,	use the Reteaching lesson on Teacher's Edition page R22.

Transparency 6–24

SMART SOLUTIONS Ramona Quimby, Age 8
Grammar Skill Adverbs

ANNOTATED VERSION

Adverbs

Beezus walks sulkily to school.
Beezus always walks to school.
Beezus walks away.

- A word that describes a verb is an **adverb.**
- Adverbs tell *how, when,* and *where* an action happens.
- Adverbs that tell *how* usually end in *-ly.*

How		When		Where	
quickly	sulkily	always	soon	here	around
slowly	beautifully	first	then	ahead	nearby
happily	softly	later	today	out	there
quietly	fast	next	tomorrow	away	upstairs
secretly	together	often	yesterday	far	
				everywhere	

1. Beezus ran upstairs angrily.
   angrily; how
2. She stomped her foot loudly.
   loudly; how
3. Beezus cried here, there, and everywhere.
   here, there, everywhere; where
4. Soon, Mrs. Quimby talked calmly to Beezus.
   Soon; when. calmly; how
5. Beezus always listens carefully.
   always; when. carefully; how

TRANSPARENCY 6–24
TEACHER'S EDITION PAGE 399I

Practice Book page 212

Ramona Quimby, Age 8
Grammar Skill Adverbs

Name _____

Circling Adverbially

Circle the adverbs in each sentence. Then write the adverbs in the chart below.

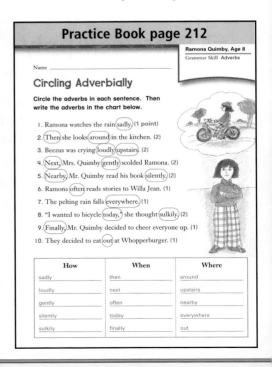

1. Ramona watches the rain sadly. (1 point)
2. Then she looks around in the kitchen. (2)
3. Beezus was crying loudly upstairs. (2)
4. Next, Mrs. Quimby gently scolded Ramona. (2)
5. Nearby, Mr. Quimby read his book silently. (2)
6. Ramona often reads stories to Willa Jean. (1)
7. The pelting rain falls everywhere. (1)
8. "I wanted to bicycle today," she thought sulkily. (2)
9. Finally, Mr. Quimby decided to cheer everyone up. (1)
10. They decided to eat out at Whopperburger. (1)

How	When	Where
sadly	then	around
loudly	next	upstairs
gently	often	nearby
silently	today	everywhere
sulkily	finally	out

Adverb Actions

Have teams create note cards show-ing adverbs that tell how an action happens. Remind students that most adverbs that tell how an action happens end in -ly. You may wish to provide examples: *quickly, softly, smartly, bravely, sadly, shyly, happily, loudly, quietly.*

- Students take turns selecting a card and demonstrating the action of the adverb shown. For example, they might act out writing a letter *quickly* or waving to a friend *happily.*

- Teammates try to guess the secret adverb. If the team guesses the adverb and uses it correctly in a sentence, they get 1 point.

- The team with the most points after 5 or 10 rounds is the winner.

Daily Language Practice
Have students correct Sentences 5 and 6 on **Transparency 6–23.**

Independent Work

Practice/Homework Assign **Practice Book** page 213.

Daily Language Practice
Have students correct Sentences 7 and 8 on **Transparency 6–23.**

Expanding Sentences

Teach Explain to students that good writers use adverbs to make their writing more descriptive and interesting.

- Show the examples at the top of **Transparency 6-25** to model how adverbs can make a sentence more interesting.

- Ask volunteers to suggest ways to add adverbs to Sentences 1–5.

- Have students review a piece of their own writing to see whether they can improve it by expanding their sentences with adverbs.

Practice/Homework Assign **Practice Book** page 214.

Daily Language Practice
Have students correct Sentences 9 and 10 on **Transparency 6–23.**

Practice Book page 213

Name _____

Ramona Quimby, Age 8
Grammar Skill Adverbs

Choosing Adverbs

Choose an adverb from the box to complete each sentence. Use the clue in parentheses to help you.

Word Bank
around
completely
inside
loudly
often
out
quickly
sharply
slowly
quietly

Mr. Quimby parked the car and the family walked inside (1) _____ (where). The customers filled the restaurant completely (1) _____ (how). Ramona and Beezus quarreled loudly (1) _____ (how). Mrs. Quimby scolded them sharply (1) _____ (how). When they were seated, they ordered quickly (1) _____ (how). Soon the waitress appeared. She carried platters of food out (1) _____ (where) of the kitchen.

The Quimbys sat at the table quietly (1) _____ (how). Ramona ate slowly (1) _____ (how). She wished the meal could last forever. She often (1) _____ (when) wished for impossible things. Ramona looked around (1) _____ (where). She wanted to remember her perfect meal.

Transparency 6–25

Expanding Sentences with Adverbs

Ramona babysits for Willa Jean.
Ramona reluctantly babysits for Willa Jean. (how)
Ramona often babysits for Willa Jean. (when)
Downstairs, Ramona babysits for Willa Jean. (where)

Answers may vary. Suggested answers are provided.

1. Ramona reads to Willa Jean.
   Ramona reads slowly to Willa Jean.

2. Willa Jean listens.
   Willa Jean listens carefully.

3. Ramona stops reading.
   Then Ramona stops reading aloud.

4. Willa Jean cries.
   Soon, Willa Jean cries loudly.

5. Ramona reads a few more pages.
   Unhappily, Ramona quickly reads a few more pages.

SMART SOLUTIONS *Ramona Quimby, Age 8*
Grammar Skill Improving Your Writing

ANNOTATED VERSION

TRANSPARENCY 6–25
TEACHER'S EDITION PAGE 399J

Practice Book page 214

Name _____

Ramona Quimby, Age 8
Grammar Skill Adverbs

Expanding Sentences with Adverbs

Add one adverb to each sentence. In the first five sentences, add the adverb in the blank. Use the clues in parentheses to help you. In the other sentences, decide where to add the adverb.
Answers may vary. Sample answers are supplied.

1. Mother talks strictly (1 point) _____ to Becky. (how)

2. Mother often (1) _____ talks to Becky. (when)

3. Becky looks everywhere (1) _____ for Fluffy. (where)

4. "I want to sleep over at Mimi's," Susan shouted angrily (1) _____ . (how)

5. Soon (1) _____ Susan was in tears. (when)

6. Susan slammed her door.
   Susan slammed her door loudly. (1)

7. Becky had listened to the quarrel.
   Becky had secretly listened to the quarrel. (1)

8. She decided to talk to Susan.
   Then she decided to talk to Susan. (1)

9. "May I come in?" asked Becky.
   "May I come in?" asked Becky quietly. (1)

10. "Sure," said Susan, "I will only talk to you and our cat."
    "Sure," said Susan quickly. "I will only talk to you and our cat." (1)

WRITING: Essay

OBJECTIVES

- Identify the characteristics of a good personal essay.
- Write a personal essay.
- Use adverbs to tell more.
- Learn academic language: *essay, adverbs.*

Writing Traits

Word Choice As students revise on Day 3, emphasize that using exact words will help a reader understand what they are saying. Provide these examples:

Without Exact Words Raindrops <u>fell</u> on the sidewalk.

Same Meaning Raindrops <u>pounded heavily</u> on the sidewalk.

DAY 1 PREWRITING

Introducing the Format

Identify characteristics of an essay.

- A personal essay is a short piece of writing that tells the writer's thoughts and feelings about a particular subject.
- The first paragraph should have a topic sentence that states the main idea.
- The essay should then explain the writer's thoughts and feelings about the main idea, providing details and examples for support.
- The concluding sentence should sum up or restate the writer's thoughts and feelings.

Start students thinking about writing an essay.

- Ask students to list three topics that they care about, such as soccer, a pet, and a favorite place.
- Have students write an opinion about each topic.
- Have them save their notes.

DAY 2 DRAFTING

Discussing the Model

Display Transparency 6–26. Ask

- What is the topic of this essay? What is the writer's opinion about it? (rainy days; why she likes them)
- Where does the writer state this opinion? (in the title and in the first paragraph)
- What reasons does the writer give to support this opinion? (She does jigsaw puzzles with her mother, bakes with her father, and makes up games.)
- What details does the writer give to support one of these reasons? (Sample answers for second reason: has tea; pretends to be a princess; talks with English accent)
- What does the last paragraph do? (sums up and restates the main idea)

Display Transparency 6–27 and discuss the guidelines.

Have students draft an essay.

- Have them use their notes from Day 1.
- Assign **Practice Book** page 215 to help students organize their writing.
- Provide support as needed.

Transparency 6–26

An Essay

Rainy Days Are Fun!
by Raina Storm

Although some people tease me because of my name, I think rainy days are fun. My mom grew up in Seattle where it rains all the time. Dad grew up in England where it also rains almost every day. They learned how to have fun indoors on rainy days.

One of Mom's favorite rainy-day activities is doing jigsaw puzzles. When the weather is horrible, she takes out a new 1,000-piece puzzle. We clear off the coffee table in the living room and spread out the pieces. I'm the fastest at finding the corner pieces. Sometimes it takes weeks to finish a puzzle, but a rainy day gets a puzzle off to a good start.

On a cold rainy day, Dad lets me help bake scones. Then we make a big pot of tea. At exactly four o'clock, we have "tea time." We drink hot tea with milk and sugar and eat scones with strawberry jam. I pretend I am an English princess and Mom and Dad are the queen and king of England. We talk with English accents and hold up our pinky fingers when we drink tea.

My favorite rainy-day activity is to make up games using empty plastic bottles or balled-up socks. I like to bowl with ten empty milk cartons and a pair of dad's sweat socks rolled into a ball.

Now you know why my family likes rainy days. I hope our ideas will make your next rainy day a fun day.

Transparency 6–27

Guidelines for Writing an Essay

- Choose a topic that you care about.
- State your opinion clearly. This will be the main point or focus of your essay.
- Include reasons that support your opinion.
- Include details that support each reason.
- Organize each reason into a separate paragraph, along with the details that support it. State the reason in the topic sentence.
- Leave out any details that don't tell more about the main idea.
- Sum up and restate the main idea in the last paragraph.

Practice Book page 215

Ramona Quimby, Age 8
Writing Skill A Personal Essay

Name _____

Planning Your Personal Essay

Use this graphic organizer to help you plan your personal essay. Write your main idea in the top box. Then write two reasons or facts about your idea in the boxes below. Think of details and examples for each reason. Then summarize your main idea in the last box.

My Main Idea:
(2 points)

Reason 1:
(2)

Reason 2:
(2)

Reason 1 Examples and Details:
(2)

Reason 2 Examples and Details:
(2)

Summary and restatement of main idea:
(2)

DAY 3 REVISING

Improving Writing: Using Exact Adverbs

Explain using exact adverbs.

- Adverbs can modify verbs. They can tell how or when an action occurs.
- Exact adverbs give readers more detailed information.

Display Transparency 6–28.

- Discuss the definition and the examples.
- Discuss the adverbs in the box that tell *how* and the adverbs that tell *when*.
- Work with students to add adverbs to each sentence. Discuss how each adverb makes the sentence clearer.

Assign Practice Book page 216.

Have students revise their drafts.

- Display **Transparency 6–27** again. Ask students to use the guidelines to revise their essays.
- Have partners hold writing conferences.
- Ask them to revise any parts of their essay that still need work. Have students look for places to add exact adverbs.
- See Writing Traits on page 399K.

Transparency 6–28

Using Exact Adverbs

Adverbs can modify verbs. Good writers use adverbs to tell more about an action. They can tell *how* or *when*.

The rainstorm began.
The rainstorm began **slowly**. (tells *how*)
The rainstorm began **yesterday**. (tells *when*)

Adverbs	
How	**When**
sadly	always
quietly	finally
fast	never
loudly	yesterday
slowly	tomorrow
completely	now

Sample answers shown.
1. Ramona watched the rain drip (how) ___slowly___ down the window.
2. Mr. Quimby worked (how) ___silently___ at the dining room table.
3. Ramona (when) ___finally___ went upstairs to clean her room.
4. Mary Jane's sleepover party takes place (when) ___tomorrow___
5. Mollycat meowed (how) ___quietly___ at the front door.

DAY 4 PROOFREADING

Checking for Errors

Have students proofread for errors in grammar, spelling, punctuation, and usage.

- Students can use the proofreading checklist on **Practice Book** page 250 to help them proofread their summaries.
- Students can also use the chart of proofreading marks on **Practice Book** page 251.

Practice Book page 216

Ramona Quimby, Age 8
Writing Skill Improving Your Writing

Name _____

Telling More with Adverbs

Adverbs can modify verbs. Good writers use adverbs to tell more about an action. They can tell *how* or *when*.

The cat is meowing.
The cat is meowing **loudly**. (tells *how*)
The cat is meowing **now**. (tells *when*)

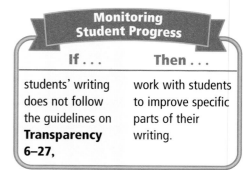

Adverbs That Tell How		Adverbs That Tell When	
sadly	patiently	always	tomorrow
silently	secretly	finally	now
loudly	quickly	never	daily
slowly		yesterday	

Rewrite each sentence by adding an adverb to tell how or when.
Sample answers shown.
1. The family ate their meals together (when) ___daily (1 point)___
2. Ginger stared (how) ___silently (1)___ out the window.
3. The log in the fireplace snapped (how) ___loudly (1)___
4. The family waited (how) ___patiently (1)___ for a table in the restaurant.
5. The man went to the store (when) ___yesterday (1)___
6. The girl (how) ___secretly (1)___ wished for a bicycle.
7. He (when) ___never (1)___ told them about it.
8. The dog ran (how) ___quickly (1)___ past the house.

DAY 5 PUBLISHING

Sharing an Essay

Consider these publishing options.

- Ask students to read their essay or some other piece of writing from the Author's Chair.
- Encourage students to collect their essays in a class book. They can organize the essays by topics or themes.

Portfolio Opportunity

Save students' essays as samples of their writing development.

Monitoring Student Progress

If . . .	Then . . .
students' writing does not follow the guidelines on **Transparency 6–27,**	work with students to improve specific parts of their writing.

Independent Activities

Language Center

VOCABULARY

Building Vocabulary

👤 Singles	🕐 20 minutes
Objective	Create a restaurant word web.

In the selection *Ramona Quimby, Age 8,* Beverly Cleary uses words about the people and objects in restaurants. Look through the selection and find as many of these words as you can. Record them in a web similar to the one below.

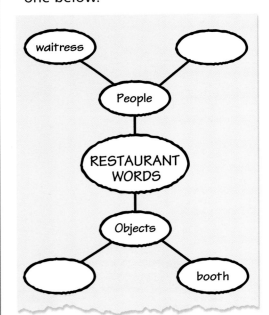

Now think of additional categories and words related to restaurants. Add them to your web.

GRAMMAR

Adverb Game

👥 Pairs	🕐 30 minutes
Objective	Use adverbs to complete sentences.
Materials	Index cards

Write these question words on separate index cards: **How? When? Where?** Mix up the cards and place them face-down in a pile. Each partner takes five blank cards. Start a sentence on each one by writing a noun and an action verb, such as

- *Ramona walks _____.*
- *Picky-picky yowls _____.*

Mix up these cards and place them face-down in another pile. Take turns to play the game:

- The first player takes a sentence card and reads it out loud.
- The same player picks up a question word card. The player completes the sentence with an adverb that answers the question on the card.
- Continue playing until all the sentence cards have been used.

VOCABULARY

Vocabulary Game

👥 Pairs	🕐 30 minutes
Objective	Identify scrambled Key Vocabulary words.
Materials	2 copies of Activity Master 6–3 on page R25

- Review the Key Vocabulary words on Anthology page 368.
- Now pick two other words from the story. Don't show them to your partner.
- Write the two words on a piece of paper and then scramble the letters of each word.
- On your Activity Master, write a sentence for each of the words on the long line after numbers 9 and 10. In your sentences, write the two words in scrambled form and underline them.
- Trade papers with your partner.
- Without looking at the Anthology, try to unscramble all ten words. Write each word correctly on the line after the sentence.
- Get back together with your partner and compare your answers.

Consider copying and laminating these activities for use in centers.

LISTENING/SPEAKING

Dramatize a Story

👥👥👥 Groups	🕐 45 minutes
Objective	Present a dramatization.
Materials	Anthology, markers, a video camera if available

With your group, perform a dramatization of a scene about the Quimbys at the Whopperburger. Reread Anthology pages 384–391. Decide how to dramatize the scene. Here are some different ways to do it:

- A narrator and actors read their parts of the story.
- One or more narrators read the story while the others pantomime the actions.
- Write a play script and perform the scene with action, costumes, props, and sets.

As a group, divide up the responsibilities for preparing and performing the scene. Then practice your parts. Perform the scene for the class.

Tips for Performing a Scene

- Listen carefully for your cues.
- Use gestures, facial expressions, and movements. Vary your tone of voice.
- Pronounce words clearly and loudly.
- Look at the characters you are addressing, but don't turn your back to the audience.

STRUCTURAL ANALYSIS

Contraction Poster

👤 Singles	🕐 30 minutes
Objective	Make a set of rules for contractions.
Materials	Anthology, drawing materials

You already know many different contractions, such as *it's, you're, haven't,* and *I'll.* Choose one or more contraction forms that use *is, are, not,* or *will.* Look for examples in the Anthology. Then make a poster that shows how to form the contractions.

You poster should

- show the two words that make up each contraction,
- include a rule for forming these contractions,
- show an example sentence in which the two words are crossed out and replaced by a contraction.

Illustrate your poster and display it on a classroom bulletin board.

Leveled Readers

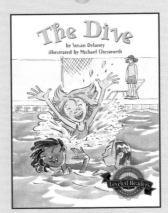

The Dive

Summary *Christy has fun at the pool—showing friends how to do split jumps—until Sara arrives and shows kids how to dive. Then everyone dives—except Christy. At home she tries to learn, with help from her brother and mother. The next day at the pool, Sara offers help as well. Everyone's advice helps Christy overcome her fear.*

Vocabulary

Introduce the Key Vocabulary and ask students to complete the BLM.

dive jump headfirst into water, *p. 4*

blowfish a spiny fish that can puff itself up to scare off enemies, *p. 7*

ruined made a mess of, *p. 10*

whined complained in an annoying way, *p. 11*

in public not private; in front of others, *p. 13*

● BELOW LEVEL

Building Background and Vocabulary

Have students discuss any swimming or diving lessons they have taken. Be sure students understand that diving in the wrong way can hurt. Preview the story with students, using the story vocabulary when possible.

Comprehension Skill: Making Generalizations

Have students read the Strategy Focus on the book flap. Remind students to use the strategy and to make generalizations as they read the book. (See the Leveled Readers Teacher's Guide for **Vocabulary and Comprehension Practice Masters**.)

Responding

Have partners discuss how to answer the questions on the inside back cover.

Think About the Selection Sample answers:

1. Christy enjoys being in the pool. She likes showing other children how to do the split jump.
2. She is being nice. She wants Christy to teach her the split jump.
3. Christy's family and friends work together to teach her how to dive.

Making Connections Responses will vary.

Building Fluency

Model Read aloud page 4. Explain the word *Then* is a transition word that is often put at the beginning of a sentence to tell what happens next.

Practice Have students work in pairs to find other sentences where *then* is used as a transition word. Have them take turns reading aloud the sentences they find.

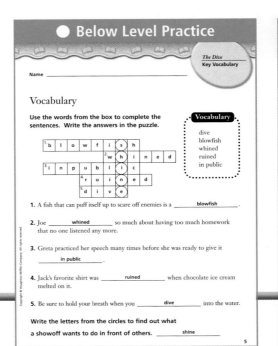

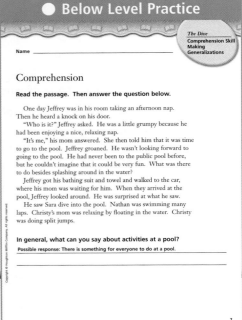

3990 **THEME 6: Smart Solutions**

▲ ON LEVEL

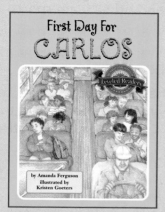

First Day for Carlos

Summary *It is Carlos's first day at his new school and he misses his best friend. Furthermore, he is certain that everyone at the new school already has a best friend and he will be all alone. In class, he is placed in a group with two girls and another boy. As they begin to work together on an assignment, Carlos quickly learns that he and the other boy have a common interest—soccer. On the bus ride home, the boys make plans to kick the soccer ball around.*

Vocabulary

Introduce the Key Vocabulary and ask students to complete the BLM.

sullenly* angrily; not happily; gloomily, *p. 2*

pelting* beating against, *p. 5*

hall monitor a person who supervises the hallway, *p. 5*

discouraged* having no hope or happiness, *p. 5*

transfer change from one place to another, *p. 9*

*Forms of these words are Anthology Key Vocabulary words.

Building Background and Vocabulary

Discuss how it feels to be in an unfamiliar situation or in a place where everyone is a stranger. Preview the story with students, using the story vocabulary.

Comprehension Skill: Making Generalizations

Have students read the Strategy Focus on the book flap. Remind students to use the strategy and to make generalizations as they read the book. (See the Leveled Readers Teacher's Guide for **Vocabulary and Comprehension Practice Masters.**)

Responding

Have partners discuss how to answer the questions on the inside back cover.

Think About the Selection Sample answers:

1. He doesn't know anyone and is afraid he won't make any friends.
2. Possible response: The students in his group seem nice, but Carlos is still worried that he won't fit in.
3. Gregg asks him to be his interview partner. They find out that they both like soccer.
4. Possible response: I think Carlos and Gregg will become good friends. They both like soccer and they take the same bus.

Making Connections Responses will vary.

Building Fluency

Model Read aloud page 2. Explain that a character's thoughts should be read differently from what the character actually says. Usually thoughts are read in a softer voice.

Practice Have students find another example of Carlos's thoughts and have them take turns with a partner reading the thoughts in a soft voice. If they have difficulty, direct them to page 10.

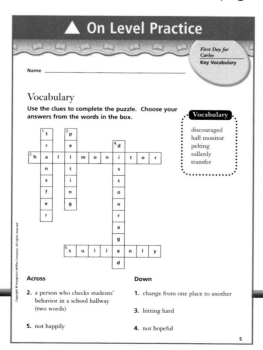

LEVELED READERS

Real Team Soccer

Summary *Soccer player Megan has all the talent to be an excellent individual player, but her coach wants her to play as part of a team. It takes an equally talented opponent to teach Megan that as part of a team, she can win in more ways than one.*

Building Background and Vocabulary

Ask students to share what they know about soccer and other team sports. Preview the story with students, using the story vocabulary when possible.

⟳ Comprehension Skill: Making Generalizations

Have students read the Strategy Focus on the book flap. Remind students to use the strategy and to make generalizations as they read the book. (See the Leveled Readers Teacher's Guide for **Vocabulary and Comprehension Practice Masters.**)

Responding

Have partners discuss how to answer the questions on the inside back cover.

Think About the Selection Sample answers:

1. Megan is a talented athlete. She feels she can win the game on her own.
2. Megan doesn't feel she plays as well when the field is muddy. Her mother points out that teammates can help with the scoring.
3. Angie is a top scorer and plays hard. But she is also willing to pass the ball.
4. Possible response: Yes. She will play team soccer from now on because she has seen that it can work.

Making Connections Responses will vary.

⟳ Building Fluency

Model Read aloud page 9. Point out the heading and explain that headings tell about the paragraphs that follow them.

Practice Have students find and read aloud each heading in the story. Then they can read the paragraphs that follow the heading and explain why the heading is appropriate.

Vocabulary

Introduce the Key Vocabulary and ask students to complete the BLM.

sullenly* angrily; not happily; gloomily, *p. 5*

dreary* gloomy, *p. 9*

dismal* gloomy, *p. 9*

pelting* beating against, *p. 9*

ceaseless* not stopping, *p. 10*

*Forms of these words are Anthology Key Vocabulary words.

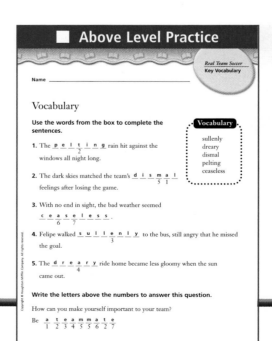

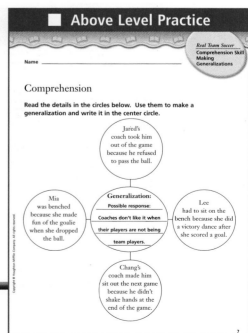

Leveled Readers

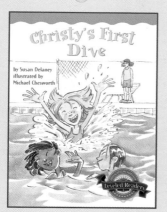

Christy's First Dive

Summary *When Christy goes to a pool party, one of the other guests teaches everyone to dive. But Christy is afraid to try it. After the party, Christy gets diving tips from her mother and brother. When she returns to the pool the next day, Christy is ready to try a dive.*

Vocabulary

Introduce the Key Vocabulary and ask students to complete the BLM.

dive to jump into the water head first, *p. 4*

silly not showing good sense, *p. 6*

scared frightened, *p. 16*

discouraged* having no hope or happiness, *p. 16*

edge the point where an area ends, *p. 17*

*Forms of these words are Anthology Key Vocabulary words.

◆ LANGUAGE SUPPORT

Building Background and Vocabulary

Have students pretend they are at a pool. Have them line up at the edge of the pool and show how they prepare to dive. Then distribute the **Build Background Practice Master** and read aloud the dialogue and questions. Have students complete the page with a partner.

Comprehension Skill: Making Generalizations

Have students read the Strategy Focus on the book flap. Remind students to use the strategy and to make generalizations as they read the book. (See the Leveled Readers Teacher's Guide for **Build Background, Vocabulary, and Graphic Organizer Masters**.)

Responding

Have partners discuss how to answer the questions on the inside back cover.

Think About the Selection   Sample answers:

1. Sara can dive.
2. Christy doesn't dive because she is scared and she does not know how.
3. Responses will vary.

Making Connections   Responses will vary.

Building Fluency

Model   Read aloud page 8 as students follow along in their books. Have them point to the character that is speaking as you read the dialogue.

Practice   Have small groups take the roles of Christy, Nathan, and the narrator. Students should practice reading the page several times before performing it for the class.

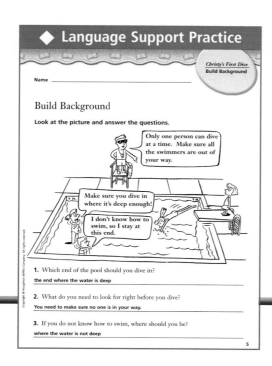

Ramona Quimby, Age 8

399R

Connecting and Comparing Literature

Check Your Progress

Use these Paired Selections to help students make connections with other theme literature and to wrap up the theme.

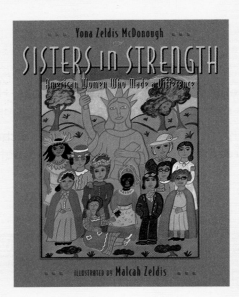

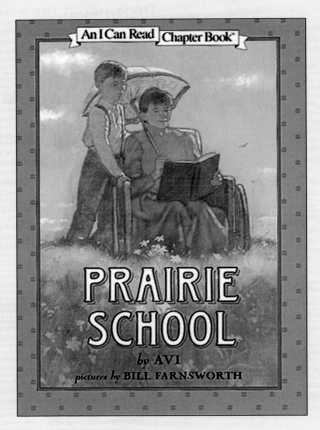

Helen Keller

Genre: Nonfiction

Born in 1880, Helen Keller lost her sight and hearing as a baby. When Helen's teacher, Annie Sullivan, taught her how to communicate using hand signs for letters, a new world opened for Helen.

Prairie School

Genre: Fiction

Aunt Dora wants to teach Noah how to read, but he would rather be outside. She uses the prairie itself to show Noah the value of gaining knowledge through books.

Preparing for Tests

Taking Tests: Strategies

Use this material to prepare for tests, to teach strategies, and to practice test formats.

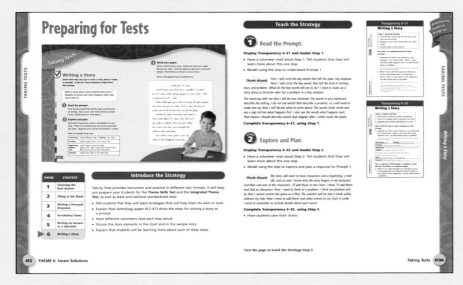

- Independent practice for skills

- Transparencies
- Strategy Posters
- Blackline Masters

Skill Review

Use these lessons and supporting activities to review tested skills in this theme.

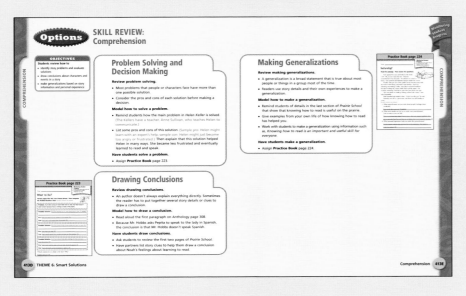

Technology

Audio Selections
Helen Keller

Prairie School

www.eduplace.com
Log on to Education Place for vocabulary support—
  e•Glossary
  e•WordGame

Theme Connections

Anthology Literature

Activities to help students think critically

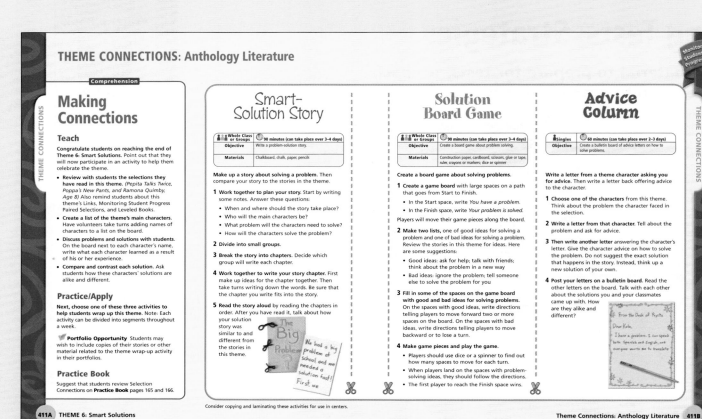

THEME CONNECTIONS: Anthology Literature

Monitoring Student Progress

Comprehension

Making Connections

Teach

Congratulate students on reaching the end of **Theme 6: Smart Solutions**. Point out that they will now participate in an activity to help them celebrate the theme.

- **Review** with students the selections they have read in this theme. (*Pepita Talks Twice, Poppa's New Pants,* and *Ramona Quimby, Age 8*) Also remind students about this theme's Links, Monitoring Student Progress Paired Selections, and Leveled Books.
- **Create a list** of the theme's main characters. Have volunteers take turns adding names of characters to a list on the board.
- **Discuss** problems and solutions with students. On the board next to each character's name, write what each character learned as a result of his or her experience.
- **Compare and contrast** each solution. Ask students how these characters' solutions are alike and different.

Practice/Apply

Next, choose one of these three activities to help students wrap up this theme. Note: Each activity can be divided into segments throughout a week.

Portfolio Opportunity Students may wish to include copies of their stories or other material related to the theme wrap-up activity in their portfolios.

Practice Book

Suggest that students review Selection Connections on **Practice Book** pages 165 and 166.

Smart-Solution Story

Whole Class or Groups	90 minutes (can take place over 3–4 days)
Objective	Write a problem-solution story.
Materials	Chalkboard, chalk, paper, pencils

Make up a story about solving a problem. Then compare your story to the stories in the theme.

1. **Work together to plan your story.** Start by writing some notes. Answer these questions:
   - When and where should the story take place?
   - Who will the main characters be?
   - What problem will the characters need to solve?
   - How will the characters solve the problem?
2. **Divide into small groups.**
3. **Break the story into chapters.** Decide which group will write each chapter.
4. **Work together to write your story chapter.** First make up ideas for the chapter together. Then take turns writing down the words. Be sure that the chapter you write fits into the story.
5. **Read the story aloud** by reading the chapters in order. After you have read it, talk about how your solution story was similar to and different from the stories in this theme.

Solution Board Game

Whole Class or Groups	90 minutes (can take place over 3–4 days)
Objective	Create a board game about problem solving.
Materials	Construction paper, cardboard, scissors, glue or tape, ruler, crayons or markers; dice or spinner

Create a board game about solving problems.

1. **Create a game board** with large spaces on a path that goes from Start to Finish.
   - In the Start space, write *You have a problem.*
   - In the Finish space, write *Your problem is solved.*
   Players will move their game pieces along the board.
2. **Make two lists,** one of good ideas for solving a problem and one of bad ideas for solving a problem. Review the stories in this theme for ideas. Here are some suggestions:
   - Good ideas: ask for help; talk with friends; think about the problem in a new way
   - Bad ideas: ignore the problem; tell someone else to solve the problem for you
3. **Fill in some of the spaces on the game board** with good and bad ideas for solving problems. On the spaces with good ideas, write directions telling players to move forward two or more spaces on the board. On the spaces with bad ideas, write directions telling players to move backward or to lose a turn.
4. **Make game pieces and play the game.**
   - Players should use dice or a spinner to find out how many spaces to move for each turn.
   - When players land on the spaces with problem-solving ideas, they should follow the directions.
   - The first player to reach the Finish space wins.

Advice Column

Singles	60 minutes (can take place over 2–3 days)
Objective	Create a bulletin board of advice letters on how to solve problems.

Write a letter from a theme character asking you for advice. Then write a letter back offering advice to the character.

1. **Choose one of the characters** from this theme. Think about the problem the character faced in the selection.
2. **Write a letter from that character.** Tell about the problem and ask for advice.
3. **Then write another letter** answering the character's letter. Give the character advice on how to solve the problem. Do not suggest the exact solution that happens in the story. Instead, think up a new solution of your own.
4. **Post your letters on a bulletin board.** Read the other letters on the board. Talk with each other about the solutions you and your classmates came up with. How are they alike and different?

Consider copying and laminating these activities for use in centers.

411A THEME 6: Smart Solutions

Theme Connections: Anthology Literature 411B

Three Main Selections

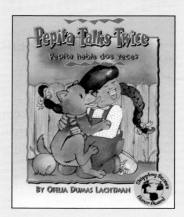

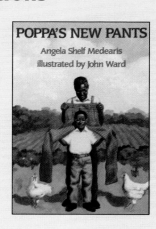

POPPA'S NEW PANTS
Angela Shelf Medearis
illustrated by John Ward

BEVERLY CLEARY
Ramona Quimby, Age 8
ILLUSTRATED BY ALAN TIEGREEN

Leveled Books

Activities to help students connect and compare

Independent Activities

While you work with small groups, students can choose from a wealth of books to complete these activities.

Leveled Readers . . .

for *Pepita Talks Twice*
Tall Tony
Talented Alex
Paul the Artist
The Tallest Boy in the Class

for *Poppa's New Pants*
A Little Bit Hotter Can't Hurt
The Mural
Gampy's Lamps
Chili for Lindy

for *Ramona Quimby, Age 8*
The Dive
First Day For Carlos
Real Team Soccer
Christy's First Dive

Leveled Theme Paperbacks
Mr. Putter and Tabby Fly the Plane
West Side Kids: The Big Idea
Stealing Home

Leveled Bibliography
pages 296E–296F

THEME CONNECTIONS:
Leveled Books

Monitoring Student Progress

THEME CONNECTIONS

A New Ending

🧑 Singles or Pairs	🕐 30 minutes
Objective	Rewrite the ending to a story.
Materials	Reference materials

Choose one of the books you have read. Think about how the story ends:

- How did the characters solve their problem?
- How did the solution make their lives different?

Think up a new ending for the story. You might decide to change one of the following:

- the solution to the problem
- the way the solution works
- the lesson the characters learn

Write your new ending. Then trade stories with a partner. After you finish reading, discuss the stories you wrote. How are your solutions different from the ones in the book? Which ending do you like better? Why?

Draw a Comic Strip

🧑🧑 Pairs	🕐 30 minutes
Objective	Draw comic strips about problems and solutions.
Materials	Paper and pencil, ruler, crayons or markers, reference materials

Choose a problem from any of the books you have read. Draw four big squares in a row on a piece of paper. Then draw a comic strip about the problem and its solution.

In the first square, draw a picture showing the problem. Use the other three squares to show how the person solves the problem.

Think about the following questions:

- What pictures will make people understand the problem and the solution?
- Can you make the pictures funny, or is this a serious comic strip?
- What will the comic strip characters say?

Display your comic strips on a bulletin board. How are the problems and solutions alike? How are they different? What pictures and words did your classmates use?

Create a Conversation

🧑🧑 Pairs	🕐 30 minutes
Objective	Role-play a conversation between two characters from different stories.
Materials	Paper, pencils, and reference materials; props and costumes (optional)

Choose two characters from two different stories. Imagine that these two characters meet and have a conversation about their problems. To refresh your memory of both characters, review the books in which they appear. You can take notes or make a simple outline as you read.

Decide which character you will role-play. Pick a setting where these two characters might meet. Then think about how their conversation might go.

- How are the characters alike and different?
- What would the characters want to tell each other about their problems?
- How are their problems alike and different?
- What advice might the characters give each other?

Then role-play the characters and discuss your problems.

> How about Hellen Keller? She had to learn to read and write.

> Noah in *Prairie School* did, too! What do you think they would say to each other?

Consider copying and laminating these activities for use in centers.

411C THEME 6: Smart Solutions

Theme Connections: Leveled Books 411D

Twelve Leveled Readers

Three Leveled Theme Paperbacks

Daily Lesson Plans

Technology
Lesson Planner CD-ROM allows you to customize the chart below to develop your own lesson plans.

T Skill tested on Theme Skills Test and/or Integrated Theme Test

 50–60 minutes

Connecting and Comparing Literature

CHECK YOUR PROGRESS

Leveled Readers
• Fluency Practice
• Independent Reading

 **DAY 1**

Introducing Paired Selections

Key Vocabulary, 401
miraculously   communicate
condemned   restored
frustrated

Reading the Selection, 402–405
Helen Keller
Comprehension Strategy, 402
Summarize **T**

Classroom Management Activities, 399Y–399Z

Leveled Readers
Tall Tony
Talented Alex
Paul the Artist
The Tallest Boy in the Class

DAY 2

Reading the Selection
Helen Keller

Connecting and Comparing
Problem Solving, 403
Making Inferences, 405

Stop and Think, 405A

Classroom Management Activities, 399Y–399Z

Leveled Readers
A Little Bit Hotter Can't Hurt
The Mural
Gampy's Lamps
Chili for Lindy

 40–60 minutes

Preparing for Tests

TAKING TESTS: Strategies

....

SKILL REVIEW OPTIONS

Comprehension

Structural Analysis

Vocabulary

Spelling

Grammar

Prompts for Writing

Introduce the Strategy, 412
Writing a Story

- -

Comprehension, 413D–413E
Skill Review Options **T**

Structural Analysis, 413F–413G
Skill Review Options **T**

Vocabulary, 413H–413I
Skill Review Options **T**

Spelling, 413J
Words Ending with *er/le* **T**

Grammar, 413L
Adjectives **T**

Prompts for Writing, 413N
Announcement/Ordering Information

Step 1: Read the Prompt, 413A

- -

Comprehension, 413D–413E
Skill Review Options **T**

Structural Analysis, 413F–413G
Skill Review Options **T**

Vocabulary, 413H–413I
Skill Review Options **T**

Spelling, 413J
Words Beginning with *a/be* **T**

Grammar, 413L
Comparing with Adjectives **T**

Prompts for Writing, 413N
Summary/Paraphrasing

Target Skills of the Week

TARGET SKILL

Comprehension
Vocabulary
Phonics/Decoding
Fluency

DAY 3

Key Vocabulary, 405B

sod	prairie
fetch	hauling
fidgeted	trunks

Reading the Selection, 406–410
Prairie School

Comprehension Strategy, 408
Summarize **T**

Classroom Management Activities,
399Y–399Z

Leveled Readers
The Dive
First Day For Carlos
Real Team Soccer
Christy's First Dive

Step 2: Explore and Plan, 413A

Comprehension, 413D–413E
Skill Review Options **T**

Structural Analysis, 413F–413G
Skill Review Options **T**

Vocabulary, 413H–413I
Skill Review Options **T**

Spelling, 413K
Contractions **T**

Grammar, 413M
Adverbs **T**

Prompts for Writing, 413O
Personal Essay/Using Exact Adverbs **T**

DAY 4

Reading the Selection
Prairie School

Connecting and Comparing
Making Generalizations,
407, 409

Think and Compare, 411

Theme Connections: Anthology Literature, 411A–411B

Classroom Management Activities,
399Y–399Z

Leveled Readers
Theme Connections: Leveled Books,
411C–411D

Step 3: Write Your Paper, 413B

Comprehension, 413D–413E
Skill Review Options **T**

Structural Analysis, 413F–413G
Skill Review Options **T**

Vocabulary, 413H–413I
Skill Review Options **T**

Spelling, 413K
VCCV Pattern

Grammar, 413M
Subject Pronouns

Prompts for Writing, 413O
Description/Writing Complete Sentences

DAY 5

Theme Connections: Anthology Literature, cont.

Rereading for Fluency,
405, 406

Classroom Management Activities,
399Y–399Z

Leveled Readers
Theme Connections: Leveled Books,
411C–411D

Writing to a Prompt Test Practice, 413C

Comprehension, 413D–413E
Skill Review Options **T**

Structural Analysis, 413F–413G
Skill Review Options **T**

Vocabulary, 413H–413I
Skill Review Options **T**

Spelling Test, 413K

Grammar, 413M
Object Pronouns

Prompts for Writing, 413O
Persuasive Essay **T**/Correcting
Run-on Sentences

Independent Activities

Assign these activities at any time during the week while you work with small groups.

Suggest that students include copies of their work in their portfolios.

Look for more activities in the Classroom Management Kit.

Language

American Sign Language

Pairs	30 minutes
Objective	Learn about American Sign Language.
Materials	A computer with Internet access

Many deaf and hearing-impaired people use American Sign Language, or ASL, to communicate. There are signs for letters of the alphabet and for numbers as well as signs for words.

Decide what you want to communicate using ASL. You might want to learn how to spell your name, ask a question, or tell something.

- Write your word, question, or message on paper.
- Visit the American Sign Language dictionary website at http://www.masterstech-home.com/asldict.html to learn about ASL.
- At the website, there are letters of the alphabet you can click on for descriptions of the signs for different words. There are also places to click on to see the signs for numbers and for the letters of the alphabet.

Use the signs you learn to communicate with a partner.

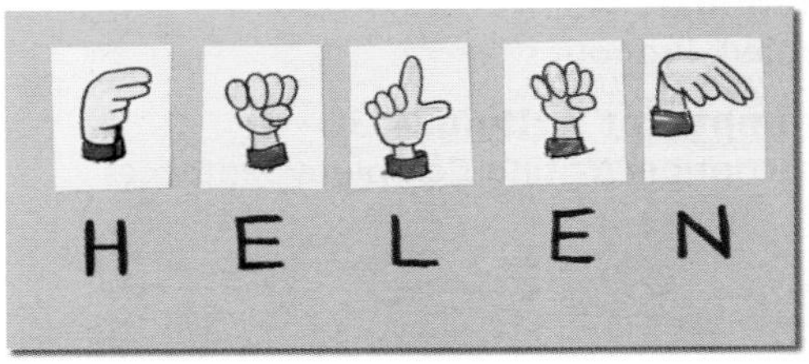

Science

Twinkle, Twinkle Little Star

Singles	45 minutes
Objective	Research stars.
Materials	Reference sources

In *Prairie School,* Aunt Dora shows Noah the Big Dipper, a group of stars that is part of a large constellation known as Ursa Major. Constellations are groups of stars that are shaped somewhat like animals, people, or objects.

Find out more about the Big Dipper, the constellations, a particular star, or stars in general.

Think about questions such as

- What are stars made of?
- How are they different from planets?
- How are they used for navigation?
- When were the constellations named, and who named them?

Decide what you want to research. Then write a paragraph to show what you learned. Include a drawing of the stars you studied.

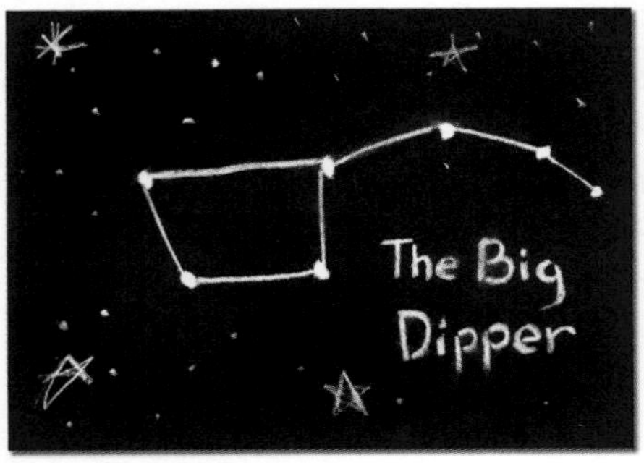

Consider copying and laminating these activities for use in centers.

Language Arts

Write to Noah

Singles	30 minutes
Objective	Write a letter to Noah.
Materials	Anthology

Think about what Noah is like. Think about the kinds of things he might be interested in. Look through the Anthology to find a selection you think Noah would enjoy reading.

Write a letter to Noah. Tell him about this selection and why you think he might enjoy it.

Include in your letter

- the name of the selection and its author
- your opinion about the selection
- the reasons you think Noah would like this selection
- facts and examples from the selection that support your opinion
- an appeal for Noah to read this selection

Career

Special Teachers

Pairs	30 minutes
Objective	List characteristics of good teachers in a word web.

Annie Sullivan taught Helen Keller to communicate. Aunt Dora taught a reluctant Noah that reading is important. Think about these women and other teachers you know.

Brainstorm with a partner a list of the qualities that good teachers have in common. Then make a word web to show your ideas.

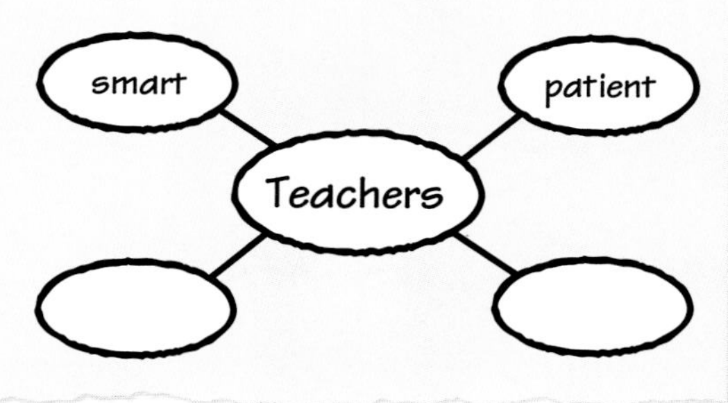

Then, on your own, write a job description for a teacher. Include what you believe are the top three characteristics a teacher should have and why. Get together with your partner and compare descriptions.

Music

A Problem-Solving Song

Groups	30 minutes
Objective	Write a song about problem solving.
Materials	A tape recorder, if available

With your group, write a song about problem solving for the theme *Smart Solutions*. Start by making a list of

- the characters in this theme and the problems they faced
- the ways they solved their problems
- characters in other stories and the ways they solved problems
- problems shared by many third-graders and how they can be solved

You can make up an original tune or make your words fit a familiar tune, such as "Old MacDonald Had a Farm," or "Twinkle, Twinkle, Little Star."

Make a clean copy of your song to post on a bulletin board. Tape-record your song if possible and play it for the class.

Connecting and Comparing Literature

Theme Wrap-Up

Check Your Progress

So far in this theme, you have read three selections about solving problems. Now you're going to read and compare two more selections. You will also practice your test-taking skills.

Before you begin, think about Ofelia Dumas Lachtman's letter on pages 299–300. Compare the way that problem is solved with the way the problems in this theme are solved.

Here are two more selections with problems that need solving. As you read, think about what makes each solution a smart one.

400

Read and Compare

Helen Keller
SISTERS IN STRENGTH
by Yona Zeldis McDonough

Read about how a blind and deaf girl learns to communicate.

Try these strategies:
Evaluate
Monitor and Clarify

PRAIRIE SCHOOL by AVI
pictures by BILL FARNSWORTH

This story is about a boy who thinks reading is not important.

Try these strategies:
Summarize
Predict and Infer

Strategies in Action *Use all your reading strategies while you read.*

401

Use Paired Selections: Check Your Progress

Have students read page 400. Discuss these questions:

- What problems do the stories' characters face? (Rain makes Ramona's family grumpy; Poppa's pants are too long; Pepita has to translate for everyone.)

- How do they solve the problems? (Ramona's family cheers up after eating at a restaurant; Grandma, Big Mama, and Aunt Viney all hem the pants and then give them to George; Pepita tries not speaking Spanish but realizes there are good things about speaking two languages.)

Have students read page 401. Ask this question:

- How might these selections be like the other selections in this theme? (Sample answer: They will probably be about people solving problems.)

Strategies in Action Remind students to use the Summarize strategy as they read the Paired Selections.

Transparency 6–29

Solution Words

On Saturday night, two thieves stole a famous ruby from the city museum. To escape, they jumped from the roof. <u>Miraculously</u>, they did not hurt themselves. A woman saw them race away from the scene.

Detective Trudy Gill was on the case the next morning. At first she was <u>frustrated</u> because she did not have enough clues to solve the crime.

Then the detective's luck changed. The thieves used pay phones to <u>communicate</u> with each other. A pizza store owner overheard one thief talking about the crime on the phone in his restaurant. The owner called the detective, and she caught the thieves at last. A judge <u>condemned</u> the thieves to ten years in prison. The ruby was <u>restored</u> to its case in the museum.

SMART SOLUTIONS *Helen Keller*
Monitoring Student Progress Key Vocabulary

ANNOTATED VERSION

TRANSPARENCY 6–29
TEACHER'S EDITION PAGE 401

Selection 1

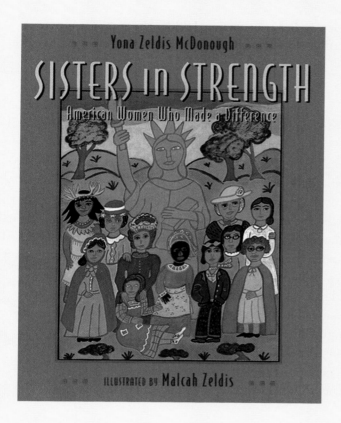

Helen Keller

Yona Zeldis McDonough

SISTERS in STRENGTH
American Women Who Made a Difference

ILLUSTRATED BY Malcah Zeldis

by Yona Zeldis McDonough

Introducing Vocabulary

Key Vocabulary
These words appear in the selection.

miraculously amazingly

condemned doomed

frustrated discouraged and upset

communicate exchange ideas by talking, writing, or other methods

restored brought back

 e • Glossary
e • WordGame

See Vocabulary note on page 404 for additional words to preview.

Have students locate Key Vocabulary words in the story.

- Have volunteers read aloud each sentence containing a Key Vocabulary word.

Display Transparency 6–29.

- Model how to use context clues to find the meaning of *miraculously*.

- Ask students to use context clues to define each remaining Key Vocabulary word.

Practice/Homework Assign **Practice Book** page 217.

Introduce the Graphic Organizer.
Tell students to fill in **Practice Book** page 218 as they read the Paired Selections.

Practice Book page 217

Name _____

Monitoring Student Progress
Key Vocabulary

Learning Word Match

Underline each vocabulary word. Then circle the word or phrase that is most like it in meaning.

Word Bank
miraculously
condemned
frustrated
communicate
restored

1. amazingly miraculously angrily (1 point)
2. frustrated hopeful (disappointed) (1)
3. complicated (write or talk) communicate (1)
4. awarded doomed (condemned) (1)
5. restored (gave back) took away (1)

Answer these questions.
6. What might make you feel **frustrated**?
Answers will vary. (1)
_____

7. Name two ways people can **communicate**.
Sample answer: talking and writing (1)
_____

8. How would Helen's story be different if a doctor had **restored** her sight?
Sample answer: She would have been able to see again
and would not have needed to learn Braille. (1)

Practice Book page 218

Name _____

Monitoring Student Progress
Graphic Organizer Problem Solving

Problem-Solution Chart

Fill in the chart as you read the stories.
Answers will vary. Accept reasonable responses.

Story	What problem do the characters have?	How do the characters solve the problem?
Helen Keller	Helen is frustrated because she is blind and deaf and has not learned a way to communicate with others. (2 points)	Miss Annie teaches Helen how to communicate using hand signs. (2)
Prairie School	Aunt Dora wants to teach Noah how to read, but he is not interested in learning, and would rather be outside. (2)	Aunt Dora teaches Noah outside and shows him how the information in books can be useful on the prairie. (2)

How are the problems and solutions in these stories similar?
Sample answers: Both problems have to do with communication (writing and
speaking); teachers find the solutions to both problems. (2 points)

Guiding Comprehension

1 **NOTING DETAILS** What led the Kellers to decide that Helen needed help? (Helen's birthday was ruined when she smashed her cake and ran into a thorny bush.)

2 **MAKING INFERENCES** Why did Helen destroy her birthday cake? (Sample answers: She didn't know what a birthday cake is for; she didn't understand that her mother was saving it for a special meal.)

3 **PREDICTING OUTCOMES** How do you think Helen will learn to communicate? (Sample answer: by using touch)

COMPREHENSION STRATEGY

Summarize

Teacher Modeling Remind students that summarizing as they read can help them keep track of what is happening. Model summarizing page 402.

Think Aloud *As a baby, Helen Keller had an illness that left her blind and deaf. That frustrated her. She hit children, broke their toys, fell, and ran into things. When she was six, she ruined her birthday cake.*

Vocabulary

miraculously amazingly

condemned doomed

frustrated discouraged and upset

communicate exchange ideas by talking, writing, or other methods

HELEN KELLER

by Yona Zeldis McDonough

Helen Keller was born in 1880. She was just nineteen months old when she had an illness that changed her life.

Captain Keller and his wife watched as their baby Helen twisted and moaned with fever. Doctors were unable to help, and the Kellers feared she would die. Miraculously, Helen recovered. But she could no longer see or hear, and was condemned to a silent, dark world.

Her early life in Tuscumbia, Alabama, was hard. Although bright, Helen was always frustrated by her condition. She fell or slammed into things when she played or ran. Other children avoided her because she hit them or broke their toys. When she smelled the cake her mother had baked for her sixth birthday, she destroyed it with her hands and stuffed chunks of it into her mouth. Her mother wanted to save the cake for a special supper, so she took it away, but Helen began to sob and kick. When her mother

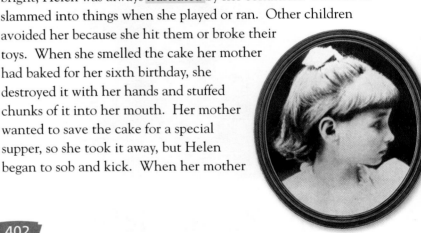

402

Challenge

Additional Reading

Students may want to read other books by Yona Zeldis McDonough. Visit Education Place at **www.eduplace.com** to find out more about the author.

tried to comfort her, Helen rushed outside, right into a thorny bush. The birthday supper was ruined. At that point, the Kellers **1** knew they had to find someone to help their daughter. **2**

Not long after this realization, the Kellers traveled to Washington, D.C., where Helen met Alexander Graham Bell, the inventor of the telephone. Dr. Bell had spent years trying to help deaf people. He took Helen on his lap. She touched his beard and held his pocket watch to her cheek to feel its ticking. Dr. Bell told her parents about a special school for the blind in Boston, where a blind and deaf girl had been taught to communicate. **3** Maybe the school would send a teacher for the Kellers.

403

Connecting and Comparing

Problem Solving

- What problem does Helen have? (She is blind and deaf and has not learned how to communicate with others.)

- What is Pepita's problem in *Pepita Talks Twice*? (Pepita can speak both English and Spanish, so people always ask her to translate for them.)

- Helen's and Pepita's problems both have to do with communicating. How are their problems different? (Helen cannot communicate at all, while Pepita can communicate in two languages.)

- Can you think of possible solutions to Helen's problem? (Sample answers: an operation to cure her blindness or deafness; learning to communicate by touch)

Extra Support/Intervention

Selection Preview

pages 402–403 These pictures show Helen Keller, a little girl who was born in 1880. Helen could not hear or see. What challenges do you think she might face?

page 404 Helen is with her teacher, Annie Sullivan. What do you think Annie might teach Helen?

page 405 Helen is holding a book with writing in Braille, a kind of writing that blind people can read by touch. What do you think she might be doing?

CRITICAL THINKING
Guiding Comprehension

4 **COMPARE AND CONTRAST** How did Helen's home life change after Miss Annie arrived? (Helen started learning hand signs; there were more rules; Helen fought with Miss Annie.)

5 **MAKING JUDGMENTS** Does Miss Annie seem like a good teacher? Why or why not? (Sample answers: yes, because Helen learns to communicate; no, because she is strict and makes Helen angry)

COMPREHENSION STRATEGY
Summarize

Teacher/Student Modeling Have students summarize the events on page 404. Remind them to describe the events in their own words and leave out minor details, such as what words Miss Annie spelled with Helen.

Vocabulary

startled surprised

restored brought back

spout an opening through which water flows

Helen was soon startled by the arrival of a young stranger, Anne Sullivan. Anne had been nearly blind before an operation restored her sight. Now she was here to help Helen. She gave Helen a doll and then took her hand and pressed strange and unfamiliar patterns on it with her fingers. Anne was making the letters D-O-L-L. Helen was confused, but soon learned to imitate the patterns. C-A-T was for when they stroked the cat. C-A-K-E meant she wanted a treat and M-I-L-K a drink. But Helen didn't understand that she was spelling words.

Life with "Miss Annie" was a roller-coaster ride. Helen liked the sewing cards and beads Miss Annie gave her, as well as their walks and pony rides in the woods. But Miss Annie was strict. No more roaming around the table, grabbing food. Helen had to sit in her chair, fold her napkin, and eat with a spoon. The rules made Helen angry. She would hit Miss Annie. Helen even locked the teacher in a room and hid the key.

4

5

404

Challenge

Learn Hand Signs
Have students learn about the American Sign Language signs for the letters of the alphabet. They can find a chart of the signs in an encyclopedia. Have them learn the signs for the letters in their names and then spell their names in sign language for the class.

Then one day, they stopped beside the outdoor pump. Helen held her hand under the spout while Annie pumped. Annie took her other hand and spelled W-A-T-E-R. All at once, something in Helen's face changed. She spelled water herself, several times. She pointed down, and Annie spelled out G-R-O-U-N-D. Suddenly, Helen understood that the signs she had been making were words, and words could be attached to objects, people, animals — anything at all! She pointed to Annie, and Annie spelled T-E-A-C-H-E-R, which became her new name.

Helen's world brightened after that day. She went on to learn Braille, a way for blind people to read. She learned how to speak, which took a long time. Later, she graduated from college with high grades. She became an author and a speaker, and spent most of her life helping blind and deaf people throughout the world.

405

Connecting and Comparing

Making Inferences

- **What was Helen like as a person? What clues tell you this?** (Sample answer: mischievous, because she locks Miss Annie in a room; determined, because she keeps practicing and learns hand signs; helpful, because she spends the rest of her life helping other blind and deaf people)

- **How would you describe Pepita's personality in** *Pepita Talks Twice*? **What clues support this description?** (Sample answers: helpful, because she translates for neighbors; determined, because she sticks with her decision not to speak Spanish through most of the story, even when others try to discourage her from doing so)

- **How are these two girls similar?** (Sample answer: Both are helpful and determined.)

Summarize Have students use what they wrote on their Graphic Organizers to summarize *Helen Keller*.

 Fluency Practice

Rereading for Fluency Suggest that students choose a favorite part of the story to reread to a partner. Encourage them to read with expression.

Stop and Think

Critical Thinking Questions

1. **DRAWING CONCLUSIONS** Why was not being able to communicate with words a problem for Helen? (Sample answers: The only way she could tell people what she wanted was by hitting or grabbing; she couldn't understand what others wanted; she was lonely.)

2. **MAKING INFERENCES** Why do you think Helen decided to spend the rest of her life helping blind and deaf people? (Sample answer: She was grateful that Miss Annie had helped her, and she wanted to help others in return.)

3. **COMPARE AND CONTRAST** This story tells about a real-life solution to a problem someone really had. How is this problem different from the problems in the other stories? (Sample answer: Helen's problem is more serious and takes more time and effort to solve than the problems in the other stories.)

Strategies in Action Have students model how they used Summarize and other strategies to help them understand this selection.

Connecting and Comparing

Problem Solving

- Help students make a list of the solutions to the problems in the theme stories. Discuss how the characters came up with these solutions. Next to each solution, write the method the characters used to come up with it.

- Have students compare and contrast these methods for finding solutions. Encourage them to focus on what the methods have in common.

- Then have students use **Practice Book** page 219 to compare the steps that the characters in each selection took to solve their problems.

Practice Book page 219

Name _____

Monitoring
Student Progress
Connecting and Comparing

Problem-Solution Checklist

In this theme you read about different kinds of problems and solutions. How well did the story characters follow the steps for solving a problem? Fill in the chart below. First read the steps. Put *yes* in the box if the character followed that step. Put *no* in the box if the character did not follow the step.

	Pepita	Poppa and His Family	The Quimbys	Helen Keller's Parents
Step 1: Think about possible solutions.	no (1 point)	no (1)	yes (1)	no (1)
Step 2: Make a list of pros and cons.	no (1)	no (1)	no (1)	no (1)
Step 3: Pick one solution and see if it works.	yes (1)	yes (1)	yes (1)	yes (1)
Step 4: If that solution doesn't work, try another one.	yes (1)	yes (1)	no (1)	no (1)

Which character do you think was the best problem-solver? Why? Answers will vary (4)

_____
_____
_____

REACHING ALL LEARNERS

Extra Support/Intervention

Review Summarize

Help students give brief oral summaries of individual selection pages. Discuss how these summaries aid in understanding the story.

Monitoring Student Progress

If . . .	Then . . .
students had difficulty answering Guiding Comprehension questions,	guide them in reading aloud relevant portions of the text and discussing their answers.

405A THEME 6: Smart Solutions

Selection 2

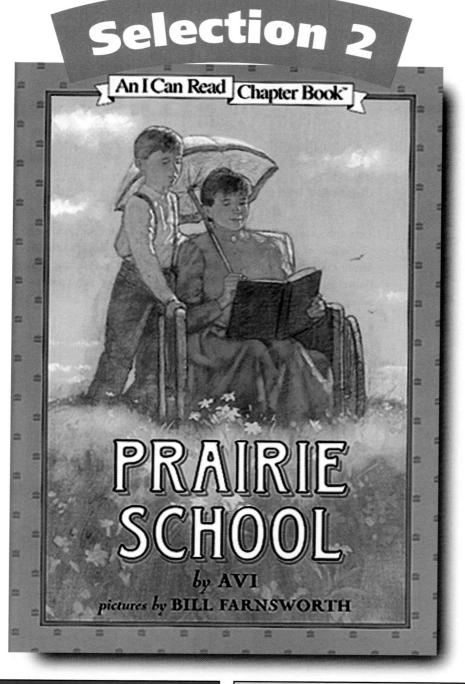

An I Can Read Chapter Book

PRAIRIE SCHOOL

by AVI

pictures by BILL FARNSWORTH

Introducing Vocabulary

Key Vocabulary
These words appear in the selection.

sod mixture of grass and soil

fetch bring

fidgeted moved around restlessly

prairie flat, grassy land with few trees

hauling carrying

trunks sturdy boxes for storing things

e • Glossary
e • WordGame

See the Vocabulary note on page 408 for additional words to preview.

Have students locate Key Vocabulary words in the story.

- Have volunteers read aloud each sentence containing a Key Vocabulary word.

Display Transparency 6–30.

- Work with students to fill in the blanks with the correct Key Vocabulary words.

Practice/Homework Assign **Practice Book** page 220.

Transparency 6–30

Prairie Words

sod fetch fidgeted prairie hauling trunks

Alice was tired of riding in the wagon. She _fidgeted_ on the wooden seat, moving her cramped arms and legs. "When will we be there?" she asked.

Papa said, "We will stop as soon as we find a good place to build our house. It won't be long now, I promise."

There were almost no trees on the _prairie_, just long grass as far as they could see. Alice wondered how they could ever come to like this flat, empty place.

Papa was right, though. Soon they found just the right spot for their house.

"Alice, please _fetch_ my shovel," Papa said. He used the shovel to dig up blocks of _sod_. Papa explained that they would make a house from these thick blocks of earth and grass.

Alice and her family started _hauling_ their things out of the wagon. They took the quilts and dishes and clothes out of the _trunks_ they had stored them in during the journey. Before Alice knew it, the prairie began to feel like home.

Practice Book page 220

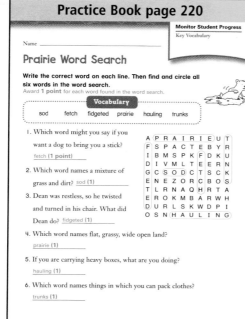

Name _____

Monitor Student Progress
Key Vocabulary

Prairie Word Search

Write the correct word on each line. Then find and circle all six words in the word search.
Award **1 point** for each word found in the word search.

Vocabulary
sod   fetch   fidgeted   prairie   hauling   trunks

1. Which word might you say if you want a dog to bring you a stick?
   fetch **(1 point)**

2. Which word names a mixture of grass and dirt? sod (1)

3. Dean was restless, so he twisted and turned in his chair. What did Dean do? fidgeted (1)

4. Which word names flat, grassy, wide open land?
   prairie (1)

5. If you are carrying heavy boxes, what are you doing?
   hauling (1)

6. Which word names things in which you can pack clothes?
   trunks (1)

```
A P R A I R I E U T
F S P A C T E B Y R
I B M S P K F D K U
D I V M L T E E R N
G C S O D C T S C K
E N E Z O R C B O S
T L R N A Q H R T A
E R O K M B A R W H
D U R L S K W D P I
O S N H A U L I N G
```

Reading the Paired Selections **405B**

READ & COMPARE

CRITICAL THINKING

Guiding Comprehension

❶ NOTING DETAILS What is Aunt Dora trying to teach Noah? (the alphabet; reading)

❷ MAKING INFERENCES Why do you think Noah never learned to read before? (Sample answers: He lives far away from any schools; the story takes place long ago, when not all children went to school.)

❸ DRAWING CONCLUSIONS A sod house is built of blocks of dirt and grass. What do you think the inside of a sod house might be like? (Sample answers: very dim; dirty; stuffy)

Continue the Graphic Organizer.
Remind students to fill in their Problem-Solution Charts as they read *Prairie School*.

PRAIRIE SCHOOL

by Avi
illustrated by Stacey Schuett

This story takes place in Colorado over one hundred years ago. Noah Bidson, who is nine years old, works hard on the family farm. He loves his chores and the freedom of prairie life. All that changes when his Aunt Dora arrives to teach him how to read. Noah is angry. What use does he have for books? **❷**

❶

ONE WEEK

MONDAY

Aunt Dora set up her school in the sod house. A lamp was lit because it was so dim.

But then Noah went to fetch water from the creek two miles away. He took a long time coming back. When he did, Aunt Dora pointed to the letter she had written on the board. "A," she said. "Please repeat that."

"A," Noah said. Then he stood up. "Aunt Dora, I forgot to feed the chickens."

❸

406

Challenge

Additional Reading

Students might enjoy reading other books by Avi. Visit Education Place at www.eduplace.com to learn more about the author.

Vocabulary

sod mixture of grass and soil

fetch bring

fidgeted moved around restlessly

prairie flat, grassy land with few trees

TUESDAY

When Noah came back from his morning chores, he sat in his chair and fidgeted. At the blackboard Aunt Dora wrote the letter B. "This is B," she said. "Can you read it?"

Just then Noah saw a snake in the front yard. "Got to get that snake!" he cried. He didn't come back all day.

WEDNESDAY

Aunt Dora wrote the alphabet on the board. She pointed to the letters with a stick. "Noah, can you find the letters for your name?"

"Nope."

"Noah, don't you ever want to read?"

"Nothing to read on the prairie," he said.

407

Connecting and Comparing

Making Generalizations

- What chores does Noah do on pages 406 and 407? (fetch water from the creek two miles away; feed the chickens)

- What chores does George do on page 344 of *Poppa's New Pants*? (beat rugs; wash windows; move furniture; go to the store)

- George and Noah both live on farms. What generalization can you make about children who live on farms and the things they have to do? (Children on farms work hard and do lots of chores.)

Fluency Practice

Rereading for Fluency Have partners reread pages 406 and 407 aloud together, alternating paragraphs. Encourage them to read the dialogue with expression.

Extra Support/Intervention

Selection Preview

pages 406–407 This story takes place on the prairie over one hundred years ago. What do you think Aunt Dora is trying to teach Noah?

pages 408–409 Aunt Dora has an idea about how to get Noah interested in learning. What do you think it might be?

page 410 Do you think Noah will decide to let Aunt Dora teach him how to read?

Guiding Comprehension

THURSDAY

Whenever Aunt Dora tried to teach, Noah excused himself to do chores. He did them as slowly as possible.

❹ **PROBLEM SOLVING** What is the problem the characters in this story must solve? (Aunt Dora wants to teach Noah to read, but he doesn't want to learn.)

FRIDAY

Aunt Dora put numbers on the board. "Would you like to learn to count?" she asked.

"Aunt Dora," Noah said, "it's too hot and dark to stay in here."

"Noah," Aunt Dora said, "you are as stubborn as a downhill mule on an uphill road."

❹

❺ **MAKING INFERENCES** Why do you think Aunt Dora decides to go out on the prairie, instead of trying to keep Noah inside? (Noah hates being inside, so Aunt Dora decides to see if he'll learn better outside.)

SATURDAY

Aunt Dora was too upset to do any teaching.

SUNDAY

"I'm afraid my kind of schooling won't work here," Aunt Dora said to her sister and brother-in-law.

"Dora," her sister said kindly, "life out here is different."

"And I'm afraid," said Mr. Bidson, "our Noah has become a regular prairie dog."

Aunt Dora laughed. "Now I know what to do!"

❻ **PREDICTING OUTCOMES** Do you think Noah will become interested in reading? Why or why not? (Sample answer: yes, because Aunt Dora is showing him how the knowledge in books can be important on the prairie; no, because he would rather do things than read about them)

408

COMPREHENSION STRATEGY

Summarize

Student Modeling Ask volunteers to summarize the events of pages 406 through 408. Remind them to tell only the main events in their own words, and leave out unimportant details.

English Language Learners

Language Support

Use the story illustrations to help students understand that Aunt Dora uses a wheelchair, and that *wheeled herself* means "moved herself in the wheelchair." You may also want to explain the expressions *as stubborn as a downhill mule on an uphill road* ("very stubborn") and *how come* ("why").

Vocabulary

stubborn not willing to change

hauling carrying

bulb the rounded underground part of certain plants

PRAIRIE SCHOOL

The next morning when Noah came back from hauling water, Aunt Dora had wheeled herself out of the sod house. On her lap was a book. "Noah," Aunt Dora said, "push me around. I need to see this prairie of yours."

5

"The ground isn't flat," he warned. He wondered how her wheelchair would ride.

"Well, then, you'd best tie me in."

When Noah pushed Aunt Dora over the prairie, the chair jumped and rolled like a bucking horse. Aunt Dora held on. "It's very beautiful here," she said. "What is the name of that yellow flower?"

Noah shrugged.

Aunt Dora looked through her book. "It's a dogtooth violet," she said, reading. "The only lily in this area. It grows from a bulb. The Indians boil the bulb and eat it for food."

Noah was surprised. "Is that true?" he asked.

Aunt Dora pointed to the page. "That's what it says here. Now show me some more prairie," she said.

All day Noah wheeled her around. All day Aunt Dora asked questions about what she saw. Noah told her what he knew. Each time, Aunt Dora looked in her book and told him more.

Noah was puzzled. "Aunt Dora, how come you're so smart?"

"I'm just smart enough to read," she said.

6

409

Connecting and Comparing

Making Generalizations

- What expressions do the characters in this story use that sound different from the way you usually hear people talk today? (*as stubborn as a downhill mule on an uphill road; a regular prairie dog*)

- What expressions does George use on page 344 of *Poppa's New Pants*? (*like a Texas tornado; sweated a bucketful*)

- What generalizations can you make about the special expressions or sayings that people use? (Sample answers: People use different expressions in different times and places; people refer to the things around them, like prairie dogs and Texas tornadoes, to help them make up expressions.)

CRITICAL THINKING

Guiding Comprehension

7 **DRAWING CONCLUSIONS** What does Aunt Dora mean when she says she sees "pictures" in the sky? (She sees constellations, or pictures made by drawing imaginary lines connecting stars.)

8 **MAKING JUDGMENTS** Do you think Aunt Dora is a good teacher? Why or why not? (Sample answers: yes, because she is starting to get Noah interested in reading; no, because she lets Noah get away with not listening to her)

Finish the Graphic Organizer.
Have students share and discuss their completed Graphic Organizers.

THE STARS

That night Aunt Dora asked Noah to take her outside. The night sky was full of stars. "Noah," Aunt Dora said, "what do you see up there?"

"Stars," he said.

"I see stars too. But I can also see pictures."

"Pictures? Where?"

"There's the mighty warrior Hercules. There is a snake. There's the Big Dipper. Nearby is the Little Dipper." **7**

Noah said, "Are you going to tell me you get all that from a book too?"

"Reading books only helps me understand what I see and hear."

Noah hung his head. "There are no books on the prairie."

"One of my trunks is full of books."

Noah said nothing.

"Noah," Aunt Dora said softly, "learn to read and you'll read the prairie. What do you say to that?" **8**

After a moment Noah said, "I might try."

410

Challenge

Make Constellation Maps
Have students find information about the constellations. Ask them to make a drawing showing the stars in one constellation. Then have them draw a picture of the image that constellation represents.

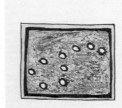

Vocabulary

trunks sturdy boxes for storing things

Think and Compare

Helen Keller
by Yona Zeldis McDonough

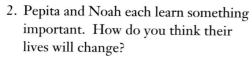

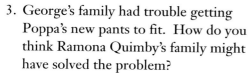

PRAIRIE SCHOOL

1. Compare the way Annie Sullivan helps Helen Keller with the way Aunt Dora helps Noah Bidson. How is their help alike and different?

2. Pepita and Noah each learn something important. How do you think their lives will change?

3. George's family had trouble getting Poppa's new pants to fit. How do you think Ramona Quimby's family might have solved the problem?

4. Think about a time you solved a problem. Compare your experience with a character's experience in this theme.

POPPA'S NEW PANTS
Angela Shelf Medearis
Illustrated by John Ward

BEVERLY CLEARY
Ramona Quimby, Age 8

Strategies in Action Which reading strategies helped you the most in this theme? Why?

Informing

Write an Interview

Have two characters in the theme interview each other. How did they each solve their problems? Write the interview.

Tips

- Write the interview as if it were a real conversation.
- Put yourself in each character's place as you write the interview.

411

Think and Compare

Discuss or Write Have students discuss or write their answers. Sample answers are provided; accept reasonable responses.

1. Both help by teaching their students ways to communicate. Annie Sullivan's help is even more valuable than Aunt Dora's, because Helen Keller could not communicate at all before Annie taught her the hand signs.

2. Pepita will probably go back to translating for people. Noah will probably learn to read, and he will learn more about prairie plants and animals by reading books.

3. Answers will vary.

4. Answers will vary.

Strategies in Action Have students take turns modeling how and where they used Summarize and other reading strategies.

REACHING ALL LEARNERS

| **Extra Support/Intervention** | **English Language Learners** |

Review Summarize

Have students discuss how they used the Summarize strategy. How did putting the story in their own words help them understand it better?

Language Development

Beginning/Preproduction Discuss with students the problems faced by the characters in the two selections they have just read. Help them explain how the problems were solved.

Early Production and Speech Emergence Have pairs of students act out their interviews with each other.

Intermediate and Advanced Fluency Have small groups discuss how they would feel if they had problems similar to those of the characters they chose for their interview.

Monitoring Student Progress

If . . .	Then . . .
students had difficulty answering Guiding Comprehension questions,	guide them in reading aloud relevant portions of the text and discussing their answers.

Reading the Paired Selections 411

Comprehension

Making Connections

Teach

Congratulate students on reaching the end of Theme 6: Smart Solutions. Point out that they will now participate in an activity to help them celebrate the theme.

- **Review with students the selections they have read in this theme.** (*Pepita Talks Twice, Poppa's New Pants,* and *Ramona Quimby, Age 8*) Also remind students about this theme's Links, Monitoring Student Progress Paired Selections, and Leveled Books.

- **Create a list of the theme's main characters.** Have volunteers take turns adding names of characters to a list on the board.

- **Discuss problems and solutions with students.** On the board next to each character's name, write what each character learned as a result of his or her experience.

- **Compare and contrast each solution.** Ask students how these characters' solutions are alike and different.

Practice/Apply

Next, choose one of these three activities to help students wrap up this theme. Note: Each activity can be divided into segments throughout a week.

✔ **Portfolio Opportunity** Students may wish to include copies of their stories or other material related to the theme wrap-up activity in their portfolios.

Practice Book

Suggest that students review Selection Connections on **Practice Book** pages 165 and 166.

Smart-Solution Story

👥👥👥 Whole Class or Groups	🕐 90 minutes (can take place over 3–4 days)	
Objective	Write a problem-solution story.	
Materials	Chalkboard, chalk, paper, pencils	

Make up a story about solving a problem. Then compare your story to the stories in the theme.

1 **Work together to plan your story.** Start by writing some notes. Answer these questions:

- When and where should the story take place?
- Who will the main characters be?
- What problem will the characters need to solve?
- How will the characters solve the problem?

2 **Divide into small groups.**

3 **Break the story into chapters.** Decide which group will write each chapter.

4 **Work together to write your story chapter.** First make up ideas for the chapter together. Then take turns writing down the words. Be sure that the chapter you write fits into the story.

5 **Read the story aloud** by reading the chapters in order. After you have read it, talk about how your solution story was similar to and different from the stories in this theme.

Consider copying and laminating these activities for use in centers.

Solution Board Game

![Whole Class or Groups]	⏱ 90 minutes (can take place over 3–4 days)
Objective	Create a board game about problem solving.
Materials	Construction paper, cardboard, scissors, glue or tape, ruler, crayons or markers; dice or spinner

Create a board game about solving problems.

1 Create a game board with large spaces on a path that goes from Start to Finish.

- In the Start space, write *You have a problem.*
- In the Finish space, write *Your problem is solved.*

Players will move their game pieces along the board.

2 Make two lists, one of good ideas for solving a problem and one of bad ideas for solving a problem. Review the stories in this theme for ideas. Here are some suggestions:

- Good ideas: ask for help; talk with friends; think about the problem in a new way
- Bad ideas: ignore the problem; tell someone else to solve the problem for you

3 Fill in some of the spaces on the game board with good and bad ideas for solving problems. On the spaces with good ideas, write directions telling players to move forward two or more spaces on the board. On the spaces with bad ideas, write directions telling players to move backward or to lose a turn.

4 Make game pieces and play the game.

- Players should use dice or a spinner to find out how many spaces to move for each turn.
- When players land on the spaces with problem-solving ideas, they should follow the directions.
- The first player to reach the Finish space wins.

Advice Column

![Singles]	⏱ 60 minutes (can take place over 2–3 days)
Objective	Create a bulletin board of advice letters on how to solve problems.

Write a letter from a theme character asking you for advice. Then write a letter back offering advice to the character.

1 Choose one of the characters from this theme. Think about the problem the character faced in the selection.

2 Write a letter from that character. Tell about the problem and ask for advice.

3 Then write another letter answering the character's letter. Give the character advice on how to solve the problem. Do not suggest the exact solution that happens in the story. Instead, think up a new solution of your own.

4 Post your letters on a bulletin board. Read the other letters on the board. Talk with each other about the solutions you and your classmates came up with. How are they alike and different?

From the Desk of Pepita

Dear Kola,

I have a problem. I can speak both Spanish and English, and everyone wants me to translate

THEME CONNECTIONS: Leveled Books

While you work with small groups, students can choose from a wealth of books to complete these activities.

Leveled Readers . . .

for *Pepita Talks Twice*
- *Tall Tony*
- *Talented Alex*
- *Paul the Artist*
- *The Tallest Boy in the Class*

for *Poppa's New Pants*
- *A Little Bit Hotter Can't Hurt*
- *The Mural*
- *Gampy's Lamps*
- *Chili for Lindy*

for *Ramona Quimby, Age 8*
- *The Dive*
- *First Day For Carlos*
- *Real Team Soccer*
- *Christy's First Dive*

Leveled Theme Paperbacks

- *Mr. Putter and Tabby Fly the Plane*
- *West Side Kids: The Big Idea*
- *Stealing Home*

Leveled Bibliography

pages 296E–296F

A New Ending

Singles or Pairs	🕐 **30 minutes**	
Objective	Rewrite the ending to a story.	
Materials	Reference materials	

Choose one of the books you have read. Think about how the story ends:

- How did the characters solve their problem?
- How did the solution make their lives different?

Think up a new ending for the story. You might decide to change one of the following:

- the solution to the problem
- the way the solution works
- the lesson the characters learn

Write your new ending. Then trade stories with a partner. After you finish reading, discuss the stories you wrote. How are your solutions different from the ones in the book? Which ending do you like better? Why?

Consider copying and laminating these activities for use in centers.

Draw a Comic Strip

👥 Pairs	🕐 30 minutes	
Objective	Draw comic strips about problems and solutions.	
Materials	Paper and pencil, ruler, crayons or markers, reference materials	

Choose a problem from any of the books you have read. Draw four big squares in a row on a piece of paper. Then draw a comic strip about the problem and its solution.

In the first square, draw a picture showing the problem. Use the other three squares to show how the person solves the problem.

Think about the following questions:

• What pictures will make people understand the problem and the solution?

• Can you make the pictures funny, or is this a serious comic strip?

• What will the comic strip characters say?

Display your comic strips on a bulletin board. How are the problems and solutions alike? How are they different? What pictures and words did your classmates use?

Create a Conversation

👥 Pairs	🕐 30 minutes	
Objective	Role-play a conversation between two characters from different stories.	
Materials	Paper, pencils, and reference materials; props and costumes (optional)	

Choose two characters from two different stories. Imagine that these two characters meet and have a conversation about their problems. To refresh your memory of both characters, review the books in which they appear. You can take notes or make a simple outline as you read.

Decide which character you will role-play. Pick a setting where these two characters might meet. Then think about how their conversation might go.

• How are the characters alike and different?

• What would the characters want to tell each other about their problems?

• How are their problems alike and different?

• What advice might the characters give each other?

Then role-play the characters and discuss your problems.

> How about Hellen Keller? She had to learn to read and write.

> Noah in *Prairie School* did, too! What do you think they would say to each other?

Preparing for Tests

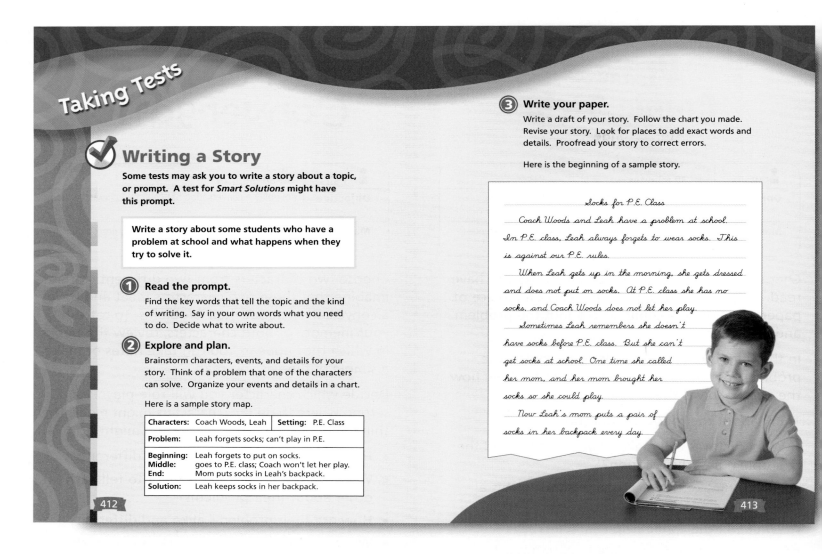

Taking Tests

✓ Writing a Story

Some tests may ask you to write a story about a topic, or prompt. A test for *Smart Solutions* might have this prompt.

> Write a story about some students who have a problem at school and what happens when they try to solve it.

1 Read the prompt.
Find the key words that tell the topic and the kind of writing. Say in your own words what you need to do. Decide what to write about.

2 Explore and plan.
Brainstorm characters, events, and details for your story. Think of a problem that one of the characters can solve. Organize your events and details in a chart.

Here is a sample story map.

Characters:	Coach Woods, Leah	Setting:	P.E. Class
Problem:	Leah forgets socks; can't play in P.E.		
Beginning: **Middle:** **End:**	Leah forgets to put on socks. goes to P.E. class; Coach won't let her play. Mom puts socks in Leah's backpack.		
Solution:	Leah keeps socks in her backpack.		

412

3 Write your paper.
Write a draft of your story. Follow the chart you made. Revise your story. Look for places to add exact words and details. Proofread your story to correct errors.

Here is the beginning of a sample story.

> ### Socks for P.E. Class
> Coach Woods and Leah have a problem at school. In P.E. class, Leah always forgets to wear socks. This is against our P.E. rules.
> When Leah gets up in the morning, she gets dressed and does not put on socks. At P.E. class she has no socks, and Coach Woods does not let her play.
> Sometimes Leah remembers she doesn't have socks before P.E. class. But she can't get socks at school. One time she called her mom, and her mom brought her socks so she could play.
> Now Leah's mom puts a pair of socks in her backpack every day.

413

THEME	STRATEGY
1	**Choosing the Best Answer**
2	**Filling in the Blank**
3	**Writing a Personal Response**
4	**Vocabulary Items**
5	**Writing an Answer to a Question**
▶ **6**	**Writing a Story**

Introduce the Strategy

Taking Tests provides instruction and practice in different test formats. It will help you prepare your students for the **Theme Skills Test** and the **Integrated Theme Test,** as well as state and national standardized tests.

- Tell students that they will learn strategies that will help them do well on tests.
- Explain that Anthology pages 412–413 show the steps for writing a story to a prompt.
- Have different volunteers read each step aloud.
- Discuss the story elements in the chart and in the sample story.
- Explain that students will be learning more about each of these steps.

Teach the Strategy

1 Read the Prompt.

Display Transparency 6–31 and model Step 1.

- Have a volunteer read aloud Step 1. Tell students that they will learn more about this one step.
- Model using the step to understand Prompt 1.

Think Aloud *First, I will circle the key words that tell the topic:* tiny airplane. *Next, I will circle the key words that tell the kind of writing:* story *and* problem. *What do the key words tell me to do? I need to make up a story about a character who has a problem in a tiny airplane.*

The word you *tells me that I will be one character. The words* in your backyard *describe the setting. I do not see words that describe a problem, so I will need to make one up. Now I will decide what to write about. The words* climb inside and see a sign *tell me what happens first. I also see the words* what happens next. *That means I should describe events that happen after I climb inside the plane.*

Complete Transparency 6–31, using Step 1.

2 Explore and Plan.

Display Transparency 6–32 and model Step 2.

- Have a volunteer read aloud Step 2. Tell students that they will learn more about this one step.
- Model using the step to explore and plan a response for Prompt 1.

Think Aloud *My story will need to have characters and a beginning, a middle, and an end. I know that the story begins in my backyard and that I am one of the characters. I'll add these to the chart. I think I'll add Mom and Dad as characters. Now I need to think of a problem. I think my problem will be that I cannot control the plane as it flies. The solution will be that it lands safely without my help. Now I need to add these and other events to my chart in order. I need to remember to include details about each event.*

Complete Transparency 6–32, using Step 2.

- Have students save their charts.

Turn the page to teach the Strategy Step 3.

Transparency 6–31
Writing a Story

> **Step 1: Read the Prompt.**
> - Find the key words that tell the topic and the kind of writing.
> - Restate in your own words what you need to do.
> - Decide what to write about.

Use Step 1 to understand both of these prompts.

1. Suppose you find a tiny airplane in your backyard. You climb inside. Write a story that tells what happens next. Include details about a problem.

   Use the Think Aloud on Teacher's Edition page 413A to model using Step 1 to understand this prompt.

2. What if you went through your television screen and became part of a television show? Write a story about what happened. Include details about a problem.

   - Key words that tell the topic: *through television screen, part of, show.*
   - Key words that tell the kind of writing: *story, problem*
   - What to do to answer the prompt: *write a story with a problem and tell how the problem is solved.*
   - What to write about: *a story with a problem that might be on a television show*

SMART SOLUTIONS
Monitoring Student Progress
Taking Tests Writing a Story
ANNOTATED VERSION

TRANSPARENCY 6–31
TEACHER'S EDITION PAGE 413A

Transparency 6–32
Writing a Story

> **Step 2: Explore and Plan.**
> - Brainstorm characters, events, and details.
> - Think of a problem that a character can solve.
> - Organize your events and details in a chart.

Work with the class to plan a response to this prompt.

1. Suppose you find a tiny airplane in your backyard. You climb inside. Write a story that tells what happens next. Include details about a problem.

   Use the Think Aloud on Teacher's Edition page 413A to model using Step 2 to complete this chart.

Characters Me	Setting my backyard, sky
Problem cannot control plane	
Beginning I climb into plane and push a red button.	
Middle The plane flies into the air. I discover that I cannot control the plane. I decide to enjoy the ride.	
End The plane lands in my backyard.	
Solution The plane lands safely in a tree.	

Plan a response to this prompt. Complete a chart like the one above on a separate paper.

2. What if you went through your television screen and became part of a television show? Write a story about what happened. Include details about a problem.

SMART SOLUTIONS
Monitoring Student Progress
Taking Tests Writing a Story
ANNOTATED VERSION

TRANSPARENCY 6–32
TEACHER'S EDITION PAGE 413A

Transparency 6–33

Writing a Story

SMART SOLUTIONS
Monitoring Student Progress
Taking Tests: Writing a Story

ANNOTATED VERSION

Step 3: Write Your Paper.
• Draft your story. Follow the chart you made.
• Revise your story. Look for places to add exact words and details.
• Proofread your story to correct errors.

Discuss a response to this prompt.

1. Suppose you find a tiny airplane in your backyard. You climb inside. Write a story that tells what happens next. Include details about a problem.

Use the questions on Teacher's Edition page 413B to discuss this model.

Beginning
Last week, I found a tiny airplane parked in my backyard. I've always loved planes, so I climbed inside. I saw a small sign that said "Press red button to fly." I buckled my seat belt and pressed the red button.
Problem (Middle)
Suddenly, the plane swooped straight up into the air. Next, it took a steep dive. I couldn't control it! My seat belt held me safely. I decided to enjoy the ride.
Solution (End)
My flight ended quickly. The plane gently drifted toward Earth and landed in a tree in my back yard. My parents ran toward me, smiling.

Write a response to this prompt on a separate paper. Use the chart you made for Step 2.

2. What if you went through your television screen and became part of a television show? Write a story about what happened. Include details about a problem.

TRANSPARENCY 6–33
TEACHER'S EDITION PAGE 413B

Teach the Strategy continued

Write Your Paper.

Display Transparency 6–33 and discuss Step 3.

• Have a volunteer read aloud Step 3.

• Tell students that they will learn more about writing a story by studying a model of a response to Prompt 1.

Discuss the model. Ask these questions.

• Where does the writer introduce the main character and the setting? (first paragraph)

• Where does the writer introduce the story problem? Where do you see its solution? (second paragraph; end of story)

• What details does the writer give about the problem and the characters? (See underscored details in the Annotated Version.)

• What exact words does the writer use? (Sample answers: *swooped, steep, safely, gently drifted*)

Complete Transparency 6–33, using Step 3.

• When students have finished, ask them to share their story with a partner and discuss places where they could add more details.

English Language Learners

Teach English language learners how to read a writing prompt before asking them to respond to one.

• Introduce students to the various kinds of writing they might find on standardized tests, such as narrative, persuasive essay, or instructions.

• Then share and discuss prompts that ask for each kind of writing. Model restating a prompt in your own words, identifying the kind of writing. Ask students to do the same for several different prompts.

• Have students write a response to a prompt you have already discussed. Later, give them practice responding to prompts you haven't discussed. Encourage them to use words they already know.

Apply the Strategy

Test Practice: Writing to a Prompt

Give students practice with timed writing.

- Many writing assessments are timed.
- If the writing assessment used in your state or district is timed, you might set a time limit for students as they work on their paper.
- This will help students get used to pacing themselves.

Discuss how to revise a story.

- Take a short break before revising your story. Stretch, stare out the window, or close your eyes and relax for a minute.
- Reread your story. Check to be sure that it fits the prompt and that it has characters, a setting, a problem, and a solution.
- Make sure your story has a beginning, middle, and end. Look for places to add details.
- Check to be sure that you told the events in order.
- Look for places to add exact words.
- Check for mistakes. Make sure you used clear handwriting.

Assign Practice Book pages 221 and 222.

- Provide students with practice responding to an additional prompt for a story.
- Emphasize that students should use all three steps to respond to the prompt.

Practice Book page 221

Monitoring Student Progress

Taking Tests Writing a Story

Name _____

Test Practice

Write a response to this prompt. Complete the chart. Then write your story on the lines below it and on page 222. Use the checklist on page 222 to revise your story.

1. A strange dog walks up to you on the street. He stands up on two legs and says, "Will you help me?" You say, "Yes." Write to tell what happens after you say, "Yes."

Characters Answers will vary	Setting
Problem	
Beginning	
Middle	
End	
Solution	

Use the Revising Checklist on page 222 to score each student's story.

_____
_____
_____
_____
_____

Continued on page 222

Practice Book page 222

Monitoring Student Progress

Taking Tests Writing a Story

Name _____

Test Practice continued

_____
_____
_____
_____
_____
_____
_____
_____
_____
_____
_____

If you need more space, use another piece of paper.

Revising Checklist
- ✔ Does my story have characters, a setting, and a problem? (5 points)
- ✔ Does my story have a beginning, a middle, and an end? (5)
- ✔ Do I need more details? Do I need more exact words? (5)
- ✔ Did I use clear handwriting? Did I fix any mistakes? (5)

Read your story aloud to a partner. Then discuss your answers to the questions on the Revising Checklist. Make any changes that will make your story better.

Additional Resources

Teacher's Assessment Handbook

Suggests more strategies for preparing students for standardized tests

Support for Writing Tests

Provides strategy instruction and practice for open-response questions and writing to prompts at Grades 1–6

COMPREHENSION

Problem Solving and Decision Making

Review problem solving.

- Most problems that people or characters face have more than one possible solution.
- Consider the pros and cons of each solution before making a decision.

Model how to solve a problem.

- Remind students how the main problem in *Helen Keller* is solved. (The Kellers have a teacher, Anne Sullivan, who teaches Helen to communicate.)
- List some pros and cons of this solution. (Sample pro: Helen might learn with an expert's help; sample con: Helen might just become too angry or frustrated.) Then explain that this solution helped Helen in many ways. She became less frustrated and eventually learned to read and speak.

Have students solve a problem.

- Assign **Practice Book** page 223.

Practice Book page 223

Monitoring Student Progress
Comprehension Skill
Problem Solving

Name _____

What to Do?

Review pages 406–407 from *Prairie School*. Then complete the Problem-Solution Chart. Sample answers are shown.

Problem: Aunt Dora comes to teach Noah how to read, but Noah doesn't want to learn because there's nothing to read on the prairie.

Possible Solution: Aunt Dora decides not to teach Noah how to read. **(1 point)**

Pro: Noah can spend all day outside on the prairie. (1)

Con: Noah can't read books about the prairie. (1)

Possible Solution: Aunt Dora forces Noah to stay inside and learn to read. (1)

Pro: Noah learns to read. (1)

Con: Noah cannot spend time outside and may not like reading. (1)

Possible Solution: Aunt Dora shows Noah that reading can help him learn about the prairie. (1)

Pro: Noah might want to read so he can learn about the prairie. (1)

Con: Noah still might not be interested in reading. (1)

Which solution do you think is the best? Why?
Answers will vary. (1)

Drawing Conclusions

Review drawing conclusions.

- An author doesn't always explain everything directly. Sometimes the reader has to put together several story details or clues to draw a conclusion.

Model how to draw a conclusion.

- Read aloud the first paragraph on Anthology page 308.
- Because Mr. Hobbs asks Pepita to speak to the lady in Spanish, the conclusion is that Mr. Hobbs doesn't speak Spanish.

Have students draw conclusions.

- Ask students to review the first two pages of *Prairie School*.
- Have partners list story clues to help them draw a conclusion about Noah's feelings about learning to read.

Making Generalizations

Review making generalizations.

- A generalization is a broad statement that is true about most people or things in a group most of the time.
- Readers use story details and their own experiences to make a generalization.

Model how to make a generalization.

- Remind students of details in the last section of *Prairie School* that show that knowing how to read is useful on the prairie.
- Give examples from your own life of how knowing how to read has helped you.
- Work with students to make a generalization using information such as, *Knowing how to read is an important and useful skill for everyone.*

Have students make a generalization.

- Assign **Practice Book** page 224.

Practice Book page 224

Name _____

Monitoring Student Progress

Comprehension Skill
Making Generalizations

Saturday!

Read the passage. Then answer the questions.

Sam opened his eyes and looked at his clock. 7:30. Oh, no, he'd miss the bus! Then he remembered it was Saturday. No school, no reason to hurry. Sam grinned and burrowed deeper under the covers.

Finally, Sam got out of bed, pulled on his favorite jeans with the holes in the knees, and went to the kitchen. Dad was whistling and making waffles. Sam liked weekend breakfasts. He liked reading the comics while Dad read the paper. On weekday mornings, Dad left so early that Sam barely saw him.

"Do you think we could go fishing at Bass Lake today?" Sam asked hopefully.

Dad stretched and winked at him. "I don't see why not," he said.

Saturday was off to a great start, and there was still Sunday to come!

Sample answers are shown.

1. What generalization can you make about people's feelings about weekends?

   Most people like weekends. **(2 points)**

2. What story details can you use to make your generalization? List as many as you can find.

   There is no school; Sam doesn't have to hurry; Sam eats special breakfasts; Sam

   gets to read with Dad; Sam and Dad can go fishing; Sam looks forward to Sunday. **(6)**

3. What personal experiences help you make this generalization?

   Sample answer: I get to relax and have fun on the weekends; I like having a

   break from school. **(2)**

STRUCTURAL ANALYSIS

VCCCV Pattern

Review the VCCCV pattern.

- In words with the VCCCV pattern (three consonants between two vowels), two of the consonants will usually be a consonant cluster or a digraph.
- When breaking VCCCV words into syllables, the consonants in the cluster or digraph stay together.

Model how to decode a VCCCV word.

- Display this phrase: *resolve the conflict*.
- Model decoding *conflict*.

Think Aloud *This word has the VCCCV pattern. I see the consonant cluster fl, so I'll divide the word between n and f. The first syllable is closed, so I pronounce it kahn. The last syllable sounds like flihkt: KAHN flihkt.*

Have students decode words.

- Have partners copy the words *dolphin, hamster, anthem, merchant, partner*, divide them into syllables, and read them aloud.

VCV Pattern

Review the VCV pattern.

- Some words with the VCV pattern are divided before the consonant, while others are divided after the consonant.
- An open syllable ends in a vowel and has a long vowel sound.
- A closed syllable ends with a consonant and has a short vowel sound.

Model how to decode a VCV word.

- Display this phrase: *subway token*.
- Model decoding *token*.

Think Aloud *I see the VCV pattern in this word. I'll try dividing it before the k. This makes the first syllable open, so I pronounce it with a long vowel sound: toh. The second syllable looks like kuhn. When I put them together I get TOH kuhn. That's what you use to pay for a subway ride.*

Have students decode words.

- Assign **Practice Book** page 225.

Practice Book page 225

Name _____

Monitoring Student
Progress

Structural Analysis VCV
Pattern

Divide the Words

Write the word from the box that matches each clue
and draw a line between the syllables.

Word Bank

rodents   final
silent   below
lemon   clever
private   locate

1. at the end fi | nal **(1 point)**

2. animals such as mice, rats, and squirrels
   ro | dents **(1)**

3. intelligent clev | er **(1)**

4. a fruit lem | on **(1)**

5. underneath be | low **(1)**

6. quiet si | lent **(1)**

7. to find lo | cate **(1)**

8. not public pri | vate **(1)**

Contractions

Review contractions.

- A contraction is a shortened form of two words.
- The apostrophe in a contraction stands for the missing letter or letters.

Model how to decode a contraction.

- Display this sentence: *She didn't see it.*
- Model decoding *didn't.*

Think Aloud *In this contraction I recognize the word* did. *The apostrophe between the* n *and the* t *stands for one or more missing letters of a word. I think the word is* not. *When I substitute the words* did not *for* didn't, *the phrase still makes sense.* Didn't *is a contraction for* did not.

Have students decode words.

- Display *you'll, I'm, wasn't, don't, they've, she's.*
- Have students read each contraction and identify the two words that make it up.

VOCABULARY

Options SKILL REVIEW: Vocabulary

OBJECTIVES

Students review how to
- identify and select synonyms
- identify and select antonyms
- use a spelling table

Synonyms

Review synonyms.

- Synonyms are words that mean almost the same thing.
- Synonyms can add different shades of meaning to writing.

Model how to select a synonym.

- Display this sentence: *All my answers were right.*
- Explain that *right* can mean "the direction opposite of left," or it can mean "correct."
- Point out that *right* refers to answers, so in this sentence a good synonym for *right* would be *correct*.

Have students select synonyms.

- Display *take, happy, fix, start.*
- Have partners write a sentence for each word.
- Ask them to rewrite each sentence, using a synonym for the word.

Practice Book page 226

Monitoring Student Progress
Vocabulary Skill Antonyms

Name ______________________

Find the Opposite

Read each sentence. Pick the antonym for each underlined word from the box. Write a new sentence using each antonym. Then circle each antonym.

Sample answers are shown.

Word Bank

quiet	quickly
dirty	late
tame	answer

1. The turtle moved slowly.
   The deer ran quickly into the woods. **(2 points)**
2. Our new clothes were clean.
   Our shoes were dirty. **(2)**
3. I need to ask you a question.
   The teacher told us the answer. **(2)**
4. The campers woke up early in the morning.
   They got home late from practice. **(2)**
5. It was noisy on the school bus.
   It was quiet last night. **(2)**
6. The girls saw wild horses.
   They fed the tame birds. **(2)**

Antonyms

Review antonyms.

- Antonyms are words that have opposite meanings.
- Antonyms are used to help readers see differences.

Model how to identify antonyms.

- Display this sentence: *Zoe's hair was short, but Yazmin's was long.*
- Explain that *short* and *long* have opposite meanings in this sentence, so they are antonyms.

Have students select antonyms.

- Assign **Practice Book** page 226.

Dictionary: Spelling Table

Review the spelling table.

- A spelling table shows the letters or combinations of letters that spell the same sound in different words.

- A dictionary spelling table helps readers look up words they don't know how to spell.

Model how to use a spelling table.

- Display a spelling table and explain that you want to figure out the correct spelling of the word *maintain*.

- Use the table to find the letters that can stand for the /ā/ sound.

- Try the different letter combinations, and check the spelling in the dictionary.

Have students use a spelling table.

- Have partners use a spelling table to find the correct spellings of *slight* and *flame*.

Options

SKILL REVIEW: Spelling

OBJECTIVES

Students review
- words that end with *er* or *le*
- words that begin with *a* or *be*
- words that are contractions
- words with the VCCV pattern

SPELLING WORDS

Basic

little	I'd
again	because
summer	he's
alive	away
purple	couldn't
around	November
I'm	shouldn't
able	apple
wouldn't	about
ago	behind
ever	wasn't
before	later
aren't	

Challenge

mumble
let's
awhile
who's
thermometer

DAY 1 — WORDS ENDING WITH *er/le*

Pretest Use the Day 5 sentences.

Review words ending with *er* or *le*.

- Display *apple*. Read it aloud. Explain that this two-syllable word ends with the /əl/ sounds. Then point to the letters *le*.
- Explain that final /əl/ sounds can be spelled *le*.
- Repeat the process with the word *winter* and the /ər/ sounds spelled *er*.

Have students identify words that end with *er* or *le*.

- Have students make a two-column chart with the headings *le* and *er*.
- Display these words: *little, summer, purple, able, ever, November, later.*
- Have students write each word in the appropriate column and underline the letters that make the /ər/ or /əl/ sounds. Repeat with the Challenge Words *mumble* and *thermometer*.

Practice/Homework Assign **Practice Book** page 245.

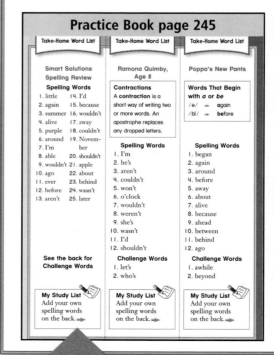

Practice Book page 245

DAY 2 — WORDS BEGINNING WITH *a/be*

Review words that begin with *a* or *be*.

- Display *ahead*, break it into syllables, and read it aloud. Point out that the second syllable is stressed and the first is unstressed.
- Explain that the unstressed /ə/ sound at the beginning of a two-syllable word can be spelled *a*.
- Display *begin*, break it into syllables, and read it aloud. Explain that the unstressed /bĭ/ sounds at the beginning of a word may be spelled *be*.

Have students identify words that begin with *a* or *be*.

- Display these words: *again, alive, around, ago, before, because, away, about, behind.*
- Have students write the words and underline the letter(s) in the first syllable that stand for either the schwa sound or the /bĭ/ sounds.

Practice/Homework Assign **Practice Book** page 227.

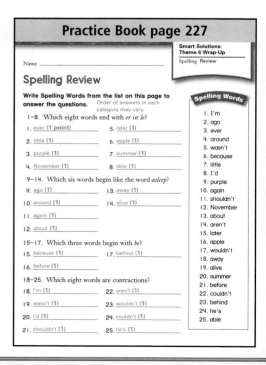

Practice Book page 227

Take-Home Word List

DAY 3 CONTRACTIONS

Review contractions.

- Write the following on the board: *I would* → *I'd*. Read the words aloud and explain that *I'd* is a short form, or contraction, of *I would*.

- Point to the apostrophe in *I'd* and guide students to understand that the apostrophe takes the place of the missing letters *woul* in *I would*.

- Repeat the process, using the words *were not* → *weren't*.

Have students write contractions.

- Display these contractions: *couldn't, shouldn't, wasn't, aren't, wouldn't, I'm, he's*.

- Have students make a two-column chart. Have them copy the contractions into the left column and write the phrases they stand for in the right column.

- Then have them circle any letters from the words in the right column that are missing in the contractions.

Practice/Homework Assign **Practice Book** page 228.

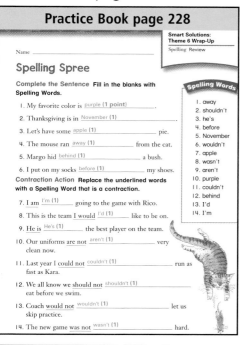

Practice Book page 228

Smart Solutions:
Theme 6 Wrap-Up
Spelling Review

Name _____

Spelling Spree

Complete the Sentence Fill in the blanks with Spelling Words.

Spelling Words

1. My favorite color is purple (1 point) _____.
2. Thanksgiving is in November (1) _____.
3. Let's have some apple (1) _____ pie.
4. The mouse ran away (1) _____ from the cat.
5. Margo hid behind (1) _____ a bush.
6. I put on my socks before (1) _____ my shoes.

Contraction Action Replace the underlined words with a Spelling Word that is a contraction.

7. I am I'm (1) _____ going to the game with Rico.
8. This is the team I would I'd (1) _____ like to be on.
9. He is He's (1) _____ the best player on the team.
10. Our uniforms are not aren't (1) _____ very clean now.
11. Last year I could not couldn't (1) _____ run as fast as Kara.
12. We all know we should not shouldn't (1) _____ eat before we swim.
13. Coach would not wouldn't (1) _____ let us skip practice.
14. The new game was not wasn't (1) _____ hard.

1. away
2. shouldn't
3. he's
4. before
5. November
6. wouldn't
7. apple
8. wasn't
9. aren't
10. purple
11. couldn't
12. behind
13. I'd
14. I'm

DAY 4 VCCV PATTERN

Review the VCCV pattern.

- Display *summer* and *winter*.

- Tell students that each word has two syllables, and point out each word's VCCV pattern.

- Tell students that separating words with this pattern into syllables can help them spell the words correctly.

- Draw lines to divide *summer* and *winter* into syllables.

- Remind students that most words with the VCCV pattern are divided between the two consonants.

Have students write words with the VCCV pattern.

- Display these words: *Sunday, wander, yellow, normal, lumber, sponsor*.

- Ask students to copy the words, underline the VCCV pattern in each one, and draw lines showing how to break each word into syllables.

Practice/Homework Assign **Practice Book** page 229.

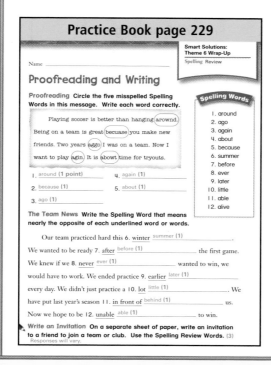

Practice Book page 229

Smart Solutions:
Theme 6 Wrap-Up
Spelling Review

Name _____

Proofreading and Writing

Proofreading Circle the five misspelled Spelling Words in this message. Write each word correctly.

Spelling Words

Playing soccer is better than hanging (arownd.) Being on a team is great (becuase) you make new friends. Two years (aggo) I was on a team. Now I want to play (agin.) It is (abowt) time for tryouts.

1. around (1 point)   4. again (1)
2. because (1)   5. about (1)
3. ago (1)

1. around
2. ago
3. again
4. about
5. because
6. summer
7. before
8. ever
9. later
10. little
11. able
12. alive

The Team News Write the Spelling Word that means nearly the opposite of each underlined word or words.

Our team practiced hard this 6. winter summer (1) _____.
We wanted to be ready 7. after before (1) _____ the first game.
We knew if we 8. never ever (1) _____ wanted to win, we would have to work. We ended practice 9. earlier later (1) _____ every day. We didn't just practice a 10. lot little (1) _____. We have put last year's season 11. in front of behind (1) _____ us.
Now we hope to be 12. unable able (1) _____ to win.

▶ **Write an Invitation** On a separate sheet of paper, write an invitation to a friend to join a team or club. Use the Spelling Review Words. (3)
Responses will vary.

DAY 5 TEST

Say each underlined word, read the sentence, and then repeat the word. Have students write only the underlined word.

Basic Words

1. She **couldn't** see **because** it was dark.
2. **I'd** like to eat lunch **before** we go.
3. We will stay from **November** until the end of next **summer**.
4. **Shouldn't** you try to call them **again**?
5. The guests **aren't** coming until **later**.
6. The **purple** shoe is **behind** the sofa.
7. The stray dog **wouldn't** go **away**.
8. **I'm** happy to be **alive** and in third grade.
9. We can talk **about** how to solve the problem.
10. Eight years **ago** you were a **little** baby.
11. Never run **around** a swimming pool.
12. That **apple** **wasn't** very ripe.
13. My brother isn't **able** to walk to school by himself.
14. **He's** only six years old.
15. Did you **ever** ride on a roller coaster?

Challenge Words

16. I cannot hear you when you **mumble**.
17. **Let's** get some ice cream.
18. **Who's** your math teacher?
19. The **thermometer** showed she had a fever.
20. If we wait **awhile**, it might stop raining.

SKILL REVIEW: Grammar

OBJECTIVES

Students review how to
- identify and use adjectives and articles
- form common comparative and superlative adjectives
- identify and use adverbs
- identify and use subject pronouns
- identify and use object pronouns

DAY 1 — ADJECTIVES

Review adjectives and display the examples.

- An adjective is a word that describes a noun: *Helen Keller had a <u>high</u> fever.*
- Some adjectives tell *what kind* or *how many*: *a <u>terrible</u> illness; <u>nineteen</u> months.*
- *A, an,* and *the* are special adjectives called *articles.*
- Use *a* before a word beginning with a consonant sound: *<u>a</u> teacher.* Use *an* before a word beginning with a vowel sound: *<u>an</u> author.*
- Use *a* and *an* before singular nouns. Use *the* before singular and plural nouns.

Have students identify adjectives.

- Assign **Practice Book** page 230.

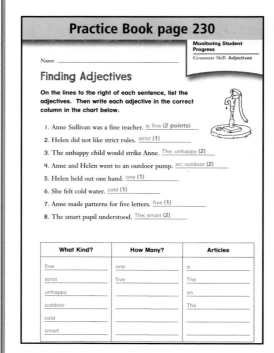

Practice Book page 230

Monitoring Student Progress
Grammar Skill Adjectives

Name _____

Finding Adjectives

On the lines to the right of each sentence, list the adjectives. Then write each adjective in the correct column in the chart below.

1. Anne Sullivan was a fine teacher. a; fine (2 points)
2. Helen did not like strict rules. strict (1)
3. The unhappy child would strike Anne. The; unhappy (2)
4. Anne and Helen went to an outdoor pump. an; outdoor (2)
5. Helen held out one hand. one (1)
6. She felt cold water. cold (1)
7. Anne made patterns for five letters. five (1)
8. The smart pupil understood. The; smart (2)

What Kind?	How Many?	Articles
fine	one	a
strict	five	The
unhappy		an
outdoor		The
cold		
smart		

DAY 2 — COMPARING WITH ADJECTIVES

Review comparing with adjectives.

- Add *-er* to most adjectives to compare two persons, places, or things.
- Add *-est* to most adjectives to compare more than two persons, places, or things.

Identify adjectives that compare.

- Display these sentences: *Miss Annie was <u>stricter</u> than Mrs. Keller was. Miss Annie was the <u>strictest</u> person in the house.*
- Point out that *stricter* is used to compare two persons.
- Point out that *strictest* is used to compare more than two persons.

Have students use adjectives that compare.

- Display these adjectives: *kind, tall.*
- Have partners write sentences, using forms of these adjectives to compare two persons, and then to compare more than two persons.

DAY 3 — ADVERBS

Review adverbs and display the examples.

- A word that describes a verb is an adverb: *Noah walked <u>slowly</u>*.

- Adverbs tell *how, when,* and *where* an action happens: *Aunt Dora spoke <u>clearly</u>. (how) Noah returned <u>later</u>. (when) He worked <u>outdoors</u>. (where)*

- Adverbs that tell *how* usually end in *-ly*.

Have students identify adverbs.

- Assign **Practice Book** page 231.

Practice Book page 231

Monitoring Student Progress
Grammar Skill Adverbs

Name _____

Finding Adverbs

Circle the adverbs in each sentence. Then write the adverbs in the correct column in the chart below.

1. Noah went outside to fetch water. (1 point)
2. Aunt Dora carefully wrote down the letters of the alphabet. (2)
3. Next, she turned to Noah. (1)
4. Then she asked him a question. (1)
5. Noah answered sulkily. (1)
6. He went out and did his chores slowly. (2)
7. Aunt Dora cleverly showed Noah the value of reading. (1)
8. Noah began to study willingly. (1)

Aa Bb Cc Dd
Ee Ff Gg Hh
Ii Jj Kk Ll
Mm Nn Oo Pp
Qq Rr Ss Tt
Uu Vv Ww Xx
Yy Zz

How?	When?	Where?
carefully	Next	outside
sulkily	Then	down
slowly		out
cleverly		
willingly		

DAY 4 — SUBJECT PRONOUNS

Review subject pronouns.

- A pronoun takes the place of one or more nouns.

- The pronouns *I, you, he, she, it, we* and *they* are subject pronouns. Pronouns can be singular or plural.

- Add *-s* or *-es* to a verb when the subject is *he, she,* or *it.*

- Do not add *-s* or *-es* to any verb when the subject is *I, you, we,* or *they.*

Identify subject pronouns.

- Display these pairs of sentences: *The teacher brings a doll.* → *<u>She</u> brings a doll. The patterns spell words.* → *<u>They</u> spell words.*

- Show that in the first pair of sentences, *she* takes the place of *The teacher.*

- Show that in the second pair, *they* takes the place of *The patterns.*

- Point out that the verb *brings,* used with *she,* ends in *-s,* while the verb *spell,* used with *they,* does not.

Have students write subject pronouns.

- Display the following, underlining the indicated words:

    1. *<u>The teacher</u> ___ the pump. (move, moves)*

    2. *<u>The water</u> ___ on the girl's hand. (splash, splashes)*

    3. *<u>The signs</u> suddenly ___ sense to the girl. (make, makes)*

- Have students rewrite the sentences, substituting subject pronouns for the underlined words and filling in the blank with the correct form of the verb.

DAY 5 — OBJECT PRONOUNS

Review subject and object pronouns.

- The pronouns *me, you, him, it, us,* and *them* are object pronouns.

- *It* and *you* are both subject and object pronouns.

- Use *I* as the subject of a sentence. Use *me* as an object pronoun.

- Always capitalize the word *I.*

- Name yourself last when you talk about another person and yourself.

Identify object pronouns.

- Display these sentences: *He learned from Aunt Dora. Aunt Dora helped him.*

- Point out that *he* is the subject of the first sentence, and that *he* is a subject pronoun.

- Point out that in the second sentence, *him* is the object of the verb *helped,* and that *him* is an object pronoun.

Have students write object pronouns.

- Display these sentences, underlining the indicated words:

    1. *Aunt Dora scolded <u>Noah</u>.*

    2. *Aunt Dora talked to <u>Noah's parents</u>.*

- Have students rewrite the sentences, replacing the underlined words with object pronouns.

Independent Activities

SKILL REVIEW:
Prompts for Writing

WRITING

Announcement

👤 Singles	🕐 30 minutes
Objective	Write an announcement.

The church that George's family attends in *Poppa's New Pants* probably posts announcements about special events and activities. An announcement can be written or spoken. It gives important information about an event.

Write an announcement about an upcoming event that you would like to attend. Make sure your announcement answers the following questions: *Who? What? Where? When? Why? How?*

- Include all important information such as date, time, place, and cost (if any).
- Use friendly, easy-to-understand language.
- Include some interesting details.

Remember to organize your information from most important to least important.

Who?	What?	Where?
When?	Why?	How?

Summary

👤 Singles	🕐 30 minutes
Objective	Write a summary.

The selections in this theme show characters and people solving problems in creative ways. Summarizing the main ideas or events in a selection can help you remember how different problems were solved and assist you in sharing what you have read.

Choose a story or nonfiction selection in which the main characters or people solved their problems in a way you admired. Write a summary of that selection.

- Before writing, make a story map to help you plan your summary.
- Briefly tell the main idea of a nonfiction selection or the main character's problem and the most important events in a story.
- Describe how the story or selection ends.

Remember to paraphrase ideas and events, restating them in your own words without changing the author's meaning.

Consider copying and laminating these activities for use in centers.

WRITING

Personal Essay

👤 Singles	🕐 30 minutes
Objective	Write a personal essay.

In *Pepita Talks Twice*, Pepita has strong feelings about having to speak in both English and Spanish. She could have expressed her thoughts and feelings about this topic in a personal essay.

Write a personal essay about something that you feel strongly about, such as an activity or event you really enjoy.

- State the main idea in the first paragraph.
- Give your thoughts and feelings about the topic in the body of the essay.
- Use the words *I* and *my*.
- Include facts and examples that support your main idea.
- Sum up and restate the main idea in the last paragraph.

Remember to use adverbs to tell how or when an action occurs.

Description

👤 Singles	🕐 30 minutes
Objective	Write a description.

In *Prairie School*, Noah learns interesting details about his surroundings from information in Aunt Dora's book and from his own observations. He could use these details to describe the prairie to someone who has never been there.

Think about a place you know well. If possible, find out more about that place by doing some research. Then write a detailed description of the place.

- Begin by introducing the topic.
- Include details that create a vivid picture in the reader's mind.
- Put the details in an order that makes sense.
- Use words that appeal to the senses.

Remember to make sure each sentence you write has a subject and a predicate.

Persuasive Essay

👤 Singles	🕐 30 minutes
Objective	Write a persuasive essay.

In *Ramona Quimby, Age 8*, both Beezus and Ramona would like to convince their parents to let them do things like sleep over at a friend's house or not have to go to the Kemps' house after school.

Think about something you would like your parents or teacher to agree with or do. Write a persuasive essay to convince them.

- Get your readers' attention with a catchy title and an interesting beginning.
- Clearly state your goal or position.
- Build an argument for your position with strong reasons.
- Support your position with accurate facts and examples.
- Restate your goal or position at the end.

Remember to correct run-on sentences by dividing them into two or more sentences, or by joining them with *and* or *but*.

Why I Like to Read

Reading is one of my favorite activities.

One thing I like about reading is

Assessing Student Progress

Monitoring Student Progress

Preparing for Testing

Throughout the theme, your students have had opportunities to read and think critically, to connect and compare, and to practice and apply new and reviewed skills and reading strategies.

Monitoring Student Progress

For Theme 6, *Smart Solutions,* students have read the paired selections—*Prairie School* and *Helen Keller*—and made connections between these and other selections in the theme. They have practiced strategies for writing a story to a prompt, and they have reviewed all the tested skills taught in this theme, as well as some tested skills taught in earlier themes. Your students are now ready to have their progress formally assessed in both theme assessments and standardized tests.

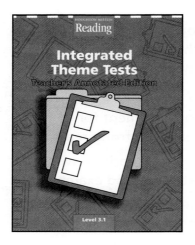

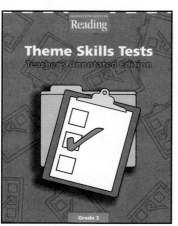

Testing Options

The **Integrated Theme Test** and the **Theme Skills Test** are formal group assessments used to evaluate student performance on theme objectives. In addition to administering one or both of these tests, you may wish to assess students' oral reading fluency.

Integrated Theme Test
- Assesses students' progress as readers and writers in a format that reflects instruction
- Integrates reading and writing skills: comprehension strategies and skills, high-frequency words, spelling, grammar, and writing
- Includes authentic literary passages to test students' reading skills in context

Theme Skills Test
- May be used as a pretest or administered following the theme
- Assesses students' mastery of discrete reading and language arts skills taught in the theme: comprehension skills, high-frequency words, spelling, grammar, writing, and information and study skills
- Consists of individual skill subtests, which can be administered separately

Fluency Assessment

Oral reading fluency is a useful measure of a student's development of rapid automatic word recognition. Students who are on level in Grade 3 should be able to read, accurately and with expression, an appropriate level text at the approximate rates shown in the table below.

Early Grade 3	Mid-Grade 3	Late Grade 3
79–110 words correct per minute	93–123 words correct per minute	114–142 words correct per minute

- You can use the **Leveled Reading Passages Assessment Kit** to assess fluency or a **Leveled Reader** from this theme at the appropriate level for each student.

- For some students, you may check their oral fluency rate three times during the year. If students are working below level, you might want to check their fluency rate more often. Students can also check their own fluency by timing themselves reading easier text.

- Consider decoding and comprehension, as well as reading rate, when evaluating students' reading development.

- For information on how to select appropriate text, administer fluency checks, and interpret results, see the **Teacher's Assessment Handbook,** pp. 25–28.

Technology

Managing Assessment

The *Learner Profile CD-ROM* lets you record, manage, and report your assessment of student progress electronically.

You can
- record student progress on objectives in Theme 6.

- add or import additional objectives, including your state standards, and track your students' progress against these.

- record and manage results from the **Integrated Theme Test** and the **Theme Skills Test** for Theme 6, as well as results from other reading assessments.

- organize information about student progress and generate a variety of student assessment reports.

- use *Learner Profile To Go* to record student progress throughout the day on a handheld computer device, and then upload the information to a desktop computer.

Using Multiple Measures

In addition to the tests mentioned on page 413P, multiple measures might include the following:

- Observation Checklist from this theme
- Persuasive Essay from the Reading-Writing Workshop
- Other writing, projects, or artwork
- One or more items selected by the student

Student progress is best evaluated through multiple measures. Multiple measures of assessment can be collected in a portfolio. The portfolio provides a record of student progress over time and can be useful when conferencing with the student, parents, or other educators.

Turn the page to continue.

Using Assessment to Plan Instruction

You can use the results of theme assessments to determine individual students' needs for additional skill instruction and to modify instruction during the next theme. For more detail, see the test manuals or the **Teacher's Assessment Handbook.**

This chart shows Theme 6 resources for differentiating additional instruction.

Differentiating Instruction

Assessment Shows	Use These Resources	
Difficulty with Comprehension **Emphasize** Oral comprehension, strategy development, story comprehension, vocabulary development	• **Get Set for Reading CD-ROM** • Reteaching: Comprehension, *Teacher's Edition,* pp. R8; R10; R12 • Selection Summaries in **Teachers' Resource Blackline Masters,** pp. 41–43	• Below Level **Leveled Readers** • *Extra Support Handbook,* pp. 196–197, 202–203; 206–207, 212–213; 216–217, 222–223
Difficulty with Word Skills Structural Analysis Phonics Vocabulary **Emphasize** Word skills, phonics, reading for fluency, phonemic awareness	• **Get Set for Reading CD-ROM** • Reteaching: Structural Analysis, *Teacher's Edition,* pp. R14; R16; R18 • *Extra Support Handbook,* pp. 194–195, 198–199; 204–205, 208–209; 214–215, 218–219	• *Handbook for English Language Learners,* pp. 198–199, 200, 202–203, 204, 206; 208–209, 210, 212–213, 214, 216; 218–219, 220, 222–223, 224, 226 • **Lexia Quick Phonics Assessment CD-ROM** • **Lexia Phonics CD-ROM: Intermediate Intervention**
Difficulty with Fluency **Emphasize** Reading and rereading of independent level text, vocabulary development	• Leveled Bibliography, *Teacher's Edition,* pp. 296E–296F • Below Level **Theme Paperback** • Below Level **Leveled Readers**	• Leveled Readers: Below Level lesson, *Teacher's Edition,* pp. 337O; 367O; 399O
Difficulty with Writing **Emphasize** Complete sentences, combining sentences, choosing exact words	• *Handbook for English Language Learners,* pp. 207; 217; 227 • Reteaching: Grammar Skills, *Teacher's Edition,* pp. R20–R22	• Improving Writing, *Teacher's Edition,* pp. 337J, 337L; 339E; 367J, 367L; 399J, 399L
Overall High Performance **Emphasize** Independent reading and writing, vocabulary development, critical thinking	• Challenge/Extension Activities: Comprehension, *Teacher's Edition,* pp. R9; R11; R13 • Challenge/Extension Activities: Vocabulary, *Teacher's Edition,* pp. R15; R17; R19 • Reading Assignment Cards, **Teachers' Resource Blackline Masters,** pp. 85–90	• Above Level **Theme Paperback** • Above Level **Leveled Readers** • Leveled Readers: Above Level lesson, *Teacher's Edition,* pp. 337Q; 367Q; 399Q • Challenge Activity Masters, **Challenge Handbook,** CH6–1 to CH6–6

Resources for Theme 6

Contents

Mr. Putter and Tabby Fly the Plane

Summary *In this fiction story about the sacrifices friends make for each other, Mr. Putter, usually content with his cat, Tabby, fulfills an old wish: He buys a remote-controlled biplane. Things that fly make Tabby nervous, but she puts up with her owner's new hobby. Then Mr. Putter befriends a shy boy who seems to need the plane more than he does, and, like Tabby, the old man finds that making someone else happy means the most of all.*

Vocabulary

biplanes airplanes with two sets of wings, one above the other, *p. 16*

monoplanes airplanes with only one set of wings, *p. 16*

Junkers early all-metal airplanes, named for German engineer Hugo Junkers, *p. 16*

● BELOW LEVEL

Preparing to Read

Building Background Ask students if they've ever put up with something they didn't like for the sake of a friend. Was it hard to make this kind of sacrifice? Then tell students that this story is about an old man and his cat who find contentment by making someone else happy. Ask students which reading strategies might be most helpful when reading fiction. Remind students to use these strategies as they read *Mr. Putter and Tabby Fly the Plane*.

Developing Key Vocabulary Before students read the book or book part, preview with them the Key Vocabulary words. Have volunteers read and define the words. Ask students how these words might be used to describe an old man rediscovering a favorite toy.

Previewing the Text

Read *Mr. Putter and Tabby Fly the Plane* in its entirety or in two segments, pages 8–33 and pages 34–45. Have students preview the book by viewing the cover, reading the chapter titles, and looking at the illustrations. Ask, What is happening on the cover? How will Tabby feel about Mr. Putter's new hobby? What will happen to Tabby? Have students read to find out if their predictions are accurate.

Supporting the Reading

pages 8–33

- Why does the author begin the story by describing Mr. Putter's visits to the toy store? (The author wants the reader to know that Mr. Putter is unusual. Toy stores are usually for kids, and he is an old man.)

- What words does the author use to describe what Tabby does when she's unhappy? (twitch, jump, and hiccup)

- What finally makes Tabby purr? (Mr. Putter's new plane won't start.)

- What else might Mr. Putter have done to get his plane to start? (He could have checked the batteries and read the directions.)

- Have students share the predictions they made before reading this section, and tell whether they were accurate. Then have them make new predictions. Will Tabby learn to like the plane?

How does Tabby's reaction to the plane change? (She gets used to it and doesn't hiccup anymore.)

- Besides the joy of flying his plane, what unexpected pleasure does Mr. Putter's hobby bring him? (Children come around, and he loves their company.)

- What words does the author use to describe the boy? (shy, clumsy, forgetful, strong, sure, happy)

What kind of person does Mr. Putter seem to be? Explain. (He seems kind and sensitive because he notices the change in the shy boy.)

Evaluate how the author tells her story. How clearly did she show the story problems? Did the characters seem true-to-life? (Answers will vary.)

Responding

Have students summarize the main events in *Mr. Putter and Tabby Fly the Plane*. Ask them to share their latest predictions and discuss which were accurate. Then have them write brief "behind the scenes" pages that tell more of the story. Options: 1) a dialogue between Mr. Putter and the boy when Mr. Putter gives him the plane; 2) a letter from the boy to Mr. Putter that describes what the plane means to him; 3) a note from Tabby to Mr. Putter that tells how she feels about his plane.

English Language Learners

Point out the phrase *her nerves weren't as good as they used to be* on page 10. Explain that in this context, *nerves* means "patience or tolerance."

THEME PAPERBACKS

The Big Idea

Summary *In this fiction story from the West Side Kids series, Luz Mendes tries to organize her neighbors to help turn an abandoned park into a garden. When people are slow to respond—especially her best friend, Rosie—Luz doesn't give up. The beautiful result is a tribute to what can happen when someone sets a good example.*

Vocabulary

bodega small grocery store, *p. 1*

stubborn not willing to change in spite of others' requests, *p. 15*

sponsor support or take responsibility for a person or thing, *p. 24*

application written request, *p. 29*

script letters or symbols written by hand, *p. 32*

Preparing to Read

Building Background Ask students if anyone has read other stories in the West Side Kids series. Then ask them to share what they know about making changes. Have they ever tried to get others to help them do something important? Explain that in this story, a young girl takes on a huge project without knowing if she'll have any help. Remind students to use their strategies as they read *The Big Idea*.

Developing Key Vocabulary Before students read the book or book part, preview with them the Key Vocabulary words. Have volunteers read and define the words. Ask students how these words might be important to a story about organizing a neighborhood.

Previewing the Text

Read *The Big Idea* in its entirety or in three segments, pages 1–27, pages 28–52, and pages 53–75. Have students preview the book by looking at the cover and inside illustrations and reading the chapter titles. Then have them predict what will happen. What will become important to Luz? How will she respond?

Supporting the Reading

pages 1–27

- Ask volunteers to give the English meanings of *mira, hola,* and *buenos días* on page 2, and *abuelito* on page 4. ("look," "hello," "good day," and "grandfather")

- Compare the personalities of Officer Carter and Officer Ramirez. **Explain your answer.** (Carter seems stricter and sterner; she just yells without asking for explanations. Ramirez is firm but more understanding because he tries to be sympathetic and helpful to Luz.)

- Have students share and evaluate their predictions. Then have them predict what will happen next. Will the Green Giants help Luz? Will Rosie come around? (Answers will vary.)

ages 28–52

Why is Rosie so angry at Luz? (Rosie is upset about moving away. She wants Luz to pay attention to her instead of the garden.)

Why do you think Mami refuses to sign the application? (Answers will vary. Some students may think Mami's reaction is consistent with how she felt at the beginning of the book: afraid for Luz's safety.)

What does the author mean when she writes, *But the word "we" sings in my ears*? (page 49) (The author wants the reader to understand how happy Luz is to have her brother's help and support.)

ages 53–75

What setback threatens the cleanup effort? (Someone dumps more trash in the lot.)

Name at least one way Luz might have worked to mend her friendship with Rosie. (Answers will vary. Some students may think she should pay special attention to Rosie, write her a letter explaining her feelings, or buy her a gift.)

Why does the author choose "Dreams Come True" as the title of the last chapter? (In the last chapter, all of Luz's hard work results in success. The community hangs a sign on the garden that reads "Luz's Garden: A Dream Come True.")

Responding

sk students to share their use of strategies while reading *The Big Idea*. ave them note which strategy was most helpful, and ask them for an xample of how they used it. Then have them share their latest predictions nd evaluate how these fit with actual story events. Finally, have students hare their reactions to *The Big Idea*.

English Language Learners

Point out and explain the following idiomatic expressions:

- *raining cats and dogs*, p. 11: raining very hard
- *tongue-tied*, p. 17: unable to speak
- *That'll go over like a lead balloon*, pp. 39–40: That idea won't be very popular.

■ ABOVE LEVEL

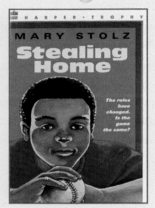

Stealing Home

Summary *Things are going fine for ten-year-old Thomas and his grandfather, who are quite used to living on their own in rural Florida. But when Grandfather's sister-in-law pays them an extended "visit," they discover how thoroughly things—and people—can change.*

Vocabulary

relenting softening in attitude, *p. 2*

disposition a person's usual mood or attitude, *p. 8*

tentatively in an uncertain way; hesitantly, *p. 29*

wistful full of wishful longing, *p. 37*

elude escape from, *p. 39*

dumbfounded filled with astonishment, *p. 61*

pretense something imagined or pretended, *p. 63*

accommodate to do a favor or service, *p. 65*

capacity mental or physical ability, *p. 121*

candor sincerity or openness, *p. 140*

Preparing to Read

Building Background Ask students if they've ever had to make sacrifices or adjustments to help a family friend or relative. What did they have to give up? How did things change—for better or worse? Tell students that this book is about a boy and his grandfather whose lives are turned upside down when a relative appears, uninvited. Ask students to review strategies useful for reading fiction. Remind them to use these strategies as they read *Stealing Home*.

Developing Key Vocabulary Before students read the book or book part, preview with them the Key Vocabulary words. Have volunteers read and define the words. Ask students which of these words might describe the way someone can act around a guest.

Previewing the Text

Read *Stealing Home* in its entirety or in three segments, pages 1–50, pages 51–103, and pages 104–153. Have students preview the book by looking at the cover and reading the summary. Have them predict what problem Thomas will face. How will he react?

Supporting the Reading

pages 1–50

- Why does the author begin the story by focusing on Thomas and his grandfather? (The author wants readers to see the close and loving relationship they have.)

- Point out the word *piscatorial* on page 38 and explain that it means "of or relating to fish." Ask students if this word choice seems typical for Grandfather. Why or why not? (Students may think that this word is typical because Grandfather uses a lot of big words.)

- Have students share and evaluate their predictions. Then have them predict what will happen next. Will Aunt Linzy's visit go smoothly?

pages 51–103

- Point out the word *abrasive* on page 67. Explain that although Grandfather tells Thomas this means "unspeakable," it actually means "rough or harsh."

- What does Thomas do to cope with the changes Linzy's visit has caused? (He talks to his friend Donny. He complains to his grandfather.)

- Have students share and evaluate their predictions. Then have them predict what will happen next. Will Linzy's painting of their house be the final straw for Thomas and Grandfather?

pages 104–153

- Why does Thomas ask Aunt Linzy to go to the planetarium with him? (He feels bad about her fight with Grandfather, and he wants to make her feel better.)

- Consider the choices Aunt Linzy has made throughout the book. Can you generalize about the type of person she seems to be? (Answers will vary.)

- Why does the author end the story with Thomas and Grandfather by themselves again? (The author wants to show that they are still close and loving, and that they've learned about each other through Aunt Linzy's visit.)

Responding

Ask students to share their use of strategies while reading *Stealing Home*. What strategy did they use most frequently with this book? Then have them share their latest predictions and summarize how these fit with actual story events. Finally, have students share their reactions to *Stealing Home*.

Bonus Have students research where each Major League baseball team holds its spring training camp. Then have them mark a map of Florida with icons that show these towns and their host teams.

English Language Learners

Some students may not know that the phrase *out of whack* on page 64 means "not running smoothly," or "broken."

Problem Solving

OBJECTIVES

- Define a problem in a story.
- Identify possible solutions to the problem.

Target Skill Trace

- Problem Solving, pp. 337A–337B

Teach

Begin by telling the students that you have a problem. Say, I want to go to a movie on Saturday, but I also need to clean my house. How can I solve my problem? Call on volunteers to offer solutions to your problem. Write a list of three or four solutions on chart paper. Then read them aloud. Choose one solution and explain to students why that would be your first choice.

Explain to students that what they helped you do is called problem solving. Tell them there are steps they can identify in the process of solving a problem. Write the following steps:

- Identify the problem.
- Think about some solutions.
- Choose the best solution.

Tell students that characters in a story often have a problem to solve. Many stories are about finding a solution to a problem. Ask students to identify the problem and solution in some fables or stories they are familiar with.

Practice

Have students return to the story *Pepita Talks Twice*. Ask, What is Pepita's problem in this story? (She is always asked to talk in both Spanish and English.) Ask, How does Pepita decide to solve her problem?

(She decides to stop speaking Spanish.) Ask, Does Pepita's solution work? (no) Have the students explain why the solution doesn't work. Make a list of examples on chart paper. Your list might include the following answers:

- Pepita can't say the names of foods she likes in Spanish.
- The dog doesn't answer to his name in English.
- Pepita can't help the new girl in her class.
- Pepita can't teach the dog tricks.
- She can't sing songs in Spanish.
- She has to think of a new name for herself.

Ask the students to repeat the three steps for solving a problem. (identify the problem, think of solutions, choose the best solution) Ask, Which steps did Pepita not follow in solving her problem? (Steps 2 and 3) Direct students to think of other ways that Pepita might solve her problem. Ask volunteers to offer other solutions to Pepita's problem. Say, At the end of the story, did Pepita solve her problem? What did she do? (Yes; she decided it was okay to talk twice.)

Apply

Have students use problem-solving skills, with an eye to following the steps in the process, as they read their **Leveled Readers** for the week. Ask students to complete the questions and activity on the Responding page.

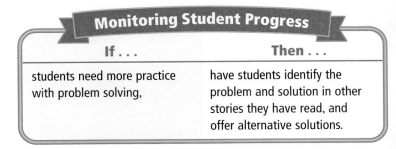

Monitoring Student Progress	
If . . .	Then . . .
students need more practice with problem solving,	have students identify the problem and solution in other stories they have read, and offer alternative solutions.

CHALLENGE/EXTENSION: Problem Solving

Use the Spanish words listed in the Get Set to Read section and in the story *Pepita Talks Twice* to write addition and subtraction story problems. You may want to brainstorm a list of words before beginning the activity. Look at one of the following examples:

- If one taco costs $ .59, how much will two tacos cost?

- Juan buys a collar and a ball for Lobo. The collar costs $3.49, and the ball costs $1.99. How much does Juan spend in all?

When you have finished writing your story problems, exchange papers with a partner. Solve each other's problems.

Form a small discussion group with a few classmates to talk about problems in your neighborhood, school, or community. Make a list of problems. If you are having difficulty thinking of topics, you may want to talk about problems such as: trash in the neighborhood, families who need clothes or food, old playground equipment. Work together to propose a solution to the problem that you can all be involved in. You may want to raise money, form a neighborhood cleanup committee, or collect canned food or clothing for a shelter.

Grade 3 Food Collection

CHALLENGE

Think about the ways in which transportation has changed over the past 100 years. Since the time of the first cars, automobiles have become faster, more comfortable, more reliable, and more efficient. However, we now have a problem because of the pollution caused by automobiles and the shortage of fuel. Look at pictures from magazines or brochures from car dealers to see how cars are changing to meet these new needs.

Design and draw a cleaner, more efficient car to solve the problems of pollution and fuel shortages. Label the features of your car. Make sure your design explains how you have improved your car.

RETEACHING: Comprehension Skills

Drawing Conclusions

OBJECTIVES
- Draw conclusions about events in a story.
- Use strategies to conclude information based on prior knowledge.

Target Skill Trace
- Drawing Conclusions, pp. 367A–367B

Teach

Read the following to the students:

As I sat on the couch, I heard the refrigerator open and close. Then I heard the cabinet doors open. There was a cracking sound, and next I heard the whir of the electric mixer. The oven door creaked as it opened, and pretty soon, the smell of chocolate drifted out to the living room.

Ask, What do you think was happening? (Someone was baking a cake or cookies.) Ask, What clues in the story help you know someone is cooking? (refrigerator door opens and closes, eggs cracking and mixer whirring, oven door opening) Ask, What do you know about baking that helps you draw your conclusion? (You bake in an oven, you find ingredients in the cabinets and refrigerator, and you use a mixer.)

Remind students that they can use clues in the story, and what they know, to help them draw conclusions.

Practice

Have students return to the story *Poppa's New Pants* on pages 284–285. Read aloud this sentence from the story:

Poppa and I had beaten so many rugs, washed so many windows, and moved around so much furniture that we'd sweated a bucketful.

Ask, What were Poppa and the speaker doing? (chores, cleaning house) Ask, Does the text say "Poppa and I cleaned house"? (no) How do you know that is what is happening? (prior knowledge of cleaning, clues in

the picture) Say, You can draw a conclusion about what Poppa and the speaker are doing to clean the house, based on what you know about cleaning a house.

Have students turn to pages 286–287. Read page 286 together. Ask, What does the storekeeper in this store sell? (farm equipment, food, pants, candy) How do you know? (from the text and illustration) Ask, Have you ever been in a store that sells all of those things? Lead students in a discussion about how this store is different from stores they know. Ask them what kind of store this might be. (a country store that has many different items for sale)

Apply

Have students draw conclusions, with an eye to using story clues and their own knowledge, as they read their **Leveled Readers** for the week. Ask students to complete the questions and activity on the Responding page.

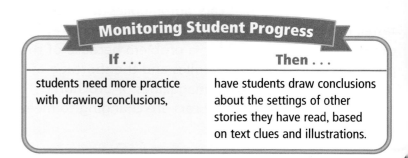

Monitoring Student Progress

If . . .	Then . . .
students need more practice with drawing conclusions,	have students draw conclusions about the settings of other stories they have read, based on text clues and illustrations.

CHALLENGE/EXTENSION:
Drawing Conclusions

Independent Activities

Work in a small group. Your group will need a large piece of chart paper or butcher paper. Think of a story that the whole class has read. Illustrate a scene from that story on the paper.

When your group has finished, come together in a large group to guess which story each illustration is from. As each scene is named, ask the student or students who guessed correctly to name individual clues that helped them to guess each story. Have a volunteer write the clues and the story name on the board in the following format:

ice and snow + sinking ship + small boats = Trapped by the Ice!

young girl + eggs + a dragon = Raising Dragons

In *Poppa's New Pants,* the story begins with everyone working together to clean the house. Make a list of chores that need to be done daily and weekly to have a clean house. Next, make a chart that shows who is responsible for each chore in your house. You may want to copy the chart at right to use as an example.

	Mom	Dad	Brother	Me
daily chores				
weekly chores				

CHALLENGE

Remember that Poppa and George spent all day cleaning the house for the visiting relatives. What chores do you do? How long does it take you to do your chores?

Make a list of chores you do at home. Next, write the number of minutes it takes you to do each chore. Add up the times taken for each chore to determine how many minutes it takes you to do all your chores.

Making Generalizations

OBJECTIVES

- Make generalizations.
- Recognize key words used in making generalizations.

Target Skill Trace

- Making Generalizations, pp. 399A–399B

Teach

Display pictures of four to five different kinds of birds. Include one bird that does not fly, such as a penguin or an ostrich. If you are unable to locate pictures, write the names of five or six birds on the chalkboard, for example, *pigeon, canary, penguin, wren, ostrich,* and *blue jay.* Then write the following sentence on the board: *All birds can fly.* Ask, Can all birds fly? (no) Have students identify which bird(s) cannot fly. Cross out the word *All* and write *Most.* Point to the new statement and ask, Is this a true statement? (yes)

Tell students that a statement that is true about most of the items in a group—most of the time—is called a *generalization.* Explain that a generalization should be based on facts, not on personal beliefs or experiences. Tell students that generalizations often include key words such as *most, all, always, generally, often, many, usually, few,* or *never.* Write the key words on the board.

Practice

Point out the picture of Ramona and the chapter title on page 312 of the story *Ramona Quimby, Age 8.* Have a volunteer read the first sentence of the story aloud. Tell students that the first part of this sentence is a generalization about the weather. Ask students to point out the key word in the first part of the sentence. (*always*) Write, *Rainy Sunday afternoons in November were always dismal.* Ask students if they agree or disagree with this statement.

Have students think of other generalizations about the weather at different times of the year. Write some more generalizations on the board. Ask students to underline the key word or words in each statement.

Read aloud the last paragraph on page 330. Write the following sentence on the board: *The Quimbys are always a nice family.* Ask, Is this statement true? (no) Ask, What word can we change to make this a true generalization? (change always to usually)

Apply

Have students identify generalizations, with an eye to noting key words, as they read their **Leveled Readers** for the week. Ask students to complete the questions and activity on the Responding page.

Monitoring Student Progress

If . . .	Then . . .
students need more practice with making generalizations,	have students make some generalizations about school or home routines, such as, "Our class usually has library on Tuesday."

CHALLENGE/EXTENSION: Making Generalizations

Use the menu on page 335 to practice rounding out numbers. Copy the menu and round each price listed to the nearest dollar. Next, decide what you would order if you were eating at the Whopperburger restaurant. Write your order with the prices as they are noted on the menu, add up your total, and round the total to the nearest dollar.

Think about how a "nice family" should behave. What are some good general rules? Work with a partner to make a list of rules for a nice family. Make an illustrated poster for display in the room. When you have finished, swap posters with another student pair. What rules appear in both your list and the other pair's list? What generalizations can you make about how members of nice families behave?

Our Family
• helps each other
• listens
• laughs together

CHALLENGE

Scientists rarely talk about the world in terms of *always* and *never*. Instead, scientists use generalizations to describe the world around them. They report observations that are usually true. Scientists repeat their experiments many times to make sure they get the same results each time.

Work in a small group to perform sink-and-float experiments with a container of water and a variety of different materials. For example, you can use a plastic cup, an eraser, a paper clip, or a pen. After you have experimented with the different objects in water, work together to write a list of generalizations based on your experiments. One example is *Cork usually floats*.

RETEACHING: Structural Analysis

VCCCV Pattern

OBJECTIVE

- Divide words with a VCCCV pattern into syllables.

Target Skill Trace

- VCCCV Pattern, p. 337C

Teach

Write the word *tremble*. Under the word, write the letters VCCCV.

tremble

VCCCV

Tell students that the letters -*emble* in the word *tremble* follow a vowel-consonant-consonant-consonant-vowel (VCCCV) pattern. Remind them that letter patterns can help divide words into syllables. Draw a vertical line between the *m* and *b* in *tremble*. Tell students that when we divide this word into syllables, we divide it between the first two consonants. Say the word *tremble* slowly, clapping each syllable. Explain that words with a VCCCV pattern are usually divided between the first two consonants. Ask, What vowel sound do you hear in the first syllable of *tremble*? (ĕ) Ask, Is this a long or short vowel sound? (short) Explain that words with a VCCCV pattern often have short vowel sounds because the syllables are closed.

Write the following words on chart paper: *little, English, fumble,* and *simple*. Have students read the words with you. Explain that all of these words have VCCCV patterns. Point out that these words also have a short vowel sound in the first syllable. Ask a volunteer to draw a line between the first two consonants in the word *little*. Have the students clap the syllables in the word while saying it aloud. Continue through

the other three words. Remind students that the VCCCV pattern can help them decode unfamiliar words when they are reading.

Practice

Revisit the story *Pepita Talks Twice*. Have students help you find words that have the VCCCV letter pattern. Write each word on chart paper. You may want to include these examples: *grumble, mumbled, instead, little, wiggle,* and *answer*.

Have volunteers use a marker and underline the letters forming the VCCCV pattern. Using a different color marker, have volunteers divide the word into syllables. Repeat the words together, clapping the syllables. Ask students if they hear a short or long vowel sound in the first syllable of each word. Help students to understand that the VCCCV pattern can help them when they read and write words.

Apply

Have students continue to look in the story for words with the VCCCV pattern. Have each student make a list of words. Tell students to skip a line between each word. Have students exchange papers and circle the VCCCV combinations. Have students exchange papers again and divide the words into syllables. Discuss words that students find that are not divided before the second consonant, and discuss words that do not have a short vowel sound in the first syllable.

Monitoring Student Progress

If . . .	Then . . .
students need more practice with the VCCCV pattern,	have them find words with the VCCCV pattern in other stories they have read, and divide them into syllables.

CHALLENGE/EXTENSION: Vocabulary

Concentration Game

Make a list of words from the story that have three or more syllables. You will need twelve 3" x 3" pieces of construction paper. Choose six words from your list and write each word on two of the construction paper cards. Then combine cards with a partner. Take your new group of cards and place them neatly face-down on a desk. Take turns turning over two cards at a time and reading them aloud. When you find a matching pair, take the cards and put them to one side.

VCCCV Word Scramble

Take words that have a VCCCV pattern and mix up the letters. Here's how. Fold paper in half lengthwise, so that the fold is on the right and the opening is on the left. Next, number your paper and write a mixed-up VCCCV word next to each number. When you have finished, unfold your paper lengthwise and write the correct answer in the column formed by the fold. Now exchange papers with a partner and try to guess the scrambled words. Look at the column underneath the scrambled words only if you cannot figure out the word without help.

Vocabulary Expansion

In the story *Pepita Talks Twice,* Pepita decides to stop speaking Spanish. Her brother reminds her that she will have to find a different way to say Spanish words that are commonly used in English. Use other words to describe the following Spanish words from the story and the Get Set to Read selection: *armadillo, guitar, tornado, taco, tamales, iguana, enchiladas, salsa.* You may have to use many words to tell the meaning of words on the list so that someone else would know what you are talking about. Try to use adjectives and adverbs, and also use all five senses to describe the words. For example, Pepita refers to a taco as a *crispy, crunchy, folded-over, round* corn sandwich.

RETEACHING: Structural Analysis

VCV Pattern

> ### OBJECTIVE
> - Students divide words with a VCV pattern into syllables.
>
> ### Target Skill Trace
> - VCV Pattern, p. 367C

Teach

Write the word *began* on chart paper. Under the word, write the letters VCV, so the word appears like this:

began

VCV

Tell students that the letters *ega* in the word *began* follow a vowel-consonant-vowel pattern (VCV). Remind students that we can use the patterns of letters in words to tell how to divide a word into syllables. Draw a vertical line between the *e* and *g* in *began*. Tell students that when we divide this word into syllables, we divide it before the consonant. Say the word *began* slowly, clapping each syllable. Explain that words with a VCV pattern are usually divided before the consonant, causing those syllables to have long vowel sounds since they are open.

Write the following words on chart paper: *again, alive, ahead, behind, ago.* Have the students read the words with you. Explain that all of these words have VCV patterns. Ask a volunteer to draw a line between the syllables in the word *again*. Have the students clap the syllables in the word while saying it aloud. Continue through the other four words.

Remind students that knowing the VCV pattern can help them decode unfamiliar words when they read.

Practice

Revisit the story *Poppa's New Pants*. Have students help you find words that have the VCV letter pattern. Write each word on chart paper. You may want to include these examples: *around, about, against, before, because, awake.*

Have student volunteers use a marker to underline the letters forming the VCV pattern. Have volunteers divide the word into syllables, using a different color marker. Repeat the words together, clapping the syllables.

Apply

Have students continue to look in the story for words with the VCV pattern. Have each student make a list of words. Tell students to skip a line between each word. Have students exchange papers and circle the VCV combinations. Have students exchange papers again and divide the words into syllables.

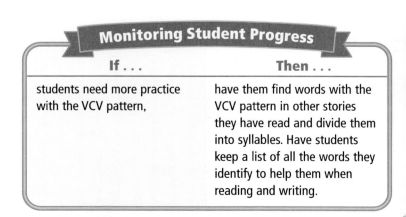

Monitoring Student Progress	
If . . .	**Then . . .**
students need more practice with the VCV pattern,	have them find words with the VCV pattern in other stories they have read and divide them into syllables. Have students keep a list of all the words they identify to help them when reading and writing.

CHALLENGE/EXTENSION: Vocabulary

Words Beginning with *a-* and *be-*

Work with a partner. Together, use a dictionary to find all the words you can that begin with the fragments *a-* and *be-* and that follow the VCV pattern. Make a word web for each fragment, with the fragment in the center and write all the words you find in circles connected to the center. Use highlighting markers to highlight words you did not know before. Share your word web with another pair.

Vocabulary Expansion

In the story *Poppa's New Pants,* Grandma Tiny tells Poppa he is a "tee-ninchy" little man. What do you think this word means? Look to see if this word is in the dictionary. Discuss with a partner ways to find the meanings of words not in the dictionary, such as using context clues. Use a dictionary and thesaurus to make a list of words that you think mean the same as "tee-ninchy." When finished, meet with other classmates as a group and discuss your lists.

CHALLENGE

Sound Words

Work with a partner. Together, use descriptive words or strings of letters to list sound words. Write the following activities on strips of paper: pushing a lawn mower, lifting weights, walking in the woods, camping out, making a cake, going on a train ride. Place the strips of paper face-down on a table, mix them up, and choose three strips each. List as many sound words as you can for the three activities you picked. Write the sound words on chart paper. Then write a paragraph about your topic, using as many sound words as you can. When you have finished, exchange paragraphs with your partner.

Contractions

OBJECTIVES

- Identify contractions.
- Differentiate between contractions and possessives.

Target Skill Trace

- Contractions, p. 399C

Teach

Write the following on chart paper:

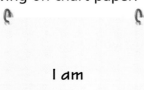

I am

you are

could not

Hold up an index card with an apostrophe on it, and ask students to identify the punctuation mark. Remind them that they have used an apostrophe to show possession. Tell students that another way to use an apostrophe is in contractions. Explain that contractions are a shortened way of writing two words. Tell students that when you make a contraction, the apostrophe takes the place of one or more of the letters. Have students say each pair of words on the chart and then replace it with a contraction. (I'm, you're, couldn't) Record student responses on chart paper.

Then ask a volunteer which letter the apostrophe replaces in the contraction *I'm.* (a) Have the student write the replaced letter next to the contraction. Follow the same procedure with the other pairs of words.

Practice

Revisit the story *Ramona Quimby, Age 8,* and ask students to help you identify the contractions in the story. As students look for words with an apostrophe, decide together whether each word indicates possession or is a contraction. Write the words on the board. Some words with apostrophes found in the story include the following:

> **page 312** *haven't, don't*

> **pages 314–315** *hasn't, I'm, don't, mother's, shouldn't, week's, you're*

> **pages 316–317** *can't, someone's, Mary Jane's, Picky-picky's*

Have students identify the two words that form each contraction.

Apply

Have students continue to look for contractions and add them to their own list. Next to each contraction, ask them to write the two words that form the contraction.

Have students choose several contractions from their charts. Ask them to write a brief dialogue between two people, using the contractions they have chosen.

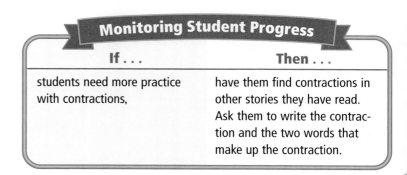

Monitoring Student Progress

If . . .	Then . . .
students need more practice with contractions,	have them find contractions in other stories they have read. Ask them to write the contraction and the two words that make up the contraction.

CHALLENGE/EXTENSION: Vocabulary

Word Wheel

You will need two pre-cut construction paper circles, one slightly larger than the other. Attach the two circles with a brad, so that the smaller circle is on top of the larger circle. Write words on the circles as if you were drawing spokes on a wheel. The words for the inner circle are *she, he, we, they, I, you,* and *it.* The words for the outer circle are *will, am, are, would,* and *is.*

Work with a partner to line up a word on the inner circle with a word on the outer circle. Take turns saying the words out loud, and then saying the contraction that can be made from those words. Remember that not all word pairs will lead to a contraction.

Vocabulary Expansion

Bring in several examples of menus to your classroom. Look at the menus and brainstorm words that have to do with taste, such as *sweet, salty, delicious,* and *mouth-watering.*

Then write a menu of your favorite foods. Include at least three different categories in your menus, such as appetizers, breakfast foods, side dishes, main dishes, drinks, and desserts. Write a description for each item. Use words that would make a customer want to order those foods. Illustrate your menu by drawing pictures or cutting pictures of food out of magazines.

Favorite Foods

CHALLENGE

Contraction Poetry

A rhyme occurs when two words end in the same sound, such as *cat* and *hat.* You could also consider two contractions to be rhyming words because the second word in the contraction is the same, as in *aren't* and *weren't.* Brainstorm a list of contractions that end in *n't.* Work in a small group to write a

rhyming poem, using some of these words. You may want to use contractions such as *couldn't, wouldn't, shouldn't, didn't, hadn't, hasn't, won't, aren't, weren't, can't, wasn't,* and *isn't.*

RETEACHING

Adjectives

OBJECTIVES

- Find adjectives in a story.
- Use adjectives to describe common objects.

Target Skill Trace

- Adjectives, pp. 337I–337J

Teach

Write the following sentences:

> A bird landed on the lawn.
>
> A huge, shiny, green-headed bird landed on the lawn.

Read each sentence aloud. Ask, Which sentence helps you picture what this bird looks like in your imagination? (the second sentence) What words help you to get a clear picture of what the bird looks like? (huge, shiny, green-headed) Point out to students that even the word *A* tells them about the bird. Explain that words like *a* and *an* tell them that there is only one thing being described. Explain that we use words called *adjectives* to *describe* objects. Authors use adjectives to help readers imagine the objects or events they are describing.

Give each student an index card with a common noun written on it. Choose nouns that students are familiar with. Tell students to think of two words that they could use to describe the object on their card. Write all the adjectives and display the list where all students can refer to it.

Repeat the activity, using new cards or having students choose two new words from the chart paper to describe the noun they have on their index card.

Practice

Tell the students you are going to talk about adjectives in the story *Pepita Talks Twice*. Reread the story together, adding more adjectives to the list as the students identify them. Some examples of adjectives from the story are: *little, new, red, old, long, sad.*

After reading the story, invite students to use adjectives to describe characters from the story. If the students use any new adjectives, add them to the list. Characters from the story include Pepita, Juan, Papa, Mama, Lobo, Miguel, Mr. Hobbs, Mr. Jones, and Miss Garcia.

When all the characters have been described, ask, What does an adjective do? (describes a noun)

Apply

Have students describe an object in the classroom without naming it. Tell them to make a list of adjectives describing the object they have chosen on a sheet of paper. Remind them to describe the object's size, shape, color, texture, and anything else they can think of. When students are done, have them exchange papers and try to guess the object being described. Allow students to exchange papers several times to read a variety of adjectives.

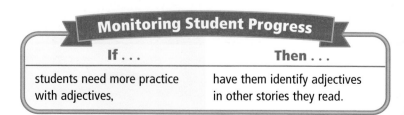

Monitoring Student Progress

If . . .	Then . . .
students need more practice with adjectives,	have them identify adjectives in other stories they read.

RETEACHING: Grammar

Comparing with Adjectives

OBJECTIVES

- Identify comparative and superlative adjectives.
- Use comparative and superlative adjectives in sentences.

Target Skill Trace

- Comparing with Adjectives, pp. 367I–367J

Teach

Write the following sentences:

A big dog dug up a bone.

A bigger dog sniffed the bone.

The biggest dog ran away with the bone.

Read each sentence aloud. Underline the words *big*, *bigger*, and *biggest*. Remind the students that we use adjectives in writing to describe things. Explain that often when we write, we need to compare objects and show ways that they are alike and different. One way to do this is by using comparative and superlative forms of adjectives. Tell students that *bigger* is a comparative form of the adjective *big*, and *biggest* is the superlative form of *big*. Explain that the comparative form compares two people, places, or things, and the superlative form compares three or more people, places, or things.

Draw a chart similar to the one shown here on chart paper:

adjective	comparative adjective	superlative adjective

Write adjectives in the first column of the chart, such as *large, scary, red, sharp,* or *thin*. For each word, call on volunteers to offer the comparative and superlative forms of the word. Continue through several examples.

Practice

Tell students that you are going to talk about comparative and superlative adjectives in the story *Poppa's New Pants*. Draw a new chart on chart paper. Reread the story together, adding adjectives to the correct columns of the chart as the students identify them. Some examples of adjectives from the story are listed here:

page 286 *shiny, soft, fattest*

pages 288–289 *sloppy, wet, new, pretty, mighty*

page 291 *good, long*

After reading the story, ask questions, using words from the chart you have created. Some possible questions are:

- Who was the oldest person in the story?
- Which character was older than Poppa?
- Who cut the pants to the shortest length?
- Which character do you think was the happiest?

Apply

Have students choose three objects and describe them. Instruct them to write at least three sentences, using comparative and superlative adjectives. You may want to remind them to use only attributes that can be measured, such as size or color.

Monitoring Student Progress

If . . .	Then . . .
students need more practice comparing with adjectives,	have them compare the attributes of classroom objects.

RETEACHING: Grammar

Adverbs

OBJECTIVES

- Identify adverbs in a story.
- Use adverbs in sentences.

Target Skill Trace

- Adverbs, pp. 399I–399J

Teach

Write the following sentences:

> Tyler walked across the bridge.
>
> Tyler walked slowly and carefully across the bridge.

Read each sentence aloud. Use the following Think Aloud to begin a discussion.

Think Aloud *The first sentence helps me form a picture in my mind of a boy crossing a bridge. The second sentence gives me more information. It changes the picture in my mind. Now I see a boy crossing a river "slowly and carefully," which makes me think that he is probably on a dangerous bridge.*

Explain that words like *slowly* and *carefully* modify the word *walked*, which is the verb in this sentence. Explain, too, that words that modify a verb, an adjective, or another adverb are called adverbs, and that adverbs often answer the question *how, when, where,* or *to what extent*. Go back to the initial paragraph, and explain that the words *slowly* and *gradually* tell *how* the boy crossed the bridge.

Practice

Engage students in a game of round robin. Make a stack of index cards labeled with verbs that are familiar to students, such as *run, dance, climb, crawl, stir, eat,* and *sing*. Ask students to choose a word from the pile, use the word in a sentence, and include an adverb that modifies the verb. Then have the next person identify the adverb and say whether it tells *how, when, where,* or *to what extent*. Display all the adverbs so students can refer to them. When finished, point out that adverbs often end in the letters *-ly*.

Ask students to find adverbs in the story *Ramona Quimby, Age 8*. Reread the story together, writing adverbs as students identify them. Some examples of adverbs from the story are *always, angrily, vaguely, sulkily, silently*.

Ask, What does an adverb do? (modifies a verb and tells how, where, when, or to what extent)

Apply

Have students write a paragraph describing an event that contains a lot of action. Suggest ideas to them, such as a dance recital, a football game, or an Olympic event. Ask students to use adverbs to modify the actions and events taking place. Have them write as if they were reporting the event on the radio to someone who was listening but could not see the action.

Monitoring Student Progress

If . . .	Then . . .
students need more practice with adverbs,	have them find adverbs in other stories they read.

The Vocabulary Restaurant

El Taco Grande/The Big Taco

1. _____ plate _____ $7.50

2. _____ plate _____ $6.50

3. Two steaming _____ $5.75

4. Five warm _____ $1.75

5. _____ (three kinds) .... $0.25 each

El Taco Grande/The Big Taco

1. **Enchilada**   a tortilla rolled around a filling, then covered with spicy sauce

2. **Taco**   a tortilla folded around a filling such as ground meat or cheese

3. **Tamales**   cornmeal dough wrapped around a filling and steamed in a corn husk or leaf

4. **Tortillas**   round, flat bread made of corn, from Mexico and Central America

5. **Salsa**   a spicy sauce usually made with tomatoes, onions, and peppers

Theme 6: **Smart Solutions**

Name _____

Spinning Vocabulary

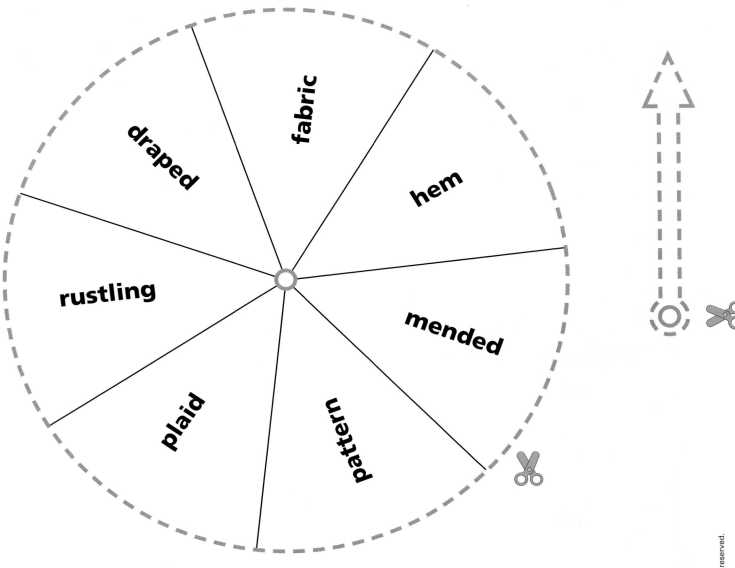

draped

fabric

hem

rustling

mended

plaid

pattern

draped hung loosely in folds	**pattern** a repeated design or decoration
fabric cloth	
hem to fold back and sew down the edges	**plaid** a pattern of stripes that cross each other
mended repaired by sewing	**rustling** quick, soft, fluttering sound

Theme 6: **Smart Solutions**

Name_____

Scrambled Words

1. It was a gray, <u>dyarer</u> day. _____

2. The rain was <u>lepgint</u> down on our heads. _____

3. Stephanie looked <u>seylulnl</u> at her mother. _____

4. "What a <u>lamdis</u> morning," Shane thought as he looked out

   the window. _____

5. They were <u>hexasudet</u> by the end of the hike.

   _____

6. After three days, the rain seemed <u>clesasees.</u> _____

7. Bingo was a very <u>panicolemoban</u> dog. _____

8. Aldo was very <u>cogdisuread</u> when his team lost the game.

   _____

9. _____.

   _____

10. _____.

    _____

1. dreary
2. pelting
3. sullenly
4. dismal
5. exhausted
6. ceaseless
7. companionable
8. discouraged
9. (Answers will vary.)
10. (Answers will vary.)

Theme 6: **Smart Solutions**

Writing Conference:

What Should I Say?

**In a writing conference, a writer reads a draft to a partner or
a small group. A listener can help the writer by discussing the
draft and asking questions such as these.**

If you're thinking . . .

- I don't understand the goal.
- Why should I think that? Why should I do that?
- This reason is not very convincing.

You could say . . .

- What do you want your audience to think or do?
- Could you give me some more reasons to support your goal?
- Could you give details that tell more about this reason?

More Questions a Listener Might Ask

**Read these questions before you listen. Take notes on the other
side of this paper. Then discuss your thoughts with the writer.**

1. What do you like about the writer's persuasive essay?

2. What is the writer's goal? What reasons does the writer give to
   support this goal? Retell what you heard.

3. What details make the writer's reasons clear?

4. Where does the writer need to add more details?

Theme 6: **Smart Solutions**

TECHNOLOGY RESOURCES

American Melody
P.O. Box 270
Guilford, CT 06437
800-220-5557
www.americanmelody.com

Audio Bookshelf
174 Prescott Hill Road
Northport, ME 04849
800-234-1713
www.audiobookshelf.com

Baker & Taylor
100 Business Center Drive
Pittsburgh, PA 15205
800-775-2600
www.btal.com

BDD Audio/Random House
400 Hohn Road
Westminster, MD 21157
800-733-3000

Big Kids Productions
1606 Dywer Ave.
Austin, TX 78704
800-477-7811
www.bigkidsvideo.com

Books on Tape
P.O. Box 25122
Santa Ana, CA 92799
800-541-5525
www.booksontape.com

Broderbund Company
1 Martha's Way
Hiawatha, IA 52233
www.broderbund.com

Filmic Archives
The Cinema Center
Botsford, CT 06404
800-366-1920
www.filmicarchives.com

Great White Dog Picture Company
10 Toon Lane
Lee, NH 03824
800-397-7641
www.greatwhitedog.com

HarperAudio
10 E. 53rd St.
New York, NY 10022
800-242-7737
www.harperaudio.com

Houghton Mifflin Company
222 Berkeley St.
Boston, MA 02116
800-225-3362

Informed Democracy
P.O. Box 67
Santa Cruz, CA 95063
800-827-0949

JEF Films
143 Hickory Hill Circle
Osterville, MA 02655
508-428-7198

Kimbo Educational
P.O. Box 477
Long Branch, NJ 07740
800-631-2187
www.kimboed.com

Library Video Co.
P.O. Box 580
Wynnewood, PA 19096
800-843-3620
www.libraryvideo.com

Listening Library
P.O. Box 25122
Santa Ana, CA 92799
800-541-5525
www.listeninglibrary.com

Live Oak Media
P.O. Box 652
Pine Plains, NY 12567
800-788-1121
www.liveoakmedia.com

Media Basics
Lighthouse Square
P.O. Box 449
Guilford, CT 06437
800-542-2505
www.mediabasicsvideo.com

Microsoft Corp.
One Microsoft Way
Redmond, WA 98052
800-426-9400
www.microsoft.com

National Geographic School Publishing
P.O. Box 10597
Des Moines, IA 50340
800-368-2728
www.nationalgeographic.com

New Kid Home Video
P.O. Box 10443
Beverly Hills, CA 90213
800-309-2392
www.NewKidhomevideo.com

Puffin Books
345 Hudson Street
New York, NY 10014
800-233-7364

Rainbow Educational Media
4540 Preslyn Drive
Raleigh, NC 27616
800-331-4047
www.rainbowedumedia.com

Recorded Books
270 Skipjack Road
Prince Frederick, MD 20678
800-638-1304
www.recordedbooks.com

Sony Wonder
Dist. by Professional Media Service
19122 S. Vermont Ave.
Gardena, CA 90248
800-223-7672
www.sonywonder.com

Spoken Arts
195 South White Rock Road
Holmes, NY 12531
800-326-4090
www.spokenartsmedia.com

SRA Media
220 E. Danieldale Rd.
DeSoto, TX 75115
800-843-8855
www.sra4kids.com

Sunburst Technology
1550 Executive Drive
Elgin, IL 60123
800-321-7511
www.sunburst.com

SVE & Churchill Media
6677 North Northwest Highway
Chicago, IL 60631
800-829-1900
www.svemedia.com

Tom Snyder Productions
80 Coolidge Hill Road
Watertown, MA 02472
800-342-0236
www.tomsnyder.com

Troll Communications
100 Corporate Drive
Mahwah, NJ 07430
800-526-5289
www.troll.com

Weston Woods
143 Main St.
Norwalk, CT 06851-1318
800-243-5020
www.scholastic.com/westonwoods

PRONUNCIATION GUIDE

In this book some unfamiliar or hard-to-pronounce words are followed by respellings to help you say the words correctly. Use the key below to find examples of various sounds and their respellings. Note that in the respelled word, the syllable in capital letters is the one receiving the most stress.

Dictionary letter or mark		Respelled as	Example	Respelled word
ă	(pat)	a	basket	BAS-kiht
ā	(pay)	ay	came	kaym
âr	(care)	air	share	shair
ä	(father)	ah	barter	BAHR-tur
ch	(church)	ch	channel	CHAN-uhl
ĕ	(pet)	eh	test	tehst
ē	(bee)	ee	heap	heep
g	(gag)	g	goulash	GOO-lahsh
ĭ	(pit)	ih	liver	LIHV-ur
ī	(pie, by)	y	alive	uh-LYV
		eye	island	EYE-luhnd
îr	(hear)	eer	year	yeer
j	(judge)	j	germ	jurm
k	(kick, cat, pique)	k	liquid	LIHK-wihd
ŏ	(pot)	ah	otter	AHT-ur
ō	(toe)	oh	solo	SOH-loh
ô	(caught, paw)	aw	always	AWL-wayz
ôr	(for)	or	normal	NOR-muhl
oi	(noise)	oy	boiling	BOYL-ihng
o͝o	(took)	u	pull, wool	pul, wul
o͞o	(boot)	oo	bruise	brooz
ou	(out)	ow	pound	pownd
s	(sauce)	s	center	SEHN-tur
sh	(ship, dish)	sh	chagrin	shuh-GRIHN
ŭ	(cut)	uh	flood	fluhd
ûr	(urge, term, firm, word, heard)	ur	earth	urth
			bird	burd
z	(zebra, xylem)	z	cows	kowz
zh	(vision, pleasure, garage)	zh	decision	dih-SIHZH-uhn
ə	(about)	uh	around	uh-ROWND
	(item)	uh	broken	BROH-kuhn
	(edible)	uh	pencil	PEHN-suhl
	(gallop)	uh	connect	kuh-NEHKT
	(circus)	uh	focus	FOH-kuhs
ər	(butter)	ur	liter	LEE-tur

Glossary

This glossary contains meanings and pronunciations for some of the words in this book. The Full Pronunciation Key shows how to pronounce each consonant and vowel in a special spelling. At the bottom of the glossary pages is a shortened form of the full key.

Full Pronunciation Key

Consonant Sounds

b	**b**i**b**, ca**bb**age	kw	**ch**oir, **qu**ick	t	**t**igh**t**, s**t**opped
ch	**ch**ur**ch**, sti**tch**	l	**l**id, need**l**e, ta**ll**	th	ba**th**, **th**in
d	**d**ee**d**, maile**d**, pu**ddl**e	m	a**m**, **m**an, du**mb**	th	ba**th**e, **th**is
f	**f**ast, **f**i**f**e, o**ff**, **ph**rase, rou**gh**	n	**n**o, sudde**n**	v	ca**v**e, **v**al**v**e, **v**ine
		ng	thi**ng**, i**nk**	w	**w**ith, **w**olf
g	**g**a**g**, **g**et, fin**g**er	p	**p**o**p**, ha**pp**y	y	**y**es, **y**olk, on**i**on
h	**h**at, **wh**o	r	**r**oa**r**, **rh**yme	z	ro**s**e, **s**i**z**e, **x**ylophone, **z**ebra
hw	**wh**ich, **wh**ere	s	mi**ss**, **s**au**c**e, **sc**ene, **s**ee		
j	**j**udge, **g**em			zh	gara**g**e, plea**s**ure, vi**s**ion
k	**c**at, **k**ick, s**ch**ool	sh	**d**i**sh**, **sh**ip, **s**ugar, ti**ss**ue		

Vowel Sounds

ă	p**a**t, l**au**gh	ŏ	h**o**rrible, p**o**t	ŭ	c**u**t, fl**oo**d, r**ou**gh, s**o**me
ā	**a**pe, **ai**d, p**ay**	ō	g**o**, r**o**w, t**oe**, th**ough**		
â	**ai**r, c**a**re, w**ea**r	ô	**a**ll, c**au**ght, f**o**r, p**aw**	û	c**i**rcle, f**u**r, h**ea**rd, t**er**m, t**u**rn, **u**rge, w**o**rd
ä	f**a**ther, k**oa**la, y**a**rd	oi	b**oy**, n**oi**se, **oi**l		
ĕ	p**e**t, pl**ea**sure, **a**ny	ou	c**ow**, **ou**t	yōō	c**u**re
ē	b**e**, b**ee**, **ea**sy, p**ia**no	ŏŏ	f**u**ll, b**oo**k, w**o**lf	yōō	**a**b**u**se, **u**se
ĭ	**i**f, p**i**t, b**u**sy	ōō	b**oo**t, r**u**de, fr**ui**t, fl**ew**	ə	**a**go, sil**e**nt, penc**i**l, lem**o**n, circ**u**s
ī	r**i**de, b**y**, p**ie**, h**igh**				
î	d**ea**r, d**ee**r, f**ie**rce, m**e**re				

Stress Marks

Primary Stress ´: bi·ol·o·gy [bī ŏl´ ə jē]
Secondary Stress ´: bi·o·log·i·cal [bī´ ə lŏj´ ĭ kəl]

Pronunciation key and definitions © 1998 by Houghton Mifflin Company. Adapted and reprinted by permission from *The American Heritage Children's Dictionary.*

414

A

an·chor (ăng´ kər) *noun* A heavy metal object, attached to a ship, that is dropped overboard to keep the ship in place: *We dropped the anchor so that our sailboat wouldn't crash onto the rocky shore.*

ap·pre·ci·ate (ə prē´ shē āt´) *verb* To enjoy and understand: *Max could appreciate that having a dog was a big responsibility.*

a·shore (ə shôr´) *adverb* On or to the shore: *The seal came ashore and then went back into the water.*

B

bar·ren (băr´ ən) *adjective* Not able to produce growing plants or crops: *Because the country's land was barren, food had to be shipped in from other places.*

bask (băsk) *verb* To rest in a pleasant warmth: *Rochelle enjoyed the summer weather as she basked in the warm sun.*

buf·fet (bŭf´ ĭt) *verb* To strike against powerfully: *Luis held his kite tightly as it was buffeted by the strong wind.*

bur·row (bûr´ ō) *noun* A hole or tunnel small animals use as an underground nest.

bus·tling (bŭs´ ling) *adjective* Full of activity; busy: *The bustling mall was full of people shopping for holiday gifts.*

C

cease·less (sēs´ lĭs) *adjective* Continuing without end: *Kim played indoors all day because of the ceaseless rain.*

com·pan·ion·a·ble (kəm păn´ yən ə bəl) *adjective* Friendly: *Maria talked to a companionable girl who was sitting next to her on the train.*

cramped (krămpt) *adjective* So small as to prevent free movement: *The travelers could not stretch out their legs in the plane's cramped space.*

cre·vasse (krĭ văs´) *noun* A deep opening or crack: *A crevasse appeared in the iceberg before it broke apart.*

cus·tom (kŭs´ təm) *noun* Something that the members of a group usually do: *It is an American custom to eat turkey on Thanksgiving.*

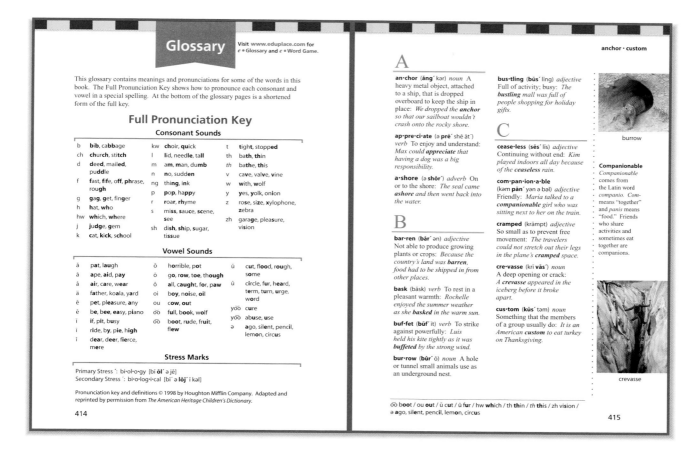

burrow

Companionable
Companionable comes from the Latin word *companio.* Com- means "together" and *panis* means "food." Friends who share activities and sometimes eat together are companions.

crevasse

ōō **boo**t / ou **ou**t / ŭ **cu**t / û **fu**r / hw **wh**ich / th **th**in / th **th**is / zh vision / ə **a**go, sil**e**nt, penc**i**l, lem**o**n, circus

415

D

de·sert·ed (dĭ zûrt´ ĕd) *adjective* Not lived in; having few or no people: *No one has lived in the deserted house for many years.*

dis·cour·aged (dĭ skûr´ ĭjd) *adjective* Less hopeful or enthusiastic: *Instead of being discouraged by his poor grade on the test, Matt decided to study more for the next one.*

dis·mal (dĭz´ məl) *adjective* Causing, feeling, or showing gloom or sadness: *It was a dismal day for Yoshiko when her best friend moved away.*

drape (drāp) *verb* To hang in loose folds: *Ellie's long skirt draped to the floor.*

drear·y (drîr´ ē) *adjective* Gloomy; dismal; without cheer: *We decided not to let the dreary weather ruin our vacation.*

E

en·chi·la·da (ĕn´ chə lä´ də) *noun* A tortilla that is folded around a meat filling and covered with a spicy tomato sauce: *Greg learned to make delicious chicken enchiladas in cooking class.*

ex·haust·ed (ĭg zôst´ əd) *adjective* Worn out; tired: *Tina was exhausted after carrying the heavy boxes.*

F

fab·ric (făb´ rĭk) *noun* Material that is produced by weaving threads, or fibers, together; cloth: *Kelly's shirt was made of a cotton fabric.*

floe (flō) *noun* A large, flat mass of floating ice: *The polar bear dove off the ice floe into the freezing water.*

for·eign·er (fôr´ ə nər) *noun* A person from a different country or place: *Americans are foreigners in Europe.*

G

graze (grāz) *verb* To feed on growing plants: *The cows were grazing on grass near the barn.*

gru·el·ing (grōō´ ə lĭng) *adjective* Extremely tiring: *Hannah went to sleep early after running the grueling ten-mile race.*

H

hem (hĕm) *verb* To fold back and sew down the edge of: *I will have to hem my new skirt because it is too long.*

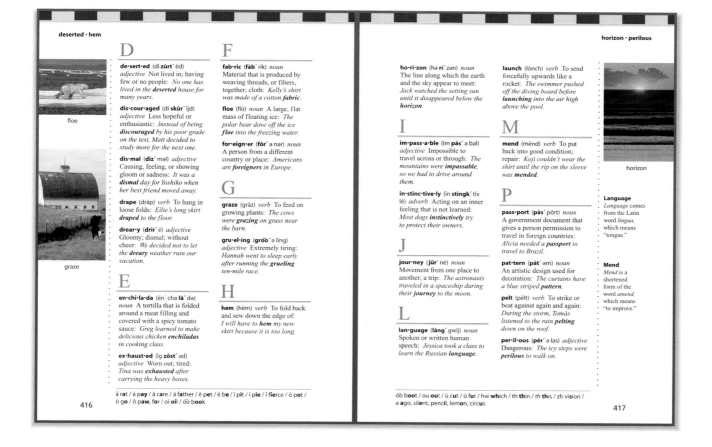

floe

graze

ă **ra**t / ā **pa**y / â **ca**re / ä **fa**ther / ĕ **pe**t / ē **be** / ĭ **pi**t / ĭ **pie** / î **fie**rce / ŏ **po**t / ō **go** / ô **pa**w, **for** / oi **oi**l / ōō **boo**k

416

ho·ri·zon (hə rī´ zən) *noun* The line along which the earth and the sky appear to meet: *Jack watched the setting sun until it disappeared below the horizon.*

I

im·pass·a·ble (ĭm păs´ ə bəl) *adjective* Impossible to travel across or through: *The mountains were impassable, so we had to drive around them.*

in·stinc·tive·ly (ĭn stĭngk´ tĭv lē) *adverb* Acting on an inner feeling that is not learned: *Most dogs instinctively try to protect their owners.*

J

jour·ney (jûr´ nē) *noun* Movement from one place to another; a trip: *The astronauts traveled in a spaceship during their journey to the moon.*

L

lan·guage (lăng´ gwĭj) *noun* Spoken or written human speech: *Jessica took a class to learn the Russian language.*

launch (lônch) *verb* To send forcefully upwards like a rocket: *The swimmer pushed off the diving board before launching into the air high above the pool.*

M

mend (mĕnd) *verb* To put back into good condition; repair: *Koji couldn't wear the shirt until the rip on the sleeve was mended.*

P

pass·port (păs´ pôrt) *noun* A government document that gives a person permission to travel in foreign countries: *Alicia needed a passport to travel to Brazil.*

pat·tern (păt´ ərn) *noun* An artistic design used for decoration: *The curtains have a blue striped pattern.*

pelt (pĕlt) *verb* To strike or beat against again and again: *During the storm, Tomás listened to the rain pelting down on the roof.*

per·il·ous (pĕr´ ə ləs) *adjective* Dangerous: *The icy steps were perilous to walk on.*

horizon

Language
Language comes from the Latin word *lingua,* which means "tongue."

Mend
Mend is a shortened form of the word *amend,* which means "to improve."

ōō **boo**t / ou **ou**t / ŭ **cu**t / û **fu**r / hw **wh**ich / th **th**in / th **th**is / zh vision / ə **a**go, sil**e**nt, penc**i**l, lem**o**n, circus

417

Glossary continued

quay

skyscraper

Skyscraper
The highest sails on a ship used to be called skyscrapers. When the world's first ten-story building was built, writers called it a skyscraper, naming it after those high sails.

Strand
Strand comes from an Old English word that meant "seashore."

plaid (plăd) *adjective* Having a pattern formed by stripes of different widths and colors that cross each other at right angles: *Gus put on his plaid scarf before he went out into the cold.*

pop·u·la·tion (pŏp´ yə lā´ shən) *noun* The total number of plants, animals, or people living in a certain place: *Our class did a population survey to learn about the people who live in our town.*

Q

quay (kē) *noun* A dock where ships are loaded or unloaded: *The boy stood on the quay watching supplies being loaded onto the ships.*

R

rus·tling (rŭs´ ling) *noun* A soft fluttering sound: *Deb heard the rustling of the leaves in the wind.*

S

sal·sa (säl´ sə) *noun* A spicy sauce made of tomatoes, onions, and peppers: *We dipped our chips in the spicy salsa.*

seep (sēp) *verb* To pass slowly through small openings; ooze: *We stuffed a towel in the crack under the door to keep the cold air from seeping in.*

set·tle·ment (sĕt´l mənt) *noun* A small community in a new place: *When they reached the new land, the pioneers built a settlement to live in.*

sight·see·ing (sīt´ sē´ ing) *verb* The act of touring interesting places: *When Marc took his visitors sightseeing in Washington, D.C., they went to the Washington Monument.*

sky·scra·per (skī´ skrā pər) *noun* A very tall building: *The Empire State Building is one of the tallest skyscrapers in New York City.*

Span·ish (spăn´ ĭsh) *noun* The language of Spain, Mexico, and most of Central America and South America: *My cousin grew up in Mexico and speaks Spanish.*

starve (stärv) *verb* To suffer or die from lack of food: *We put seeds in the feeder so the birds wouldn't starve in the winter.*

strand·ed (strănd´ əd) *adjective* In a difficult or helpless position: *When our car ran out of gas, we were stranded on the side of the road.*

å rat / ā pay / â care / ä father / ĕ pet / ē be / ĭ pit / ī pie / î fierce / ŏ pot / ō go / ô paw, for / oi oil / ōō book

418

---

sul·len·ly (sŭl´ ən lē) *adverb* Angrily or unhappily: *When his parents wouldn't let him have a cookie, the little boy sullenly refused to eat dinner.*

surf (sûrf) *verb* To ride on waves, often on a surfboard: *During summer vacation, Doug surfed at the beach.* —*noun* The waves of the sea as they break on a shore or reef: *Lucy swam in the surf.*

sur·round·ing (sə roun´ ding) *adjective* On all sides of: *The surrounding trees shaded the house from the sun.*

sur·vive (sər vīv´) *verb* To stay alive or continue to exist: *A whale cannot survive out of water.*

swell (swĕl) *noun* A long rolling wave in open water: *The swimmer was lifted gently by the ocean swell.*

swoop (swōōp) *verb* To move with a sudden sweeping motion: *The seagull swooped down to catch a fish.*

T

ta·co (tä´ kō) *noun* A tortilla that is folded around a filling, such as ground meat or cheese: *We added lettuce and tomato to our tacos.*

ta·ma·le (tə mä´ lē) *noun* A steamed cornhusk that is wrapped around a meat filling made with red peppers and cornmeal: *When I go to my favorite Mexican restaurant, I love to order tamales.*

ter·rain (tə rān´) *noun* Any piece of land; ground, soil, earth: *It was difficult to hike across the rocky terrain.*

ter·ri·to·ry (tĕr´ ĭ tôr´ ē) *noun* An area of land; region: *Bears roam their territory in search of food.*

tor·til·la (tôr tē´ yə) *noun* A round, flat bread made from cornmeal and water and baked on a grill: *My grandmother showed me how to make a tortilla.*

U

un·in·hab·i·ted (ŭn´ ĭn hăb´ ə tĭd) *adjective* Having no people living there: *The explorer was the first person to visit the uninhabited island.*

V

vend·or (vĕn´ dər) *noun* A person who sells something: *In Chicago, Carl bought a hot dog from a street vendor.*

surf

Terrain
Terrain comes from the Latin word *terra*, which means "earth." Other words that come from *terra* are *territory*, *terrace*, and *terrier*.

vendor

ōō boot / ou out / ŭ cut / û fur / hw which / th thin / th this / zh vision / ə ago, silent, pencil, lemon, circus

419

venture

ven·ture (vĕn´ chər) *verb* To do something in spite of risk: *We decided to venture out to the edge of the cliff.*

W

wan·der (wŏn´ dər) *verb* To move from place to place without a special purpose or goal: *People in shopping malls often wander from store to store.*

wea·ry (wîr´ ē) *adjective* Needing rest; tired: *After climbing the mountain, the weary hikers took a nap.*

å rat / ā pay / â care / ä father / ĕ pet / ē be / ĭ pit / ī pie / î fierce / ŏ pot / ō go / ô paw, for / oi oil / ōō book

420

Acknowledgments

Pronunciation key and definitions © 1998 by Houghton Mifflin Company. Adapted and reprinted by permission from The American Heritage Children's Dictionary.

Main Literature Selections
Across the Wide Dark Sea: The Mayflower Journey, by Jean Van Leeuwen, illustrated by Thomas B. Allen. Text copyright © 1995 by Jean Van Leeuwen. Illustrations copyright © 1995 by Thomas B. Allen. Reprinted by permission of Dial Books for Young Readers, a division of Penguin Books Inc.
Alejandro's Gift, by Richard E. Albert, illustrated by Sylvia Long. Text copyright © 1994 by Richard E. Albert. Illustrations copyright © 1994 by Sylvia Long. Reprinted by permission of the publisher, Chronicle Books LLC, San Francisco. Visit http://www.chroniclebooks.com.
"Helen Keller" from *Sisters in Strength,* by Yona Zeldis McDonough, illustrated by Malcah Zeldis. Text copyright © 2000 by Yona Zeldis McDonough. Reprinted by permission of Henry Holt and Company, LLC.
The Island-Below-the-Star, written and illustrated by James Rumford. Copyright © 1998 by James Rumford. Reprinted by permission of Houghton Mifflin Company. All rights reserved.
Nights of the Pufflings, by Bruce McMillan. Copyright © 1995 by Bruce McMillan. Reprinted by permission of Houghton Mifflin Company. All rights reserved.
Pepita Talks Twice/Pepita habla dos veces, by Ofelia Dumas Lachman. Copyright © 1995 by Ofelia Dumas Lachman. Reprinted with permission from the publisher Arte Público Press/University of Houston.
Poppa's New Pants, by Angela Shelf Medearis, illustrated by John Ward. Text copyright © 1995 by Angela Shelf Medearis. Illustrations copyright © 1995 by John Ward. Reprinted by permission of Holiday House, Inc.
Selection from *Prairie School* by Avi. Text copyright © 2001 by Avi. Reprinted by permission of HarperCollins Publishers.

Selection from *Ramona Quimby, Age 8,* by Beverly Cleary, illustrated by Alan Tiegreen. Copyright © 1981 by Beverly Cleary. Reprinted by permission of HarperCollins Publishers.
Seal Surfer, by Michael Foreman. Copyright © 1996 by Michael Foreman. Reprinted by permission of Harcourt Inc.
Trapped by the Ice!: Shackleton's Amazing Antarctic Adventure, by Michael McCurdy. Copyright © 1997 by Michael McCurdy. Reprinted by arrangement with Walker & Co.
Two Days in May, by Harriet Peck Taylor, pictures by Leyla Torres. Text copyright © 1999 by Harriet Peck Taylor. Illustrations copyright © 1999 by Leyla Torres. Reprinted by permission of Farrar, Straus and Giroux, LLC.
"A Wild Ride," by Thomas Fleming, from the March 2002 issue of *Boy's Life* magazine. Text copyright © 2002 by Thomas Fleming. Cover copyright © 2002 by the Boy Scouts of America. Reprinted by permission of the author and Boy's Life, published by the Boy Scouts of America.
Yunmi and Halmoni's Trip, by Sook Nyul Choi, illustrated by Karen Dugan. Text copyright © 1997 by Sook Nyul Choi. Illustrations copyright © 1997 by Karen Dugan. Reprinted by permission of Houghton Mifflin Company. All rights reserved.

Focus Selections
Cinderella, by Charles Perrault, retold by Amy Ehrlich. Text copyright © 1985 by Amy E. Ehrlich. Published by arrangement with Dial Books for Young Readers, a member of Penguin Putnam Inc.
Selection from *Yeh-Shen: A Cinderella Story from China,* retold by Ai-Ling Louie, illustrated by Ed Young. Text copyright © 1982 by Ai-Ling Louie. Illustrations copyright © 1982 by Ed Young. Reprinted by permission of Philomel Books, a division of Penguin Young Readers Group, a member of Penguin Group (USA) Inc. Electronic rights granted by the author for the text and by McIntosh and Otis, Inc. for the illustrations. All rights reserved.

421

Links and Theme Openers

"Big Apple Birding," by Radha Permaul, reprinted from the March 1992 issue of *Ranger Rick* magazine. Copyright © 1992 by the National Wildlife Federation. Reprinted with the permission of the National Wildlife Federation.

Calvin and Hobbes comic "Let's go Calvin…" reprinted in the *No Problem! Media Link.* Copyright © 1988 by Bill Watterson. Reprinted by permission of the Universal Press Syndicate. All rights reserved.

Calvin and Hobbes comic "Oh no, I lost my quarter. . ." reprinted in the *No Problem! Media Link.* Copyright © 1987 by Bill Watterson. Reprinted by permission of the Universal Press Syndicate. All rights reserved.

Foxtrot comic "Anyone seen the leaf blower?" by Bill Amend. Reprinted in the *No Problem! Media Link.* Copyright © 1996 by Bill Amend. Reprinted by permission of the Universal Press Syndicate. All rights reserved.

"Henry and Ramona," based on the books by Beverly Cleary, dramatized by Cynthia J. McGean. Copyright © 1952 by Beverly Cleary. Dramatized play copyright © 1964 by Cynthia J. McGean. Used by permission of HarperCollins Publishers.

"I Like to Ride My Bike/Me gusta montar mi bicicleta" from *Sol a Sol: Bilingual Poems,* written and selected by Lori Marie Carlson. Text © 1998 by Lori Marie Carlson. Reprinted by permission of Henry Holt and Company, LLC.

"I Work in the Ocean," by Kristin Ingram from *SPIDER* magazine, January 1998 issue, Vol. 5, No. 1. Copyright © 1998 by Kristin Ingram. Cover copyright © 1998 by Carus Publishing Company. Reprinted by permission of the author. Cover reprinted by permission of SPIDER magazine.

"January Deer" from *Turtle in July,* by Marilyn Singer. Copyright © 1989 by Marilyn Singer. Reprinted with the permission of Atheneum Books for Young Readers, an imprint of Simon & Schuster's Children's Publishing Division, and the author.

"Little Piece of Prickly Pear/Pedacito de nopal" from *My Mexico/Mexico Mio,* by Tony Johnston. Copyright © 1996 by Tony Johnston. Reprinted by permission of G.P. Putnam's Sons, a division of Penguin Putnam.

"My Grandmother's Songs/Las canciones de mi abuela" from *Laughing Tomatoes and Other Spring Poems,* by Francisco X. Alarcón. Text copyright © 1997 by Francosco X. Alarcón. Illustrations copyright © 1997 by Maya Christina Gonzalez. Reprinted by permission of Children's Book Press, San Francisco, CA.

Peanuts comic "Snoopy, This has been a bad week for me…" reprinted in the *No Problem! Media Link* is from *Stop Snowing on my Secretary,* by Charles Schulz. PEANUTS © United Feature Syndicate. Reprinted by permission of United Feature Syndicate.

Peanuts comic "The wilderness is . . ." reprinted in the *No Problem! Media Link* is from *Nothing Echoes Like an Empty Mailbox,* by Charles Schulz. PEANUTS © United Feature Syndicate. Reprinted by permission of United Feature Syndicate.

"Puffin-Stuff," by Joan Peronto from *LADYBUG* magazine, June 1996 issue, Vol. 6, No. 10. Copyright © 1996 by Joan Peronto. Reprinted by permission of LADYBUG magazine and the author.

"Seal" from *Laughing Time: Collected Nonsense,* by William Jay Smith. Copyright © 1990 by William Jay Smith. Reprinted by permission of Farrar, Straus & Giroux, LLC.

"Travellers," by Arthur St. John Adcock. Copyright by Arthur St. John Adcock. Reprinted by permission of Hodder & Stoughton Ltd.

"Under the Trees" from *In the Woods, In the Meadow, In the Sky,* by Aileen Fisher. Copyright © 1965, 1993 by Aileen Fisher. Used by permission of Marian Reiner for the author.

"The Ways of Living Things," by Jack Prelutsky from *The Random House Book of Poetry for Children.* Copyright © 1983 by Jack Prelutsky. Reprinted by permission of Random House Children's Books, a division

of Random House, Inc. and the author.

"Young Voyagers: A Pilgrim Childhood." Grateful acknowledgment is given to the Plimoth Plantation for the printed resource materials that were provided for informational purposes.

Additional Acknowledgments

Special thanks to the following teachers whose students' compositions appear as Student Writing Models: Cindy Cheatwood, Florida; Diana Davis, North Carolina; Kathy Driscoll, Massachusetts; Linda Evers, Florida; Heidi Harrison, Michigan; Eileen Hoffman, Massachusetts; Bonnie Lewison, Florida; Kanetha McCord, Michigan.

Credits

Photography

1 (t) © Royalty-Free/Corbis. (m) V.C.L./Taxi/Getty Images. (b) © JIStock/Masterfile. 3 © Royalty-Free/Corbis. 4 © Corbis/Bettmann. (m) Jeff Arnold/Bill Melendez Productions. (r) AP/New York Times Pictures. 6 V.C.L./Taxi/Getty Images. 9 © JIStock/Masterfile. 10–11 ©Michio Hoshino/Minden Pictures. 11 (t) © Royalty-Free/Corbis. 12–14 Courtesy of Bruce McMillan. 16–17 (bkgd) ©Hubert Stadler/CORBIS. 17 (t) ©Sigurgeir Jonasson. (b) ©James P. Rowan. 18 (tc) Benner McGee, ©1995 Bruce McMillan. 18-19 (bkgd) © Catherine Karow/ Corbis. 19–33 ©Bruce McMillan. 35 (br) Arthur C. Smith III/Grant Heilman. 36–9 (all) ©Arthur Morris/BIRDS AS ART. 40 ©Kit Kittle/CORBIS. 41 ©Clem Haagner; Gallo Images/CORBIS. 42 ©Lynda Richardson/ CORBIS. 43 (t) ©James L. Amos/ CORBIS. 44 (starfish) © PhotoDisc/Getty Images. (c) ©Rick Rusing/Stone/Getty Images. (bl) ©Roger Tidman/CORBIS. 44–5 ©Bill Ross/CORBIS. 45 (cl) ©Art Wolfe. (br) ©Phil Schermeister/CORBIS. 46 ©Ron Sutherland. 46-47 (bkgd) © Doug Wilson/Corbis. 65 (br) A.K.G., Berlin/SuperStock. 66–9 (all) ©Norbert Wu. 70 (banner) W. Cody/CORBIS. (bl) ©Erwin and Peggy Bauer. 70–1 (inset) ©Daniel J. Cox/Natural Exposures. 71 (inset) ©Daniel J. Cox/Natural Exposures. 72-73 (bkgd) © Bohemian Nomad Picturemakers/Corbis. 93 (bl) John Crispin/

Mercury Pictures. (tr) Eric Bakke/Mercury Pictures. 100-11 (bkgd) © Joseph Van Os/The Image Bank/Getty Images. 100 (b) © Royalty-Free/Corbis. 114–16 (border) Corbis Images/Picturequest. 115 (bkgd) Larry Ulrich/DRK Photo, (tl) Francois Gohier/Photo Researchers, Inc., (bl) Craig Lorenz/Photo Researchers, Inc. 116 (t) Stephen Krasemann/Photo Researchers, Inc., (b) Rod Planck. 122Corbis/Bettmann. 123 Corbis/Bettmann. 124 Corbis/Bettmann. 125 (t) Corbis/Bettmann. (b) Underwood & Underwood/CORBIS. 126 (tr) AP/Wide World Photos. (bl) Corbis/Bettmann. 127 Zaharias Collection, Special Collections/Mary & John Gray Library/Lamar University, Beaumont, Texas. 128 Jeff Arnold/Bill Meléndez Productions. 129 Photofest. 130 © PhotoDisc/Getty Images. 131 Photofest. 132 Photofest. 133 Everett Collection. 134 Underwood & Underwood/CORBIS. 135 Security Pacific Collection/Los Angeles Public Library. 136 CORBIS. 137 Museum of Flight/CORBIS. 138 The Lilly Library, Indiana University, Bloomington. 139 USPS. 140 Corbis/Bettmann. 141 AP/New York Times Pictures. 142 Corbis/Bettmann. 143 AP/New York Times Pictures. 144 AP Wide World Photos. 145 (t) Corbis/Bettmann. (b) AP/Wide World Photos. 146 (l) AFP/Corbis. (cl) Flip Schulke/CORBIS. (cr) NASA/CORBIS. (r) Corbis/Bettmann. 148-49 (bkgd) © Kelly Harriger/CORBIS. 149 (m) V.C.L./Taxi/Getty Images. 150–51 Courtesy of Sook Nyul Choi. 152 Courtesy of Manhattanville College, (b) Courtesy of Sook Nyul Choi. 154 (bl) Courtesy of the Pilgrim Society, Plymouth, Massachusetts. 155 (t) Courtesy of Bert Lane/Plimoth Plantation. (b) Courtesy of the Pilgrim Society, Plymouth, Massachusetts. 156 (t) Photo by David Gavril from Growing Ideas published by Richard C. Owens Publishers, Inc., Katonah, NY 10536. (tr) Courtesy, Thomas B. Allen. 156-57 (bkgd) Kaz Mori/The Image Bank/Getty Images. 179 (br) SuperStock. 182 (tl) Photo by Ted Curtain/Plimoth Plantation. (b) Photo by Ted Avery/Plimoth Plantation. 183 (t) ©Dorothy Littell Greco/Stock Boston. (c) (b) ©Russ Kendall. 186 (b) ©Wolfgang Kaehler/

Index

Boldface page references indicate formal strategy and skill instruction.

Compare/contrast. *See* Comprehension skills.

Comparing. *See* Connections.

Comprehension skills
author's viewpoint, TE2: **157A–157B,** **185A–185B,** 160, 162, **171,** 176, 178, 180, 223, 229, **279D,** R8–R9; TE3: 373; TE4: 25, 34, 61, 79; TE6: **309,** 316, 332, 337, 361
categorize and classify, TE1: 91, 150; TE2: **190, 203,** 213A–213B **225, 279D,** R10–R11
cause and effect, TE1: **18,** 34, **39,** 42, **49A–49B,** 58, 70, 116, 137D, R8–R9; TE2: 169, 192, 284, 293; TE3: 347, 310, **377;** TE5: 192, 196, **205,** 208, 230; TE6: 310, 332, **349,** 358, 362, 390, 399
compare and contrast, TE1: 36, 72, 100, 116, 121, 121H, 148, 150, 151A; TE2: 170, 174, 180, 185, 200, 208, 223, 230, 233, **253,** 256, 259, 289, 299, 300; TE3: 321, 323, 333, 354, 366, 374, 375, 405, 413, 419; TE4: 39, 46, 49, 54, 56, 63, 64, **69A–69B,** 94, 99, R4–R5, R10, R11; TE5: 160, 176, 178, 222; TE6: 320, 337, 353, **355,** 366, 372, 274, 381
conclusions, drawing, TE1: 22, 24, 28, 30, 38, 40, 42, 44, 49, 56, 58, 60, 62, 64, 66, 68, 69, 70, 76, 80, 82, 84, 96, 98, 100, 102, 104, 106, 108, 110, 112, 114, 116, 121, 146, 149; TE2: 164, 166, 168, 170, 174, 178, 179, 180, 185, 192, 194, 196, 198, 202, 204, 206, 208, 213, 220, 222, 224, 226, **227,** 230, 238, 250, 252, 254, 256, 259, 284, 299, 300; TE3: 329, 340, 342, 354, 356, 364, 366, **371,** 372, 380, 384, 393, 393A–393B, 398, 402, 404, 407, 408, 410, 412, 414, 419, **439E,** R12–R13; TE4: 20, 24, 26, 32, 34, 39, 48, 52, 58, 60, 62, 64, 69, 74, 76, 80, 86, 88, 92, 94; TE5: 158, 164, 168, 170, 172, 174, 190, 192, 196, 198, 202, 206, 208, 218, 220, 222, 234, 236, 244, 250; TE6: 306, 312, 314, 320, 322, 326, 330, 331, 344, 350, 352, **359,** 360, 362, **367A–367B,** 374, 377, 382, 386, 388, **391,** 394
details, noting, TE1: **27,** 30, 44, 49, 58, 64, 66, 68, 78, 82, 84, 89, 94, 98, 100, 102, 105, 112, 121; TE2: 162, **163,** 164, **171,** 172, **175,** 176, 204, 206, 208, 213, **216, 219,** 220, 226, 233, **233A–233B,** 238, 240, 242, 246, 248, 252, 255, 256, 259, 293, R12–R13; TE3: 312, 314, 322, 326, 333A, 335, 360, 370, 374, 376, 378, 380, 382, 386, 388, 393, 399, 400, 404, 406, 408, 410, 414, 419; TE4: 22, 28, 48, 50, 54, 58, 62, 64, 69, 76, 82, 84, 86, 90, 92, 94, 99; TE5: 160, 162, 165, 166, 168, 178, 199, 200, 204, 238, 242; TE6: 332, 337, 350, 354, 362, 376, 382
directions, following, TE1: 47, 121; TE2: **232–233, 258–259;** TE3: 333, **338, 349, 361A–361B, 439D,** R10–R11
fact and opinion, TE2: **184,** 185, 198; TE4: **18, 23, 39A–39B,** R2–R3, R8, R9

fantasy/realism, TE1: 83, **95,** 96, 102, **105;** TE3: 310, **263C, 323,** 330, **333A–333B,** 345, 333, 346, 347, **439D,** R8–R9
generalizations, making, TE1: 46, 86, 89; TE2: 180, 245, 256, 293; TE3: 315, 318, 330, 361; TE4: **29,** 34, 54, 63; TE5: **197,** 178, 183; TE6: 332, 370, **385,** 399, **399A–399B,** R12–R13
inferences. *See* Inferences, making.
judgments, making, TE1: 43, 49, **63,** 72, 84, 89, 94, 106, 108, 114, 115, 116, 149, 150; TE2: 176, 207, 228, 230, 244, 254, 255, 300; TE3: 309, 310, 320, 326, 340, 341, 356, 359, 368, 387, 400, 405; TE4: 33, 34, 55, 62, 64, 69, **72,** 74, **77,** 82, 94, 99, **99A–99B,** R6–R7, R12, R13; TE5: 164, **171,** 176, 183, 204, 207, 208, 238, 240, 245, 250; TE6: 312, 314, 318, 326, 332, 346, 361, 381, **383,** 394
predicting outcomes, TE1: 22, 26, 33, 44, 69, 83, 84, 101, 103, 110, 115, 116, 149; TE2: 179, 199, **201,** 254, 286, 296, 299; TE3: 320, 329, 330, 348, 356, 364, 368, 374, 375, 378, 386, 388, 413, 414; TE4: 25, 33, 64, 90, **91,** 93; TE5: **188, 203,** 208, **213A–213B,** 226, R4, R10–R11; TE6: 324, 331, 393
problem solving, TE1: 102; TE2: 230, 300; TE3: **327,** 330, 338, 356; TE4: 34, 83, **87;** TE5: 178; TE6: 306, 316, **319,** 322, 337A, 362, 366, 393, 399, **301A–301B,** R8–R9
sequence of events, TE1: **92, 109,** 112, 113, 116, **121A–121B,** R12–R13; TE2: 285; TE4: 22, **57,** 94; TE5: **221,** 208
story structure, TE1: **25, 101;** TE2: 300; TE3: 396, **396,** 403, **419A–419B,** R14–R15, **439E;** TE5: **159,** 207
text organization, TE1: **48;** TE3: **333,** 391, 371, 417; TE5: 183, **216, 233, 251A–251B,** 245, 250; TE6: 399
topic/main idea/supporting details, TE2: 180, 182, 183, **259A–259B, 236, 241,** R14–R15; TE3: 342, 358, 361; TE4: **27,** 66; TE5: 177, **223**
understanding biographies, TE4: 147A–147B
understanding fairy tales, TE5: 295A–295B
understanding poetry, TE1: 151A–151B
understanding trickster tales, TE2: 301A–301B
See also Lessons, specific; Strategies, reading.

Comprehension strategies. *See* Strategies, reading.

Computer activities. *See* Technology resources; Writing skills.

Concepts of print
bold print, TE4: 39L
capitalization
for emphasis, TE1: 108; TE3: 322, 354
to represent a sign, TE1: 22
italics, TE4: 39L
punctuation
end of sentence
exclamation point, TE1: 96
foreign words in italics, TE3: 341

italics for emphasis, TE3: 322
See also Mechanics, language.

Connections
between art works, TE5: 210–213
between expository selections, TE2: 213, 233; TE4: 39, 69
between grammar and writing, TE1: 51E; TE2: 187E; TE3: 335E; TE4: 43E
between individuals/story characters, TE5: 162, 168J
between literature and life experience, TE1: 21, 68, 97; TE2: 169, 188, 191, 199, 205, 245, 254; TE3: 392; TE4: 15C, 34; TE5: 107C; TE6: 332
between narrative and expository selections, TE1: 121; TE2: 185, 259; TE3: 361, 347; TE4: 64, 94
between narrative selection and poetry, TE1: 51, 118
between narrative selections, TE1: 51X, 70, 86, 91, 92J, 116; TE3: 356, 368, R5; TE5: 183, 139X, 246
between photo essay and narrative selection, TE5: 251
between poems, TE6: 337
between reading and writing, TE1: 50–51, 62; TE2: 186–187; TE3: 333S, 335; TE4: 40–43
between strategies and skills, TE2: 160, 190, 216, 236; TE3: 310, 338, 364, 396; TE4: 18, 46, 72
connecting/comparing, TE1: 44, 49, 84, 89; TE3: 307B, 331, 333, 335T, 361, 361DD, 389, 393, 393DD, 415, 419; TE5: 153B, 178, 185T, 208, 213DD, 246, 267CC, 294; TE6: 301B, 339T, 367DD, 411A–411B, 411C–411D
selections, TE1: 10P; TE2: 181, 209, 231, 257; TE3: 302P; TE5: 148P; TE6: 296P
theme connections, TE1: 15A, 15B, 16, 46, 51S, 51T, 52, 86, 92G, 92K; TE2: 180, 185, 208, 213, 230, 233, 256, 259; TE3: 308, 336, 356, 362, 394, 437A–437B, 437C–437D; TE4: 15B, 16, 39, 44, 64, 70, 94, 99, 100, 101, 105, 107, 111; TE5: 154, 186, 168G, 214, 265A–265B, 265C–265D; TE6: 302, 340, 368

Constructing meaning from text. *See* Comprehension skills; Decoding skills; Language concepts and skills; Phonics; Strategies, reading.

Content areas, reading in the
art, TE5: 210–213
careers, TE2: 210–213; TE3: 416–419; TE4: 66–69
fine arts, TE3: 308–309, 416–419
home economics, TE2: 232–233; TE6: 340–341, 368–369
language arts, TE1: 86–91
media, TE5: 248–251; TE6: 364–367
multicultural, TE1: 57–85; TE2: 161–179, 182–185, 217–229, 237–255, 214–215,

161, **185G,** R17, R19, R21; TE3: 318, 397; TE4: 73; TE5: 183G; TE6: 355

multi-syllabic words, TE2: 193, 201A; TE3: 311, 344, 361D, 393D, 397, R3, R5, R7, R9; TE4: 30, 47, 69C, 99C, 99D

phonics/decoding strategy, TE1: **19,** 36, 49D, 73, 89D, 93, 101, 121C, 121D, 141, 142, 151D; TE2: **161,** 175, 185C, 185D, 191, 193, 213C, 213D, 217, 225, 233C, 233D, 237, 241, 259C, 259D, 283, 290, R2, R3, R4, R5, R6, R7, R8, R9; TE3: **311,** 318, 333C , 333D, 339, 344, 404, 361C, 361D, 365, 371, 393C, 393D, 397, 403, 419D; TE4: **19,** 30, 39D, 47, 57, 69D, 73, 81, 99D, R2, R3, R4, R5, R6, R7; TE5: **157,** 169, 183D, 189, 194, 213D, 217, 251D, R3, R5, R7; TE6: **305,** 314, 337C, 337D, 343, 355, 367C, 367D, 371, 377, 399C, 399D

See also Phonics; Structural analysis; Vocabulary, selection.

Details, noting important, related, and sufficient. *See* Comprehension skills.

Diagrams. *See* Graphic information, interpreting; Graphic organizers.

Dialogue. *See* Writer's craft.

Diaries and journals. *See* Journal.

Dictionary skills

alphabetical order, TE1: **49G, 121G, 137H;** TE3: 361G

antonyms, TE6: **367G**

base words and inflected forms, TE4: **99G**

bilingual dictionary, TE6: **337H**

choosing the correct meaning, TE3: **361G**

definitions, TE1: 28, **121G;** TE2: **259G;** TE3: 361G

entry and guide words, TE1: **121G;** TE3: 361G, R19

geography and map section, TE1: **121G**

guide words, TE2: **213G**

homographs, TE4: 39F

inflected forms, TE1: **121G**

multiple-meaning words, TE1: **89H, 121F, 137H;** TE3: 361G; TE4: **69G**

parts of speech, TE1: **89H, 121G;** TE3: 361G; TE4: **39G,** 99G

parts of the dictionary, TE1: **121G, 137I**

pronunciation key, TE1: **89H, 121G;** TE3: **393G**

root form, TE3: 361G

sample sentence, TE4: 39G

spelling and phonics key, TE1: **121G**

spelling table, TE6: **339G**

syllables, TE5: **183G**

synonyms, TE6: **337G**

word beginnings -*a, -be,* TE6: R17

Directions, following. *See* Comprehension skills; Information skills.

Drafting. *See* Reading-Writing Workshop, steps of; Writing skills, drafting.

Drama. *See* Creative dramatics.

Drawing conclusions. *See* Comprehension skills.

Editing. *See* Reading-Writing Workshop, steps of, proofreading; Writing skills, proofreading.

English Language Learners, activities especially helpful for

beginning/preproduction, TE1: 16, 44, 52, 84, 90, 116, 138; TE2: 158, 180, 188, 208, 214, 230, 234, 256, 280; TE3: 308, 330, 336, 356, 362, 388, 394, 414; TE4: 16, 34, 44, 70; TE5: 154, 178, 186, 208, 214, 246; TE6: 302, 332, 340, 362, 368, 394

early production and speech emergence, TE1: 16, 44, 52, 84, 90, 116, 138; TE2: 158, 180, 188, 208, 214, 230, 234, 256, 280; TE4: 16, 34, 44, 70; TE5: 154, 178, 186, 208, 214, 246; TE6: 302, 332, 340, 362, 368, 394

intermediate and advanced fluency, TE1: 16, 44, 52, 84, 90, 116, 138; TE2: 158, 180, 188, 208, 214, 230, 234, 256, 280; TE3: 308, 330, 336, 356, 362, 388, 394, 414; TE4: 16, 34, 744; TE5: 154, 178, 186, 208, 214, 246; TE6: 302, 332, 340, 362, 368, 394

language development, TE1: 52, 60, 80, 106, 111, 117, 120, 144, 151G; TE2: 174, 202, 243, 251, R3, R5, R7; TE3: 317, 322, 346, 353, 376, 394, R3, R5, R7; TE4: 78, 80; TE5: 153, 159, 174, 239, R5, R7; TE6: 314, 361, 386

supporting comprehension, TE1: 20, 26, 30, 34, 36, 48, 52, 56, 59, 63, 67, 68, 74, 77, 78, 83, 88, 94, 96, 97, 102, 115, 116, 138, 143, 146, 149, R3, R5, R7; TE2: 158, 162, 164, 167, 176, 179, 180, 184, 188, 192, 197, 200, 205, 208, 212, 214, 218, 220, 224, 229, 230, 233, 234, 239, 240, 244, 248, 256, 259, 280, 289, 293, 295, 299; TE3: 308, 312, 314, 320, 325, 330, 336, 341, 344, 350, 356, 362, 366, 369, 373, 379, 385, 388, 391, 394, 398, 401, 403, 407, 410, 413, 414, 418; TE4: 16, 22, 25, 31, 33, 34, 44, 50, 52, 58, 70, 74, 76, 87, 93, 94, 98; TE5: 154, 158, 160, 173, 177, 178, 182, 186, 191, 193, 196, 198, 204, 208, 212, 214, 218, 222, 227, 232, 236, 245, 246, 250; TE6: 302, 306, 309, 317, 318, 323, 324, 332, 336, 340, 344, 346, 351, 356, 362, 366, 368, 372, 375, 376, 380, 383, 389, 390, 391, 394, 398

See also Reaching All Learners

Ethnic diversity. *See* Literary analysis; Multicultural activities/information.

Evaluating literature. *See* Literature, evaluating.

Evaluating writing. *See* Reading-Writing Workshop.

Evaluation. *See* Assessment options, choosing.

Evaluation. *See* Assessment, planning for.

Expanding literacy. *See* Skills links.

Experience story. *See* Writing, shared writing.

Expository text, TE1: 16–17, 54–55, 46–49, 54–55, 86–89, 46–49, 90–91, 118–121; TE2: 158–159, 182–185, 188–189, 210–213, 214, 232–233, 234–235, 237–255, 258–259, R6–R7, R8–R9; TE3: 308–309, 332–333, 336–337, 358–361, 362–363, 394, 416–419; TE4: 16, 18–33, 36–39, 44, 66–69, 70, 96–99; TE5: 154, 180–183, 186, 210–213, 214, 216–245, 248–251; TE6: 302–303, 340–341, 364–367, 396–399

Extra Support/Intervention. *See* Reaching All Learners.

Fact and opinion. *See* Comprehension skills.

Fantasy and realism. *See* Comprehension skills.

Fiction. *See* Literary genres; Selections in Anthology.

Fiction/nonfiction, distinguishing, TE2: 182

Figurative language. *See* Writer's craft.

Fluency

assessing, TE1: 37, 71, 107, 147; TE2: 167, 197, 225, 249, 287; TE3: 315, 343, 379, 411; TE4: 21, 51, 89; TE5: 169, 193, 241; TE6: 327, 351, 379

modeling, TE1: 15A, 49O–49R, 51S, 89O–89R, 89CC, 107, 121O–121R, 137CC, 151O–151R; TE2: 157A, 185O, 185P, 185Q, 185R, 187S, 213O, 213P, 213Q, 213R, 213CC, 233O, 233P, 233Q, 233R, 233CC, 259O, 259P, 259Q, 259R, 279CC, 301O, 301P, 301Q, 301R; TE3: 307A, 333O, 333P, 333Q, 333R, 335S, 361O, 361P, 361Q, 361R, 361CC, 393O, 393P, 393Q, 393CC, 419O, 419P, 419Q, 419R; TE4: 15A, 39O–39R, 43SM, 69O–69R, 69CC, 99O–99R, 119O–119R, 119CC; TE5: 153A, 183O, 183P, 183Q, 183R, 185S, 213O, 213P, 213Q, 213R, 213CC, 251O, 251P, 251Q, 251R, 267CC, 295O, 295P, 295Q, 295R; TE6: 301A, 337O, 337P, 337Q, 337R, 339S, 367O, 367P, 367Q, 367R, 367CC, 399O, 399P, 399Q, 399R

practice for, TE1: 15A, 37, 49O–49R, 51S, 71, 89O–89R, 89CC, 107, 121O–121R, 137CC, 147, 151O–151R; TE2: 157A, 185O–185R, 187S, 213O–213R, 213CC, 233O–233R, 233CC, 259O–259R, 279CC, 301O–301R; TE3: 315, 343, 379, 411; TE4: 21, 51, 89; TE5:

TE6: 334
"Lost" by Bruce Lansky, TE1: 49
"My Grandma's Songs/Las canciones de mi
    abuela," TE6: 336–337
"Puffin, The," TE4: 98
"Puffin-Stuff," TE4: 98
"Seal," TE4: 97
"September Yearning" by Joyce Carol Thomas,
    TE1: 50
"Show Fish" by Shel Silverstein, TE1: 149
"Sneeze" by Maxine Kumin, TE1: 142
"Spaghetti! Spaghetti!" by Jack Prelutsky, TE1:
    145
"Under the Trees," TE4: 99
"Ways of Living Things, The," TE4: 10K

Poetic devices
alliteration, TE1: **120, 147, 151A;** TE4: 96
imagery, TE4: 69L
meter, TE4: 96
patterns, TE1: **120, 151A**
repetition, TE1: **120,** 145, 147, **151A;** TE4: 69K,
    69L, 96
rhyme, TE1: 118, **120, 145;** TE4: 69K, 69L, 96,
    97; TE6: R19
rhythm, TE4: 69K, 69L, 96, 97
stanza, TE4: 69K, 69L, 96

Poetry
analyzing, TE1: 118–121, **120, 151A**
characteristics, TE6: 336
Focus on Poetry, TE1: **138–151K**
free verse, TE4: 69L, 97, 99
introducing, reading, responding to, TE1:
    118–121, 140–149; TE4: 69K–69L
reading, TE6: 334–337
rhymed verse, TE4: 99
writing. *See* Writing activities and types.

Poets in Anthology
Alarcón, Francisco X., TE1: 148, TE6: 336–337
Brooks, Gwendolyn, TE1: 146
Carlson, Lori Marie, TE6: 335
Fisher, Aileen, TE4: 99
Florian, Douglas, TE1: 147
Hughes, Langston, TE1: 141
Johnston, Tony, TE6: 334
Kumin, Maxine, TE1: 142
Lewis, J. Patrick TE1: 144
McCord, David TE1: 142
Mora, Pat TE1: 143
Peronto, Joan, TE4: 98
Prelutsky, Jack, TE1: 145, TE4: 10K
Silverstein, Shel TE1: 149
Singer, Marilyn, TE4: 96
Smith, William Jay, TE4: 97
Takeshi, Hitomi, TE1: 147
Wood, Robert Williams, TE4: 98

Point of view. *See* Writer's craft.

Predicting outcomes. *See* Comprehension
skills.

Predictions, making and checking
checking, TE1: 18, 32, 42, 68, 82, 114, 148; TE2:
    161, 179, 191, 199, 200, 207, 223, 229, 245,
    254, 292, 298, R6; TE3: 328, 354, 386, 412;
    TE4: 19, 24, 25, 32, 33, 55, 62, 63, 93, 143;
    TE5: 176, 206, 228, 244, 292; TE6: 330, 360,
    392
from previewing, TE1: 19, 55, 93; TE3: 312, 344,
    R2, R4, R6; TE5: 157, 176, 189, 206, 228,
    244, 292; TE6: 305, 343, 371
from previewing. *See* Previewing.
review, TE1: 32, 33, 43, 69, 69, 83, 115, 149;
    TE2: 169, 179, 199, 200, 207, 223, 228, 229,
    230, 245, 255, 292, 298, 299; TE3: 329, 355,
    386, 413; TE4: 25, 33, 55, 63, 83, 93, 143;
    TE5: 165, 177, 199, 207, 229, 245; TE6: 315,
    331, 353, 361, 381, 393
while reading, TE4: 91; TE5: 202

Prefixes. *See* Structural analysis.

Previewing
author, illustrator, cover, TE1: R2, R4, R6; TE2:
    161, 191, 217, 237, R2, R4, R6, R8; TE3: 310,
    332, 338, 358, 364, 390, 396, 416, R2, R4,
    R6; TE4: 18, 46, 72
extra support for, TE1: 18, 19, 32, 42, 55, 68,
    82, 93, 114, 148; TE2: 178, 206, 229, 254,
    298; TE3: 329, 355, 386, 413; TE4: 33, 63, 93,
    145; TE5: 157, 176, 189, 206, 228, 244, 292;
    TE6: 305, 343, 371
headings and titles, TE4: 36, 66, 69H, R6
illustrations, TE1: 19, 141; TE2: 158, 188, 191,
    217, 283; TE4: 72, R6; TE5: 217
photos and captions, TE4: 16, 18, 66, 69H, 70A
picture walk, TE1: R2, R4, R6; TE2: R2, R4, R6;
    TE4: 72, R2, R4, R6
text, TE1: 19, 55, 141; TE2: 161, 191, 217, 237,
    283, 288, 294; TE3: 339, 365, 397, R2, R4,
    R6; TE4: 19, 47, 69H, 73; TE5: 157, 189, 202;
    TE6: 305, 343, 371

Prewriting. *See* Reading-Writing Workshop,
steps of; Writing skills, prewritng.

Prior knowledge. *See* Background, building.

Problem-solving and decision making. *See*
Comprehension skills.

Process writing. *See* Reading-Writing
Workshop, steps of; Writing skills.

Pronunciation Guide, TE5: R29; TE6: R28

Proofreading. *See* Reading-Writing Workshop,
steps of; Writing skills, proofreading.

Publications, student-produced, TE3: 357;
TE4: 39

Publishing. *See* Reading-Writing Workshop,
steps of; Writing skill, publishing.

Punctuation. *See* Mechanics, language.

Purpose setting
for reading, TE1: 19, 55, 86, 93, 118, 141; TE2:
    161, 182, 191, 210, 217, 232, 237, 258, 283,
    288, 294; TE3: 339, 347, 358, 365, 390, 397,
    416; TE4: 19, 36, 47, 66, 73, 95; TE5: 157,
    180, 189, 210, 217, 248; TE6: 305, 334,
    343, 364
reviewing, TE1: 33, 43, 83; TE2: 169, 179, 199,
    207, 223, 229, 245, 255; TE3: 321, 329, 355,
    387; TE5: 165, 177, 199, 207, 229, 245; TE6:
    315, 331, 353, 361, 381, 393

Purposes for reading
another book by author, TE3: 416; TE5: M10
another book on topic, TE5: R7
answer questions, TE1: 19, 55, 93; TE4: 66
determine feelings, TE6: 334, 371
enjoyment, TE2: 161, 191, 210, 223, 283, 288,
    294; TE3: 319, 397; TE4: 22; TE6: 305, 364
find out more, TE1: 19; TE2: 161, 182, 210, 217,
    232, 237, 258; TE4: 19, 22, 37, 47, 73; TE5:
    157, 189
for information, TE1: 46, 86
identify solution, TE6: 396
learn more, TE5: 180, 211
to answer questions, TE3: 358
reviewing, TE4: 25, 33, 55, 63, 82, 83, 92, 93

Questions, formulating, TE1: 27, 30, 44, 84,
114, 119, 149C; TE2: 169, 179, 190, 191, 192,
194, 196, 198, 202, 203, 204, 206, 207, 210, 228,
232, 254, R4; TE3: 321, 338, 344, 345, 347, 350,
352, 354, 355, 358, 366, 370, 386, 358, 366, 401,
R9; TE4: 36, 37, 66, 69H; TE5: 156, 161, 162, 164,
168, 170, 177

Quotations
direct, TE2: 211

Reaching All Learners
Challenge, TE1: 42, 47, 49E, 82, 89, 89E, 113,
    114, 120, 121E, 145, R9, R11, R13; TE2: 163,
    166, 169, 177, 178, 185, 199, 204, 206, 213,
    213E, 221, 223, 227, 228, 233E, 245, 247,
    254, 259E, 284, 287, 289, R9, R11, R13, R15,
    R17, R19, R21, R23; TE3: 319, 321, 323, 328,
    342, 347, 349, 351, 354, 361, 361E, 382,
    386, 393, 393E, 404, 412, 419, 419E, R9,
    R11, R13, R15, R17, R19, R21, R23; TE4: 24,
    28, 32, 39, 39E, 53, 55, 60, 62, 69, 69E, 79,
    83, 88, 92, 99, 99E, R11, R13, R15, R17, R19,

Reading across the curriculum. *See* Content areas, reading in the; Links, content area.

Reading fluency. *See* Fluency.

Reading log. *See* Journal.

Reading modes

See also Rereading; Leveled Readers; Leveled Theme Paperbacks.

Reading strategies. *See* Strategies, reading.

Reading Traits

Critiquing for Evaluation, TE2: 185B; TE4: 39B, 99B

Decoding Conventions, TE1: 151B; TE3: 333B; TE5: 251B

Developing Interpretations, TE1: 89B; TE3: 393B; TE5: 183B; TE6: 367B, 399B

Establishing Comprehension, TE1: 121B; TE2: 233B, 259B; TE3: 361B, 419B

Integrating for Synthesis, TE1: 49B; TE2: 213B; TE4: 69B

Realizing Context, TE5: 213B; TE6: 337B

Reading-Writing Workshop (process writing)

conferencing, TE1: **51A, 51E;** TE2: **187A, 187E,** R33; TE3: **335A, 335E;** TE4: **43A, 43E;** TE5: **185A, 185E;** TE6: **339E**

evaluating, TE1: **51G–51H;** TE2: **187G–187H;** TE3: **335G;** TE4: **43G–43H;** TE5: **185G;** TE6: **339G–339H**

reading as a writer, TE1: **51;** TE2: **187;** TE3: **289;** TE4: **43;** TE5: **185;** TE6: **339**

steps of, TE6: **339A–339H**

drafting, TE1: **51C–51D;** TE2: **187C–187D;** TE3: **335D;** TE4: **43C–43D;** TE5: **185C–185D;** TE6: **339C–339D**

prewriting, TE1: **51A–51B;** TE2: **187A–187B;** TE3: **335A–335C;** TE4: **43A–43B;** TE5: **185A–185B;** TE6: **339A–339B**

proofreading, TE1: **51E–51F;** TE2: **187E–187F;** TE3: **335F;** TE4: **43E–43F;** TE5: **185E–185F;** TE6: **339E–339F**

publishing, TE2: **187G**

publishing and sharing, TE1: **51G;** TE3: **335G;** TE4: **43G;** TE6: **339G**

revising, TE1: **51E;** TE2: **187E;** TE4: **43E**

student model, TE1: **50–51;** TE2: **186–187;** TE3: **334–335;** TE4: **40–43;** TE5: **184–185;** TE6: **338–339**

subjects

description, TE5: **183S–183T, 184–185H**

instructions, TE2: **185S–185T, 186–187H**

personal narrative, TE1: **49S–49T, 50–51H**

persuasive essay, TE6: **337S–337T, 338–339H**

research report, TE4: **39S–39T, 40–43H**

story, TE3: **333S–333T, 334–335H**

See also Writing skills.

Reads on and rereads. *See* Strategies, reading monitor/clarify.

Reference and study skills

book, parts of a

copyright page, TE3: 393H

glossary, TE1: **121H**

index, TE1: **121H;** TE3: 361H

table of contents, TE1: **121H;** TE3: 361H

title page, TE1: **121H**

electronic encyclopedia, TE4: 39H

electronic sources

CD-ROMs, TE4: 39H, 43C

electronic dictionary, TE4: 39H

Internet, TE1: 18, R9; TE2: 185, 233H; TE3: 315, 343, 347, R11; TE4: 39H, 40, 43C, 69; TE5: 179, 209, 213, 247, 295

encyclopedia, organization of

cross-references, TE3: 393H

entries, TE3: 393H
  guide words, TE3: 393H
  update volume, TE3: 393H
  volume, TE3: 393H
graphic sources. *See* Graphic information,
  interpreting.
information, gathering
  for multimedia report, TE5: **183H**
  See also Information skills.
information, organization of
  classified ads, TE3: 333H
  headlines, TE3: 333H
  K-W-L chart, making a, TE1: 46, **49H**
  map, TE3: 357
  sections, TE3: 333H
  table of contents, TE3: 333H
  See also Graphic information, interpreting.
information skills. *See* Information skills.
library
  card and electronic catalog, TE2: **185H;**
    TE4: 43C
  fiction and nonfiction books, TE2: **185H**
  periodicals, TE2: **185H**
  using, TE2: **185H, 233H;** TE4: 69P
reference resources
  atlas, TE1: 48; TE4: 67
  books, TE2: 185, **185H;** TE3: 361, 347, 419H,
    R11; TE4: 40, 43C
  dictionary, TE6: **337H**
  encyclopedia, TE1: 47, R9; TE2: 185, 233H;
    TE3: 312, 393H, 393E, 419H; TE4: R11;
    TE5: 213
  Internet, TE3: 361, 347, R11
  interview, TE3: 418
  magazines, TE4: 40, 43C
  newspaper, TE3: 333H
  primary sources, TE5: 249
  reference books, TE5: 213
  thesaurus, TE2: R17, R19, R21
  See also Graphic information.
study strategies
  adjusting reading rate, TE4: **99H**
  K-W-L Strategy, TE3: 358; TE4: 66
  notes, taking. See Notes, taking.
  outlining, TE2: **259H;** TE4: 40
  real-life reading, TE6: **399H**
  research skills, TE5: 183
  skimming and scanning, TE2: 210–213; TE3:
    370; TE4: **69H**
  SQRR, TE5: **213H**
  summarizing information graphically,
    TE3: 419H
  test-taking strategies, TE1: 122; TE4: 100
  time lines, using, TE5: **251H**
  See also Graphic information, interpreting;
    Research activities.
See also Information skills; Research activities.

Rereading
  cooperatively, TE1: 83, 69; TE2: 167, 197, 223,

225, 249, 293; TE3: 315, 343, 333; TE4: 21,
  51, 55, 83, 89; TE5: 165, 199, 229; TE6: 315,
  353, 381
for comprehension, TE1: 62, 105, 115, 121A;
  TE2: 236, 258, R10, R12, R14, R16; TE3: 329,
  361A; TE4: 75, 76, 82, 83, 86, 90, 93; TE6:
  337A, 367A, 399A
for extra support, TE1: 72, 115
for fluency, TE2: 167, 197, 225, 249, 287
independently, TE2: 167, 197, 223, 293; TE3: R3,
  R5, R7, R9; TE4: 25, 36, 55, 83; TE5: 165, 199,
  229; TE6: 315, 353, 381
orally, TE1: 37, 105, 107, 120, 147; TE2: 167,
  197, 287; TE3: 343, 333; TE4: 21, 39L, 51, 89;
  TE6: 327, 337O–337R, 351, 367O–367R, 379,
  399O–399R
to support answers, TE1: 29, 39, 51, 65, 107,
  149; TE2: 165, 185, 195, 299; TE3: 314, 393A,
  372; TE4: 34, 64, 94, 99A; TE5: 141, 199, 207,
  217; TE6: 337A, 367A, 399A
with expression and intonation, TE1: 37, 71,
  120; TE3: 315, 333, 333O–333R, 343,
  361O–361R, 419O–419R
with feeling and expression, TE2: 167, 197,
  225, 249, 287; TE4: 21, 51, 89; TE5: 169,
  183O–183P, 193, 213O–213P, 241,
  251O–251P, 295O–295P; TE6: 327,
  337O–337R, 351, 367O–367R, 379,
  399O–399R

Research activities, TE1: 47, 117, 121H, 151H,
R9, R11; TE2: 185, 185H; TE3: 343, 372, 393, R11;
TE4: 39, 39L, 40–43G, 69, 69H; TE5: 183, 213

Responding to literature, options for
  art, TE1: 45, 85, 116, 117, 120, 143, 145;
    TE3: 357, 389, 369
  discussion, TE1: 33, 42, 43, 44, 69, 114, 150,
    R3, R5, R7; TE2: 169, 178, 180, 199, 206,
    208, 223, 228, 230, 231, 245, 254, 256, 257,
    300, R3, R5, R7, R9; TE3: 321, 328, 330, 356,
    375, 386, 388, 358, 366, 368, 375, 405, 412,
    414, R3, R5, R7; TE4: 24, 32, 34, 390–39P,
    55, 62, 64, 83, 92, 94, R3, R5, R7; TE5: 165,
    176, 177, 178, 229, 244, 245, 246, 198, 199,
    206, 207, 208; TE6: 314, 315, 330, 331, 332,
    353, 360, 361, 362, 380, 381, 332, 393, 394
  drama, TE3: 389, 369
  Internet, TE1: 45, 85, 117, 151; TE2: 181, 209,
    231, 257, 300; TE3: 331, 357, 389, 415; TE4:
    35, 65, 95, 147; TE5: 179, 209, 247, 295; TE6:
    333, 363, 395
  listening and speaking, TE1: 117, 143
  personal response, TE1: 45, 85, 117, 151; TE2:
    181, 209, 231, 257, 283, 288, 294, 300; TE3:
    331, 357, 389, 415; TE4: 35, 65, 95, 147; TE5:
    179, 209, 247, 295; TE6: 333, 363, 395
  writing, TE1: 44, 84, 116, 150; TE2: 180, 208,
    230, 256, 300; TE3: 330, 342, 356, 357, 388,
    415; TE4: 34, 64, 94, 146; TE5: 178, 208, 246,

294; TE6: 332, 362, 394
  viewing, TE1: 85

Reteaching. TE1: R8, R10, R12, R14, R16, R18,
R20–R22; TE2: R8, R10, R12, R14, R16, R18, R20,
R22, R24–R27; TE3: R8, R10, R12, R14, R16, R18,
R20, R22, R24–R27; TE4: R8, R10, R12, R14, R16,
R18, R20–R22; TE5: R8, R10, R12, R14, R16, R18,
R20–R22; TE6: R8, R10, R12, R14, R16, R18,
R20–R22

Retelling
  information, TE1: 16
  story, TE1: 45, 84, 121A; TE2: 286, 293, 299;
    TE3: 361B, 367, R9

Revising. *See* Reading-Writing Workshop, steps
of; Writing skills, revising.

Rhyme. *See* Poetic devices.

Rhythm. *See* Poetic devices.

Root words. *See* Structural analysis.

Science activities. *See* Cross-curricular
activities.

Selecting books. *See* Independent reading.

Selections in Anthology
  art
    "Journeys Through Art," TE5: 210–213
  article
    "Have You Seen the Lost and Found?!" TE1:
      90–91
    "Rock Climbing" TE1: 16–17
    "Mulan Legend, The" TE1: 52–53
    "A Healthy Recipe from Ghana" from
      The Kids' Multicultural Cookbook,
      TE2: 232–233
    "Nesting Dolls" from *Hopscotch for Girls*
      magazine by Marie E. Kingdon,
      TE2: 182–185
  biographical sketches
    "Talented Kids" from *National Geographic
      World* and *Appleseeds,* TE2: 210–213
  comic strips
    "Calvin and Hobbes," by Bill Watterson,
      TE6: 366
    "Fox Trot," by Bill Amend, TE6: 365
    "Peanuts," by Charles M. Schulz, TE6:
      364, 367
  expository nonfiction
    "Celebrating Chinese New Year," by Diane
      Hoyt-Goldsmith, photographs by Lawrence
      Migdale, TE2: 274–276
    Dancing Rainbows, TE2: 237–255
  fantasy
    Dogzilla by Dav Pilkey, TE3: 311–328
    Dinosaur Bob and His Adventures with the

TE5: 148G–148H; TE6: 296G–296H

Think Aloud. *See* Modeling.

Thinking
creatively. *See* Creative thinking.
critically. *See* Critical thinking.

Topic, main idea, and supporting details. *See* Comprehension skills.

Topics, selecting. *See* Reading-Writing Workshop, steps of, prewriting; Research activities.

Usage. *See* Grammar and usage.

Venn diagrams. *See* Graphic organizers.

Verbs. *See* Speech, parts of.

Videotapes, TE4: 10D, 39H, 40, 69O

Viewing
art, TE3: 319
books, magazines, newspapers, TE4: 69O
computer sources, TE4: 69O
films, TE1: 87; TE4: 69O
fine art, TE5: **210–213**
illustrations, TE5: 201; TE6: 364, 371. *See also* Picture clues.
illustrations for a purpose, TE2: **163, 193.** S*ee also* Picture clues.
internet web sites, TE4: 69O
maps, TE1: **118–121**
mass media, TE6: 364–367
photographs, TE1: 48; TE4: 28, 38; TE5: 248–251
purpose
for amusement, TE6: 364
for entertainment, TE4: 69O
for information, TE4: 69O
tips for viewing, TE4: 69O
to access information, TE4: 38
to analyze, TE1: 118, 119, 121; TE4: 69O, 69P
to appreciate art, TE3: 319, 373
to compare film and book, TE1: 87
to compare print and nonprint, TE1: 87; TE3: 373
to compare several works by artist, TE3: 319
to compare/contrast, TE3: 319, 373; TE4: 69O
to convince people about something, TE4: 69O
to evaluate media, TE4: 69O–69P
to evaluate photographs, TE4: 28, 69
to identify main idea, supporting details, TE5: 248–251
to make observations, TE3: 319, 373

to note details, TE2: 163, 221, 242
to respond, TE3: 319, 373
television, TE4: 69O
videotapes. *See* Videotapes.

Visual literacy
analyzing an illustration, TE4: 53
artist's style, TE1: **59**
comic strips, TE6: **366**
cubism, TE5: 212
details chart, TE5: 248
foreground, TE4: 75
illustrator's craft, TE3: **319, 373**
interpreting details, TE2: 242
noting details, TE2: **163**
photography, TE5: 250
scene, picturing, TE5: **201**
silhouettes, TE2: **221**

Visualizing, TE1: 31, 36, 117, 118, **143,** 145; TE2: 213K, **298,** R13; TE4: R17; TE5: 185B

Vocabulary, building
action verb, TE5: R19
action words, TE2: R19
antonyms, TE1: **R19;** TE3: R19, R23; TE5: R15
battle words, TE1: **91J**
camping words, TE1: **121J**
commands, TE1: 46
compound words. *See* Structural analysis.
context, using. *See* Decoding skills.
compound words, TE2: R17, R23
descriptive language, TE1: 151G, 151K–151L, R7, R15, R17
feeling words, TE5: R17
historical terms, TE1: 51T
idiom/expression, TE3: 338, R5, R7
-less or -ness, words ending in, TE5: R15
multiple-meaning words, TE2: R5, R23
opposites. *See* Vocabulary, building: antonyms.
possessives, TE5: R17
sea creatures, TE1: **51J**
slang, TE2: **233F**
special language, TE3: 332
synonyms, TE1: **151F, R15,** R19; TE2: 289; TE3: 419G, R17, R19, R23; TE5: 195, R17
word families, TE1: **49C, 91J**
word origins, TE1: **91J**
word web, TE5: R19
word webs. *See* Graphic organizers, word webs.
words that suggest sounds, TE1: **89E**
See also Language concepts and skills; Vocabulary skills.

Vocabulary, expansion
opposites. *See* Vocabulary, expanding: antonyms.
See also Language concepts and skills.

Vocabulary, extending
compound words. *See* Structural analysis.
context, using. *See* Decoding skills.

words related to water and swimming, TE4: R15
See also Language concepts and skills.

Vocabulary, selection
key words, TE1: 17, 20, 22, 24, 26, 28, 30, 32, 36, 38, 40, 46, 48, 53, 56, 58, 60, 62, 64, 66, 68, 70, 72, 74, 80, 86, 91, 94, 96, 98, 100, 102, 106, 108, 110, 114, 118, 120, 139, 142, 146, 148, R2, R4, R6; TE2: **159,** 162, 164, 166, 168, 170, 176, 184, **189,** 192, 196, 198, 200, 202, 210, 212, **215,** 218, 220, 222, 224, 226, 232, **235,** 238, 240, 246, 248, 250, 252, 258, 282, 284, 288, 294, R2, R4, R6; TE3: 309, 314, 316, 318, 320, 324, 326, 332, 336, 337, 340, 342, 346, 348, 352, 354, 358, 360, 362, 363, 366, 368, 370, 376, 378, 380, 384, 390, 392, 394, 395, 398, 354, 356, 404, 406, 408, 410, 416, 418, R2, R4, R6; TE4: 15A, 15B, 17, 20, 22, 26, 28, 30, 32, 36, 38, 43V, 44, 45, 48, 50, 52, 54, 56, 58, 60, 62, 66, 68, 70I, 70, 71, 74, 76, 78, 80, 82, 84, 86, 90, 94, 96, 98, R2, R4, R6; TE5: 107A, 155, 158, 160, 162, 164, 166, 168, 170, 172, 176, 180, 182, 139V, 139W, 186, 187, 190, 192, 194, 196, 198, 200, 204, 163, 168H, 168I, 214, 217, 218, 220, 222, 224, 226, 228, 230, 232, 234, 236, 238, 240, 242, 250, R2, R4, R6, R15, R17, R19; TE6: 302, 303, 306, 308, 310, 312, 314, 316, 318, 328, 330, 334, 336, 340, 342, 344, 346, 348, 350, 352, 354, 356, 358, 360, 364–367, 366, 369, 372, 374, 376, 378, 380, 382, 384, 386, 388, 390, 392, 396
See also Context, using; Daily Language Practice; Decoding skills.

Vocabulary skills
action words, TE1: 97
adjectives with *-ed* endings, TE1: 80
alphabetical order to the first letter, TE1: **51C, 51D, 51I, 51J**
analogies, TE5: **213G**
antonyms, TE2: R17; TE4: R17; TE5: R15; TE6: **367G**
collective nouns, TE4: 69J
days of the week, TE1: **91L**
descriptive language, TE1: **151G, 151K–151L,** R7, R15, R17
dictionary, TE3: 333G, R23
dictionary, using the, TE1: **49G, 121G,** R9
exact words, TE2: **213F**
family words, TE5: **213G**
homographs, TE4: 39E
homophones, TE3: **419D, 419E–419F;** TE5: **251G**
humorous words, TE3: R17
idioms/expressions, TE1: 102, R5, R7
language games, TE5: R15, R19; TE6: R15, R17, R19
Latin word roots, TE1: **91J**